PREPARING FOR ULYSSES
Politics and Veterans During
World War I I

Contemporary American History Series
William E. Leuchtenburg, General Editor

PREPARING FOR ULYSSES

Politics and Veterans During

World War II

by Davis R. B. Ross

Columbia University Press
New York and London   1969

89596

Davis R. B. Ross is Assistant Professor of History at Columbia University.

SBN: 231–03222–6
Copyright © 1969 Columbia University Press
Library of Congress Catalog Card Number:
78–94513
Printed in the United States of America

ACKNOWLEDGMENTS

MANY DEBTS have been incurred in the preparation of this study. I am particularly grateful to Professor William E. Leuchtenburg for his innumerable comments and patient direction, to Professor Robert D. Cross for his keen substantive and stylistic insights, and to Professors Henry F. Graff, Richard Polenberg, Wallace D. Sayre, and Bruce Smith for their helpful comments. Their suggestions have borne fruit, so to speak, precisely at the spots the soil appeared most barren. Others have read portions of the essay in its early form; to John Duff, H. Draper Hunt, Daniel Leab, and George Lankewich, a special note of thanks is extended. The responsibility for following or ignoring their wise counsel, of course, remains mine.

It is impossible to name and thank all those who have ferreted out the files and answered inquiries during research. Archivists and librarians invariably and cheerfully have extended their aid, no matter how vague or importunate the request. I am especially grateful to Philip Lagerquist and Harry Clark at the Harry S. Truman Library; to Jerry Finster, Joseph Howerton, Donald Mosholder, and Mike Simmons at the National Archives; and to Fred Paul at the Veterans Administration. I thank V. L. Bedsole at Louisiana State University and Richard C. Berner at the University of Washington for microfilming materials at their libraries, obviating special trips.

Grants-in-aid from the Harry S. Truman Library Institute for National and International Affairs have made possible more extensive research than otherwise; I am grateful to Dr. Philip C. Brooks and to the members of the Institute's committee on grants-in-aid for their generous actions. Finally, to my wife Esther—and to our friend, Mrs. Monique Roeth, who has done so much of the typing chores— a special note of appreciation for their unfailing support.

May 1969.   DAVIS R. B. ROSS

CONTENTS

CONTENTS

PREPARING FOR ULYSSES
Politics and Veterans During
World War II

INTRODUCTION

HOMER'S *Odyssey* lives for all the ages. Odysseus—or, to use the Latinized form—Ulysses, with Menelaeus and other Greek companions-in-arms, journeys to Troy to recapture Menelaeus' wife, Helen. Ulysses distinguishes himself by arms and guile during the ten-year war that culminates with Greek victory. He then begins what turns out to be a long trip home. Almost reaching the beloved Ithacan shores, Ulysses' fleet is blown off course. Nine years later, after encounters with Lotus Eaters, a Cyclops, Aeolus, Laestrygonians, Circe, spirits of the dead, sirens, Scylla and Charybdis, herds on the Island of the Sun, Calypso, and Phaeacians, the hero returns alone to his homeland. There he learns that his wife, Penelope, has been faithful to him; but local suitors for her hand have camped in his ancestral home, feasting on the absent master's provisions. Ulysses proceeds in a workmanlike manner to kill all the suitors, and defeat an angry detachment of their relatives. The story closes with the disclosure that the hero's foot-weary course has not ended; more adventures, undisclosed, await him.

For some readers Homer has told a true story about the real trials of a real man visiting real places, the prototype, as it were, of all travelogues. For others, Ulysses personifies moral perfection, the triumph of reason, virtue, and endurance over the lures of lust, luxury, and greed. Still others scoff at such pretensions; the *Odyssey* is an adventure story. And for some, it is a dull, repetitious story inflicted upon captive students by humorless professors of the classics.

Another interpretation may be added without straining unduly the story's capacity to bear significant meaning. It may be said to be a classic description of how societies treat their war veterans. To put it more grandly, every society has its Troy, its Ulysses, its Penelope, and its suitors. The analogical meaning may be depicted as follows: Too often nations send their best sons to battle at Troy. Just as frequently, as soon as peace succeeds the clangor of strife, two attitudes develop in the homeland. Suitors discard rapidly (if ever they held them) feelings of obligation and gratitude to veterans. Penelope, however, remains loyal. When the veteran, Ulysses, returns, feelings of mutual animosity spring up between him and the suitors. The clash generates bad feelings that persist long after the veterans wreak their vengeance; full tranquillity can come only long after the initial return. Reconciliation is a slow and painful task.

For the United States, four great wars have tested this pattern. The first three—the American Revolution, the Civil War, and the First World War—follow the form. This is particularly true in regards to the latter part of the analogy. Each of the three conflicts fathered distinct, unified, and significant veterans' movements, from the Society of the Cincinnati, to the Grand Army of the Republic, to the American Legion. Whatever their dissimilarities, these movements shared one important characteristic. They have tended to foster and maintain a veteran's identity separate from and superior to the remainder of the society. Born of the frustration of seeing legitimate demands spurned, "veterans' separateness" was a natural response. This clannishness of the veterans, in a democratic republic, has contributed to real or ascribed political power. In turn, political power has brought to veterans concessions and special privileges— each of which has reinforced for veterans the desirability of a separate identity.

But the Homeric pattern is broken by the United States' experience following World War II. The reintegration of the veterans of that conflict has been a large success. No organization has emerged as an aggressive and militant agent for all or most of the World

War II veterans. The exception from the Ulysses legend forces us to seek out the cause.

THIS STORY OF the origins of the United States' policy for able-bodied veterans of World War II ends happily.[1] American veterans of that conflict have returned and assumed their peacetime roles almost without breaking stride. More than sixteen-million men and women whose lives had been disrupted by the call to arms (in some cases for as many as five years) have switched from khakis and blues to civilian garb with unparalleled ease.

Why was this so? Why did traditional conflict between veterans and civilians fail to break out in 1945 or 1946? Postwar prosperity may be the most important reason. A postwar slump, widely predicted during the war, did not materialize, despite an inflationary flutter in 1946. From 1946 to 1948 unemployment figures hovered at a satisfying level of approximately 4 per cent of the total work force. Even the 1949 recession saw the rate rise to 5½ per cent—hardly alarming when viewed against prewar experiences. At the same time the civilian work force expanded from 56.5 to 60.8 millions.[2] Personal income, already large due to wartime prosperity, continued to climb when peace came. Good times undoubtedly forestalled ugly veteran-civilian clashes.

The chapters that follow concentrate on another speculative lead. Never has a nation lavished so many material benefits upon its heroes. From subsidized education to privileged ocean travel for their war brides, World War II veterans received a rich bounty. Rather than ignoring them, society came close to smothering them. These gifts, perhaps, sowed the seeds of amity. This cannot be proved; but it does not seem rash to assume that (along with prosperity) the many benefits granted to veterans—even the able-bodied on whom this study concentrates—made transformation from military to civilian life easier.

[1] Throughout this study the term "veteran" will be used in its broadest sense, denoting any former military serviceman or woman.
[2] U.S. Bureau of the Census, *Historical Statistics of The United States, Colonial Times to 1957* (Washington, D.C., 1960), 72–73.

The present work focuses on the formation of a national policy for veterans from 1940 to 1946. Of course the substantial programs for veterans established by states, municipalities, and private organizations share credit for easing the heroes' return. Ultimately, success or failure for a veteran's reabsorption occurred in his home town. But it was the Nation's responsibility to provide the initiative and, of course, the bulk of the funds for veterans' benefits.

The story emphasizes decisions made during the years 1940 to 1946. True, some World War II nondisabled veterans' benefits were adopted with few changes from pre-1940 laws. Other policy decisions were made after 1946. Still, the first benefits to World War II veterans came with passage of the Selective Training and Service Act in August, 1940; and President Harry S Truman rang down the curtain for new benefits in his Annual State of the Union Message in January, 1947.

During the period covered by this study, the Federal Government, with little opposition, provided a wide range of benefits for its nondisabled World War II veterans. This was a departure from the historical pattern. Formerly, pensions and other programs for the disabled ex-serviceman had been the central concern of policymakers. Americans had tended up to World War II to restrict the application of Abraham Lincoln's phrase "to care for him who shall have borne the battle" to the wounded and their families. Responsibility for other ex-servicemen, when assumed, was done so reluctantly, often years after the conflict. Yet, government officials, congressmen, and representatives of veterans' organizations showered the new Ulysses with "readjustment" benefits. The present essay seeks to examine that basic shift in veterans' policymaking.

Veterans' policymaking is but another chapter in the political history of the United States. The familiar ingredients are present: bugle calls of political campaigns, legislative debates, exertions of special-interest groups, and Presidential proclamations all form parts of the story. But the full texture of policymaking cannot be appreciated without an account of a less dramatic element, the role of what can be called the "bureaucracy." Often the bureaucracy is considered as an extension of the President's will; for general purposes, of course, such an idea has the merit of simplicity—one can speak of the President and his "Administration" as representing one view. Thus, in describing the evolution of policy, the analyst may portray the process as a series of compromises among Administration, Congress, and special-interest groups. Moreover, it is tempting to describe fully divisions of opinion that occur within Congress, and assume either that the Administration acts monolithically or that internal differences are of little importance. Yet, both assumptions are false. One does not have to minimize the importance of Congress's role by suggesting that differences of opinion within the Executive department or among special-interest groups also merit analysis. Veterans' policymaking offers a good opportunity to do this. This study will demonstrate what most people acknowledge yet often do not fully understand: namely, that the process of policymaking is exceedingly complex—a compound of plans, hopes, fears, and accidents.

1

ULYSSES: VINTAGE 1919

VETERANS "saved the country, and now they want it." [1] So quipped one phrasemaker as he viewed veterans of the Civil War rush to the public pensions trough. The quip has proved durable; it can be applied with equal justice to veterans' demands after World War I. By 1931, in fact, one observer said that veterans already had the nation; the question had then become: What were they going to do with it? [2]

From 1919 to the outbreak of war in 1941, veterans demanded that society repay them for their wartime sacrifices. Each successful demand seemed to increase, not decrease, their sense of unredeemed sacrifice. Ulysses imagined he saw suitors—wartime profiteers, radicals on the left, and forgetful politicians—threatening to plunder his homestead. The fragrant twist of smoke rising from the shore that had symbolized Ithaca for Ulysses had by 1932 turned into an ominous cloud billowing over the Anacostia flats.

From 1919 to the outbreak of war in 1941, Federal Government officials attempted to convince veterans to forego special appeals. Each unsuccessful attempt seemed to increase official belief in the

[1] Thomas Brackett Reed (R-Me.), Speaker of the House of Representatives (1889–91 and 1895–99), quoted by Dayton David McKean, *Party and Pressure Politics* (Boston, 1949), p. 507. Cited hereafter as McKean, *Pressure Politics*.

[2] Marcus Duffield, *King Legion* (New York, 1931), p. 2. Cited hereafter as Duffield, *King Legion*.

veterans' "unpatriotic" attitude. To government leaders Ulysses soon lost his heroic mantle; he became instead the brute who wrought his senseless and unprincipled vengeance upon innocent and well-meaning men; a brute whose hand could not be stilled by Reason's tongue.

These abrasive confrontations form the historical background to policymaking for veterans from 1940 to 1946. Each clash crystallized opinions so that, by 1941, two conflicting viewpoints concerning veterans had emerged. One, voiced primarily by veterans' spokesmen, maintained that former servicemen had earned a paramount claim upon society.[3] They formed a separate class; all doubts concerning an individual veteran's claim should be resolved to the veteran's advantage. No one ought to suffer during hard times; but if anyone had to suffer let the veterans be the last.

The other viewpoint, although first expressed during the Harding Administration, later became associated with the New Deal. Veterans, the argument ran, could never be repaid fully for their wartime sacrifices. That principle led to the next: the best way to attempt to repay would be to treat the veteran as an ordinary citizen. If hard times came, all should be helped, not just a select few. At times this second theme incorporated two other, related overtones. It would be argued that service to the country was a civic responsibility; its performance, like jury duty, did not earn the individual special solicitude. Sometimes, the attitude implied that the very combination of veterans into special interest groups was undemocratic and unnatural, if not evil. The rank-and-file veterans, it was argued, would never have pressed for enlarged bounties if they had not been manipulated by a handful of power-hungry, demagogic, and despotic leaders.[4]

THE AMERICAN LEGION, the largest veterans' organization emerging from World War I, became the main protector of veterans' interests during the interbellum period. The Legion had been founded by a

[3] Of course there existed also a preferential hierarchy within the veterans' group. It is possible, although fruitless, to construct a "preference scale" with permanently and totally disabled combat veterans with large, dependent families receiving the highest "score," etc.

[4] See, for example, Talcott Powell, *Tattered Banners* (New York, 1933), pp. 252–53; cited hereafter as Powell, *Tattered Banners;* and Roger Burlingame, *Peace Veterans* (New York, 1932), p. 6.

group of officers and enlisted men in Paris during February and March, 1919.[5] The Allied Expeditionary Force's General Headquarters (GHQ) staff had desired to halt the growth of bolshevism in the AEF's ranks; the rapidly deteriorating morale of the soldiers, it was thought, needed an antidote. The GHQ permitted a select group of officers to meet to discuss remedies. These officers— Theodore Roosevelt, Jr., Ogden Mills, W. J. "Wild Bill" Donovan, Franklin D'Olier, George Ared White, and Joel Bennett "Champ" Clark, to name a few of the more prominent—decided to attract men from the enlisted ranks in order to broaden their movement's appeal. The officers' efforts met limited success at first, although some enlisted men like Harold D. Ross, Alvin C. York, and Alexander Woollcott participated in the so-called Paris caucus, March 15 to 17, 1919. Eager to remove suspicions that the whole affair was a GHQ "plot," the Legion founders maintained that the idea for their organization had arisen more to counter the development of bogus veterans' groups in the United States than to fight bolshevism.[6] Perhaps all had in mind the success of the Grand Army of the Republic, formed after the Civil War. The preamble adopted at the Paris caucus spoke of other, more general, motives:

To perpetuate the principles of justice, freedom and democracy for which we have fought; to inculcate the duty and obligation of the citizen to the State; to preserve the history and incidents of our participation in the war; and to cement the ties of comradeship formed in service.[7]

The final form of the preamble emerged later, at the "Continental caucus" held in St. Louis from May 8 to 10, 1919. This preamble,

[5] For the pro-Legion accounts of the organization's origins, see Richard Seelye Jones, *A History of the American Legion* (Indianapolis and New York, 1946), pp. 22–34. Cited hereafter as Jones, *The Legion*. See also, George Seay Wheat, *The Story of the American Legion* (New York and London, 1919), pp. 1–30; Marquis James, *A History of the American Legion* (New York, 1923), pp. 11–40; and Raymond Moley, Jr., *The American Legion Story* (New York, 1966), pp. 41–59. Cited hereafter as James, *The Legion*, and Moley, *The Legion*. For more critical views, see William Gellermann, *The American Legion as Educator* (New York, 1938), pp. 3–15; and Duffield, *King Legion*, pp. 1–12. Cited hereafter as Gellermann, *The Legion as Educator*.

[6] George A. White, "Cradle Days in the Legion" [mimeographed reprint of an article from], *The American Legion Weekly*, November 19 and 26, and December 10 and 17, 1920; p. 2. Cited hereafter as White, "Cradle Days."

[7] Jones, *The Legion*, p. 29; and Moley, *The Legion*, p. 56.

dubbed by an enthusiast as "one of the greatest documents in American history," added other Legion aims.[8] In short, the preamble dedicated Legionnaires to uphold the Constitution, defend law and order, develop "a one hundred per cent Americanism," combat autocracy of the "classes and the masses," "make right the master of might," promote "peace and good will on earth," and work to help others.[9]

Whatever motivated early Legionnaires to form the organization, they soon assumed the role of spokesman for all former doughboys. The Legion's claim to leadership stemmed partly from its large membership. By 1920 the Legion boasted 843,013 Legionnaires; this amounted to approximately 18.5 per cent of the estimated 4,566,000 veterans of World War I. Although the Legion's popularity waned during the first years of its existence (falling to a low in 1925 of 609,407, or 13.7 per cent of possible enrollees), its fame and influence began to attract more members during the late 1920s. By 1930 Legionnaires for the first time outnumbered the 1920 total; in that year of the Great Depression the count reached 887,754—20.5 per cent of those eligible. Membership exceeded one million for the first time in 1931, but a two-year decline ensued. Beginning in 1933, the Legion grew consistently, if unevenly, during the remaining pre-1941 years. In 1940 the 1931 peak was surpassed; 1,078,119 Legionnaires had been enrolled—26.6 per cent of the eligibles.[10]

[8] White, "Cradle Days," p. 8. If inclusion in Henry Steele Commager's bulky *Documents of American History* be a reliable guide to immortality, then White's claim, alas, has not been borne out. Ironically, Professor Commager does include another preamble of the same vintage—that of the Industrial Workers of the World, one of the Legion's arch-enemies.

[9] Duffield, *King Legion,* p. 10. Much of the following sketch of the Legion is based on Duffield's work. David B. Truman's *The Governmental Process* (New York, 1951) provides insights into the Legion.

[10] The Legion's membership claims are based on its tallies of dues-paying members; see chart prepared by the American Legion, "The American Legion National Membership Record—1920–1962"; Archives of The American Legion, Indianapolis, Ind. Percentages are computed from figures for estimated number of World War I veterans in civil life, U.S. Bureau of the Census, *Historical Statistics of the United States, Colonial Time to 1957* (Washington, D.C., 1960), p. 738. Figures for the number of veterans are:

1925	4,453,000	1935	4,201,000
1930	4,336,000	1940	4,040,000

It should be noted that the Legion restricted its membership to honorably discharged veterans; so the percentage figures may be slightly higher.

The Legion's effectiveness as the veteran's spokesman rested on firmer ground than its claim to one in four eligible veterans as members. The organization's presence throughout the United States enhanced its influence. Few American communities did not have a local Legion post by 1941; many of these posts had become a focal point of the town's social activities, joining the Rotary, the Lions Club, and other fraternal organizations as centers of influence and prestige.[11] Although virtually autonomous on local matters, the posts were bound tightly to the state organization (the department level) and ultimately to the National Headquarters, located at Indianapolis. The rule that forbade local posts to speak out on national issues without prior clearance from upper hierarchical reaches gave the Legion the appearance of solid unity. This may have impressed lawmakers at all governmental levels. As one writer noted in 1932, "the feeling is that opposing a Legion measure is like poking one's political head out of a train window. Maybe nothing would happen; but still it isn't wise." [12]

Other features of the Legion's structure added to the illusion of unity. Theoretically, the national conventions made all the policy decisions for the Legion. Representatives from each department assembled annually for the four-day proceedings. The delegates had a full agenda: elect national officers, decide Legion policy on intricate veterans' benefits, voice opinions on other important issues, and enjoy themselves. This latter item apparently loomed large for most delegates; they paid only cursory attention to other matters. As a result, the National Commander and the National Executive Committee (the group that rules the Legion during the intervals between conventions) guided the delegates on important questions. The national convention's actions became a mandate for the entire organization.

The Legion's ability to assist individual veterans helped the organization to gain influence. The Legion served all veterans, not only its members. Legionnaires gave expert advice and assistance to

[11] One writer has estimated that there were 12,000 posts in the '30s; Jones, *The Legion*, p. 214. Gellermann puts the figure as 11,248 at the beginning of 1936; *The Legion as Educator*, p. 26.
[12] Knowlton Durham, *Billions for Veterans* (New York, 1932), p. 58.

veterans who experienced difficulties in filing claims with the government. Service officers knew the intricacies of bureaucratic procedure; they knew the laws; and, most important, they knew the right person to contact. It was easier to go to the Legion's local post to get help than to tackle the Veterans Administration. Thus, service as an intermediary between the individual needy veteran and big government helped to enhance the Legion's appeal.

Over the years leading to 1941, the Legion followed its preamble's precepts. It exerted pressures to improve physical "rehabilitation" programs for disabled veterans. It helped to force an administrative reorganization of federal agencies dealing with veterans, culminating with establishment of the Veterans Administration in 1930. It worked zealously to promote child welfare; no less ardently, Legionnaires expended countless hours and ergs of energy in the difficult task of defining and defending "Americanism." [13] One constitutional clause forbade the Legion's participation in political activity—eschewing both partisanship and indorsement of candidates to political office. The Legion's main "bread-and-butter" accomplishments during the period 1920–1941, however, resulted from its activities as a pressure group. So effectively did the Legion operate that some commentators consider the group "as the most powerful pressure group of any sort." [14] On three key questions concerning veterans—the bonus, pensions, and administration of benefits—the American Legion played a leading role.

Allied with the Legion, two smaller veterans' organizations earned a share of the lawmakers' respect for their techniques. The Veterans of Foreign Wars of the United States (VFW), formed in 1913 by a merger two Spanish-American War veterans' groups, permitted only servicemen who had seen duty outside America's continental limits to join.[15] By 1941 the VFW claimed 201,268 members.[16]

---

[13] See Jones, *The Legion,* pp. 255–95 for a favorable account of the Legion's child welfare, education, and "Americanism" activities. For a conflicting view on education, see Gellermann, *The Legion as Educator;* and on "Americanism," Rodney G. Minott, *Peerless Patriots* (Washington, D.C., 1962), pp. 55–89. Cited hereafter as Minott, *Peerless Patriots.*

[14] McKean, *Pressure Politics,* p. 511; see also, Jones, *The Legion,* ch. iv.

[15] Minott, *Peerless Patriots,* pp. 27–28.

[16] U.S., House of Representatives, 77th Cong., 2d Sess., *House Document*

The VFW's dedication to promote "fraternal, patriotic, historical, and educational" aims led the organization into political pressure group activity. One critic of veterans' organizations asserted that the VFW "is even more greedy [than the Legion] in its demands upon the taxpayers." [17] The second group, the Disabled Veterans of America (DAV), as its title indicates, restricted membership to war-disabled veterans. Founded in 1920, DAV claimed 41,547 members by 1941.[18] Some observers believed that DAV's limited aim of promoting the welfare of disabled veterans enhanced the organization's effectiveness.[19] By and large, however, DAV members tended to share the larger organizations' views on "nonveterans' " matters.[20] As a result, the Legion, VFW, and DAV frequently presented a united front in putting demands to Congressmen.

THE MEN who returned to civilian life in 1919 received sixty dollars and allowances for train fare to their home towns.[21] But mustering-out pay had come almost as an afterthought; Congress passed the measure three months after the Armistice. Close to one-and-one-third million men had already been released before the bill's enactment.[22] The act was tardy and the sixty dollars a paltry sum. Stories of workers wearing silk shirts and war profiteering by civilians angered the returning doughboys. Common laborers had received large pay increases during the war; navy and government arsenal employees had received six to twelve dollars a day, compared to the doughboy's one dollar; and civil service employees had been given a gratuity of $240 for each year of war-time service.[23]

537, "Proceedings of the 42d National Encampment of the Veterans of Foreign Wars of the United States" (Washington, D.C., 1942), p. 169.

[17] Powell, *Tattered Banners*, p. 252.

[18] U.S., House of Representatives, 78th Cong., 1st Sess., *House Document 39*, "Twenty-Second National Report, Disabled American Veterans, 1942" (Washington, D.C., 1943), p. 42.

[19] Powell, *Tattered Banners*, pp. 252–53.

[20] Minott, *Peerless Patriots,* pp. 51–52.

[21] Dixon Wecter, *When Johnny Comes Marching Home* (New York, 1944), p. 312. Cited hereafter as Wecter, *When Johnny Comes Marching Home.*

[22] John C. Sparrow, *History of Personnel Demobilization in the United States* (Washington, D.C., 1952), p. 453.

[23] Arthur Hennessy, Jr., "Bonus March of 1932" (Unpublished Ph.D. dis-

Discontent about the alleged inequality of sacrifice led to demands for "adjusted compensation" for servicemen. Adjusted compensation or "bonus" would, its advocates argued, help equalize the sacrifices of war; they proposed that servicemen be presented with cash bounties depending upon the duration and rigor of their service. Shortly, the American Legion (having eschewed an interest in similar proposals at the St. Louis caucus) adopted the bonus issue as its own on November 13, 1919 at its Minneapolis convention.[24] From 1920 to 1924 the proposal remained one of the Legion's principal legislative objectives.[25]

The aura of sympathy for veterans in the immediate postwar years failed to insure the bonus campaign's early success. The hard times during 1920–1921 levied their toll on veterans' hopes; as Dixon Wecter later observed: "The Keys to the City had turned out to be only a pass to the flophouse" for some veterans.[26] Relief from unemployment joined equality of sacrifice as a reason for adjusted compensation. But Federal Government officials hardened their countenances to the veterans' pleas. Andrew Mellon, Secretary of the Treasury under Presidents Warren G. Harding, Calvin Coolidge, and Herbert Hoover, particularly disliked the bonus plan. It would, the aluminum trust magnate believed, interfere with the Republican administration's attempts to achieve "fiscal integrity." The high cost of the plan (some predicted it eventually would reach $4.5 billion) and initial suggestions that it be financed in large part by more business taxes appalled Mellon. "War service," he admonished, "should be performed as the highest duty of citizenship and is a sacrifice that can never be measured in terms of money."[27] Mellon attacked the bonus plan by suggesting that it could be financed only by non-business taxation. He proceeded to suggest a series of nuisance taxes on

sertation, Georgetown U., 1957), p. 18. Cited hereafter as Hennessy, "Bonus March of 1932."

[24] James, *The Legion,* pp. 83–87.

[25] Dixon Wecter has suggested that the Legion's leaders had become disturbed about declining membership. With interest in anti-Red activity on the wane, the bonus became the new cohesive force for the Legion. *When Johnny Comes Marching Home,* pp. 446–47.

[26] *Ibid.,* p. 345.

[27] Mellon to Sen. P. Frelinghuysen (R-N.J.), July 2, 1921; quoted in Hennessy, "Bonus March of 1932," 11.

tobacco, public documents, bank checks, and auto licenses to raise the funds.[28] Congress, needless to say, objected to his remedy. Harding and Coolidge, however, shared his views. Harding warned that "this menacing effort to expend billions in gratuities would imperil the restoration of normalcy." [29] More than normalcy was at stake for Coolidge; "we must," he said, "stop this bill or revise our definition of patriotism." [30]

The American Legion pressed on—undaunted by the frigid attitudes of Mellon, Harding, and Coolidge. Legionnaires had other visions of normalcy and patriotism. The Legion mounted a formidable "grass roots" campaign to arouse public support for the bonus—the first in a long series of similar efforts.[31] The National Legislative Committee, the Legion's lobbyists in Washington, asked local post members to write their Congressmen, rally public support, and agitate generally for the Legion's adjusted compensation measure. The campaign met its first test in 1922; Congress passed a bonus bill, only to have it vetoed by Harding. Members of the House of Representatives, perhaps because 1922 was an election year for them, heeded the Legion's appeal to override the Presidential negative. But the Legionnaires' effort fell short in the Senate. This turned out to be but a temporary rebuff. In 1924 the Senate proved more tractable when faced with another veto (this time Coolidge's); on May 19, 1924, the bonus became law and "Silent Cal" had to redefine patriotism.[32]

The bonus act, although giving a handsome bounty, authorized cash payment in only a few cases; most received adjusted compen-

[28] Philip H. Love, *Andrew W. Mellon: The Man and His Work* (Baltimore, 1929), pp. 50–52. Executives of firms in which Mellon had large interests, coincidently, supported the Ex-Servicemen's Anti-Bonus League. Harvey O'Connor, *Mellon's Millions: The Biography of a Fortune* (New York, 1933), p. 269.

[29] Quoted by Andrew Sinclair, *The Available Man* (New York, 1965), p. 212. Sinclair notes also that J. P. Morgan on July 15, 1921 wrote a letter of "personal thanks" to Harding for his "extremely courageous action" after Harding had spoken out against the bonus. *Ibid.*, p. 200.

[30] Quoted by McKean, *Pressure Politics*, pp. 513–14.

[31] Jones, *The Legion*, p. 173.

[32] William Pyrle Dillingham, *Federal Aid to Veterans, 1917–1941* (Gainesville, Fla., 1952), pp. 145–54. This thorough study of World War I benefits is cited hereafter as Dillingham, *Federal Aid to Veterans*.

sation certificates.[33] These bonus certificates soon became the center of critical domestic controversies. As the twenties drew to a close and good times turned to bad, the demand for cash redemption of the policies grew. Veterans once again petitioned Congress; again, in 1931, Congress overrode a Presidential veto (this time Herbert Hoover's) to liberalize the loan provisions of the certificates to permit loans up to 50 per cent of face value, regardless of the reserve accumulated.[34] But even this did not suffice. The Great Depression continued unabated. Veterans stationed themselves on streetcorners vending apples, pencils, and poppies.[35] Soon groups gathered together; simultaneously veterans who had been hardest hit by the economic collapse began the march to the nation's capital during the spring of 1932 with "Adjustment Now" as their goal.

Veterans poured into Washington on foot, by car, and by rail; they hailed from both near and far—New Jersey, Pennsylvania, Oregon, Texas, and California—giving abundant evidence of the universality of the individual veteran's plight.[36] By July, 1932, the num-

[33] The World War Adjusted Compensation Act authorized payments for service between April 5, 1917 and July 1, 1919 of $1 and $1.25, respectively, for each day of domestic and overseas duty served in excess of 60 days. Officers with rank of major or above were excluded. Maximum amounts of $500 for home, and $625 for overseas service were set. Soldiers eligible for $50 or less received the bonus in cash. Those who qualified for larger amounts received bonus certificates in lieu of cash. These certificates were actually twenty-year endowment insurance policies. The policy's face amount depended upon how much insurance an individual could buy at his age if he paid a single lump sum premium that equalled his bonus, increased by 25 per cent. The certificates matured in twenty years, i.e., in 1945; the veteran could, however, after two years, borrow up to 22½ per cent of the certificate's face value. *Ibid.,* p. 154.

[34] *Ibid.,* p. 161.

[35] One writer, seeking to absolve Hoover from responsibility for almost everything, states that the apple-vending of veterans was a "dismal project worked up by Oregon and Washington apple-growers." Eugene Lyons, *Our Unknown Ex-President* (New York, 1948), p. 288.

[36] The brief summary that follows in the next five paragraphs is based primarily on the excellent accounts of the bonus march in Irving Bernstein, *The Lean Years: A History of the American Worker* (New York [Pelican Book edition], 1966), pp. 437–55; William E. Leuchtenburg, *Franklin D. Roosevelt and the New Deal* (New York, 1963), pp. 13–16; Powell, *Tattered Banners,* pp. 215–48; Arthur M. Schlesinger, Jr., *The Crisis of the Old Order,* Vol. I of *The Age of Franklin D. Roosevelt* (New York, 1957), pp. 257–65; and Harris Gaylord Warren, *Herbert Hoover and the Great Depression* (New York, 1959), pp. 227–36. For Hoover's bitter reminiscences and attempt

ber of discontented "hunger marchers" had swelled to approximately 20,000. Despite the attempts of President Hoover and Secretary of War Patrick Hurley to brand the movement as Communist-inspired and led, probably no more than 500 of the dread persuasion participated; indeed, the Reds consistently needed police protection against the menacing threats of the veterans. As it entered Washington, the "Bonus Expeditionary Force (B.E.F.)"—94 per cent of which was composed of veterans—housed itself as best it could. Some abandoned government buildings on Pennsylvania Avenue, hastily built huts on a large plot of land across the river on the Anacostia Flats, and nearby vacant Army posts provided shelter. The generosity of Washington's police and citizens, as well as contributions from other cities, gave the men and their families food and medical supplies. The B.E.F. set up its own police force and attempted to follow military procedures. The veterans behaved well; they claimed their sole purpose was to persuade Congress, and then the President, to pay the bonus at once.

The House of Representatives responded to the veterans' plea. On June 15, 1932, the so-called Patman bill passed the lower body by a vote of 211–176. But the Senate refused to agree; the B.E.F.'s hopes had been in vain. "President Hoover, He's a Bum" and "My Bonus Lies Over the Ocean" became anthems for the disgruntled former servicemen.

At this point, the Administration began to act. President Hoover had decided to remove the veterans from Washington. He asked Congress for funds as loans for B.E.F. members to return to their homes. The legislature complied; some 5,160 veterans took advantage of the loan. The majority however, lingered on. As one veteran explained: " 'No use going back home, because there's nothing to do and nothing to eat. They've got to feed me here.' "

Over the objections of Washington's police superintendent, Pelham

---

at absolution, see Herbert Hoover, *The Cabinet and the Presidency, 1920–1933*, Vol. II of the *Memoirs of Herbert Hoover* (New York, 1951), pp. 225–32. Cited hereafter as Hoover, *Memoirs*. For more detailed views see the solid narrative of Hennessy "Bonus Army of 1932"; and, less valuable, Maurice P. Sneller, Jr., "The Bonus March of 1932: A Study of Depression Leadership and its Legacy" (unpublished Ph.D. dissertation, U. of Va., 1960).

D. Glassford, the District of Columbia Commissioners ordered the evacuation of the buildings on Pennsylvania Avenue. Glassford began this operation on July 28, 1932. In the ensuing fracases, two veterans were mortally wounded, and a policeman was seriously injured. The District commissioners panicked; again, they ignored Glassford's appeals for moderation. The commissioners asked President Hoover to call out the regular Army troops.

Hoover was ready. He dispatched his chief of staff, General Douglas MacArthur, to quell the "riot" on Pennsylvania Avenue. MacArthur, four companies each of infantry and cavalry, a mounted machine gun squadron, and six tanks descended on the former doughboys. After clearing the government buildings, MacArthur, exceeding his instructions, moved his troops on to the mud flats.[37] The B.E.F. fled before the tear gas and the better disciplined troops. The huts of Anacostia flats, fired by troops and veterans alike, went up in a blaze. The dull red glow lit up the sky—even the President in his study could see the over-enthusiastic execution of his orders. MacArthur had done his job well; only a few suffered injuries, minor at that. The B.E.F. had been dispersed. Its immediate goal had been frustrated; yet the marchers represented only the pinched vanguard of the World War I veterans.

Driving veterans out of Washington proved to be temporary.[38] Drummers for cash redemption beat a steady tattoo during the early days of the New Deal. Representative Wright Patman (D-Tex.), a self-styled "serviceman's friend," spearheaded the drive in Congress to pay the bonus in cash. Patman, with generous support from the Legion and the Veterans of Foreign Wars, succeeded in 1935; Congress sent to President Roosevelt a bill that provided for cash redemption through the issuance of more paper currency. This put the Administration in a difficult position. President Franklin D. Roosevelt

[37] See James F. and Jean H. Vivian, "The Bonus March of 1932: The Role of General George Van Horn Moseley," *The Wisconsin Magazine of History,* LI (Autumn, 1967), 26–36; and Donald Lisio, "A Blunder Becomes Catastrophe: Hoover, the Legion, and the Bonus Army," *ibid.,* pp. 37–50.
[38] President Roosevelt and his wife Eleanor treated a subsequent group to coffee (rather than tear gas) in 1933; it also proved a temporary expedient. Frances Perkins, *The Roosevelt I Knew* (New York, 1946), pp. 111–12.

did not approve of the bonus.[39] At first, Roosevelt agreed that he should veto the bill and then allow the negative to be overridden; this would put the burden of any ill effects of cash redemption on Congress.[40]

At this point Henry Morgenthau, Secretary of the Treasury—following Mellon's tradition—intervened. "The veterans," he argued, "had no special claim on the government." [41] Despite Vice President John Nance Garner's earlier warning that "that damn thing's got a lot of strength down in the Senate," Morgenthau continued to view the Patman bill's "premature payment as an unsound, unwarranted, even immoral subsidy to a special-interest group." [42] On May 16, 1935, Morgenthau preached his sermon to Roosevelt in a session that lasted into early morning. Finally the President's face "lit up in a great smile. He raised his two fists in the air and shook them and said 'My God, if I win I would be on the crest of the wave!' " [43]

To rise to the crest, Roosevelt decided to read his veto message to Congress in person, the first time a President had done so. On May 22, 1935, he said that recovery from the depression would be impeded, the debt structure weakened, other interest groups would be enticed to rush to the federal till, and energy would be drained from more permanent and helpful recovery measures if the bonus redemption plan were adopted.[44] The President observed:

Able-bodied veterans should be accorded no treatment different from that accorded to other citizens who did not wear a uniform during the World War. . . . There is before this Congress legislation providing old-age benefits and a greater measure of security for all workers against

[39] Frank Freidel, *Franklin D. Roosevelt, The Triumph* (Boston and Toronto, 1956), p. 363, note. Samuel I. Rosenman tells of Roosevelt's refusal to indorse cash redemption during the Democratic convention at Chicago in 1932. Huey Long had urged Roosevelt to do so; the Kingfish claimed that FDR would not get the nomination if he ignored his advice. *Working With Roosevelt* (New York, 1952), pp. 69–70.

[40] James Farley, *Jim Farley's Story* (New York, 1948), p. 53; and Harold L. Ickes, *The Secret Diary of Harold L. Ickes* (3 vols.; New York, 1953–1954), I, 356, cited hereafter as Ickes, *Diary*.

[41] John Morton Blum, *From the Morgenthau Diaries* (Boston, 1959), p. 250.

[42] *Ibid.*

[43] *Ibid.*, pp. 251–52.

[44] Neil MacNeil, *Forge of Democracy* (New York, 1963), pp. 223–24.

the hazards of unemployment. We are also meeting the . . . need of immediate relief. In all of this the veteran shares.[45]

The vigorous veto message and his personal appearance indicated that the President meant business; it would not be "a veto with a wink." The House, nevertheless, voted to override, 322 to 98. The Senate, as in the case of Harding's veto of the original bonus bill, upheld the President.

Following this negative action, Legionnaires met to survey the field. They did not heed the Administration's pleas to call the dogs off. After lopping Patman's unpleasant monetary inflation features from the proposal, the Legion came right back in 1936, an election year, with another bill. The President had other worries by this time. When Congress passed the new measure providing for payment in savings bonds, he vetoed it; his message, according to one New Dealer, "was totally lacking in vigor or argument of any sort." [46] To no one's surprise, both houses overrode the veto—and veterans flocked in, exchanged their certificates for savings bonds, and promptly cashed most of the bonds.[47]

Final victory on the bonus in 1936 meant that an issue, alive for almost twenty years, had been laid to rest, or so it appeared. Actually, the bonus fight had a lasting impact on those who had joined the fracas. The series of vetoes by four Presidents convinced officials of the American Legion and other veterans' organizations that legislation benefiting veterans could be won only through great effort and organization. It made them more receptive to suggestions that secret forces conspired to frustrate legitimate veterans' demands. In a like manner, those who had opposed these appeals viewed the activities of Legionnaires and others as "treasury raids." And for some observers, the success of the veterans' importunities for a bonus in 1924, and for its cash redemption in 1936, represented a pattern that would likely be repeated if the United States should engage in another war.

[45] Samuel I. Rosenman, comp., *The Public Papers and Addresses of Franklin D. Roosevelt* (13 vols.; 1938–1950), IV, 187 and 189. Cited hereafter as Rosenman, *Roosevelt Public Papers*.

[46] Ickes, *Diary*, I, 525.

[47] Not all veterans exchanged the certificates. On the eve of the original redemption date, the VA estimated that approximately 30,000 veterans still held the bonus certificates. *The Washington Post,* December 18, 1944.

"THE AMERICAN idea of war is to take the farmer from his plow, and return him to his plow—with a pension." [48] This half-humorous appraisal typifies a major goal of the American Legion after World War I. Securing the bonus, after all, took up only part of their time. Other more long-lasting conduits to the treasury were being laid. Although the bonus finally cost the Government approximately $3.8 billion, it at least had the merit of being a one-time proposition. But pensions were a different matter; they tended to stretch on unbelievably. As late as 1942 the pension rolls still listed one beneficiary from the War of 1812.[49] From 1920 to 1941, the Legion led the fight to liberalize the basis for awarding pensions as well as to widen the number of beneficiaries. Like the bonus question, the continuing battle between the Legion and New Deal over pensions was remembered in the post-1941 period.

When the men and women returned after World War I, virtually no one disputed the claims of the war disabled for pensions. The gassed, the maimed, and the blinded bore physical witness to the horror of war; the community could not deny them pecuniary assistance. Before the conflict in France had ended Congress had passed a compensation law allowing $30 monthly for the single veteran totally and permanently disabled—a niggardly sum, to be sure.[50] To raise that amount became one of the early tasks of veterans, able-bodied and disabled alike. Their success in December, 1919, when Congress raised the monthly base amount to $80, gave them the satisfaction of a job well done.[51]

If the veterans' organizations earned just praise for awakening the national legislators to a shameful condition, their subsequent efforts

[48] Thomas B. Reed again; quoted by V. O. Key, Jr., *Politics, Parties, and Pressure Groups* (5th ed., New York, 1964), p. 106.

[49] Alfred G. Buehler, "Military Pensions," *The Annals of the American Academy of Political and Social Science*, CCXXVII (May, 1943), 132.

[50] Public Law 90, 65th Cong., October 6, 1917. Dependents qualified the totally disabled veteran to additions to the base allowance: $15 for his wife, $10 for each dependent child, $10 for a dependent, widowed mother. If the veteran required the full-time services of a nurse or an attendant $20 more was added. For partial disability, rated at 10 per cent or more, the monthly amounts were a corresponding percentage of the compensation for total disability. Dillingham, *Federal Aid to Veterans*, p. 39.

[51] Public Law 104, 66 Cong., December 24, 1919. For the Legion's role, see James, *The Legion*, pp. 99–101; and Jones, *The Legion*, pp. 47–48.

received less approbation. Having succeeded once, the veterans' organizations began an onslaught on the compensation principle that had been adopted to forestall repetition of the abuses of the Civil War pensions system. This principle declared that only those individuals who could link their physical disability to honorably performed war service by medical proof would receive compensation. The term "compensation" had been used deliberately to denote indemnity for loss, rather than "pension" to signify a gratuity.[52]

The citadel resisted onslaughts until 1921. Then the Sweet bill declared that active tuberculosis or a neuropsychiatric disease that broke out within two years of a veterans' discharge would be presumed to be service-connected.[53] The adoption of statutory proof, rather than medical evidence, had begun. Pressures from the Legion, the VFW, and DAV continued; partly because of their efforts another major revision came in 1924, when Congress codified the veterans' laws.[54] The result, the World War Veterans' Act, permitted (among other provisions) compensation to veterans hospitalized due to venereal disease. Prior to this, contraction of the disease stood as a priori proof of misconduct; therefore, the debilitating effects were noncompensable. The act also added more diseases to the presumptive service-connected list: paralysis agitans, encephalitis lethargica, and amoebic dysentery. Another noteworthy liberalization came with the increase of the additional monthly allowance for veterans needing the services of a nurse or an attendant to $50.

In 1930 the veterans' organizations found a strong ally within the House: John Elliott Rankin (D-Miss.), chairman of the Committee on World War Veterans' Legislation. Rankin began to press for further changes in veterans' pensions. The Mississippian was increasingly influential over the next fourteen years in establishing policies for ex-servicemen.[55] Rankin had come to the House of Representatives in

[52] Other safeguards had been erected; disabilities had to occur within one year after discharge from service to be compensable. Claims had to be filed within five years. No claim was retroactive for more than one year. *Ibid.,* p. 40.
[53] Public Law 47, 67 Cong., August 9, 1921.
[54] Public Law 242, 68 Cong., June 7, 1924.
[55] The following sketch is based on Rankin's biography in *Current Biography* (February, 1944), pp. 555–58; Walter Davenport, "Big Wind from the South,"

1921, at the age of 38. His home town of Tupelo and Mississippi's First Congressional District returned him regularly to Washington for the next thirty-two years. During that period Rankin became both the joy and the *bête noire* of conservative and liberal alike—although as the years progressed more the darling of the former. One recent historian of the House of Representatives views Rankin as one of the body's "most controversial twentieth-century members and also one of its ablest parliamentarians." [56]

Rankin had strong passions. These passions seemed to radiate from a central emotional core of his brand of "Americanism." The outlines of his "Americanism" are clearly shown by the chief causes he championed: anti-monopolies, especially in regard to electric power "trusts"; anti-Negro; anti-Jew; anti-Labor; anti-communist; and pro-veteran. His distaste for private utilities led him to co-author, with Senator George Norris (R-Neb.), the Tennessee Valley Authority Act; Rankin, baiting the "Power Trust," continued to champion public power throughout his career. Northern liberals castigated him as a Negro-hater and Jew-baiter.[57] When Harlem voters first elected Adam Clayton Powell (D-N.Y.) to represent them in 1944, Rankin said he would not sit next to the Negro Congressman: "In my opinion sending this individual to Congress is the worst thing that could happen to the members of his race. It just shows what certain Communistic elements are trying to bring about in this country." [58] To a Jewish critic, he wrote:

You say that, being a Jew, you have been on the sore end of my cudgel. I am not after American Jews who believe in the American way of life; but I am anti-Communist, and I don't care whether those Communists

---

Collier's, CXVI (December 1, 1945), 66, 81–83; and Russell Whelan, "Rankin of Mississippi," *The American Mercury*, LIX (July, 1944), 31–37.

[56] Neil MacNeil, *Forge of Democracy* (New York, 1963), p. 44.

[57] Sen. Joseph F. Guffey (D-Pa.), for example, after classing Rankin with John Randolph and Thaddeus Stevens as a legislative leader, went on to say: "Today we have a third leader who is dominating both branches of Congress —Jew baiting, Negro hating John Rankin of Mississippi is against popular education and says so and he is against the Negro and boasts of it." Quoted from Guffey's Jefferson-Jackson Day dinner at York, Pa., on April 15, 1944, by *The Washington Post*, April 16, 1944.

[58] Rankin to John Lynch, editor of the Greenville [Miss.] *Delta-Democrat Times*, quoted in *ibid.*, January 9, 1945.

are Jew, Gentile, or what-not. Frankly, I think that those of them who go after that stuff are doing you American Jews an irreparable injury— and when I say that I am expressing the opinion of my Jew friends who are real Americans and have no patience with Communism.[59]

One admirer summed up Rankin's qualities in a missive that Rankin rated as a "splendid letter":

On my recent trip through Miss., I heard many well deserved complimentary references to your record on the race issue, Poll taxes, Marshall Field III, and the arched [sic], south hater, "nigger" lover, Chameleonic candidate for the presidency, who deadbeat his way on a world trip and now pretends such great love for "My fellow Americans." [60]

Rankin usually denied that he abhorred Negroes and Jews; as the examples indicate, he rationalized his position by saying, in effect, that he had nothing against Negroes "in their place," or against Jews who were "Americans." Nonetheless, the fiery Mississippian earned the label of "bigot."

In his later years as a lawmaker, Rankin derived his greatest personal satisfaction from close association with the anti-communism "crusade." He assessed his stunning tactics in 1945 in making the House Un-American Activities Committee a permanent house organ "as one of my greatest services to my country." [61] Negroes desiring greater freedom, Jews upholding liberal causes, CIO Political Action Committee officials attempting to influence elections, Fair Employment Practice Committee supporters—all these Rankin thought were communists or communist-inspired. Of course his anti-communism cannot be separated from his bigotry; it became merely another tool in his well-stocked arsenal of racist weapons.

These qualities involved him in many verbal scrapes—and more

[59] Rankin to Mort Gittleman, February 5, 1946; "John Stelle vs. Gen. Bradley—79th Cong." Folder, HR 79 A-F 38.2, Tray 17809, Records of the House Committee on World War Veterans' Legislation, Record Group 233, National Archives. Cited hereafter as Rankin Committee Records, RG 233, NA.

[60] Lloyd T. Binford to Rankin, October 23, 1943, and Rankin to Binford, October 28, 1943; "B" Folder, HR 78 A-F 39.1, Tray 17010, ibid. Field, a liberal, published PM (New York), a newspaper that Rankin despised.

[61] Rankin to Walter Johnson, January 31, 1946; "Military Order of the Liberty Bell—79th Cong." Folder, HR 79 A-F 38.2, Tray 17807, ibid.

than one exchange of fisticuffs.[62] Drew Pearson, who considered
Rankin a charter member of the "hate group" in Congress, featured
the "Rankin superstition" in one of his "Washington Merry-Go-
Round" columns: some Congressmen apparently believed that those
who tangled with Rankin shortly would die.[63] Despite these run-ins,
or perhaps because of the superstition, Rankin apparently got along
well with most of his colleagues; for example, no one opposed him
more bitterly than Vito N. Marcantonio (American Labor Party-
N.Y.). Yet, Marcantonio and Rankin, after a sharp exchange, often
would leave the House chambers arm in arm.[64]

Rankin's entry into the 1930 fray over pensions is an early indica-
tion of his identification of ex-servicemen with patriotism. The specific
issue was whether to extend compensation to veterans whose disabilities commenced after January 1, 1925, the earlier cut-off date
for presumptive proof of service connection. Rankin and the veterans' organizations urged that the date be extended. Arrayed against
this proposal stood the adherents of Herbert Hoover's economy measures. The 1929 Crash had come; but the costs of veterans' benefits
remained high. In 1930 the Treasury expended 24.7 per cent of the
total federal budget on veterans' services—only slightly below the
26 per cent average from 1924 to 1929.[65] Hoover, faced with the
bleak prospect of continued hard times, strove to beat back the "professional money-hunting veterans." [66]

Rankin, however, won the first skirmish when the House approved

[62] In 1945 the 140-pound, 62-year-old Rankin landed a stiff left jab on
the chin of Rep. Frank Hook (D-Mich.). Hook, 10 years his junior and 55
pounds heavier, did not fight back—fortunately for Rankin. Rankin had in-
timated that Hook was a Communist; Hook replied that Rankin was a "God
damn liar," or a "dirty liar" depending upon whose version is used. *The
Washington Post,* February 23, 1945.

[63] *Ibid.,* March 11, 1945.

[64] MacNeil, *Forge of Democracy,* p. 146.

[65] U.S., The President's Commission on Veterans' Pensions, *A Report on
Veterans' Benefits in the United States, Staff Report No. II: Veterans' Benefits
Administered by Departments and Agencies of the Federal Government, Digest
of Laws and Basic Statistics,* printed as U.S., House of Representatives, 84th
Cong., 2d Sess., *House Committee Print No. 262* (Washington, D.C., 1956),
Table 26, 190.

[66] Hoover, *Memoirs,* II, 285. A year later Hoover journeyed to Detroit to
"point out the path of service" to Legionnaires on the bonus question; *ibid.,*
288.

his bill extending the presumptive date to January 1, 1930. After Hoover's veto had been upheld, an Administration-backed substitute measure was passed.[67] Although the time extension requested by Rankin and the veterans' organizations failed of adoption, all shreds of the service-connected principle were discarded by the new act. For the first time, World War I veterans whose disabilities were not connected with wartime duty could receive compensation.[68] Twelve years following the Armistice the compensation principle had been scrapped; the veterans' organizations seemed to have won.

Legionnaires, however, could not rest on their laurels. The election of Franklin D. Roosevelt brought a fresh opponent who visualized his 1932 campaign promises to reduce federal outlays as a mandate.[69] The expenditure of $985 million for veterans' services in fiscal year 1932 could not have escaped his eye. The new President's belief in budget balancing—a view shared by many in his party—led him to a head-on clash with the American Legion and other veterans' organizations. Roosevelt probably believed also that veterans already were receiving substantial benefits not shared by other Americans. Desiring to help all, Roosevelt was prompted to level his aim on the high privileges enjoyed by veterans.[70]

On March 10, 1933, shortly after his inaugural, Roosevelt asked Congress to approve an "economy" plan; he desired, among other proposals, to cut $400 million from veterans' payments. "Too often," he warned, "in recent history liberal governments have been wrecked

[67] Public Law 522, 71 Cong., July 3, 1930. Dillingham, *Federal Aid to Veterans*, pp. 51–52.

[68] By this measure, veterans with a permanent non-service connected disability rated at 25 per cent or more, who served more than 90 days during the war, some time of which had to fall before November 11, 1918, and who had been exempt from filing a federal income tax the year before applying for disability compensation—could receive up to $40 monthly. *Ibid.*, pp. 52–53.

[69] During the campaign, Roosevelt vowed that "I shall approach the problem of carrying out the plain precept of our Party, which is to reduce the costs of current Federal Government operations by 25 per cent." Quoted by Freidel, *FDR: The Triumph*, p. 363.

[70] See *ibid.*, p. 363, and Leuchtenburg, *Franklin D. Roosevelt and the New Deal*, p. 37, for Roosevelt's views on the budget. For the President's attitude about the preferred position of veterans, see his address at the dedication of the Roanoke, Va. veterans' hospital, October 19, 1934, in Rosenman, *Roosevelt Public Papers*, III, 427–30.

on rocks of loose fiscal policy." [71] The words might have been Mellon's; no matter who said them, veterans fought back vigorously. The Democratic Party caucus listened to the veterans' howls; it refused to indorse Roosevelt's request. James F. Byrnes (D-S.C.), a Senate floor leader of the bill, recalls that "all the parliamentary skill we could command" was brought to bear.[72] After four days of strenuous battle the bill passed, borne along in part by the generally irresistible tide of legislation of those first one hundred days. On March 20, 1933 Roosevelt signed the bill.[73]

The measure gave the President sweeping power. All former pension and compensation laws were repealed; in their place the President could make his own. Subsequently, he promulgated twelve executive orders. The more important features show how radical the changes were: the orders discarded the term "compensation" and returned to the older "pension" reference. They changed the complicated rating schedules to a simple five-step scheme (10, 25, 50, 75, or 100 per cent) for disabilities, with $80 monthly as the highest award for total permanent disability. Disability percentages rated between these "steps" were set at the next lower level.[74] The order limited the basic monthly death benefits for widows to $30, with maximum monthly amount (basic pension plus allowances for dependents) set at $75. The Administration eliminated, with few exceptions, statutory presumption of service-connected disabilities. Officials also repealed outright the $50 monthly statutory award for life for arrested tuberculosis; in its place a new rating schedule was set up. The Administration also imposed limits on pension amounts a veteran could receive while undergoing domiciliary or hospital care. Finally, the decision of the Veterans Administrator was made final, no longer subject to judicial review.[75]

[71] Quoted by Leuchtenburg, *Franklin D. Roosevelt and the New Deal*, p. 45.
[72] James F. Byrnes, *All in One Lifetime* (New York, 1958), p. 75.
[73] Public Law 2, 73 Cong., March 20, 1933.
[74] Jones, *The Legion*, p. 152.
[75] U.S., The President's Commission on Veterans' Pensions, *A Report on Veterans' Benefits in the United States, Staff Report No. 1: The Historical Development of Veterans' Benefits in the United States*, printed as U.S., House of Representatives, 84th Cong., 2d Sess., House Committee Print No. 244 (Washington, D.C., 1956), 85–86.

The new orders made Congressmen blanch at the thought of the reprisals that might be made in their home districts. The Grand Rapids (Mich.) *Herald* gave one clue to the reaction outside of Washington: "If in order to balance the budget we have to take the bread out of the mouths of men who are suffering because of patriotic service, then let the Treasury go down with the flag waving." [76] But most editorials wanted Congressmen to keep their hands off. *The Baltimore Sun* moralized that politicians "ought not to be allowed to masquerade as champions of the battle-scarred soldiers, when . . . they are merely urging the perpetuation of a system of disgraceful abuses in which battle-scarred veterans have no part." [77] Despite this kind of admonishment, Congress entertained second thoughts about giving President Roosevelt unlimited power over veterans' pensions. Three months after the Economy Act, the lawmakers passed the Independent Offices Appropriation Act of 1934, decreeing that no service-connected disability pension be reduced more than 25 per cent, that no reduction for death compensation be made, and that the presumptive service-connected cases be reviewed by a board before elimination. During the period of review a veteran would be carried at 75 per cent of his former compensation. [78]

In October, 1933, Roosevelt followed in his predecessor's footsteps—this time to Chicago—to address the American Legion's annual convention. It was a brave move; Chicago's Mayor Edward Joseph Kelly had doubted whether he could protect the President during his stay. [79] What the President told the Legionnaires was even more courageous. For it was in this speech that (after agreeing the government had the obligation to aid veterans with war-connected disabilities) Roosevelt stated, "That no person, because he wore a uniform, must thereafter be placed in a special class of beneficiaries over and above all other citizens." [80]

The appeal to the Legionnaires to accept the changes made in the pension laws went for naught. The Legion helped get passed the Inde-

[76] Quoted in *The Literary Digest*, CXV (July 17, 1933), 3.
[77] Quoted in *ibid.*, 4.
[78] Public Law 78, 73 Cong., June 16, 1933.
[79] Ickes, *Diary*, I, 104.
[80] Rosenman, *Roosevelt Public Papers*, II, 375–76.

pendent Offices Appropriations Act of 1935, which restored almost all of the pre-economy veterans' allowances.[81] Congress overrode Roosevelt's veto; he "suffered his first serious political setback" as chief executive.[82] Ungraciously, Harold L. Ickes noted that "like so many scared rabbits [the Representatives] ran to cover out of fear of the soldier vote." [83]

The pension struggle had now ended. All the service-connected disabled had been put back at the pre-economy rates; the "presumptives" had been returned to 75 per cent levels; the term "compensation" had been restored; even the "misconduct" cases found their way back by 1939.[84]

What had Roosevelt accomplished? A 25 per cent reduction in compensation for the "presumptives." "Non-war" veterans, veterans with disabilities arising from pre-existing conditions, and cases of fraud, once lopped from the rolls, were not replaced. More important, the President had enunciated clearly a principle concerning veterans' benefits that, if not followed consistently, would at least remain as the ideal, or the standard, during the New Deal and war periods. Of equal importance, of course, was the heritage of bitterness that grew out of the economy fight. Representatives of the veterans' organizations would never forget the traumatic experience of seeing fourteen years of painstaking gains swept aside by the stroke of a pen. During World War II, for example, representatives of veterans' organizations warned Congressmen that an overly generous civil service preference policy would lead to another "whirlwind economy act." [85] On the other hand, the experience undoubtedly taught that if demands for special benefits were granted without check, a reaction surely would set in. Ten years later, Brigadier General Frank T. Hines, the Veterans Administrator, advised a group of representatives from veterans' organizations:

Let's be cautious! Let's not have another Economy Act! I survived one of them, but I am not sure that I could survive another, I should prefer

[81] Public Law 141, 73 Cong., March 28, 1934.
[82] Ickes, *Diary*, I, 158.
[83] *Ibid.*
[84] Dillingham, *Federal Aid to Veterans*, p. 98.
[85] See below, ch. viii.

not to take the chance and I think we can chart out [our] course so that there will be no necessity for such a thing.[86]

THE INDOMITABLE veterans of World War I also faced the problem of reshaping the Federal Government's bureaucratic apparatus to meet their special needs. Specifically, they strove to centralize all responsibility for veterans in one responsive agency. They wanted one tuning fork, pitch set at a sympathetic frequency, so that their demands might be met by harmonious acquiescence.

One event stands out as a cause for unified administration: the unfortunate result of the dual control of vocational rehabilitation for disabled veterans.[87] This program had been set up in the closing days of 1917. It sprang from the lofty motive of Congress to do something valuable for the war injured. Rather than place men with broken bodies on a permanent dole, it was believed both more economical and humane to attempt to train them for jobs which they could perform despite their handicaps—more economical, because the veteran would soon be earning income, making him less reliant upon the government; more humane, since a man who worked obviously benefited from that experience; he became, in effect, a stronger person, no longer an object of pity.

But vocational rehabilitation of World War I veterans proved to be a near disaster. The program suffered from mismanagement, excessive costs, and improper planning. Administrators did not exercise enough care in approving veterans' training courses. Unfortunately, the examples of the right-handed veteran trained to be a barber although unable to raise his right arm above his waist, and of the man taught to be an automobile mechanic even though he could not stoop without falling, were numerous.[88]

[86] "Minutes of Fourth Annual Meeting, National Council of American Veteran Organizations, held November 10, 1944," mimeographed copy in "National Council of American Veteran Organizations" Folder, HR 79 A-F 38.2, Tray 17807, Rankin Committee Records, RG 233, NA.

[87] See Dillingham, *Federal Aid to Veterans*, pp. 131–44; Wecter, *When Johnny Comes Marching Home*, pp. 393–403; and Willard Waller, *Veteran Comes Back* (New York, 1944), pp. 238–40. The following account leans heavily on these fine summaries of the vocational rehabilitation program.

[88] Dillingham, *Federal Aid to Veterans*, p. 138; and Powell, *Tattered Banners*, p. 183.

A plethora of red tape emerged from the administrative arrange-ments under which the program operated. The Bureau of War Risk Insurance determined the eligibility of veterans applying for training. Then the Federal Board for Vocational Education (also within the Treasury Department) set up the specific training course, as well as approved the institutions where veterans actually took the training. Often training programs did not start quickly since the War Risk In-surance Bureau, swamped with applications for veterans' benefits during demobilization, could not keep up with its certification func-tions. In 1919 Congress unified the certification and supervision under the Board for Vocational Education. This did not work well; the pro-gram did not begin to operate satisfactorily until after the legislators switched entire responsibility to the newly established Veterans' Bu-reau in 1921. But the move came too late. The program did linger on for seven more years; yet most of that time was spent in its liqui-dation. Still, when the final figures were computed in 1928, the Vet-erans' Bureau could report that 128,747 disabled veterans had com-pleted their work satisfactorily; the total cost came to approximately $645,000,000.[89]

One important lesson emerged from the vocational rehabilitation program. The division of authority during the program's early days had added to the distress of disabled veterans. Unification of func-tions under the Veterans' Bureau in 1921 established a precedent that veterans' organizations elevated into a principle.

The principle, to be sure, underwent its greatest test in 1921. Charles R. Forbes had charmed President Harding during a vacation trip to Honolulu; Harding then appointed his genial acquaintance to head the War Risk Insurance Agency, the Veterans' Bureau's prede-cessor. Forbes brought few credentials to his task. He had served briefly in the Signal Corps; he deserted, was captured, and permitted to serve out his enlistment after a short incarceration. Forbes later earned the Distinguished Service Medal.

It was a short burst of glory. Under his mismanagement from 1921

[89] Dillingham, *Federal Aid to Veterans,* p. 143. Dillingham points out that the total includes disability compensation that would have been paid at any rate, vocational rehabilitation program or not.

to 1923, approximately one-quarter of the funds appropriated for his agency was stolen or wasted. Some of the details surpass belief. Floor wax purchases exceeded the bureau's needs for a century; much of the huge supply became a fire hazard and had to be destroyed. Under Forbes's orders the bureau sold at one door 85,000 sheets worth $1.25 each for $.20 apiece—at the same time new shipments were being delivered at another entrance. One hard-worked employee received $4,800 for two hours labor annually. The failure to build adequate hospital facilities, however, remains Forbes's greatest sin. This and a host of other irregularities came to light officially under a senatorial investigation in 1923. Forbes resigned, was tried, convicted, and sent to Leavenworth, where he served one-and-a-half years. But the damage had been done; the veterans' cause had been injured by the scandals within the Veterans' Bureau.[90]

Public confidence had to be restored; at the same time a genuinely responsive and honest administrator needed to be appointed. Both needs were met with Harding's choice of Brigadier General Frank T. Hines as the new director. Hines soon made over the Veterans' Bureau—and its successor, the Veterans Administration—into an efficient and tightly run agency. One of his most successful moves was to take the organization out from under the glare of publicity; by adhering to a scrupulously honest policy (therefore undramatic), Hines performed a valuable service for the veterans.

In a manner of speaking, the agency began to mirror Hines's personality.[91] Born at Salt Lake City, Utah, in 1879, Hines had begun his long, but not continuous, military association during the Spanish-American War. He saw action in the Philippines; his bravery there earned him a recommendation for the Congressional Medal of Honor. During World War I he served as Chief of Staff of the Embarkation Service. In 1920, two years after having been promoted to brigadier

[90] The above two paragraphs on Forbes follow Wecter's and Waller's descriptions.

[91] The following is based on Dillingham, *Federal Aid to Veterans*, p. 15; the article on Hines in *Current Biography* (April, 1944); 296–99; "People of the Week," *The United States News*, XVI (June 2, 1944), 62–64; and personal interview with Guy H. Birdsall and Robinson E. Adkins, February 3, 1965, Wash., D.C. Messrs. Birdsall and Adkins held important posts under General Hines.

general, Hines resigned from the Army. He capitalized on his war-time experience and contacts by entering the shipping business. During the Senate's investigation of Forbes, Hines reluctantly accepted Harding's offer to head the Veterans' Bureau. He continued as head of the agency until replaced by General Omar N. Bradley, twenty-two years later.

As head of the Veterans' Bureau, General Hines earned the respect of observers in Washington for his unusual devotion to hard work and long hours. Years later, associates recalled that the General avoided using the chauffeured limousine to which his job entitled him; he preferred instead to travel to work by bus. He often arrived at his desk at seven o'clock in the morning and left eleven hours later with a briefcase stuffed with papers for work at home.

An able administrator, quiet-spoken, undemonstrative, and austere, Hines hewed closely to his conception of his job—that of an informed, nonpartisan, and totally trustworthy adviser to his superiors. Although the latter ostensibly were the five Presidents under whom he served, Hines's relationships with members of Congress and leaders of the veterans' organizations probably made him more aware of and sensitive to their wishes. He nurtured carefully his "image" with influential and durable Congressmen like John Rankin. During the dark days of his last unhappy months as Veterans Administrator, for example, Hines would send copies of letters that praised him to the Chairman of the House Committee on Veterans' Legislation.[92]

---

[92] See Hines to Rankin, June 4, 1945, with enclosure, Mrs. Wales Latham to Hines, May 31, 1945; "L" Folder, HR 79 A-F 38.1, Tray 17793, Rankin Committee Records, RG 233, NA. Even after he had been "promoted" to the post of Ambassador to Panama in 1945, he continued to curry favor. In December, 1945, he told Rankin of his pleasure in learning that Tupelo had been chosen as a Veterans Administration hospital site; he reminded the Mississippian that he had been the one to make the initial recommendation. Rankin, let it be said, reacted positively to Hines's attention. Concerning the hospital, Rankin replied: "I cannot tell you how grateful I am for your kindness in this matter, as well as in all other matters. Nor can I tell you how much I miss you here now." The General must have been pleased to read Rankin's assertion that "since I have been a member of Congress, no public servant deserves a higher praise than you do for the excellent work which you have done for the ex-serviceman, as well as the country as a whole." See Hines to Rankin, December 14, 1945; and Rankin to Hines, December 17, 1945, and January 8, 1946; "Hines, General Frank T." Folder, HR 79 A-F 38.2, Tray 17805, *ibid*.

Over the two decades of his service, Hines learned to approach Congress cautiously. Although he would press for statutory changes that would make his job of administering benefits easier, he preferred to give information rather than dictate policy. His insistence upon standing and speaking without notes while testifying before Congressional committees impressed seasoned lawmakers who knew the complexity of veterans' laws. By remaining "nonpartisan"—he was a registered Republican—he enhanced his image as a fact-giver. He was, in short, a superb selection to replace Forbes.

By 1941 the American Legion and its sister organizations had attained most of their goals. Bonuses, pensions, unified and sympathetic administration of benefits—these were the tangible assets. The memories of difficulties in attaining them would not be forgotten easily. The Roosevelt Administration also had established a principle: that able-bodied veterans would be viewed as part of the American community—not a separate class.

The background and setting for veterans' policymaking can now be summarized briefly. The officials in power during 1941 to 1946 inherited a threefold legacy. One was that of Ulysses, the ancient sense of an obligation to veterans and the equally age-old tradition of civilian-veteran clashes. Second, that of the World War I doughboy, the record of a series of forays upon the public treasury and the sharp sense that veterans deserved far more than they got. Third, that of general welfare orientation of the New Deal—the deeply ingrained notion that veterans could be helped best by helping all Americans. This legacy, as can be seen, carried with it contradictory elements. The attempts to reconcile internal inconsistencies provided the tensions under which policymaking evolved.

2

ITHACA BEGINS TO PLAN

"WHEN DEMOBILIZATION DAY comes we are going to suffer another Pearl Harbor, a Pearl Harbor perfectly foreseeable—now—a Pearl Harbor of peace, not of war." This glum prognostication came during the summer of 1943 from the pen of T.R.B., Washington correspondent for the liberal periodical, *The New Republic*.[1] Many Americans shared the columnist's uneasiness. For, although he used a wartime symbol, T.R.B. suffered from a bad case of what John Kenneth Galbraith has called the "Depression Psychosis."[2] To Americans of the war years, the bitter memories of the Great Depression had not yet faded. Time and prosperity, the great anodynes of bitter memories, had scarcely begun to work their magic. The belief lingered that America had not righted itself from the economic blow of the depression, except through heavy defense and war spending beginning in 1939. Removal of the war-created federal fiscal activity when peace came would lead to widespread unemployment; it was "likely to be one of the most serious in American history."[3] The "Depression Psychosis"

[1] "When Demobilization Comes," CIX (August 2, 1943), 139. Congress' termination of the National Resources Planning Board provided the immediate stimulus of T.R.B.'s gloom.

[2] *American Capitalism* (Cambridge, Mass., 1952), ch. vi.

[3] Max Lerner, writing in January, 1944; Lerner, *Public Journal: Marginal Notes on Wartime America* (New York, 1945), p. 357.

provides part of the intellectual setting for the period.[4] In brief, fear of a postwar economic collapse impelled Americans—latter day Ithacans—to plan for Ulysses' return.

Of course not all observers believed that massive unemployment lurked immediately beyond victory. Early in the war, for example, Luther Gulick, a political scientist, expressed mild optimism about the future. Writing to Representative Lyndon B. Johnson (D-Tex.), Gulick noted: "In fact I am inclined to think that there will be a very high level of employment" after the war.[5] To be sure, Gulick hedged his bet; if the movement toward that "high level" of employment were delayed, then government, labor, and business would have to combine to insure "work for all." President Roosevelt himself apparently believed that the "hangover" of unfulfilled consumer wants would carry the nation forward prosperously in the immediate postwar years.[6] Others agreed with the President; Representative James W. Wadsworth, Jr. (R-N.Y.) foresaw not only the "hangover effect," but also the demand for goods that rehabilitation of war-torn countries in Europe and Asia would bring, as well as the development of new industries such as commercial aviation and plastics.[7]

Yet, according to the public opinion polls, as many people feared resumption of high unemployment as those who did not. For example, in July 1944, a Gallup poll recorded that only 12 per cent of the interviewees thought unemployment would be three million or less; 24 per cent pegged the jobless figure at somewhere between seven to ten million, 11 per cent at eleven to nineteen million, and 8 per cent

[4] This point is stressed in Stephen Kemp Bailey's excellent *Congress Makes a Law* (New York, 1950), ch. ii. Cited hereafter as Bailey, *Congress Makes a Law.*

[5] Gulick to Johnson, February 18, 1943; 830.31 File, Central Office Correspondence, Records of the National Resources Planning Board, Record Group 187, National Archives. Cited hereafter as NRPB Records, RG 187, NA.

[6] Vice President Henry Wallace tried to convince Roosevelt that hard work and planning for postwar employment be commenced early in 1943. In the course of a letter, Wallace commented: "I agree with you that because of shortages there will be a certain amount of hangover prosperity for the first year or two." Wallace to Roosevelt, February 5, 1943; Official File 4351, White House Papers of Franklin D. Roosevelt, Franklin D. Roosevelt Library, Hyde Park. Cited hereafter as OF . . . , Roosevelt Papers, FDRL.

[7] Wadsworth to Harold A. Aron, March 22, 1943; "Demobilization" Folder, House of Representatives Files, Wadsworth Papers, Library of Congress.

at twenty million or more.[8] Five months later another Gallup poll elicited the information that 68 per cent of those questioned believed that not everyone who wished to work would be able to find a job when the war ended.[9] This concern helped to shape three early efforts by Ithacans to get ready for Ulysses: the Selective Training and Service Act of 1940, the Vocational Rehabilitation Act of 1943, and the work of the Post-War Manpower Conference during 1942 and 1943.

SEPTEMBER 16, 1940, set an unhappy precendent. On that day President Franklin D. Roosevelt approved the Selective Training and Service Act.[10] The new statute was America's first peacetime military conscription law. Under the terms of the act—and its revisions—sixteen million citizens went off to war.

No one knew in September 1940 that war would come in fifteen months, or that four years would pass before it would end. The uncertainty had added to the gravity of the setting as Congress considered the bill. The debate was distinguished by such large concerns as national security, the fear of being drawn into Europe's war, and the attempts to make the burden of service fall justly.

These weighty considerations tended to obscure another precedent being set by the draft bill. For, by Section 8 of the act, Congress had presented to would-be veterans the first benefit on what would grow to be a long and varied list. The lawmakers granted veterans reemployment rights to nontemporary jobs that they had vacated to enter the service. Senator Elbert D. Thomas (D-Utah) claimed paternity for Section 8.[11] The section required employers (both private and the Federal Government) to rehire their former employees to the same position or to one of like seniority, status, or pay. To qualify, the veteran had to have completed satisfactorily his military service and still be able to perform the duties of the old position. The veteran had

[8] *The Washington Post,* July 28, 1944. Thirty-one per cent of those polled said the level would be four to six million, with 14 per cent noncommittal.

[9] *Ibid.,* December 27, 1944.

[10] Public Law 783, 76th Cong., September 16, 1940. The principle had been introduced in the National Guard Act, Public Resolution 96, 76th Cong., August 27, 1940.

[11] Thomas to General Omar N. Bradley, February 7, 1946; "Veterans Administration (Ind.-12a)" Folder, Thomas Papers, FDRL.

to apply for his old position within forty (changed to ninety in December, 1944) days of his release from the armed services. Once rehired, he could not be discharged, except for cause, during the first year of his reemployment. Congressmen, aware that business conditions might fluctuate greatly, inserted a clause to protect employers. Thus, reinstatement would not be mandatory if the employer's circumstances had "so changed as to make it impossible or unreasonable to do so." Finally, the statute directed the new Selective Service System to set up a personnel division to service veterans' reemployment needs. If disputes arose about a veteran's reemployment rights, the Selective Service System would turn the case over to the Federal District Attorney; the law specified that these cases be placed at the top of the Federal District Court dockets.

Congress' right to direct Federal Government agencies to adhere to a veteran's reemployment policy could not be doubted; but how could it require private enterprise to do likewise? During the debate on the bill, Senator Thomas patiently answered this question. Congress, he explained, derived its authority over private employers under the Constitution's Article III, Section 8 provision "To raise and support Armies." Resourcefully, the former political science professor pointed out that Congress needed to assure inductees that their tour of military duty would not impair their hard-earned civilian job rights. The morale of the military forces concerned Congress; how else could it "maintain" an army or navy? Section 8 of the selective service act would help fulfill this constitutional obligation. Senator Thomas anticipated that someone could claim that the section denied an employer's right to due process under the Constitution's fifth amendment. He reasoned, however, that the employer could (if necessary) demonstrate the "unreasonableness" of being forced to rehire a veteran; hence, his fifth amendment rights remained intact.[12]

The legislators did not debate Section 8 intensively. Reemploy-

---

[12] U.S., *Congressional Record,* 76th Cong., 3rd Sess. (August 20, 1940), 10572–74; cited hereafter as *Cong. Rec.* followed by Congress and Session numbers, date, and page. The Federal District Court for Eastern Kentucky upheld Thomas's views in Hall v. Union Light, Heat & Power Co. in 1944. "Veterans' Reemployment Litigation: Need for an Administrative Process," *Harvard Law Review,* LIX (April, 1946), 594.

ment rights obviously seemed less important during the cloud-filled days of 1940 than peacetime conscription. Indeed, some Congressmen may have considered Section 8 not much more than a gesture. This prompted one member, like St. Luke, to plead: "not to give [veterans] . . . a stone when promising them bread." [13] Nonetheless, few could dispute the justice or political wisdom in enacting such a provision, gesture or not. The scant debate on reemployment rights may have helped the bill's managers to achieve their main goal of a peacetime draft more rapidly; it also contributed to the controversy that arose four years later over the section's meaning. For, aside from Senator Thomas's lucid exposition on the section's constitutionality, there emerged from the debate few clear aids to interpret Congressional intent. For example, did Congress desire to give veterans more rights than those they would have earned had they not been inducted? No one could be sure. The law, in brief, was vague. As a result, a stubborn stalemate developed later between the Selective Service System, some business and veterans' groups on the one hand, and the Department of Labor and labor unions on the other.[14]

THE JAPANESE ATTACK on Pearl Harbor made potential disagreements over Section 8 of the draft act seem remote. The war called on all hands. Men who could not serve on Africa's hot sands could build tanks; women who customarily perused morning tabloids over a leisurely cup of coffee could operate drill presses; even children could rummage for scrap metals, bundle their mothers' tabloids, and scramble for milkweed pods in weed-choked lots. With factories consuming men and materials insatiably, the pre-defense worry about unemployment had vanished. Now government officials feared that they could not obtain enough men for war industries' work. From this setting grew the second major benefit for veterans of World War II: the program to train disabled servicemen to perform new jobs.[15]

[13] Fred C. Gilchrist (R-Iowa); *Cong. Rec.* 76:3 (September 7, 1940), 11699.
[14] See below, chapter 7.
[15] World War II veterans with service-connected disabilities had received hospitalization rights by virtue of the extension of Public Law 2, 73d Cong. Compensation was granted by Public Law 359, 77th Cong., December 19, 1941. Discussion of this benefit for disabled veterans is included since it demonstrates well the tensions that accompanied later policymaking for the able-bodied.

Five days after Pearl Harbor, President Roosevelt initiated the drive that would be completed a year-and-a-half later. He asked Paul V. McNutt, head of the Federal Security Agency and a former National Commander of the Legion, to coordinate the Administration's efforts to bring forth a program that would, in effect, restore disabled persons' ability to work.[16] People who possessed physical handicaps constituted a large pool of potential war workers. Each disabled person brought back to the labor force freed an able-bodied man for military service. Job training for the disabled coincided, moreover, with the humanitarian notions of President Roosevelt and his New Deal staff. Government officials strove, of course, to minimize this latter motive; McNutt, for example, protested that "today's need for manpower justifies immediate expansion [of job training for the handicapped] . . . , not as a social gain, but as a wartime necessity." [17]

The prime mover behind the government program was Harold D. Smith, director of the Bureau of the Budget. A quiet, unobtrusive man, Smith enjoyed wide influence within the Administration. His agency acted as clearing house for the executive branch on all proposed legislation, as well as serving as the President's watchdog over the federal budget. The admonitions of the Budget Director—an official who enjoyed privileged access to the chief executive—merited serious consideration.

Smith championed two ideas relevant to veterans' policy formulation. With a quiet but determined passion, he advocated government economy and efficiency. In practical terms this meant he indorsed efforts to eliminate duplication of government services. He also had a special interest in the welfare of the physically handicapped. Throughout the sometimes bitter controversy over job training for the disabled during 1942 and 1943 Smith maintained a keen interest. At times he must have regretted that his job as a coordinator precluded him from becoming more active in the battle.[18]

[16] *The New York Times,* December 14, 1941.
[17] U.S., Senate, Committee on Education and Labor, 77th Cong., 2d Sess., *Hearings on Vocational Rehabilitation of War-Disabled Individuals,* October 9, 1942 (Washington, D.C., 1942), 9.
[18] See article on Smith in *Current Biography,* 1943, 710–12. Herbert Miles Somers, *Presidential Agency, OWMR* (Cambridge, Mass., 1950), pp. 66–70, has perceptive comments on Smith.

The President's request in December 1941 brought little response, despite the idea's attractiveness. Divergence of interest within Mc-Nutt's organization made unified action on that front difficult. The Federal Security Agency (FSA), for example, ruled the activities of the Office of Education. The Office of Education in turn controlled the Vocational Rehabilitation Bureau, which had charge of a modest grant-in-aid program then in effect. It had a lively interest in pending projects affecting handicapped persons. Members of the Bureau believed that the Office of Education staff treated them as stepchildren; the professional educators, it was thought, did not understand the vocational group's needs. The gulf between "educators" and "rebuilders" mirrored similar cleavages in many states. Frequently vocational and trade schools warred with State educators over questions involving accreditation and standards. To put it simply: the Vocational Rehabilitation Bureau and the Office of Education served two different, frequently competing clienteles. The Bureau viewed the war-accentuated demand for its services as an opportunity to achieve independence from the "educator" group. At the same time, it should be noted, it continued to advocate greater federal financial contributions, with minimum federal control.[19] The War Manpower Commission (WMC), moreover, had been set up in April 1942 to oversee all manpower questions. Headed by McNutt, WMC tended to urge increased federal control over job training as well as more funds. This brought the top of the bureaucratic pyramid into conflict with one of its own building blocks. Not unexpectedly the whole project became stalled.

The Veterans Administration presented an even greater obstacle. That organization had agonized its way through the job training program after World War I.[20] Some officials doubted whether it had been worth the trouble. R. L. Jarnagin, Chairman of the Board of Veterans' Appeals, for example, had been more impressed with the failures of the first program than with its successes. In any event, the

[19] For an excellent, detailed account see Mary E. MacDonald, *Federal Grants for Vocational Rehabilitation* (Chicago, Ill., 1944), pp. 332–73. Also see Henry Redkey, "Rehabilitating the War Injured," *Survey Midmonthly*, LXXXIX (May 1943), 131–33.

[20] See chapter 1, above, pp. 29–30.

existing job counseling and training program of the United States Employment Service seemed adequate to him. Why hurry into a headache? [21] Lingering memories of the World War I experience gave the Veterans Administration yet another reason to be reluctant. The agency staff members, from General Frank T. Hines down, believed that all matters dealing with veterans should remain in their bailiwick. The training of disabled veterans belonged with the VA, not with a "civilian" agency.[22]

By late spring 1942 the program had run aground on the reef of administrative bickerings. Smith decided to intervene; he drafted Leonard Outhwaite from the Office of Emergency Management and Floyd W. Reeves, an educator from the University of Chicago and former chairman of the President's Advisory Committee on Education, to prepare legislation. Outhwaite had worked on personnel classification during World War I; he had returned to Washington in 1939 on the request of Edward R. Stettinius to assist in the stock-piling of strategic "defense" materials.[23]

By early summer, 1942, Outhwaite and Reeves had drafted legislation for preliminary discussion purposes. The key feature of the budget plan centered on the proposal to establish within the Federal Security Agency a separate Federal Rehabilitation Service to coordinate and administer all job training of disabled and handicapped civilians and veterans. Wayne Coy, a protegé of McNutt who became Assistant Budget Bureau Director in May 1942, obtained the green light from President Roosevelt to promote legislation along those lines.[24] Shortly after Coy met with the President on August 5, 1942,

[21] R. L. Jarnagin to Edward O. Odom, July 27, 1942; "15 P.L. 16, 78th Cong. and Extensions, Part I" Folder, Office of Legislative and Liaison Records, Central Office, Veterans Administration, Washington D.C. Cited hereafter as VA records.

[22] See, for example, General Hines's testimony; U.S., Senate, Finance Committee, Subcommittee on Veterans' Legislation, 77th Cong., 2d Sess., *Hearings on Veterans' Rehabilitation,* October 9, 1942 (Washington, D.C., 1942), 10.

[23] Personal interview with Leonard Outhwaite, March 30, 1965, New York City. Cited hereafter as Outhwaite Interview, March 30, 1965.

[24] Wayne Coy to Franklin D. Roosevelt, July 17, 1942; and Harold D. Smith to Roosevelt, October 5, 1942; "V88 (3) Vocational Rehabilitation" Folder, Series 39.1, Legislative and Reference Division Files, Bureau of the Budget Records, Record Group 51, National Archives. Cited hereafter as Budget Records, RG 51, NA.

Representative Graham A. Barden (D-N.C.) and Senator Robert M. La Follette, Jr. (Progr.-Wisc.) introduced companion measures that became the genesis of a coordinated program.[25]

These comprehensive proposals galvanized the veterans' organizations into action. One of their two basic tenets was threatened: unification of responsibility for veterans under the Veterans Administration. The Administration plan, however, did reinforce the other principle, the desire to broaden and increase veterans' benefits. The American Legion, Veterans of Foreign Wars (VFW), and Disabled Veterans of America considered the violation of the first basic principle more important than the gains under the second; therefore, each organization opposed the bill. The big three suspected that unseen forces conspired to "destroy the identity of veterans as a group for special consideration." [26]

They were right; but the "force" could be seen clearly. President Roosevelt, as noted in the preceding chapter, had long urged that able-bodied veterans be treated the same as other citizens. His words before the American Legion's convention in 1933 certainly had not been forgotten by the veterans' organizations ten years later.[27] Nor had his actions in the Bonus and Economy fights been unnoticed.

The budget program also encountered the suspicions of the enemies of the New Deal's social reform. Representative John E. Rankin stated:

I do not want to make the World War veterans the common carriers for the enormous appropriations that I can see in the distance for all the social uplifting that we will have and all the social and physical rehabilitation that may be undertaken.[28]

[25] HR 7484, 77th Cong., August 13, 1942, and S. 1714, 77th Cong., August 13, 1942.

[26] Omar N. Ketchum, the VFW's Legislative Director; U.S., House of Representatives, Committee on Education and Labor, 78th Cong., 1st Sess., *Hearings on Vocational Rehabilitation,* February 12, 1943 (Washington, D.C.), 180; see also 182–86. Cited hereafter as House, *Barden Committee Vocational Rehabilitation Hearings.*

[27] Republicans would not let them forget. At their 1944 meeting, Legionnaires heard Governor John W. Bricker of Ohio, the Republican Vice Presidential candidate, denounce Roosevelt's 1933 statement. "Legionnaires at Work," *Newsweek,* XXIV (October 2, 1944), 47

[28] U.S., House of Representatives, Committee on World War Veterans' Leg-

A colleague, Bertrand W. Gearhart (R-Calif.)—a founder of the American Legion, a past commander of his department, and a former National Executive Committee member—echoed Rankin's attitude:

The thing we have to fight down is the crafty effort of so many different groups to use the war for the reorganization of the world after the war; to capitalize upon the war sentiment to accomplish their objectives which have to do with social uplift and which are, to them, far more important than the rehabilitation and vocational training of our returning war disabled.[29]

Rankin and Gearhart were members of a wrecking team in Congress that hoped to demolish the remaining vestiges of the New Deal. During 1942 and 1943 the conservatives succeeded in uprooting the National Youth Administration, the Civilian Conservation Corps, the Works Progress Administration, and the National Resources Planning Board. Although officials in the New Deal readily admitted that some of these agencies' functions had outlived their usefulness, the loss of the NRPB was a blow.

The two attitudes—expressed by veterans' organizations and conservatives—went hand in hand on this issue of job training. Both were anti-New Deal. Conservatives feared the use of the "veterans" appeal as a guise to obtain general liberal reforms; spokesmen for veterans' organizations feared use of broad welfare programs to diminish veterans' exclusiveness. The first opposed the New Deal on all its fronts; the second focused its ire on one sector. The latter could rely almost automatically on support of the former when "veterans' exclusiveness" was at stake; it cannot be said, however, that conservatives enjoyed an equivalent leverage in reverse. Obviously, conservatives and veterans' groups would part company when the gain in benefits seemed greater than loss in central responsibility.

One other group joined conservatives and the big three of the veterans' organizations later in opposition to the budget program. The nation's private business, secretarial, and trade schools generally preferred to have the Veterans Administration handle the job train-

---

islation, 77th Cong., 2d Sess., *Hearing on . . . Rehabilitation of Disabled Veterans*, October 7, 1942 (Washington D.C., 1942), 14. Cited hereafter as House, *Rankin Committee Vocational Rehabilitation Hearing, 77:2.*

[29] *Ibid.*, 36.

ing program. Willard J. Wheeler, president of the Wheeler Business College of Birmingham, Alabama wrote to Rankin that "the Veterans Administration, in my opinion, can do this work much more effectively than if put in the hands of the educational department of each state." [30] At least forty-two school officials from twenty-two other states agreed with Wheeler. They represented a small, but highly organized, lobby which provided handy support for the opponents of the budget program.[31]

The veterans' organizations, recovering from the initial shock dealt by the budget bill, launched a counterattack. They urged that Congress pass a separate disabled veterans' job training bill that had been introduced on September 30, 1942 jointly by David I. Walsh (D-Mass.) and J. Bennett "Champ" Clark (D-Mo.) in the Senate; the companion bill was filed on October 2, 1942 by Rankin in the House. Francis M. Sullivan, the Legion's Legislative Director, later told Congressmen:

Some of our folks have made a canvass, and they are wondering if a huge, expensive bill will be accepted by the Congress, one which includes civilians and disabled veterans. Therefore, our concern is to try to have some legislation put on the books for those men now being discharged, and let the other program come along and be considered by Congress also, but let them be decided apart.[32]

Faced with this opposition, the Budget Bureau had to revise its bill. After a series of interagency conferences, a new draft was ready —but one that retained the single rehabilitation service feature. Smith asked President Roosevelt to forward the bill to Congress along with a message that stressed the need for a coordinated service.[33] The President agreed. He told Congress:

[30] Wheeler to Rankin, February 22, 1943; "Rehabilitation, Letters & Bills" Folder, HR 78 A-F 39.2, Tray 17017, House Committee on World War Veterans' Legislation Records, Record Group 233, National Archives.

[31] See communications in *ibid.,* February 9 to March 13, 1943 and February 16 to 23, 1943 in "P" Folder, HR 78 A-F 39.1, Tray 17013, *ibid.*

[32] House, *Barden Committee Vocational Rehabilitation Hearings,* 78:1, February 11, 1943, 176.

[33] Smith to Roosevelt, October 5, 1942; "V88 (3) Vocational Rehabilitation" Folder, Budget Records, RG 51, NA.

In order to secure the most effective utilization of the capabilities of the physically handicapped it is important that a single Rehabilitation Service be established for both veterans and civilians.[34]

But he also indicated that the Veterans' Administration should determine which veterans were eligible; then it would refer them to the Rehabilitation Service. The President further weakened the appeal for a single service when he told Smith privately:

I cannot send a bill up with the message. . . . I suggest that you take legislation to the Committee Chairmen and tell them that I have asked you to do so as a sample of the kind of legislation the Administration feels should be passed.[35]

The President's cautious attitude may have been dictated by signs of compromise shown by the veterans' organizations. On the day that Smith importuned his chief to support explicitly a strong central rehabilitation service, representatives of the American Legion, Veterans of Foreign Wars, and Disabled Veterans of America met to revise the Walsh-Clark bill.[36] Rankin and some VA officials joined them. The new bill that emerged from this conference once again dealt only with disabled veterans' job training; but now the bill instructed the Veterans Administrator to use the services of the Federal Security Agency to avoid possible duplication of efforts. Although a purist like R. L. Jarnagin objected that the new bill violated the veterans' exclusiveness principle, the compromise worked.[37] After a one-day public hearing Rankin rammed the bill through the House on October 19, 1942. With Congressional elections a scant two weeks off, few members were on the floor. Although the bill probably would

[34] The President sent the message to Congress on October 9, 1942. For the complete text, see Samuel I. Rosenman, comp., *The Public Papers and Addresses of Franklin D. Roosevelt*, vol. XI, *1942—Humanity on the Defensive* (New York, 1950), 411–12.

[35] Roosevelt to Smith, October 8, 1942; "VII (3) Vocational Rehabilitation" Folder, Budget Records, RG 51, NA.

[36] They met on October 5, 1942; see statement by Millard Rice, National Service Director of Disabled Veterans of America; House, *Rankin Committee Veterans' Rehabilitation Hearing, 77:2*, October 7, 1942 (Washington, D.C., 1942), 21.

[37] Jarnagin to Edward O. Odom, October 8, 1942; "15 P.L. 16, 78th Cong., and Extensions, Part I" Folder, VA Records.

have passed even if the full membership had been present, Rankin's tactics irritated his colleagues.[38]

Empty chambers or no, the House had indorsed the veterans' organizations' views. Chances for a comprehensive bill dimmed. Still, all was not lost. The Senate probably would not have time during the closing days of the session to act affirmatively on the House bill.[39] There would be time, perhaps, for the Budget Bureau to iron out differences that still existed between executive agencies. Also, maybe the Veterans Administration could be brought into line to solidify the Administration's front.

By the end of October, after long consultations, Harold D. Smith apparently believed that he had settled all differences. He erred, however; Watson Miller, Acting Director of the Federal Security Agency and former head of the Legion's National Rehabilitation Committee, shattered Smith's hopes. Miller told the Budget chief that he was "not prepared to agree that so far as this agency is concerned negotiations have been satisfactorily completed." [40] Smith brooded quietly for a month; then he bitterly reproached the Federal Security Agency:

I have spent as much time personally in getting the principals together concerning this matter, beginning last May, and then finding it falling apart all around me that I am not very happy about what occurred. . . . It seems to be quite a problem to get the forces in the administration to-

[38] Four years later, in a similar situation, Rankin brought legislation before the House in the closing moments of the 79th Congress' second session. The bill, affecting training allowances for veterans undergoing vocational education training, passed because of low attendance of House members. Representative John Taber (R-N.Y.) was indignant about the way Rankin forced legislation through the House. See John Taber to John T. Andrews, September 12, 1946, and to George McDonough, September 13, 1946; "Veterans' Affairs 1947" Folder, Box 161, Taber Papers, Cornell U. Library, Ithaca, N.Y.

[39] Congress adjourned on December 16, 1942.

[40] Miller to Smith, November 10, 1942; "V88 (3) Vocational Rehabilitation" Folder, Budget Records, RG 51, NA. The Budget Bureau's power in this instance flowed from its position of influence over emergency requests for funds. Hence, in June, 1942, not long after the Bureau first interested itself in the legislation, it had extracted a promise from President Roosevelt that no special or emergency funds be granted to the Federal Security Agency for vocational rehabilitation until the general bill had passed Congress. This was one way in which the unwilling FSA might be made to cooperate more readily. From Miller's comment it is clear that this method failed.

gether on something that everybody agrees ought to be done without quibbling over a lot of details. It is no wonder that Congressmen get disgusted.[41]

Miller tried to mollify Smith by noting philosophically that "none of us who have responsibilities correlative one to the other should permit mountains to groan for the delivery of mice." [42]

Not even a tiny mouse could be produced, however, until a new Congress—the Seventy-Eighth—met in January 1943. The struggle resumed on January 7, 1943 when both sides filed their bills: Rankin and Clark for the veterans' organization,[43] and La Follette and Barden for the overall plan.[44] Again Congress held hearings. This time, the American Legion would not agree to the revised La Follette bill, even though the measure preserved veterans' exclusiveness by vesting all authority in the Veterans Administrator.[45] The veterans' organizations probably believed that with the new Congress they did not need to compromise further. The dramatic decrease in the Democratic majority in both Houses (from a margin over Republicans of 106 during the Seventy-Seventh Congress to 10 during the Seventy-Eighth, in the House of Representatives; and from 38 to 21 in the Senate) might have influenced the organizations also. Although the question had not yet taken any partisan significance, the Administration obviously could not easily gain its way. Whatever the reasons, the veterans' organizations refused to budge from their position.

Supporters of the La Follette bill made a last-ditch effort for their cause. Representative Barden enlisted the aid of his state's Commission for the Blind to coordinate a lobbying program in favor of the overall rehabilitation bill. The executive secretary of that organization informed Barden that "the Lions Clubs and the State Federation of Women's Clubs are getting out their letter to the officials

[41] Smith to Miller, December 16, 1942; *ibid.*
[42] Miller to Smith, December 30, 1942; *ibid.*
[43] H.R. 801, 78th Cong., and S. 786, 78th Cong.
[44] S. 180, 78th Cong., and H.R. 699, 78th Cong.
[45] The Veterans Administration Legislative Counsel met with Legion officials on January 8, 1943, only to learn of that organization's continued opposition. Memo of meeting, January 8, 1943; "15 P.L. 16, 78th Cong., and Extensions—Part I" Folder, VA Records.

in all of the other states, so that they can write personal letters to their Congressmen and Senators supporting this bill." [46]

The momentum, however, of conservatives, private schools, and veterans' organizations could not be checked.[47] Senator Clark rose in mighty wrath when the La Follette bill appeared before the Senate for debate. He claimed that the bill would destroy preferential treatment of veterans. He continued:

I have never seen the veterans' organizations of the United States as much wrought up, as unanimous, and as bitter, about any proposition, as they are about the proposal to take a simple matter of veterans' rehabilitation and pitchfork it into a general scheme of social rehabilitation affecting all the people of the United States, which, whether it is justifiable or not, has nothing in common with the question of military rehabilitation.[48]

Clark dismissed the significance of General Hines's support of the measure by suggesting that the Budget Bureau had put the "heat" on the Veterans Administrator. Clark said he opposed the La Follette bill in part because of an earlier attempt [by S. 2714, 77th Congress] to strip the Veterans Administration of jurisdiction—the VA had been "boldly raped" by that attempt. He insisted that his bill, S.786, be considered in lieu of La Follette's comprehensive measure.[49]

Sensing that the Senate shared Senator Clark's views, the majority leader suggested that the separate veterans' bill, S.786, be considered before La Follette's.[50] After a futile attempt by La Follette to amend that measure by substituting his own, the separate veterans' bill passed.[51] The House of Representatives followed suit with a unanimous vote, on March 15, 1943.

[46] Roma Sawyer Cheek to Barden, January 18, 1943; "Dr. Roma Sawyer Cheek . . . Correspondence on Rehabilitation" Folder, Education and Labor Committee Files, Graham A. Barden Papers, Duke U. Library, Durham, N.C.

[47] Dr. Cheek noted that "it does not seem possible to satisfy this group [of veterans organizations]." *Ibid.*

[48] *Cong. Rec.,* 78:1 (March 5, 1943), 1605–606.

[49] *Ibid.,* 1606.

[50] It took little prescience to come to this conclusion; for not only had the House already passed a "veterans" bill during the 77th Congress, its Committee on Education had also eliminated the veterans' portion from the companion bill of La Follette's comprehensive version only the day before debate began in the Senate.

[51] La Follette's bill providing vocational rehabilitation for civilians later passed as Public Law 113, 78th Cong., July 6, 1943.

Nine days later the President signed the measure—Public Law 16 —at long last giving disabled veterans the opportunity to receive special training to restore their employability. To qualify, veterans had to have served on active duty since December 6, 1943,[52] to have been "honorably" discharged, to have received a service-connected disability rated at 10 per cent or greater, and to need "vocational rehabilitation to overcome the handicap." Eligible veterans could receive training for a period not to exceed four years, nor to extend beyond a period six years after termination of hostilities.[53] During the period of training, plus two months, the veteran would receive an allowance that would increase his basic disability compensation to an amount equivalent to rates paid for temporary total disability.[54] Thus, technically, all who would participate in the program would be considered totally disabled.

THE LEGISLATIVE maneuverings behind vocational rehabilitation presaged a pattern that would be repeated as benefits for World War II veterans were decided upon. On most of the major readjustment policies a basic cleavage of opinion, similar to that shown in the vocational rehabilitation struggle, would emerge: should veterans be considered as a separate group, or as a part—albeit an important segment—of the entire population? This question would recur time and time again as the various planners within the executive branch persisted in trying to link the needs of veterans with those of the whole population. Just as persistently, the veterans' organizations could be

[52] Liberalized by the GI Bill of Rights to include all who served since September 16, 1940.

[53] Congress extended the six-year limit to nine years by Public Law 268, 79th Cong., December 28, 1943. The legislators declared hostilities ended on July 25, 1947 with the passage of Public Law 239, 80th Cong. Hence, July 25, 1956 became the terminal date for the entire program.

[54] At the time of passage of Public Law 16, disabled veterans received disability compensation at the same rates as for World War I veterans—namely, for temporary disability, $8 per month for each 10 per cent rated disability, and for permanent disability $10 per month for each 10 per cent rating, plus (in both cases) increments for anatomical losses and dependents. Thus, single veterans with a 10 per cent temporary disability would receive $72 per month while in training to bring their basic compensation to the full rate of $80. Congress increased these amounts by 15 per cent by Public Law 312, May 27, 1944, effective June 1, 1944.

counted on to stand at the breach in defense of veterans' exclusiveness.

The struggle to bring forth job training legislation for disabled persons demonstrated the resourcefulness and competence of the veterans' organizations. Not strong enough alone to generate sufficient pressure for passage of a disabled veterans' job training bill, they obtained their goal by capitalizing on the initiative of executive agencies who desired a more comprehensive program. Their technique of appealing to the sanctity of the veterans' exclusiveness principle proved successful. To paraphrase Senator Clark, quoted above: serve the veterans first and then, if anything else remained, the rest of the population could get theirs.

Finally, the loss of the original Administration program had its own negative lesson. After all, the President of the United States had indorsed explicitly the comprehensive plan. But it did not pass. Its loss could be attributed only in part to the clever tactics of the veterans' organizations. The lack of unity among the various executive agencies provided another reason. While components of the Federal Security Agency argued among themselves, for example, the opposition gained strength. At the same time, President Roosevelt temporized, refusing to indorse wholeheartedly the Budget Bureau's proposal. Proponents of the Administration plan, moreover, had not countered the charges of their opponents effectively. With so much time wasted on settling interagency quarrels, little attention could be given to weaving a comprehensive, rational, and entirely justifiable veterans' readjustment program. Until that task had been accomplished, the Administration had no real alternatives to offer that could compete successfully with the potent appeal of the veterans' organizations.

WORKING on the Budget Bureau's job training bill for disabled citizens reminded Leonard Outhwaite of the hectic days in Washington when World War I drew to a close.[55] Then, President Woodrow Wilson, transfixed by his vision of world leadership, had ignored postwar

[55] Outhwaite interview, March 30, 1965.

domestic planning.[56] As a result, the veterans' readjustment programs suffered delays; this in turn left veterans with bitter memories. This disenchantment had many ramifications. Twenty-four years later, Vice President Henry A. Wallace concluded that Wilson's failure to prepare adequately for domestic postwar problems had contributed more to the defeat of American entry into the League of Nations than had the diversionary tactics adopted in the 1919 Senate debate. Writing to President Franklin D. Roosevelt to urge the adoption of a "Domestic Lend Lease" plan, Wallace noted: "You can't expect men who are losing their jobs, their farms and their businesses to respond with an altruistic glow to an international idea." [57] Wallace, New Deal to the core, had begun to articulate the liberal program for the postwar period. He told Congress of Industrial Organization (CIO) members that the nation had to plan to avoid a dark future of "roving bands seeking food where there is no food, seeking jobs where there are no jobs, seeking shelter where there is no shelter." [58] Central to his thought—and to the periodical *The New Republic*'s policy as well—was the need for America to achieve a full employment policy. Sixty million jobs became a magic goal; the President, New Dealer though he was, required reminders that the first postwar task was at home. Thus, shortly after Roosevelt's reelection in 1944, *The New Republic* cautioned:

Every possible effort must be made to prepare for a smooth reconversion to civilian production when the war is over, and to maintain full employment thereafter. It would be fatal to sacrifice these ends for success in achieving international political organization.[59]

Outhwaite had drawn a more practical conclusion from the World War I experiences. With the first drafts of vocational rehabilitation legislation completed, he interested his co-worker in the Budget Bu-

---

[56] As one writer has observed: "The nation simply stumbled into the postwar period of readjustment wholly unprepared and essentially unaware of the great tasks ahead." E. Jay Howenstine, Jr., *The Economics of Demobilization* (Washington, D.C., 1944), p. 90; see also pp. 92–100.
[57] February 4, 1943; OF 4351, FDRL Papers.
[58] Quoted by *The New York Times,* November 4, 1943.
[59] "Mr. Roosevelt and the Future," *The New Republic,* CXI (November 20, 1944), 648.

reau, Floyd W. Reeves, in a plan for a government conference on postwar planning.[60] From this initial suggestion grew the single most important effort on the part of the executive department to provide a comprehensive policy for World War II veterans: the work of the National Resources Planning Board's (NRPB)[61] Postwar Manpower Conference.

Outhwaite's suggestion fell on fertile ground. Paradoxically, "post defense" planning had been on the minds of some individuals even before the United States had entered the war. More than a year before Pearl Harbor the President had selected the NRPB to coordinate post defense planning.[62] Nine months later, the NRPB, in one of its pamphlets, asked: "Should there be a dismissal allowance for all demobilized men?" The booklet also raised the subject of veterans' reemployment rights, already broached by the Selective Training and Service Act of 1940.[63] By early spring, 1942, the NRPB (with the approval of the President) had followed up its questioning by initiating a full-scale planning program.[64]

The NRPB planners agreed with Outhwaite's idea that an interagency conference on postwar planning should be held. As one NRPB staff member later noted, the time had come "to bring postwar planning out of the cloister of secluded studies by government experts, and into the market place of pro and con discussion by the interested

[60] Outhwaite interview, March 30, 1965.
[61] The Board's ancestry went back to the early days of the "First" New Deal. It served as the National Planning Board under the Public Works Administration; in 1934 it became the National Resources Board, and by the Presidential Reorganization Plan No. I effective July 1, 1939, it received its final form and title. It continued in operation as the President's chief planning group until its formal liquidation on January 1, 1944. See Edward H. Hobbs, *Behind the President: A Study of Executive Office Agencies* (Washington, D.C., 1954), pp. 77–85.
[62] Roosevelt to the National Resources Planning Board, November 12, 1940; cited by Bailey, *Congress Makes a Law,* p, 26, note 20; and Frederic A. Delano to Frances Perkins, December 23, 1940; "National Resources Committee, 1941" Folder, Office of the Secretary Files, Department of Labor Records, Record Group 174, National Archives.
[63] NRPB, *After Defense—What?* (Washington, D.C., August, 1941), pp. 9–10.
[64] NRPB, "Status of Work," June 30, 1942; "Administration" Folder, General and Technical Correspondence and Reports, Division A Files, NRPB Records, RG 187, NA.

public." [65] The government, it was reasoned, had to ease the public's insecure feeling about the future. Why not demonstrate that the Federal Government had both civilian and military personnel's post-war welfare in mind? A conference of responsible public officials would help accomplish this.

The Board's executive director, Charles W. Eliot, cleared the way for a conference by enlisting the support of other Government agencies.[66] With this preparatory work completed, NRPB Chairman Frederic A. Delano (the President's uncle) presented the ambitious proposal to the President. He requested President Roosevelt to approve the plan and issue a short news release publicizing the decision. Delano told his nephew: "Announcement of such a program will give assurance to young men interrupting their normal occupations or training that at the end of war service they will have substantial assistance in adjusting to, and engaging upon, their civil pursuits." [67] But the President did not agree with the avuncular advice:

This is a little like the problem put up to me by the State Department. They wanted a full-fledged, publicized survey on post-war international economic and other problems, and said that they had many people in and out of the Government who are "rarin" to go.

I finally decided that this is no time for a public interest in or discussion of post-war problems—on the broad ground that there will not be any post-war problems if we lose this war. This includes the danger of diverting people's attention from the winning of the war.

I am inclined to think, therefore, that any publicity given at this time to the future demobilization of men in the armed forces or industry would be a mistake.[68]

The chief executive's concern about the war had a real basis. Shipping losses due to the effective German submarine attack exceeded Amer-

[65] Luther Gulick to Assistant Directors and Section Chiefs, NRPB, August 28, 1942: "Memoranda from Luther Gulick and John D. Millett" Folder, Intra-Office Memoranda, Correspondence and Reports; Post War Agenda Section, Office of the Director Files, NRPB Records, RG 187, NA.

[66] Eliot to Dr. Robert Leigh (a NRPB Special Adviser), July 1, 1942; "Demobilization" Folder, General and Technical Correspondences and Reports, Division A, NRPB Records, RG 187, NA. Grandson of the famous president of Harvard University, and an expert on city planning, Charles W. Eliot (1899–   ) had been with the Board since its founding in June 1933.

[67] Delano to Roosevelt, July 1, 1942; OF 1092-D, Roosevelt Papers, FDRL.

[68] Roosevelt to Delano, July 6, 1942; *ibid.*

ica's new construction; as late as May, U-Boats found America's Atlantic coast a bountiful hunting ground. Less than a month prior to the President's reply to Delano, for example, Floridians at Virginia Beach witnessed the sinking of two freighters close off shore. Consistently, bad news flowed in from convoys running the Lend Lease gauntlet to Murmansk, Russia; in the summer of 1942, the Germans sank twenty-two merchant vessels out of a convoy of thirty-three. News from the Pacific had matched the grim tales from the Atlantic. Bataan had fallen as recently as April 9th; Corregidor on May 6th. The Tokyo raid on April 18th and the American victory at the Battle of the Coral Sea buoyed morale somewhat; but the initiative still remained with the Japanese. Moreover, the high hopes for a major offensive in Europe had been frustrated; even the alternative plan for landings on North Africa had been delayed. From the President's viewpoint, the summer of 1942 presented a gloomy scene.[69]

Still, the President did consent to a "wholly unpublicized, 'off the record' preliminary examination . . . without any form of an official set-up." To emphasize his intent he suggested that "four or five people . . . work on this in their spare time in order that they may be better prepared for an official study and report and recommendations later on." [70]

The negative tone of the President's response was misleading—perhaps deliberately so. The President, in fact, welcomed the NRPB plan; after all, he had authorized preliminary work, as noted above, as early as November, 1940. Moreover, he had favored the earlier State Department proposal for an Advisory Committee on Post-War Foreign Policy. Sumner Welles, Under Secretary of State, had conveyed the President's approval of that project to the Agriculture Department:

The President has decided that vigorous and intensive work needs to be done now in preparation for this country's effective participation in the solution of the vast and complicated problems of international relations which will confront us and the world after the final defeat of the forces of aggression.[71]

[69] A. Russell Buchanan, *The United States and World War II* (New York, Evanston, and London, 1964), I, chs. iv, v, and x.
[70] Roosevelt to Delano, July 6, 1942; OF 1092-D, Roosevelt Papers, FDRL.
[71] Welles to Paul Appleby, February 9, 1942; "Committees 2 Interdepartmen-

So the letter to Delano did not mean exactly what it said; the President's marked sensitivity to premature publicity may have led him to understate his real desires.

At any rate, the planners went ahead with their original proposal; they heeded only the admonition against publicity. A conference, headed by Floyd W. Reeves and with Leonard Outhwaite as executive secretary, met for the first time on July 17, 1942.[72] Rather than "four or five" people working in their "spare time," the Postwar Manpower Conference met regularly during 1942 and early 1943, usually with at least fifteen members present.[73] The participants naturally agreed about the need for the planning venture. For example, General Hines thought the Conference's purpose "second only to the question of winning the war." [74]

The conferees faced one persistent and difficult question: whether to recommend rapid discharge of servicemen immediately upon cessation of hostilities,[75] or to hold them in the armed forces until postwar economic conditions favored their assimilation into the labor force.[76]

---

tal" Folder, Office of the Secretary, Department of Agriculture Records, Record Group 16, National Archives.

[72] The formal title was Conference on Post-War Readjustment of Civilian and Military Personnel. However, members of the Conference preferred the shorter Post-War Manpower Conference designation. Hereafter it is referred to as the PMC. As the formal title suggests, the Conference dealt with other questions beyond the purview of this study. Such problems as war industries' personnel demobilization, postwar agriculture, and postwar fiscal policy received notice.

[73] Outhwaite interview, March 30, 1965. The Agriculture, Labor, Navy, and War Departments, the Veterans Administration, the Selective Service System, the War Manpower Commission, the Federal Security Agency, and the NRPB sent representatives to the Conference.

[74] NRPB, Conference on Post-War Readjustment of Civilian and Military Personnel, "Summary of 1st Meeting, July 17, 1942," 2, hereafter referred to as PMC, "Summary of 1st Meeting," File 830.31, Central Office Classified Correspondence and Related Records, NRPB Records, RG 187, NA.

[75] When conference members referred to "rapid and immediate" release of the armed forces, they tacitly added two significant qualifications: the limitations imposed by shipping capacity and the requirements of national defense.

[76] The question had been brought up at the first meeting, *ibid.*, 3; it received full discussion at subsequent sessions, particularly the ones held on September 10 and 24, and on October 8, 1942. See PMC, "Summary of . . . 5th, 6th, and 7th Meetings," *ibid.* This whole matter had been under serious consideration in both the NRPB and War Department as early as March, 1942. See Dr. Robert Leigh to Floyd Reeves, March 10, 1942. "Mr. Reeves Folder," Intra-Office Memoranda, Correspondence, and Reports; Post-War Agenda Section, Office of the Director Files, *ibid.*

Conference members discussed three possible answers to this question. The first, advocated by General Hines and others, argued that men should be retained in the service to allow for their gradual absorption into civilian life. Hines argued:

In the long run it was both better socially and cheaper economically, to keep the men in service than to create a period of unemployment which would necessitate large expenditures for relief and welfare.[77]

The fear that economic distress would follow immediately the war— as after World War I—buttressed this argument. Proponents of Hines's position doubted the ability of the economy to make the transition from war to peace rapidly and smoothly; postwar unemployment seemed likely. All signs, they thought, pointed to an economic crisis: the cessation of military contracts, the time-consuming job of retooling industries for civilian consumer production, the mass migration of war workers returning to their former locations, and the prospects of large numbers of demobilized servicemen looking for employment. Since its rate could be controlled, military personnel demobilization loomed large as a possible aid to avert disaster. As Outhwaite put it,

If we now abandon all attempts to control the rate of Military Demobilization then we are surrendering the one possible, positive, control that may turn the margin between economic equilibrium or unemployment crisis.[78]

As if anticipating the certain criticism of the servicemen themselves, Outhwaite added: "Would we . . . trade the illusion of personal liberty for the certain hell of an unemployment depression? Compared with this the restraints of army life are child's play in a rosy garden." [79]

Colonel Francis T. Spaulding of the War Department suggested a second alternative.[80] After urging that servicemen be demobilized

[77] PMC, "Summary of 1st Meeting," July 17, 1942, 3, *ibid.*
[78] PMC, "Summary of 6th Meeting, September 24, 1942," 3, *ibid.*
[79] *Ibid.*
[80] Spaulding headed the Education Section, Office of the Chief of Special Service, Services of Supply. Allen Drury characterized the former Dean of Harvard's Graduate School of Education as "that perfect academic type, smooth as butter and sharp as a knife, ingratiating, reasonable, courteous, shrewd, ambitious." Allen Drury, *Senate Journal, 1943–1945* (New York, Toronto, and London, 1963), p. 25.

rapidly, he proposed that veterans be granted a three-month furlough prior to final mustering out. During that period (the first two weeks of which he would receive his normal pay), the individual would have an opportunity to seek employment. If successful, he would be mustered out; if not, he could return to service and embark on a training or education program, conducted by the military.[81] This view appeared more practical than Hines's. The first plan had not addressed itself directly to the basic question of what to do with servicemen while they waited in the armed forces for civilian job chances to improve. Yet, like the first group, Spaulding anticipated bleak postwar economic conditions.

Some conferees believed that Spaulding's plan did not go far enough to equalize veterans' benefits with those of the civilian war worker—most notably in unemployment compensation. Spaulding's critics thought that the two-weeks pay proposed did not compare favorably even with the inadequate provisions of the state unemployment benefit plans. They wanted a comprehensive federal unemployment compensation program. Perhaps their goal could be attained by first providing a program for veterans and then expanding that plan to cover war workers and others. Critics like Charles W. Eliot tended to view veterans' benefits as a lever for broader domestic policy reforms—a characteristic of most of the later New Deal-Fair Deal veterans' programs.[82]

The third approach to a military personnel demobilization policy varied slightly, but significantly, from the second: release the men rapidly and make available to them post-discharge training or education to permit them to re-enter civilian life effortlessly. This seemed most realistic to those who believed that any policy of retention would be resisted with vigor by the servicemen and the public. Even Colonel Spaulding had swung around to this view by October 1942. He observed that a serviceman "would be sore as a pup, in fact as a whole litter of pups, if he could not get out of the armed forces and look

[81] PMC, "Summary of the 5th Meeting, September 10, 1942, 11, Central Office Classified Correspondence and Related Records, NRPB Records, RG 187, NA. Spaulding explained that the limited pay period during the "furlough" would give the veteran "a chance to find out what civil employment conditions were really like."
[82] See Eliot's views summarized in *ibid.,* 11–14.

for a job on his own." [83] Adherents of the third plan doubted that the pressure for rapid demobilization could be alleviated by molding public opinion; they reasoned that it would be difficult, perhaps impossible, for a political administration to resist the plea to "bring the boys home." Some of these skeptics expressed concern that the other plans under discussion suggested that "strings" would still bind the ex-servicemen and the military during the post discharge period. With ears cocked to future clamor, they warned that the planners' desire to protect the former warriors would be viewed as an attempt to foster militarism and political opportunism.

Deadlocked on the question of demobilization policy, the Conference sought a way out of its dilemma. Perhaps the President would now be willing to resolve the question? But the President disappointed them. Repeating his earlier objections about premature policy statements, the President gave no clues to the uncertain planners. Charles Eliot reported that the President "hoped the Conference would have a statement or report ready which would indicate the scope of the problem and the type of questions that would have to be dealt with." [84]

With the problem thus tossed back to them by their nimble (but cautious) leader, the planners had no recourse but to work out their own policy statement. By remaining aloof and by keeping the work of the Conference confidential, Roosevelt retained his freedom of independent action. Not closely identified with the planners' efforts, he could decide after the report had been made whether, and to what extent, he would accept its recommendations. Although this policy created problems for Floyd Reeves and the Conference members, under the circumstances it seemed to be a sensible approach. The President had made clear his administrative and executive views. He would not direct policy planning, nor leave it in the hands of one agency. Instead, he would receive the conferees' views and, after soliciting the opinions of others, would then determine his own course of action.[85]

[83] PMC, "Summary of 7th Meeting, October 8, 1942," 11, *ibid.*
[84] PMC, "Summary of 8th Meeting, November 5, 1942," *ibid.*
[85] Characteristically, at about this time the President, despite the work of the

THE REGULAR group meetings of the Postwar Manpower Conference ended in November 1942. Work began on drafting the policy statement. Leonard Outhwaite, directed by Floyd Reeves, whipped the formal report into shape during the spring of 1943. When finally submitted by the President to Congress in June 1943, the report outlined comprehensive goals for the handling of veterans' problems.[86]

On the basic question of military personnel demobilization, the report's authors urged adoption of a program similar to Colonel Spaulding's original proposal. Demobilization should be speedy, the planners thought; but at the same time a three-month "leave" or "furlough" with pay should be granted to each serviceman following separation. The planners concluded that once soldiers and sailors learned of the steps taken by a grateful nation for their postwar welfare, and, in addition, understood how large a task it would be to withdraw the far-flung troops rapidly, they would be "more likely to view with patience any unavoidable delay in the process of their release from the services." [87]

The PMC planners thought that servicemen should be released on an individual basis; a combination of democratic and economic criteria should determine priority of discharge.[88] Thus, after suggesting that the armed forces release individuals according to the type of their service and to the nature of their family obligations, the civilian planners urged that the occupational status of the servicemen also be considered. That is, no man should be released unless he had a job waiting for him.[89] Moreover, if a particular industry needed men of special skills, those individuals should be released preferentially.

NRPB, appointed another committee (The Armed Forces Committee on Post-War Educational Opportunities for Service Personnel) to report on a veterans' educational program.

[86] NRPB, *Demobilization and Readjustment* (Washington, D.C., 1943). Hereafter referred to as *PMC Report.*

[87] *Ibid.,* 37.

[88] *Ibid.,* 53.

[89] The American Legion also indorsed this view: "We should oppose the outright demobilization of those in service unless a proper job is awaiting them upon their discharge." The American Legion, *Digest of Minutes, National Executive Committee Meeting, May 6 and 7, 1943* (Indianapolis, Ind., 1943), 42.

The conferees concluded by suggesting early releases for servicemen who as civilians would employ others. The PMC conferees proposed, in short, that those who had served longest and hardest, who had a job, and who provided others with either jobs or support should be the first to doff their khakis and blues.[90]

Here the planners' views harmonized with those of top War Department officials. Assistant Secretary of War Robert P. Patterson, speaking at Northwestern University on January 25, 1943, pledged that his department would "do its best to see [that] no man is mustered out of military ranks into a breadline." [91] He continued:

We may be a war-weary people by the time we have shattered the Axis. . . . There will be an urge to let down after the fast pace we maintained to win this war, to dump men willy-nilly back into civilian life, to let them find a job as best they can and where they can. . . . But the Army will not take that easy way. Its responsibility is too great.

The specific recommendations about priority of military discharges proved to be controversial—despite broad support—during early 1943. The priorities set up would surely offend many people. It would be difficult, for example, to reconcile the difference between draft and discharge policies. Men had been inducted during the early years of the war without regard to occupational status. Why change that democratic procedure? Moreover, the recommendation would provide fuel for attacks that the government planned to hold GIs in the service against their will. Once the report had been submitted, uneasiness about this became evident:

I am afraid we may have been indiscreet in talking about delays and timing in demobilization and have done something to create the impression that our remedy for idle veterans is keeping them in the service. Carried to the logical conclusion, we might as well say, leave them in indefinitely and let them all die in service. My point is that we should protect our position in this whole thing very carefully because reaction among men in service against a plan to hold them in the army in-

[90] *PMC Report,* p. 53.
[91] *The New York Times,* January 26, 1943.

definitely will be terrific. In fact, they don't want to be held in a day longer than necessary.[92]

The conference report dealt with other crucial matters. The conferees urged that federal programs of education, employment, and social security be expanded to help meet the inevitable strains that would be caused by military demobilization. After reminding that demobilization did not end when the individual GI boarded the train destined to carry him to his home, the authors of the report went on to describe what still had to be done.

In education, the PMC recommended that all veterans be given the opportunity to embark on one year's education or training with substantial federal aid. It urged, moreover, the creation of a supplemental system of competitive federal scholarships. These grants would permit individuals whose education had been interrupted by military service to continue their education, up to a maximum of three additional years. In both plans, however, the planners imposed one major limitation. No training or education should "be provided in those fields or for those occupations in which the supply . . . is already large enough to meet anticipated employment demands." [93] This qualification demonstrated how the planners emphasized the interdependence of all the elements of the demobilization program. Thus, one obviously needed a strengthened United States Office of Education to supervise the program; the Department of Labor's fact-finding into employment conditions could not be slighted; nor, finally could the United States Employment Service's ability to locate jobs for veterans be weakened.

These links of the nexus extended still farther. Not only did education benefit the country in traditional ways, the authors of the PMC report thought, but veterans' education would also help alleviate unemployment after the war. If unemployment rose, a system of federal scholarships would help cushion the impact. Finally, although it was

[92] George F. Yantis (a member of the three-man National Resources Planning Board) to Charles W. Eliot, August 4, 1943; File 830.31, Central Office Classified Correspondence, and Related Records, NRPB Records, RG 187, NA.

[93] Recommendation No. 53, *PMC Report,* 53; and in similar wording Recommendation No. 63, *ibid.,* p. 60.

not stated explicitly, the planners believed that aid to veterans would strengthen the nation's schools and colleges.[94]

The report also dealt with unemployment compensation (under the general heading of social security). Although some state plans provided adequate benefits, the planners reasoned, the peculiar nature of national responsibility for the welfare of its fighting men argued for a Federal Unemployment Compensation system.[95] Lest readers might think that this responsibility could be limited to veterans, the authors' report noted once again that the issue loomed larger than that of providing for one special group:

Social security legislation must receive attention in a program for demobilization because any proposals for special measures for veterans must be coordinated with the existing framework of security measures applicable to the civilian population as a whole, including members of the armed forces before and after, although not during the war.[96]

The authors of the report considered employment the focal point of any demobilization program.[97] In this area the Federal Government agencies had to work together to make known to veterans what job opportunities existed. Again the report's authors sounded the plea for continuing and strengthening the federally operated United States Employment Service.[98]

Farming as a possible postwar occupation for veterans also caught the planners' attention. They warned that there could be no "back to the land" movement. Good farm land was scarce; farming could not be a cure-all for the problem of unemployed veterans as it had been after past wars. Only those who had the necessary skills should be encouraged to embark on farming careers. Yet some opportunities did exist; to that end the planners recommended disposal of lands acquired by the Federal Government during the war to deserving and apt veterans.[99]

The PMC report, in one respect, came too late. The entire effort

[94] Outhwaite interview.
[95] *PMC Report*, 57.
[96] *Ibid.*, 41.
[97] *Ibid.*, 46.
[98] *Ibid.*, 48.
[99] *Ibid.*, 98–99.

had been overshadowed by the extremely controversial "cradle to the grave" report on social security; that report, like the PMC, had been written under National Resources Planning Board aegis.[100] Partly as a result of this "American Beveridge" report, Congress had killed the NRPB.[101] Led by individuals like Everett M. Dirksen (R-Ill.) in the House and Robert A. Taft (R-Ohio) in the Senate, Congress had proclaimed itself opposed to unauthorized and "utopian" planning. Congress wanted to do the planning; only it had the practical vision. Actually, Dirksen, Taft, and others wished to end the New Deal-type national planning. Representative John M. Vorys (R-Ohio), for one, viewed the NRPB as merely "another planning board." Vorys justified his opposition to NRPB by observing:

The New Deal theory of planning and administration seems to be to have a number of agencies covering the same ground with a personal appeal to the President as the only way to settle their differences. . . . Thus we do not stop any function of government, but merely eliminate some over-lapping when we lop off a bureau or board.[102]

To paraphrase a Dirksen remark during the House debate, Gabriel had blown his fiscal horn.[103]

Despite the NRPB's demise, its work in coordinating postwar planning provided the careful preparatory steps necessary for a coherent veterans' policy. Although the final PMC report underestimated the intensity of pressures that would build up for the immediate release of GIs and sailors when peace came, the planners nonetheless had provided meaningful guidelines for future veterans' policy—most notably in education benefits. Most important, perhaps, the report gave the President what he had desired from the first: a cogent statement of the outstanding problems to be faced in respect to personnel demobilization.[104]

[100] NRPB, "Report in Security, Work, and Relief." See summary of the report's recommendations, *The New York Times,* March 11, 1943.

[101] Independent Offices Appropriations Act of 1944, Public Law, No. 90, June 26, 1943. The law, to be effective August 31, 1943, further provided that the Board's functions could not be transferred to any other agency.

[102] Vorys to Howard Dwight Smith, April 26, 1943; "NRPB Legislative—78th Cong." Folder, Vorys Papers, State Historical Society of Ohio, Columbus, Ohio.

[103] *Cong. Rec.,* 78:1 (February 16, 1943), 1027.

[104] Other correspondents reinforced the report's findings. Ward Canaday, the

THE PMC REPORT came to the President at an opportune moment. The North African campaign had been successfully completed; Mussolini had resigned; and the President's plans for conferences to pave the way toward a Big Three meeting seemed on the verge of consummation. Roosevelt could now speak for the first time about postwar plans for veterans without jeopardizing the nation's ability to fight. With Congress in recess for the summer, moreover, he could test the winds of public opinion before presenting specific plans to that somewhat hostile group.[105]

On July 28, 1943, the chief executive resorted to one of his favored political devices, the fireside chat. In this talk, entitled "First Crack in the Axis," Roosevelt devoted most of his time to the war's progress; he suggested that the Allies could now view the military situation with cautious optimism.[106] Turning from his sketch of recent Allied victories, Roosevelt broached the question of postwar planning:

> While concentrating on military victory, we are not neglecting the planning of things to come, the freedoms which we know will make for more decency and greater justice throughout the world.
>
> Among many other things we are, today, laying plans for the return to civilian life of our gallant men and women in the armed services. They must not be demobilized into an environment of inflation and unemployment, to a place on the bread line or on a corner selling apples. We must, this time, have plans ready—instead of waiting to do a hasty, insufficient and ill-considered job at the last moment.[107]

The President urged Congress to provide necessary "minimum" legislation for mustering-out pay, education, unemployment and social security, hospital, and pension benefits.

> The members of the armed forces have been compelled to make greater economic sacrifice and every other kind of sacrifice than the rest of us,

Chairman of the Board of Willys-Overland Motors, Inc., for example, urged consideration of a plan for postwar education for servicemen that closely resembled the NRPB's recommendations. Canaday to Roosevelt, June 7, 1943; OF 4351, Roosevelt, FDRL.

[105] See Samuel I. Rosenman, *Working with Roosevelt* (New York, 1952), pp. 382–85 for an account of the background of the July 28, 1943 speech.

[106] Samuel I. Rosenman, comp., *The Public Papers and Addresses of Franklin D. Roosevelt*, vol. xii, *The Tide Turns: 1943* (New York, 1950), Item 83, 326–36.

[107] *Ibid.*, 334.

and they are entitled to definite action to help take care of their special problems.[108]

Judging from the overwhelmingly favorable mail that arrived at the White House in response to the President's radio speech, the NRPB's reiterated position that Americans desired to learn of post-war planning had been vindicated. Naturally, labor union locals— particularly maritime workers—strongly applauded the President's plan. The Greater New York Industrial Union Council (CIO) printed 200,000 copies of a pamphlet entitled "A People's War . . . A People's Peace" containing the President's address, along with one made three days earlier by the Vice President at Detroit.[109] The educational features of the President's program drew wide comment. Howard Mumford Jones, Dean of the Harvard Graduate School of Arts and Science, wrote the President supporting the plan; but he, along with the deans of four other prominent graduate schools, urged that advanced education also be included.[110]

A few listeners, predictably, objected to the radio address. One dissenter complained that the President had been using his high position to promise benefits for soldiers "in return for their votes to perpetuate [himself] . . . in the White House." [111] This correspondent echoed the charge made by Harrison Spangler, Chairman of the Republican National Committee, that the beaming of the President's address to troops abroad had been done for partisan purposes.[112] But perhaps the simple statement of a Hollywood, California listener summed up the dominant feeling of the public: "My revered President: You have just gone off the air. All I can say is thank you, and thank God for such a man." [113]

Despite the rebuff suffered at the hands of Congress over con-

[108] *Ibid.*, 334.

[109] Saul Mills, Secretary of CNYUC to Roosevelt, August 16, 1943; President's Personal File (PPF) 200—Radio Address, July 28, 1943, Roosevelt Papers, FDRL.

[110] Jones to Roosevelt, September 27, 1943; OF 4351, *ibid.*

[111] Paul Stewart to Roosevelt, July 30, 1943; PPF 200—Radio Address, July 28, 1943, *ibid.*

[112] See Spangler's open letter to various government officials, July 28, 1943; *Current History*, n.s. V (September, 1943), 69–70.

[113] Pauline G. Simonds to Roosevelt, July 28, 1943; PPF 200—Radio Address, July 28, 1943, Roosevelt Papers, FDRL.

tinuance of the National Resources Planning Board, the President's broad veterans' program had cleared the first hurdle: articulation and presentation to the public. But that initial accomplishment merely presaged new challenges; now general recommendations had to be hammered into specific legislative proposals. That accomplished, the proposals needed to be guided through the Congressional labyrinth to enactment. To maintain leadership over this entire process would require energy, patience, and unity within the executive department —qualities found lacking in the struggle over job training for disabled veterans. Perhaps the lesson had been learned.

3

BONUS RUMBLES

FROM 1940 to 1946, a bonus for the new Ulysses seemed a certainty. Bonuses had the indorsement of hoary tradition. For sixteen years following World War I, adjusted compensation, or bonus, had stirred domestic political controversies.[1] Like Prohibition, it had been a creature of the 1920s; unlike the great social experiment, the bonus could not be shrugged off as a bad dream. After 1940 a new crop of Ulysseses had been planted; reaping its harvest might bring bitterness again. Few politicians could ignore the potential vote-drawing power of the bonus. The nation's veterans' organizations would not forget how the bonus had, in part, helped to swell their membership ranks. Somehow, the bonus question for World War II veterans would emerge; public officials had to face it.

A variety of individuals and groups promoted, or used, the bonus question. Opponents of the draft act in 1940, for example, predicted that if peacetime conscription became law, another bonus crisis would follow inevitably.[2] A former führer of the Christian Mobilizers, Joseph Ellsworth McWilliams, proposed in 1942 that the government grant a whopping $7,800 bonus for each soldier and sailor.[3] A

---

[1] See chapter 1, above.

[2] Senator Ernest Lundeen (R-Minn.); U.S., *Congressional Record*, 76th Cong., 3d Sess. (August 27, 1940), 10967. Cited hereafter as *Cong. Rec.*, followed by Congress and Sessions numbers, date, and page.

[3] Joseph E. McWilliams, "The Serviceman's Reconstruction Plan" (printed

group of veterans' organizations in 1944 indorsed a bonus plan that would give veterans as much as $5,000, partly to counteract the American Legion's comprehensive veterans' benefit program.[4] Even liberals suggested a bonus to insure "equality of sacrifice." [5] Marquis Childs, for one, saddened that "no master umpire could have said at the beginning of 1941, 'still pond, no more moving,' " reluctantly admitted the merits of a bonus.[6] Finally, Frank T. Hines, whose views certainly were influential on this matter, believed a bonus to be inevitable. During the early years of the war he favored continuance of regular pay into the post-discharge period.[7] He also agreed with a subordinate's view that "there will . . . inevitably be a demand for an adjustment." He went so far as to authorize his agency to prepare an adjusted compensation bill.[8]

Significantly, one group of New Deal planners had not been infected by this bonus fatalism. In 1942 the National Resources Planning Board (NRPB) considered it "premature" to emphasize "a bonus specifically for soldiers . . . when we consider that a large part of our civilian population may feel like war veterans by the time the war is over." [9] By 1943 the Post-War Manpower Conference

pamphlet; Barrington, Ill., November 1942); copy in "Post-War Planning [P-4]" Folder, Box 62, Elbert D. Thomas Papers, Franklin D. Roosevelt Library, Hyde Park, N.Y. Cited hereafter as FDRL.

[4] See chapter 4, below.

[5] "Equality of sacrifice" referred to the insistence that all groups in American society (labor, business, farmer, etc.) should share equally in the "costs" of the war. It implied that no group's relative position to the others would be allowed to be affected adversely as a result of the war. See Roland Young, *Congressional Politics in the Second World War* (New York, 1955), pp. 6–7.

[6] *The Washington Post,* May 19, 1944

[7] Hines to Rep. Andrew J. May (D-Ky.), December 8, 1943; U.S., House of Representatives, Committee on Military Affairs, 78th Cong., 1st Sess., *Hearing on . . . Mustering-out Pay,* December 8, 1943 (Washington, D.C., 1944), 21–23. Cited hereafter as House, *May Committee Mustering-Out Pay Hearings,* 21–23.

[8] The bill was introduced for the Veterans Administration by Rep. Marion T. Bennett (R-Mo.) as HR 4695, 78:2, April 27, 1944. See draft bill with notations, and Edward E. Odom to Hines, April 14, 1944; "17 Servicemen's Readjustment Act, General, Part IVa" Folder, VA records.

[9] NRPB, "Suggestions for Gaining Increased Public Acceptance of Post-War Planning," (mimeographed), May 15, 1942; National Resources Planning Board Records, Record Group 187, National Archives. Cited hereafter as NRPB Records, RG 187, NA.

(acting under NRPB aegis) wished to move away from the concept of a lump-sum bonus or adjusted service compensation payment. Instead, conferees promoted the idea of a nominal disbursement at discharge; they coupled it with an unemployment benefit allowance that would last for an extended period. They thought, moreover, that a bonus would not be needed if other benefits, such as education and training, also had been provided. Hence the PMC's recommendations to the President in June 1943 called for separation pay during a three-month "furlough" period following demobilization, to be limited to a maximum of $300.[10] The relatively small initial furlough pay would provide funds, the planners believed, for men to travel home to visit their families, to seek employment, and "to acquire civilian clothing and meet reasonable living expenses." [11] The PMC's final report concluded:

The payments are explicitly made in lieu of any other grants for such purposes to avoid making large payments at any one time, which might be dissipated and fail to fulfill the social purposes for which they are granted.[12]

The struggle that developed in 1943 and 1944 over veterans' benefits fell into two overlapping stages. The first lasted from the summer of 1943 until February 1944; the second from autumn 1943 until June 1944. The first, covered in this chapter, featured the Administration's ad hoc and at times confused response to bonus demands, the clarification of committee jurisdiction on veterans' matters in the House of Representatives, and the enactment of the mustering-out pay bill. The second, treated in the next chapter, involved the passage of the famous GI Bill of Rights. During these stages the focus broadened from the relatively narrow question of post-discharge payments to one that embraced the wider question of the readjustment of soldiers and sailors to civilian life.

[10] NRPB, *Demobilization and Readjustment* (Washington, D.C., 1943), 56.
[11] *Ibid.*
[12] *Ibid.* One soldiers's wife urged that no money be issued to a discharged soldier until he had been released at the city from which he had been inducted, "instead of giving him money to disappear forever." A Soldier's Wife to Post-War Planning Committee, August 1, 1943; 830.3 File, Central Office Correspondence, NRPB Records, RG 187, NA.

PRESIDENT ROOSEVELT's July 28, 1943, fireside chat had asked for, among other things, legislation to provide veterans with mustering-out pay. It took almost four months before the chat could be made into a program.

An inadequate federal bureaucracy was a chief reason for the delay. The huge administrative bureaucracy that had been gathered at the banks of the Potomac to meet demands born of depression and war did not include a policymaking or coordinative body for veterans' affairs. Other areas of more pressing concern in 1943, such as war material and personnel procurement, had been covered by ad hoc agencies. But veterans' affairs coordination frequently fell into an administrative no man's land bounded by the Veterans Administration, the War and Navy departments, the Selective Service System, and the Federal Security Agency. All were interested; but in the autumn and winter of 1943 none of the first four agencies seemed to want to take the lead in following up the July speech. Only the Federal Security Agency (FSA) enthusiastically promoted early action to implement Roosevelt's speech. Paul V. McNutt, head of the FSA, commenting on a bill to provide loans to veterans for education, for example, argued that it would take a long time to draft legislation. The need to uphold the morale of the servicemen compelled the Administration to act, he thought; waiting until the war ended was an undesirable alternative.[13] But McNutt stood alone.

The Veterans Administration (VA), on the surface a likely candidate for the job, did not qualify. In Frank T. Hines, the VA had a leader with great knowledge of veterans' benefits; but his knowledge was matched by his reluctance to indorse new departures. When McNutt urged action for veterans' education benefits in August, 1943, Hines observed somberly that loans for education were unprecedented, as well as costly. Hines indorsed the veterans' organizations' demand "that veterans of World War II receive no less than those of World War I." [14] This may have made Hines view possible bene-

[13] McNutt to F. J. Bailey, August 25, 1943; "V69 (2)-Veterans-Benefits-Loans" Folder, Series 39.1, Legislative and Reference Division Files, Bureau of the Budget Records, Record Group 51, National Archives. Cited hereafter as Budget Records, RG 51, NA.
[14] Hines to Harold D. Smith, August 25, 1943; *ibid.*

fits for the new Ulysses through eyeglasses ground by the experience with World War I veterans. Hines, to be brief, was a conservative. Moreover, he held inviolable the principle that veterans should receive benefits that bore close relation to the sacrifice actually incurred while in service. This left him cool, not to say unresponsive, to some of the newer proposals advanced in 1943. He mirrored the legalistic and conservative view of his aides. For example, three of Hines's closest advisers in the VA, Assistant Administrators George E. Ijams and Omer E. Clark, and the Solicitor, Edward E. Odom, all thought talk of educational benefits was premature. Six days after the President's July speech Clark noted that "the need for this legislation [referring to loans for education] is not apparent and its passage is not recommended." [15] The General and his agency remained in the background of policy-making in 1943 and 1944.

Leadership had to come from above. But from whom? The Office of War Mobilization, headed by former Supreme Court Associate Justice James F. Byrnes, was committed totally to prosecution of the war.[16] Except for one occasion, Byrnes did not have time for the peripheral issue of veterans' affairs.[17] Another arm of the President, the Bureau of the Budget, might well have filled the need. Traditionally, however, it did not enter the picture until major disagreements separated executive agencies on an issue, or until legislation had been referred to it for coordination. In neither case did it have an initiating responsibility.

As for the President himself, he could do little more than provide the oratory. In the winter of 1943–44, wartime diplomacy increas-

---

[15] Odom drafted the letter that went over Hines's signature to F. J. Bailey on August 25, 1943; Hines marked on the file copy "very excellent letter." Ijams to Odom, July 27, 1943; Clark to Odom, August 3, 1943; and draft, Hines to Bailey, August 25, 1943; "17 Servicemen's Readjustment Act, Part I" Folder, Office of Legislative and Liaison Files, Central Office, Veterans Administration Records, Washington, D.C.

[16] Isadore Lubin, however, an adviser to Byrnes, immediately after the July speech drafted letters for FDR to send to various agencies requesting a report on accomplishments "while the issue is still fresh in the minds of the folks in Washington." Lubin to Roosevelt, July 28, 1943; Official File 4675-A, Roosevelt Papers, FDRL.

[17] He makes only passing references to veterans' affairs in his published memoirs. Byrnes, *All in One Lifetime* (New York, 1958), pp. 207 and 210.

ingly captured his time and imagination. Away for more than a month at the Teheran and Cairo conferences, and occupied on his return (December 17, 1943) with plans for the Normandy invasion, the President had no time to devote to this phase of the postwar domestic program. Engaged in global affairs, FDR may have had little inclination to risk a donnybrook over domestic policy with a recalcitrant Congress.[18]

The first full-scale discussion of plans for veterans following the July speech demonstrated how ill-prepared were the executive agencies. James F. Byrnes held a meeting on October 11, 1943, with various department heads to follow up suggestions tentatively advanced at a cabinet session.[19] Since little was accomplished, the meeting concluded with Byrnes's request for more detailed information concerning what the departments had been doing in planning for veterans, and what they recommended for future action.

The answers revealed that very little had been accomplished. The Treasury Department had given no "real consideration" of the subject and could only present general recommendations.[20] John Blandford, Jr., National Housing Administrator, claimed that current programs would be adequate for the veterans who returned during the war; in addition, he advised against a special program just to meet the postwar needs of veterans alone. He thought a broad policy bene-

[18] Rexford Guy Tugwell, although not on the immediate scene at the time, confirms Roosevelt's transfer of interest from domestic affairs to concern over "global" matters. *The Democratic Roosevelt: A Biography of Franklin D. Roosevelt* (Garden City, N.Y., 1957), pp. 624–26. Roosevelt himself indicated one side of this shift with his famous reference to the changing of "Dr. New Deal" to "Dr. Win-the-War" at a Press Conference on December 28, 1943. Samuel I. Rosenman, *Working with Roosevelt* (New York, 1952), pp. 414–16. Cited hereafter as Rosenman, *Working with Roosevelt*.

[19] See "Summary of Meeting Called by Director of War Mobilization on October 10 [*sic*], 1943 to Consider Assistance to Veterans," n.d.; "Postwar and War Adjustment, 6-Program for Aiding Discharged Veterans" Folder, Office of War Mobilization Records, Record Group 250, National Archives. Cited hereafter as OWM Records, RG 250, NA.

[20] Daniel W. Bell to Byrnes, n.d. [pencil marked October 1943] "Postwar and War Adjustment, 6-Program for Aiding Discharged Veterans" Folder, OWM Records, RG 250, NA. Bell did emphasize, however, that it would be folly to plan solely for one aspect of the problem without any consideration of the interdependence of all various elements.

fiting all citizens would be more desirable.[21] Finally, Claude Wickard, the Secretary of Agriculture, admitted that his department had "formulated no specific plans." [22]

The indecisive nature of the meeting held by Byrnes made a comprehensive expansion of the "First Crack in the Axis" speech difficult. The loss of the National Resources Planning Board's (NRPB) services dramatized the paucity of suggestions offered by other agencies. Had the defunct NRPB been represented at the Byrnes meeting, that session might well have been more productive. As it turned out, Roosevelt had to rely more on his former planning group's suggestions than on his departmental advisers.

AFFAIRS WERE EQUALLY as tangled at the other end of Pennsylvania Avenue. The House of Representatives could handle proposed veterans' legislation no more effectively than the executive department could dream it up. A myriad of committees competed for jurisdiction over legislation affecting veterans. By the beginning of October, 1943, twenty-six veterans' bills had been introduced in the House during the 78th Congress and assigned to committees other than the Committee on World War Veterans' Legislation, which by its title at least was the most natural choice.[23] These bills ranged from proposals for bonuses (in the form of continuance of military pay) assigned to the Military Affairs Committee to bonuses (in the form of adjusted service compensation) referred to the Ways and Means Committee. Other standing committees, such as Banking and Currency, Naval Affairs, Agriculture, Education, Labor, and Irrigation and Reclamation, also had claims on bills affecting veterans. But the most serious controversy between rival committees pitted John Lesinski (D-Mich.), Chairman of the Invalid Pensions Committee, against John E. Rankin, Chairman of the World War Veterans' Legislation Committee.

[21] Blandford to Byrnes, October 7, 1943; *ibid.*
[22] Wickard to Byrnes, October 13, 1943; *ibid.*
[23] "Bills Providing Continuation of Pay . . . [etc.]," October 1, 1943, "Post-War Bills and Programs, 78th Cong." Folder, HR 78 A-F 39.2, Tray 17018, House Committee on World War Veterans' Legislation Records, Record Group 233, National Archives. Cited hereafter as Rankin Committee Records, RG 233, NA.

Rankin, "a little man with bushy hair and a Hallelujah voice," [24] soon exhibited his parliamentary skill. Shortly after the war began, he introduced a resolution designed to give his committee full jurisdiction over World War II veterans' legislation.[25] Although the Rules Committee refused to sustain Rankin's position and did not report the resolution, Rankin's claims for jurisdiction alarmed Lesinski. The latter considered all veterans' pensions (except those already specifically excluded by amendments to the House rules of procedure) to fall within his committee's exclusive province. Lesinski wished to restrict his opponent to the care of World War I beneficiaries. With his own Invalid Pensions Committee on the verge of extinction because of the rapidly decreasing number of veterans and their dependents over whom it had jurisdiction, Lesinski quite naturally fought desperately to save it—and, at the same time, insure the continuance of his preserve of power. Rankin was not discouraged by his failure with the Rules Committee during the 77th Congress. At the outset of the 78th Congress, undaunted by Lesinski's countermove to change the name of the Invalid Pensions Committee to Committee on Veterans' Affairs, Rankin reintroduced his resolution (now numbered H.R. 29).[26] Again, the Rules Committee sat on it. As 1943 neared its close, Rankin seemingly had been stymied; but Lesinski had fared no better. The jurisdictional issue hung in the balance; as long as it did, the House could not deal effectively with a comprehensive veterans' program.

Meanwhile, Rankin's cause had attracted influential recruits: the American Legion and the Veterans of Foreign Wars (VFW). Francis M. Sullivan, executive director of the Legion's National Legislative Committee, had informed Rankin early in 1943 of his organization's willingness to support the Mississippian's move to discharge the Rules Committee.[27] The Veterans of Foreign Wars (VFW) soon after had

[24] Allen Drury, *A Senate Journal,* 1943–1945 (New York, Toronto, and London, 1963), p. 8.
[25] H.R. 387, 77:1, December 12, 1941.
[26] See *Cong. Rec.,* 78:2 (January 21, 1944), 586, for Lesinski's accurate summary of the problem. Rankin's new resolution was dated January 6, 1943.
[27] Sullivan to Rankin, February 18, 1943; "The American Legion—78th Cong." Folder, HR 78 A-F 39.2, Tray 17016, Rankin Committee Records, RG 233, NA.

joined the Legion in drumming up the 218 signatures required.[28] Individual House members received a barrage of letters, petitions, and telegrams importuning them to sign House Petition number 8 to force the Rules Committee to bring Rankin's bill before the full House.

The experience of one Congressman, John M. Vorys (a Republican from Columbus, Ohio), provides a glimpse of this effective lobby at work. On March 31, 1943, Martin V. Coffee, the Legion's Ohio Department Commander, wrote Vorys urging him to support Rankin's resolution, H.R. 29. Two weeks later Coffee asked Vorys to sign the discharge petition. To this Vorys responded:

Due to a number of angles inside Congress, involving the prestige of the different committees, in which a number of good Legionnaires are involved, I don't want to sign Congressman Rankin's discharge petition at this time.[29]

As if by signal Vorys then heard from a Legion auxiliary on May 11, 1943 and received a weighty petition signed by 563 Columbus, Ohio, voters in June. In July Vorys, succumbing to the pressure, signed the petition. Coffee praised the Congressman for taking the reluctant step; many Congressmen, he said, shared Vory's scruples about bypassing the committee structure. But, Coffee consoled:

We must have our house in order to take care of . . . [veterans'] legitimate requirements promptly and efficiently so that crack-pots, long-haired professors, and radicals will have as little ground as possible to work on in an effort they will undoubtedly make to influence the thinking of today's discharged Army.[30]

These efforts still fell short of the goal, and the Legion intensified pressure when the 78th Congress' second session met in January 1944. Between January 6 and 21, 1944, Vorys, despite his positive action of the previous July, received pleas in the form of postcards from local Legion auxiliaries, a letter from the Columbus unit of the "Forty and Eight" (the Legion's social organization), communica-

[28] Omar B. Ketchum to National and Department Officers, VFW, March 27, 1943, attached to Ketchum to Rankin, April 2, 1943; "Veterans of Foreign Wars—78th Cong." Folder, HR 78 A-F 39.2, Tray 17020, *ibid.*

[29] Coffee to Vorys, March 31, 1943 and April 13, 1943; Vorys to Coffee, April 16, 1943; "Veterans Legislation" Folder, 78th Cong., Vorys Papers, Ohio State Historical Society, Columbus, Ohio.

[30] Coffee to Vorys, July 15, 1943; *ibid.*

tions from the various Columbus posts, a letter from his county
Legion council, and another from the new Ohio Department Commander.[31] These tactics—multiplied many times for different Congressmen—demonstrated the potency of the "grass roots" techniques
of veterans' organizations. Perhaps not all departments followed
their instructions so zealously as Ohio, but Congressmen had to be
extraordinarily thick-skinned to misjudge the force of the message.[32]

At any rate, at least 218 Congressmen heeded Rankin's advice to
discharge the Rules Committee. When on January 24, 1944, the
House voted formally to release his resolution, Rankin seemingly
had won. Yet as befitted an already complicated situation, the af-
firmative vote actually vexed matters even more.

Rankin, in his eagerness to obtain his objective, had submitted his
resolution before the 78th Congress had adopted its rules. Hence the
resolution specifically referred to the rules of the 77th Congress. When
Rankin asked for unanimous consent, after adoption of H.R. 29, to
change the wording to affect the 78th Congress, one of his public
archenemies in the House, Vito Marcantonio, objected. This spiteful
move enraged the Mississippian. He then formally moved to make the
change. Adolph Sabath (D-Ill.), Chairman of the Rules Committee
(also no friend of Rankin's), asked the Speaker whether the motion
was in order. Rankin, unable to contain himself, asserted that it was.
The Speaker, Sam Rayburn (D-Tex.), piqued at Rankin's interjection,
noted that he would determine what "is in order here today," and proceeded to sustain the impropriety of Rankin's motion. Thus, although
H.R. 29 had passed, it technically referred to the 77th Congress and
apparently had no formal standing with the successor Congress.[33]
Rankin, not to be outdone, corrected the wording and refiled it as
H. R. 410 on the same day. Although the Rules Committee once again
ignored Rankin's pleas for prompt consideration, his prediction that
"the Speaker would comply with H. R. 29" and refer most veterans'

[31] "Veterans Legislation—Discharge Petition Re Referring Bills" and "Veterans Legislation" Folders, *ibid.*
[32] Even in the case of the Ohio Congressmen, however, these pressures were
not overly effective. The delegation of twenty-three split evenly; twelve signed
the petition, eleven did not.
[33] This tangled parliamentary course of events may be followed in *Cong.
Rec.*, 78:1 (January 24, 1944), 633.

legislation to his committee proved correct.[34] In March, 1944, the Speaker sent the whole so-called GI Bill of Rights to the Committee on World War Veterans' Legislation. His committee had won a partial, but important victory.

Lesinski failed for several reasons. For one, Lesinski's appeal to tradition lost force in face of his move to change his own committee's 137-year-old name. For another, although the Detroit Democrat urged his fellow committee members "to use your very best efforts to defeat the adoption of this Resolution [H.R. 29]," [35] he had less influence on other committee chairmen. The loss of jurisdiction over veterans' affairs would not really hurt Military Affairs or Education. Rankin's resolution, moreover, would not strip Ways and Means of its adjusted compensation legislation. Lesinski could expect little more than sympathy from those sources.

Finally, Lesinski's miscalculation of the force of the Legion plays an important role. In retrospect, late 1943 and early 1944 proved to be a turning point for the Legion. Some people agreed with Lesinski when he predicted the new Ulysses would desire his own organization. The Legion, if that were true, would face inevitable demise. After all, the doughboys, although durable, were not immortal. Legionnaires had to decide whether to open their doors to World War II veterans or to commit suicide.

Perhaps alarmed by the success of the VFW's recruitment of new members, legionnaires elected the former course. At the annual convention held in September 1943, the Legion made three moves in that direction. The convention authorized the setting up of a special committee to develop an overall program for World War II veterans. It also provided for the indefinite continuance of an hitherto temporary group to explore new methods by which word of the merits of the Legion could be brought to the individual GI. Lastly, the convention chose Warren G. Atherton, an advocate of aggressive recruiting of new legionnaires, as its chief executive for the coming year. The

---

[34] Rankin to Adolph Sabath, January 28, 1944; "Rules Committee—H.R. 29, etc. . . . 78th Cong." Folder, HR 78 A-F 39.2, Tray 17019, Rankin Committee Records, RG 233, NA.
[35] Lesinski to R. A. "Lex" Green, January 22, 1944; Miscellaneous Correspondence, Box 59, Green Papers, U. of Florida, Gainesville, Fla.

constitution of the Legion, unlike that of the VFW, barred membership to individuals still on active military duty. Atherton, chafing
under this restriction, tried his best to alter Legion policy. Appealing
to state and local commanders on July 27, 1944, Atherton hoped
that pressure from below within the Legion would force the Constitutional and By-Laws Committee to reverse an earlier negative decision. The stratagem failed when the committee again declined to recommend the constitutional change to the National Convention for
approval. That the whole attempt bordered on the "unconstitutional"
highlights Atherton's desire to put the Legion in a favorable competitive position in the veterans' "market." [36]

Thus Lesinski faced an expansionist not only in Rankin, but also
in the Legion. The Legion had begun to adjust itself to its transformation into a continuing, "universal" veterans' organization. This move
was reflected in the Legion's area of influence in the legislative branch
of the Federal Government: Rankin's committee on World War Veterans' Legislation.

THE AMERICAN LEGION did not limit its aggressive activities to the
jurisdictional battle in the House of Representatives. It made a bolder
move. On December 2, 1943, Warren H. Atherton charged that World
War II disabled veterans constituted America's "unwanted battalion." [37] These wounded men, he complained, had been discharged
from the armed forces and, due to excessive red tape, had received no
compensation during the period in which the Veterans Administration
adjudicated their claims. Atherton listed heartbreaking details: "Bill
Smith," his left side paralyzed from wounds sustained at Guadalcanal,
waiting four months after his discharge to receive his first compensation payment; "Case No. 12," totally blind, also waiting four months

---

[36] The American Legion, Digest of Minutes, *National Executive Committee
Meeting, April 30 and September 17, 1944* (Indianapolis, Ind., National Headquarters, the American Legion, 1944), 34–36 and 23–25, respectively.

[37] *The Washington Post,* December 3, 1944, and *The New York Times,* December 4, 1944. Three times within the next two weeks Atherton's statement
was reprinted in the *Congressional Record* for the benefit of the short-memoried
legislators. *Cong. Rec.* 78:1 (December 6, 7, and 15, 1943), 10328–29, 10396–
98, and 10678–79.

for payments to begin; and 1,533 others uncared for by a preoccupied and over-extended Veterans Administration.[38]

The Legion's charges did not take Washington totally by surprise. Five months before, the Veterans of Foreign Wars (VFW) had anticipated Atherton. Omar B. Ketchum, the VFW's Legislative Representative, told Rankin of "numerous instances" where delays had adversely affected World War II disabled veterans. "They were forced to let their government insurance policies lapse, and some actually became dependent upon local welfare services," he had reported.[39] One month before Atherton's announcement, thirty-six-year-old Representative Walter C. Ploeser, one of the Republican Party's "Young Turks" from St. Louis, Missouri, had startled his colleagues with a spirited denunciation of the House leadership on veterans' affairs.[40] He angered many Democrats with his charge that Roosevelt's veterans' program was mere lip service; he irritated many more by attacking the Committee on Military Affairs for failing to report out a mustering-out bill. He thought political reasons prompted the Democrats' procrastination—presumably they desired to wait until 1944 when favorable action on veterans' legislation would be remembered better by voters. "The Democratic leadership of the House of Representatives should commemorate this Armistice Day—in shame," he declared.[41]

Thus, the Legion's trumpet call had not been first. But it was by far the loudest. It also remained in the air the longest. For with typi-

[38] David Camelon, "I Saw the GI Bill Written," mimeographed reprint of articles that originally appeared in *The American Legion Magazine*, XLVII (September–November 1949), 1–5. Camelon, a correspondent for the Hearst papers, had been assigned by his publishers to assist legionnaires in their lobbying to obtain veterans' legislation late in 1943.

[39] Ketchum to Rankin, June 22, 1943; "Veterans of Foreign Wars—78th Cong. . . ." Folder, HR 78 A-F 39.2, Tray 17020, Rankin Committee Records, RG 233, NA.

[40] *Cong. Rec.*, 78:1 (November 11, 1943), 9419–21.

[41] *Ibid.*, 9421. For later reverberations and scornful denials of Ploeser's charges see *ibid.* (December 15, 1943), 10722–29. The Administration itself was aware of the plight of some disabled veterans. On November 2, 1943, Selective Service System officials, for example, pointed out that veterans experienced hardships. But the dramatic news of Lieutenant General George S. Patton's slapping of a hospitalized GI crowded the stories of the Administration's solicitude for veterans from the front page. *The Washington Post,* November 24, 1943.

cal efficiency, the Legion linked its campaign with a national newspaper chain, the Hearst press. Although other papers, like *The Washington Post*, would at first label Atherton's statements as "sound and fury," [42] the Hearst press loyally supported the Legion's national commander.[43] To William Randolph Hearst the moment probably seemed opportune. Like the Republican "Young Turks," he enjoyed harassing the Roosevelt Administration. He had long dictated a rabid anti-New Deal policy for his newspaper chain. Finally, Hearst consistently had championed "Americanism"; stories of maltreatment of disabled veterans were tailor-made.

Hearst's campaign was relentless. The Hearst press assigned two correspondents to cover full time the daily events in Washington concerning the "unwanted battalion." [44] Daily editions carried clip coupons that urged Congress to act. Editorials appeared regularly— blasting, cajoling, needling, and thundering that justice be granted to disabled veterans. Hearst himself, on Christmas Eve, 1943, wrote a letter to the editor of *The New York Journal American:*

We cannot do what the Government can do and should do for America's disabled veterans, but we can do some things promptly to alleviate their lot while the Government is waiting and debating and wondering whether paying a debt of honor is good politics. . . . Let us continue to urge our great political leaders to think less about their own personal "place in history" and think more about the men whose heroism and self-sacrifice make that place possible.

By January, 1944, the editorial tone had become strident. On January 12, 1944: "The country will not tolerate further procrastination by Congress. . . . There is nothing to DEBATE about, nothing to BARGAIN about, nothing to justify a further WASTE OF TIME." [45] On January 30, 1944:

Republics are proverbially ungrateful. But this great and once rich republic is peculiarly and especially ungrateful. It fights its wars with chil-

[42] December 2, 1943.

[43] On December 1, 1943, the *Los Angeles Examiner,* for example, had echoed Ploeser's remarks in the House. *Cong. Rec.,* 78:2 Appendix (August 24, 1944), A3709. *The New York Journal American* carried Atherton's statement as front page news on December 4, 1943.

[44] Frank Reilly from *The Boston American* and David Camelon from *The New York Journal American.*

[45] *The New York Journal American.*

dren mainly—in violation of its solemn pledges—and then when it has mutilated them or blinded them, refuses to care for them adequately, or even to try properly to rehabilitate them and make their lives more endurable and useful.[46]

On February 2, 1944: "Why is it that it is only the veterans and always the veterans who must bear the brunt of the New Deal Administration's sole economy?" [47]

The Hearst papers used the political cartoon as another technique in their publicity drive. Between December 16, 1943, and March 11, 1944, *The New York Journal American* printed fourteen cartoons about the "unwanted battalion." They ranged from the inocuous to the vicious. A typical example of the former appeared on December 16, 1943. Entitled "The Shame of a Nation," the cartoonist, "Plascher," showed a disabled veteran (crutch supporting him on right, and a hanging empty left sleeve suggesting an amputated hand) standing in snow and silhouetted against the Capitol, whose dome radiates the word "politics." A side caption read: "Sick, Wounded and Penniless Veterans of World War II." The more stinging varities, however, predominated. On December 29, 1943, one appeared bearing the title "Merely Our Son." It depicted a disabled veteran with crutches (left foot gone), standing in snow looking into a store window marked: "Ye New Deal Globalony Shoppe; Goodies for Good Neighbors." On February 17, 1944—after the mustering-out bill had passed —an ambitious two-part drawing labled "Hands Across the Sea" was published. The upper portion showed a bespectacled man standing behind the Capitol. He wears an academic mortarboard, and has tufted sideburns. With a possibly anxious expression, he holds out in his elongated arms a large money bag labled "Billions for International Rehabilitation." The lower half of the drawing showed the same character at a paywindow marked "Veterans Rehabilitation." He is dropping three coins into the right hand of a disabled veteran. The latter stands, crutch in left hand, with head bowed. The official says: "We pledged ourselves to economize, you know."

The Legion's disclosures thus served many purposes. They helped

[46] *Ibid.*
[47] *Ibid.*

the Legion in its new publicity campaign to keep the organization in the public eye as a protector of the new Ulysses. They gave the Hearst press another opportunity to flagellate the New Deal. They gave young Republicans a chance to sound off against the Democrats' leadership in the House and—by implication—to grumble about their own leader, Joseph Martin (R-Mass.). The disclosures gave long-time bonus zealots, such as William Lemke (R-N.D.), another weapon in their continuing effort to force bonus legislation through Congress. They also moved people who simply wanted to help the distressed veterans.

EVEN BEFORE the Hearst campaign had begun, the Roosevelt Administration had been acting. The President already had asked for veterans' education legislation on October 27, 1943.[48] His mustering-out pay message had been ready before his departure to Teheran and Cairo on November 13, 1943. His advisers had delayed its submission, however, until the 23rd, partly because they wished to "cover up" the President's absence from the country.[49] Eleanor Roosevelt herself had chimed in. On the day her husband returned from the conferences, she said: "I'd like to see us pass all legislation for veterans as soon as possible. It would add to the confidence of the men to have such legislation an accomplished fact." [50] The Administration was moving, with education as the first emphasis.

But the combination of Republican "Young Turks," legionnaires, long-time bonus zealots, and bitter anti-New Dealers forced the Administration to shift its priorities. The bonus drive had to be headed off; perhaps mustering-out pay would do the trick. Roosevelt had observed in his November 23, 1943, speech that:

To help service men and women tide over the difficult period of readjustment from military to civilian life, mustering-out pay will be needed. It will relieve them of anxiety while they seek private employment or make their personal plans for the future.[51]

[48] See chapter 4, below.
[49] Rosenman, *Working With Roosevelt*, p. 405.
[50] *The New York Times*, December 18, 1943.
[51] Samuel I. Rosenman, comp., *The Public Papers and Addresses of Franklin D. Roosevelt* (13 Vols., New York, 1938–1950), XII, 53. Cited hereafter as Rosenman, *Roosevelt Public Papers, 1943.*

He asked for a uniform and reasonable mustering-out pay, to be made in monthly installments. He discarded the NRPB's recommendations for three months' furlough pay. Instead, Roosevelt heeded advisers within the Justice Department and the Bureau of the Budget who advocated mustering-out pay.[52]

After the message went to Congress, proposed legislation was drawn up and given to Senate Majority Leader Alben Barkley to handle.[53] This draft followed the principle that all servicemen (up to and including the rank of captain), regardless of their length of service, would face some financial problems during the period of transition from military to civilian life. Hence the bill provided for $300 payment to be made in three monthly installments. Administration leaders hoped to move the bill through the legislative maze before the imminent adjournment of the Seventy-Eighth Congress' first session.[54]

The Senate Finance Committee, acting with appropriate haste, reported a bill out on December 15, 1943—less than three weeks after its introduction.[55] But its altered form boded ill for the bill's speedy passage. The Finance Committee's version, despite its authors' protests that they intended only to provide mustering-out payments, opened the door for a frontal assault in favor of a bonus. For the bill now provided a sliding scale of payments ranging from $200 for less than twelve months' service in the United States to a maximum of $500 for individuals who had served overseas for over eighteen months. By changing the Administration's draft, the Senators diluted the basic principle of equal treatment to all and contributed to the

[52] F. J. Bailey to Harold D. Smith, November 11, 1943; "M123(7) Military-Naval Services-Pay Continuance" Folder, Budget Records, RG 51, NA. This decision came in spite of the fact that several veterans' organizations were leaning in the direction of the NRPB proposals. See Rep. Overton Brooks's (D-La.) reference to the plans of the National Council of American Veterans' Organizations Conference held at Washington, November 9, and 10, 1943; in *Cong. Rec.*, 78:1 (December 8, 1943), 10481.

[53] Milton Handler to F. J. Bailey, November 17, 1943; and Harold D. Smith to Samuel I. Rosenman, November 20, 1943; "M176(1) Mustering-out Pay Act" Folder, Budget Records, RG 51, NA.

[54] See statement of Rep. Andrew J. May (D-Ky.), Chairman of the Committee on Military Affairs and the House manager of the bill. *Cong. Rec.*, 78:1 (December 7, 1943), 10387.

[55] S. 1543, 78th Cong.

ensuing confusion.[56] The Senate, perhaps harkening to their majority leader's "sentimental" desire to have the bill enacted in time so that it could be considered a "Christmas gift," [57] passed the bill on December 17, 1943. No voice was heard in dissent, although Senator Alexander Wiley (R-Wisc.) warned that mustering-out pay would not be enough for veterans whose "souls have been singed and . . . mentalities burned." [58]

The House acted more slowly. The Military Affairs Committee, under the leadership of Andrew Jackson May (D-Ky.), was unhappy with the Senate's precipitate action.[59] Rather than rush the legislation through, May decided on December 20, 1944, the day before the House recessed for Christmas, to hold it over until the new session convened in January, 1944. He had another reason to leave Washington; a nephew had been killed in an airplane crash.

Bonus advocates and others who desired quick action in the House protested against May's decision. Mrs. Edith Nourse Rogers (R-Mass.), a leading champion of veterans' benefits, charged that it was "cruel" and "inexcusable" to permit the bill to languish.[60] The next day, the day the House adjourned, Mrs. Rogers continued her crusade. She was sorry about May's nephew, she said, but some other veterans might die if no mustering-out bill passed immediately.[61] Mrs. Rogers made a desperate last-ditch move to get the House to act. She asked for unanimous consent to have the bill taken from the Speaker's table and passed. The Speaker quelled her rebellion by announcing simply that she had not been recognized for that purpose and that her time had expired.[62] The House adjourned shortly after-

[56] The differential imposed by the committee followed the plausible idea that those individuals in service longest and farthest away from home would suffer the greatest dislocation of their civilian affairs; as a result they would need additional funds. See Senator Warren Austin's (R-Vt.) explanation; *Cong. Rec.,* 78:1 (December 17, 1943), 10816–17.

[57] *Ibid.* (December 17, 1943), 10815.

[58] *Ibid.* (December 17, 1943), 10819.

[59] See comments of R. Ewing Thomason (D-Tex.), an influential member of May's committee; *ibid.* (Dec. 20, 1943), 10923.

[60] *Ibid.* (December 20, 1943), 10920.

[61] *Ibid.* (December 21, 1943), 10971.

[62] *Ibid.* (December 21, 1943), 10998.

ward; the Congressmen left Washington to find out what the people back home wanted.

WHEN LEGISLATORS returned to Washington from the holiday recess, "with the advice of constituents presumably fresh in mind," they put mustering-out pay high on the list of priority items.[63] The results of a Gallup poll reinforced their decision. George Gallup claimed the American people overwhelmingly supported mustering-out pay; his tabulation showed that 88 per cent of those polled approved giving "a certain sum of money" to discharged servicemen. Only 8 per cent disapproved.[64]

An ad hoc committee of House members, chaired by Lemke, provided the cadre to lead the movement for bonus legislation.[65] When the Committee on Military Affairs reported its bill on January 13, 1944, Administration leaders paged Democratic members to their posts to hold the line against the predicted amendments.[66] The committee bill discarded the Senate's version and returned more closely to the original modest concept embodied in the Administration's draft—namely, $300 for all who served more than sixty days and $100 for the remainder.[67]

At this point, the advocates of adjusted service compensation made their move. Lemke proposed that each veteran should receive $100

[63] *The New York Times,* January 11, 1944.

[64] *The Washington Post,* January 23, 1944.

[65] The organization carried the cumbersome, but descriptive, title "Congressional Committee for Immediate and Adequate Mustering-Out Pay." Formed during the first session, it had forty-five members. By the second session Lemke listed a net gain of six new recruits. Although bipartisan in composition, more Republicans than Democrats joined: twenty-eight and twenty-three, respectively, with one Progressive.

[66] R. A. "Lex" Green (D-Fla.), the Assistant Democratic Whip, for example, received the call to duty at his home in Florida. Arline Mann [Green's secretary, transmitting the message of the Majority Leader John W. McCormack (D-Mass.)] to Green, January 15, 1944; Misc. Correspondence, Green Papers, U. of Florida. McCormack should not have been so eager, perhaps, to have Green return; as it turned out, the Floridian spoke in support of a "bonus" amendment.

[67] May's committee also defined eligibility more rigorously. They excluded, for example, veterans who had been discharged, upon their own request, to accept employment in war industries.

plus continuance of monthly pay (at the lowest military rank's rate) for up to one year for those with nine months' service, or more.[68] "Mr. Speaker, America's generosity is on trial," Lemke proclaimed.[69] Earlier, Lemke had cautioned that "we should not be too peanutish with them." [70] Representative Thomas Rolph (R-Calif.) sounded a theme to be repeated by others with variations: "Here we are a Nation with wealth beyond the dreams of Midas. . . . Here we are appropriating billions upon billions for people of other lands, and still we are hesitating about our own." [71] But some opponents of the Lemke amendment questioned the Midas-like capacity of the United States. Representative Dewey Short (R-Mo.) warned of the high costs:

Have we gone completely crazy? Have we lost all sense of proportion? Who will have to pay this bill? You who think you are going to bribe the veterans and buy his vote, you who think you can win his support by coddling him and being a sob sister with a lot of silly, slushy sentimentality are going to have a sad awakening.[72]

Supporters of the May Committee bill argued that World War II veterans would receive an amount five times that received by the World War I veterans; that the push for greater cash benefits came not from servicemen, but only from the older veterans' organizations; and finally, that a bonus bill should come after, not during the war.[73]

Despite Lemke's exhortations to his fellow committeemen ("Let every Member work with his colleagues for this amendment and be on the floor. . . . *Let us do justice to the discharged veterans.*")[74] his amendment lost 71 to 137.[75] Having temporarily disposed of the

[68] The proposed schedule called for pay continuance for three, six, and nine months respectively for individuals who served at least one but less than three, three but less than six, and six but less than nine, months.

[69] *Cong. Rec.*, 78:2 (January 18, 1944), 339.

[70] House, *May Committee Mustering-Out Pay Hearings*, 78:1 (December 10, 1943), 61.

[71] *Cong. Rec.*, 78:2 (January 18, 1944), 340.

[72] *Ibid.*, 345.

[73] Along with Reps. May and Short, Leslie C. Arends (R-Ill.) and John M. Costello (D-Calif.) argued for the May Committee bill, *ibid.*, 345–47.

[74] Lemke to Colleagues, January 15, 1944; A13 Files, Lemke MSS., U. of North Dakota, Grand Forks, N.D. Lemke's emphasis.

[75] *Cong. Rec.*, 78:2 (January 19, 1944), 421. No roll call was taken; but it seems reasonable to assume that the amendment drew substantial support from Democrats—at least from those twenty-three who belonged to the Lemke Committee.

bonus question, the House then unanimously approved the May Committee bill.[76] May, who had fasted during the long day of debate, munched a tangerine in satisfaction. The bonus had been staved off.

The final revisions emerged from the ensuing conference with the Senate. Instead of retaining the simple differential of $100 or $300 depending on length of service, the conferees inserted an intermediate sum of $200 and restored distinctions based on overseas service. Hence the bill now granted $100 to individuals who served less than sixty days; $200 for those who served more than sixty days, all of which was spent in the United States; and $300 for those who served overseas. After a brief but bitter debate, the House agreed to the Conference bill, 276 to 103, with 48 members not voting.[77] President Roosevelt signed the bill on February 3, 1944.[78]

THE MUSTERING-OUT PAY ACT represented a victory for President Roosevelt. He had beaten back, if only temporarily, the bonus forces. The success gave the Administration more time to work for other portions of the broad veterans' program. The more benefits it could fashion, in lieu of the bonus, the weaker the bonus demand would become. Mustering-out pay, in that sense, tended to enervate the potent appeal of a bonus.

The American Legion also had won. It enjoyed an enviable position. It could claim that its disclosures brought about the mustering-out pay bill. The Legion could also deny, if necessary, responsibility for the precise form of the act. If events proved the law inadequate, the Legion could blame Congress or Administration or both; if the bill aroused no ill feelings, the Legion could claim paternity with safety.

The history of the enactment of the mustering-out pay act may be likened to a foot-race. Only two runners had entered, adherents to the New Deal in one lane and of the bonus in the other. The American Legion, having started the race with its pistol, stood on the side-

[76] 389–0–38. *Ibid.*, 427.
[77] *Ibid.* (January 26, 1944), 750. Approximately 83 per cent of the House Democrats who voted supported the conference report; 62 per cent of the Republicans also went along.
[78] P.L. 225, 78th Cong.

lines rooting on both racers. The New Deal sprinted home first. No sooner had the winded victor triumphed, than it found itself pitted against the Legion, a fresh competitor, in a new race—a distance event that culminated in the highly celebrated "GI Bill of Rights."

4

THE GI BILL OF RIGHTS

THE MUSTERING-OUT PAY BILL met veterans' immediate needs. By February, 1944, thousands of Ulysseses had already returned from their Troy. Private Nicholas Smolak of Pittsburgh, for example, received his first installment of mustering-out pay only two days after the President had signed the bill. Smolak's wife expected a baby in May: "The money will come in mighty handy for that," he told a reporter.[1] Former staff sergeant David E. Harris, a Guadalcanal veteran, told questioners how he would spend his newly acquired cash: "When you've just become a married man . . . you never worry much about what to do with money." [2] Smolak, Harris, and countless others probably would have agreed with the editors of *The New York Times* that "the measure is as necessary as it is just." [3]

The mustering-out pay bill's speedy passage obscured the preparations already underway to provide the new Ulysseses with a broader range of benefits. As early as October 27, 1943, President Roosevelt had presented his outline for veterans' education benefits to Congress.[4]

[1] *The New York Journal American,* February 6, 1944.
[2] *The Washington Post,* February 10, 1944.
[3] February 28, 1944.
[4] "Message to the Congress on Education of War Veterans," October 27, 1943; in Samuel I. Rosenman, comp., *Public Papers and Addresses of Franklin D. Roosevelt* (13 vols., 1938–1950), XII, 449–55. Cited hereafter as Rosenman, *Roosevelt Public Papers.*

Less than a month later he submitted the remaining parts of his veterans' program.[5] On the strength of these actions, some commentators have credited the President with paternity for the GI Bill of Rights, passed in June, 1944.[6] A review of the legislative history of the GI Bill will help to evaluate that claim. Before that tangled story is related, however, a brief reminder of the state of legislative-executive relations during the 1943–1944 winter should be made.

BY DECEMBER, 1943, two general conditions vexed Roosevelt's relations with Congress. First, an election year peeked around the corner; although the war muted the full fury of normal partisan maneuverings, Republicans and Democrats still had to have issues to attack or defend when they went on the hustings the following November. Second, Congress stirred restlessly as the President by executive order alone established the many agencies made necessary by the war. Congressmen naturally resented the expansion of presidential power. In many ways the legislature could act only as a "rubber stamp" for the executive; national security requirements, for example, made impossible the exact disclosure of how war funds would be spent. Congress, in short, frequently had to sign a blank check.[7]

Specific events during the winter of 1943–1944 demonstrated the delicacy of congressional-executive relations. The "soldier vote" controversy, for one, exacerbated those relations. President Roosevelt had proposed to extend the franchise privilege to absent servicemen by means of a uniform federal short ballot for use in the 1944 elections. His plan met fierce resistance from "states rights" defenders in both parties in Congress; they argued that traditional electoral responsibility of the states would be violated. Anti-Rooseveltians, in addition, saw in the President's proposal an attempt by the commander-in-chief to order servicemen to vote for him; his reelection would be assured, they feared. The defeat on December 3, 1943 in the Senate of the

[5] *Ibid.*, 522–27.
[6] Samuel I. Rosenman, *Working With Roosevelt* (New York, 1952) pp. 394–95; and Rexford G. Tugwell, *The Democratic Roosevelt* (Garden City, New York, 1957), p. 614.
[7] See Roland Young, *Congressional Politics During the Second World War* (New York, 1956), pp. 231–32.

Administration's plan, the first Scott Lucas bill, prompted Allen Drury (a United Press correspondent) to note that "there is a very real bitterness on this issue." [8]

The President's veto of the tax bill on February 22, 1944, moreover, burst the smouldering resentment of the legislators against "That Man" into open flame, with Senator Alben W. Barkley (D-Ky.) going as far as to resign his post as majority leader. Then, after enthusiastically reelecting Barkley, Democrats joined Republicans in overriding Roosevelt's "tax relief for the greedy not for the needy" veto. Perceptively, Drury noted: "The effect has been to create, for the first time, perhaps, of all the times in which he has differed from the Congress, a really grave crisis in the relations between the Executive and the Legislature." [9] The Senate minority whip, Kenneth S. Wherry (R-Neb.), exultantly informed a correspondent:

I do think that we have had quite an awakening and I think that the Senate realizes that we must cause a halt to government by Executive order. . . . The New Deal and this Administration is having its wings clipped and from now on you can expect Congress to continue the clipping.[10]

The bitterness shown in the mustering-out pay debates, in addition, had been symptomatic of the hardening attitude. One Congressman, Lyle Boren (D-Okla.), had thought that Administration leaders deliberately kept the mustering-out benefits low so that requests for funds for the United Nations Relief and Recovery Administration (UNRRA) would be more palatable.[11] To sum up, the congressional mood, while not "ugly," called for close attention.

AGAINST THIS BACKGROUND of darkening skies in legislative-executive relations, the President launched his program for veterans with his plea to Congress for education benefits on October 27, 1943. Osten-

---

[8] Entry for December 7, 1943; Drury, *A Senate Journal, 1943–1945* (New York, Toronto, and London, 1963), p. 17.

[9] *Ibid.*, p. 86.

[10] Wherry to W. R. Maloney, March 29, 1944; "Whip Correspondence" Folder, Wherry Papers, U. of Nebraska Library, Lincoln, Neb.

[11] U.S., *Congressional Record,* 78th Cong., 2d Sess., Appendix (January 26, 1944), A-402. Cited hereafter as *Cong. Rec.,* followed by Congress and Session numbers, date and page.

sibly, he had relied upon a report submitted to him by his Armed Forces Committee on Post-War Educational Opportunities for Service Personnel. Roosevelt had founded this committee on November 13, 1942; he had appointed Brigadier General Frederick G. Osborn to head its work. Thus the Osborn Committee's efforts overlapped those of the National Resources Planning Board's Post-War Manpower Conference (PMC). Parenthetically, this move of the President's appears to have been a stroke of administrative "genius." Although the report of the PMC contained educational recommendations that roughly paralleled those of the special committee, the President could cite the latter without incurring the certain resistance that would have ensued if he had used the tarnished PMC's efforts. The aim of the proposals remained the same; but the stigma had been cleverly removed. The Osborn Committee's preliminary report, dated July 30, 1943, furthermore, had not included controversial features that, although peripheral to the question of education, would have been handy targets for trigger-quick critics in Congress. It should also be noted that two of the more influential members of the Osborn Committee, the Army's Colonel Francis T. Spaulding and Lieutenant Commander Ralph A. Sentman of the Navy, both had served their "apprenticeship" on veterans' policy planning with the Postwar Manpower Conference.

In the October speech the President urged "that the time to prepare for peace is at the height of war." [12] Specifically, he had proposed that the Federal Government give financial aid to every member of the armed forces who had served honorably for at least six months since September 16, 1940 (the date of the Selective Training and Service Act); this would provide the veteran the opportunity to study for at least one calender year. He had suggested, moreover, that the government subsidize a select group of veterans for additional training up to a maximum of three years. Once again he had touched on a favorite sales technique: education would not only benefit the country by providing enlightened leadership in all walks of life in the coming years, but also it would cushion the impact of possible unemployment on the returning heroes. To cap his argument, the President had

[12] "Message to the Congress on Education of War Veterans," October 27, 1943; in Rosenman, *Roosevelt Public Papers, 1943,* 449–55.

spoken of the moral obligation of the Nation to provide for its veterans. He had insisted that the Federal Government be cast in the role of supervisor only; states and local educational institutions should have the direct control of the program.

On November 23, 1943, Roosevelt had presented the Congress with the remaining elements of his veterans' program. He had repeated his cautionary note about concentrating on the "primary objective of winning this war." [13] Then, he had proceeded to enumerate benefits that veterans already enjoyed: government life insurance,[14] guarantees on commercial life insurance premiums,[15] hospitalization and medical care,[16] vocational rehabilitation for the disabled,[17] pension rights,[18] suspension of certain civilian-incurred obligations for servicemen,[19] and reemployment rights.[20] To these benefits, he had requested Congress to add mustering-out pay, a uniform system of federal unemployment benefits, and credit under the Social Security System for the period spent in the armed forces. He had closed his address with a customary appeal:

The Congress will agree, I am sure, that this time, we must have plans and legislation ready for our returning veterans instead of waiting until the last moment. It will give notice to our armed forces that the people back home do not propose to let them down.[21]

First fruits of the President's two pleas came in September and November 1943 with the introduction of bills covering education and mustering-out pay benefits.[22] At first, the job of coordinating executive support for these bills fell to Judge Samuel I. Rosenman, the

[13] "A Message to the Congress on Providing for the Return of Service Personnel to Civilian Life," *ibid.*, 522–27.

[14] Public Law 360, 77th Cong., December 19, 1941.

[15] Soldiers' and Sailors' Civil Relief Act, Public Law 861, 76th Cong., October 17, 1940.

[16] Public Law 10, 78th Cong., March 17, 1943.

[17] Public Law 16, 78th Cong., March 24, 1943.

[18] Public Law 359, 77th Cong., December 19, 1941.

[19] Soldiers' and Sailors' Civil Relief Act, Public Law 861, 76th Cong., October 17, 1940.

[20] Selective Training and Service Act, Public Law 783, 76th Cong., September 16, 1940.

[21] Rosenman, *Roosevelt Public Papers, 1943*, 527.

[22] S. 1509, 78th Cong., 1st Sess., and S. 1543, 78th Cong., 1st Sess., November 26, 1943. Mustering-out pay is handled separately in chapter iii, above.

President's special counsel and one of FDR's principal speech-writers. Rosenman relied heavily on the services of Milton Handler, an attorney in the Assistant Solicitor General's office; he used members of the Budget Bureau staff as well.[23] By December the legislative situation had grown so complex, however, that the Budget Bureau set up an intraagency committee.[24] Chaired by General Hines, this small group met frequently during the months that followed in a vain attempt to maintain control over the rapidly moving legislative events.

The most difficult problem centered on the education bill (S.1509) introduced by an Administration stalwart, Senator Elbert D. Thomas. Incorporating recommendations from the Osborn Committee and, indirectly, from the earlier suggestions of the Postwar Manpower Conference, the Administration bill attempted to link educational opportunities for veterans with an overall national employment policy. Section 2 of the proposed statute extended benefits to qualified individuals[25] "in any one of the fields or branches of knowledge . . . in which the number of trained personnel is or is likely to be inadequate under conditions of full utilization of manpower." Here the Administration's tendency to foster national economic planning blended with an appreciation of the experience with World War I veterans. Hence the measure retained the features of the PMC report that proposed to use veterans' education as an instrument to help achieve full employment and, at the same time, avoid repetition of the unhappy results of training men for jobs for which no demand existed.

The Administration proposal did not offer aid to all veterans beyond the first year of study. Only persons of "exceptional ability or

[23] See "Education for Discharged Soldiers and Vocational Rehabilitation" Folder, Samuel I. Rosenman Papers, Franklin D. Roosevelt Library, Hyde Park, N.Y. Cited hereafter as FDRL.

[24] Budget Committee on Veterans' Legislation, formed December 29, 1943. The Federal Security Agency, War and Navy Departments, Budget Bureau, and Veterans Administration were represented. Memo, Harold D. Smith to Frank T. Hines, December 29, 1943; "O-2 Budget Committee on Veterans' Legislation" Folder, Office of Legislative and Liaison Records, Central Office, Veterans Administration, Washington, D.C. Cited hereafter as VA Records.

[25] Qualified by their having served on active duty in the armed services or in the merchant marine since September 16, 1940, for at least six months, and "on the basis of their intelligence, aptitude, skill, interest, prior training, education and experience."

skill" would receive additional benefits for up to three more years. The Osborn Committee had proposed to limit the additional benefits to the "elite" because of the expected high cost.[26] The Budget Bureau chief, Harold Smith, agreed with the committee. In October, 1943, he had expressed concern about the "virtually . . . unlimited commitment for what may be a large expenditure of funds." [27] The original Administration bill, as a result, provided that the total number of servicemen eligible for supplementary benefits be allotted to the states in proportion to each state's contribution of military personnel during the war.

On one crucial point—who should administer the benefits?—the bill was silent. This question touched on two thorny problems. First, to designate the United States Office of Education (USOE), for example, as the responsible agency, would wave a red flag before an easily enraged bull. The vociferous champions of the veterans' organizations in Congress would bellow at any attempt to give a bureaucratic New Deal agency responsibility over veterans. Second, the question had not even been answered within the executive branch. Milton Handler, when he had drawn up a draft of the bill, had omitted specific reference to an agency. He had reasoned that to place all administrative responsibility with the President would "remove any basis for jurisdictional disputes at this time." [28]

Handler was too optimistic. General Hines advised the Thomas Committee that all benefits should be handled by one agency. He declared that it need not be necessarily the Veterans Administration, but obviously he hoped the legislators would opt for his agency.[29] How could the Senators avoid the logic of his case? Veterans' vocational rehabilitation, hospitalization, pensions, and insurance all fell in the bailiwick of the Veterans Administration. To avoid shunting

[26] See Colonel Francis T. Spaulding's statement; U.S., Senate, Committee on Education and Labor, 78th Cong., 1st Sess. *Hearings on S. 1295 and S. 1509,* December 13, 1943 (Washington, D.C., 1943), 31. Cited hereafter as Senate, *Thomas Committee Veterans' Education Hearings.*

[27] Smith to Samuel I. Rosenman, October 19, 1943, "War Veterans' Education" Folder, Rosenman Papers, FDRL.

[28] Memo, "Servicemen's Education and Training Act of 1943," September 16, 1943, attached to Handler to Rosenman, September 17, 1943; "War Veterans' Education Folder, *ibid.*

[29] Senate, *Thomas Committee Veterans' Education Hearings,* December 14, 1943, 54–56.

the hapless veteran from agency to agency it seemed only natural that Hines's organization should have control over educational benefits as well. Hines's ideas did not go long unchallenged. Three days after the VA chief's views were presented to the Thomas Committee, the Commissioner of Education, John W. Studebaker, publicly proclaimed that his agency should have that jurisdiction.[30]

Hearings on the Administration's measure (held from December 13 to 15, 1943) brought out two important considerations concerning its future. In the first place, some of the provisions irritated "double-dyed" New Dealers. Senator Claude D. Pepper (D-Fla.), an ardent supporter of the President, objected strenuously to limiting the number of veterans eligible for education benefits; he also disliked the state quota system. Pepper's opposition presaged liberal discontent.[31]

The hearings also manifested the near unanimity of educators' opinions on the desirability of having the United States Office of Education (USOE) control the program. Although Thomas did not invite the testimony of USOE officials, many of the major private educational groups appeared before his committee. The Association of American Colleges, National Education Association, American Association of Junior Colleges, American Council on Education, American Association of Teachers Colleges, the National Home Study Council, War Emergency Council of Private Business Schools, and the National Council of Technical Schools, all sent representatives to the three-day hearings. All supported giving USOE jurisdiction.

George F. Zook, representing the American Council on Education, made valuable suggestions to Thomas's Committee. Relying on his association's special committee's recommendations,[32] Zook urged

[30] The New York Times, December 18, 1943. Studebaker was addressing the annual convention of the American Vocational Association, on December 17, 1943.

[31] See his questioning of Administration witnesses in Senate, Thomas Committee Veterans' Education Hearings, December 13, 1943, 18 ff.

[32] This group, carrying the cumbersome title of "Committee on Relationships of Higher Institutions to the Federal Government of the American Council on Education," had an imposing membership. Cornell, Hamilton, Harvard, New York U., Pembroke, Tuskegee, Vanderbilt, and Wisconsin had sent their presidents to wrestle with the problem of veterans' education. The committee had

that the unwieldy state quota system, as well as availability of employment opportunities, be eliminated as eligibility criteria. The individual educational institution should select students. Zook thought that the USOE should be in charge since, through experience and type of personnel, it best understood educational matters. Instead of having the President alone promulgate regulations for the program, Zook urged creation of an advisory commission, to be selected from "appropriate governmental agencies and nongovernmental education associations." [33] By the close of the public hearings these objections coming from individuals who agreed on fundamentals indicated that the bill needed extensive revision.

Although Senator Thomas periodically informed the press of substantial progress during December and even into January, 1944, the chances for rapid passage evaporated by the close of 1943.[34] For one thing, support within the executive branch for the bill seemed shattered when, at the third meeting of the Budget coordinating committee, the Federal Security Agency (FSA) announced it could not accept the Administration's measure.[35] It appeared as if the story of vocational rehabilitation legislation would be repeated.

Five months after the President's fireside chat, the Administration's education plans for veterans seemed imperiled by lack of unity within the executive branch. One reason for the poor showing during 1943 derived from the failure to establish an authoritative administrative apparatus to guide legislative measures embodying the President's proposals to enactment. No one rode herd over the unruly agencies. As a result, the FSA (with the USOE as one of its constituent units) waited until January 17, 1944, to indicate unequivocal objection to the Thomas bill; it did not offer a substitute plan until four days later.[36]

---

been meeting since the summer of 1943. For a complete membership list and its report, see *ibid.*, 113–15.

[33] *Ibid.*, December 15, 1943, 114–15.

[34] On January 2, 1944, Thomas predicted early passage: "I don't think anybody can be against this bill in its present form." *The New York Times,* January 3, 1944.

[35] "Minutes of Third Meeting, Monday, January 17, 1944, of Advisory Committee on Legislation for Veterans"; "O-2 Budget Committee on Veterans' Legislation" Folder, VA Records.

[36] "Minutes of Fourth Meeting, Friday, January 21, 1944, of Advisory Committee on Legislation for Veterans"; *ibid.*

Hines and his advisers in the VA, considering themselves administrators rather than policymakers, lagged even farther behind.

WHILE EXECUTIVE AGENCIES straggled without leadership, another reminder of the vocational rehabilitation struggle of 1943 cropped up. As in the case of the earlier policymaking, once the Administration provided the initial momentum, a new force emerged. Once again the veterans' organizations began to play a significant role. This time it was the American Legion acting on its own. On January 10, 1944, the Legion presented a novel plan to Congress. Rather than have the veterans' program parceled out in a series of individual bills, each subject to the vagaries of the legislative process, the Legion proposed an omnibus bill that would provide the statutory basis for the "readjustment" of the veterans of World War II. Departing from its past legislative strategy, the Legion gambled that wartime patriotism, as well as the disinclination of Congressmen publicly to oppose veterans' benefits, would overcome traditional objections to omnibus measures. The Legion maintained, moreover, that its action merely complemented the President's own general program.[37] As it turned out, the Administration did permit the Legion to carry the ball. Roosevelt did not attempt to wrest the banners from the veterans' organization; federal agencies, moreover, played only a minor role—discussed later.

Legionnaires' interest in the welfare of the World War II veterans arose in large part from a sincere desire to help prevent GIs from experiencing what they—the veterans of the Great War—had undergone. But the natural wish of the Legion to attract the new veterans helps explain the timing of its move. The move, of course, was related to the accusations voiced by the Legion's commander, Warren G. Atherton, that disabled veterans did not receive proper care. Yet, unlike the other veterans' group which galloped off to do battle for a bonus, the Legion had busied itself on more momentous matters.

---

[37] Ironically, the idea of a unified Administration program had been put forward tentatively when early legislative drafts referred to other, related bills. But VA and War Department officials opposed this method. See, for example, U.S., House of Representatives, Committee on Military Affairs, 78th Cong., 1st Sess., *Hearings on . . . Mustering-Out Pay,* December 8, 1943 (Washington, D.C., 1944), 19.

On November 30, 1943, Atherton appointed a special committee to draft a "master plan" for the readjustment of World War II veterans. For the chairman's post he chose a former Democratic Governor of Illinois, John Stelle. He included on the committee Harry Colmery, a past Legion national commander, and Robert W. Sisson, head of the Legion's National Rehabilitation Committee.[38]

Meeting in Washington, the committee, after a short, yet intensive, period beginning on December 15, 1943, finished the first draft of a proposed bill on December 31, 1943.[39] The draft embodied, its sponsors claimed, three basic principles indorsed by the Legion's National Convention. First, the Legion urged that benefits be centralized under one agency, the Veterans Administration—so that veterans would not be led from pillar to post; second, benefits for World War II veterans should be at least equal to those for their World War I counterparts; and third, any legislation should insure that the returning servicemen could resume their civilian status right at the point at which the war had disrupted their lives.[40]

The Legion publicized its bill on January 8, 1944 as "a bill of rights for G.I. Joe and G.I. Jane." [41] Within four days this had been shortened to "G.I. Bill of Rights." [42] The Legion sponsors strove to

[38] David Camelon, "I Saw the GI Bill Written," mimeographed reprint of article that originally appeared in *The American Legion Magazine,* XLVII (September–November 1949), 11–12. Cited hereafter as Camelon, "GI Bill." See also Richard Seelye Jones, *A History of the American Legion* (Indianapolis and New York, 1946), pp. 217–21; and Raymond Moley, Jr., *The American Legion Story* (New York, 1966), p. 273. Cited hereafter as Jones, *The Legion,* and Moley, *The Legion.*

[39] Camelon gives the completion date as January 6, 1944; "G.I. Bill," 25. The VA Records show, however, that the Legion committee sent the first draft to that agency on December 31, 1943. See Edward E. Odom to Guy H. Birdsall, January 1, 1944; "17 Servicemen's Readjustment Act General, Part III" Folder, VA Records.

[40] See Atherton's statement in U.S., Senate, Committee on Finance, Subcommittee on Veterans' Legislation, 78th Cong., 2d Sess., *Hearings on Veterans' Omnibus Bill,* January 14, 1944 (Washington, D.C., 1944), 19–20, cited hereafter as Senate, *Clark Subcommittee GI Bill Hearings.*

[41] *The New York Times,* January 9, 1944.

[42] The official Legion version of the origin of the term gives credit to Jack Cejnar, the Legion's acting publicity director. Cejnar presumably thought of the catchy phrase on January 7, 1944. Camelon "GI Bill," 27. But in presenting the bill to Congress, the Legion sponsors were not the first to use it. Omar Ketchum of the VFW called it the "GI Bill of Rights" on January 12, 1944,

impress Congressmen that their bill did not represent the final word on benefits for World War II veterans. They also pointed out that they would not resent changes—as long as the basic principles remained intact. They requested Senator J. Bennett "Champ" Clark (D-Mo.) to introduce the bill in the upper chamber; John E. Rankin (D-Miss.) was asked to perform the same service in the House.

The Legion measure contained titles covering hospitalization, claims, and appeals procedures; mustering-out pay; education; home and farm loans; employment; and unemployment compensation.[43] The first title reflected Atherton's charges that disabled veterans' claims had not been receiving prompt attention. The bill proposed that no serviceman be discharged without receiving first a substantial amount of the pay due him and second, an explanation of his rights. The first section of the title also proposed that the Veterans Administration be accorded priority second only to the War and Navy departments in requisitioning its construction materials and other supplies.

Title II dealt with mustering-out pay; when a separate bill was passed this title was dropped. Title III contained the Legion's education plan for veterans. In keeping with the Legion's desires to restore the returning servicemen to a *status quo ante bellum,* the bill limited benefits to honorably discharged servicemen whose education or training had been interrupted by military duty. The proposal further added a nine-month service requirement; all qualified individuals would be eligible for one full year of benefits. At the expiration of that year the Veterans Administrator would choose those to continue for a maximum of three more years. Single and married veterans engaged in full-time education would receive a subsistence allowance of $50 and $75 per month, respectively. The relatively low amounts authorized were thought necessary to discourage vet-

during the House hearings. U.S., House of Representatives, Committee on World War Veterans' Legislation, 78th Cong., 2d Sess., *Hearings on H.R.3817 and S.1767 to Provide Federal Government Aid for the Readjustment in Civilian Life of Returning World War II Veterans,* January 12, 1944 (Washington, D.C., 1944), 30. Cited hereafter as House, *Rankin Committee GI Bill Hearings.*

[43] S.1617, 78th Cong., 2d Sess., January 11, 1944.

erans with little interest in education from "cashing in" on the benefits. Married female veterans, however, had to prove their husbands' dependence upon them for support in order to receive the $75. Tuition costs, up to a maximum of $300, would be paid to institutions approved by the Veterans Administration. The Legion authors obviously had benefited from the debates on veterans' education, particularly those aired before the Thomas committee.

The fourth title opened the door to relatively unexplored areas. It proposed that veterans be granted loans for homes and farms. The states should establish these programs subject to the approval of the Veterans Administrator. Loans for homes up to 95 per cent of the appraised value with $7,500 as the maximum—or $12,500 for farms—could be made. The Federal Government would provide $4 for each $1 donated by the state; the maximum allowable interest rate could be 1 per cent on the former and 5 per cent on the latter. To insure that a state's inability to participate would not deprive benefits for needy veterans, the bill allowed the Veterans Administrator to advance the entire amount, requiring only that the state portion be repaid by July 31, 1949. Although this title would be altered substantially, it did not lead to as much controversy as the final two titles of the bill.

The first of these proposed that all functions relating to veterans' employment be centralized under the Veterans Administration— with one significant exception. The Selective Service System's responsibility over reemployment rights for veterans would remain with that agency. The United States Employment Service fared less well in the proposed legislation. The Veterans' Employment Service (established in 1933 by the Wagner-Peyser Act) would be shifted to the Veterans Administration. An elaborate employment referral system would then be the responsibility of the Veterans Administration. This proposal touched on a sensitive issue—the return of the entire United States Employment Service to state control. The fuse on the dynamite of this proposal led to an explosion after V-J Day; the fuse on the bill's concluding title, however, was considerably shorter.

The Legion closed its proposals with one dealing with unemployment allowances. This title provided benefits of up to $25 per week for a maximum period of fifty-two weeks. Individuals who left work without suitable cause would be barred from benefits for a maximum of four weeks; such period of debarment would also count against total eligibility for benefits, thus imposing a double penalty. Former servicemen who participated in a strike, either directly or indirectly, would be disqualified for benefits during that work stoppage. In addition, veterans who were suspended or discharged from a job for misconduct, or who failed to report for, or accept suitable work, or who failed to attend free training periods authorized for them, would be ineligible for benefits until they had substantially full-time employment for a period of two weeks. Finally, the Veterans Administration could bar repeat violators indefinitely.

To sum up, although the Legion's version of the bill would be modified in important particulars, it did have the merit of logical internal consistency. All the benefits revolved around the dual themes of centralization of administration and facilitation of veterans' readjustment to civilian life. Nothing in it—with the exception of the loan features—departed from ideas and plans already formulated by the Roosevelt Administration. If not original in that sense, the method of its presentation and its form as an omnibus measure represented shrewd tactical insight into legislative maneuvering that contrasted favorably with the Administration's piecemeal approach.

The similarity of the Legion's program and that of the Administration's should not conceal dissimilarities in intent. The hope of linking veterans' benefits with the overall task of domestic reconversion had been a polestar for Roosevelt's planners. The drafters of the Legion's measure, however, had a simpler, but no dimmer guiding light: serve the veteran directly, unequivocally, and with no shenanigans.

WHEN PUBLIC HEARINGS on the Legion's bill commenced in both House and Senate,[44] a minor obstacle emerged. In their eagerness to appear first with the bill, the Legion sponsors had not consulted with their colleagues in other veterans' organizations. Perhaps un-

[44] January 12 and 14, 1944.

willing to share the limelight, the legionnaires ran the risk of jeopardizing their program by alienating the Veterans of Foreign Wars (VFW) and the Disabled Veterans of America (DAV).

The Legion's precipitate action irritated the VFW's legislative representative, Omar Ketchum. He doubted the wisdom of introducing an omnibus bill, declaring this frequently had led to the defeat of important constituent measures. Captiously, he reminded the legislators that the Legion's bill repeated much that had already been enacted into law. The implication that the Legion alone supported GI benefits seemed to bother Ketchum most. The Legion's proposal, he grumbled, "is not a miraculous cure-all which has suddenly been discovered." [45] After all, he pointed out, the VFW had been working just as hard in the past as the Legion to achieve the same goals. Ketchum might have had in mind the memory of working closely with Francis M. Sullivan, his counterpart in the Legion, as late as November 6, 1943. At that time the two had agreed upon a veterans' education bill—introduced by Rankin as H.R.3634 on November 8, 1943.[46] Since the VFW later indorsed the GI Bill (after conferences with the Legion sponsors had cleared up their points of disagreement) there is little reason to believe that this could not have been accomplished before its introduction in January. As a result, one of the Legion's stated goals of bringing the legislation to fruition quickly may have been delayed due to the VFW's hurt feelings.[47]

The Disabled Veterans of America (DAV) also questioned the Legion's tactics. In fact, unlike the VFW, the DAV doggedly opposed the GI Bill of Rights throughout the entire course of its legislative history. The organization believed that the Veterans Administration had its hands full with the problems of the disabled. The Legion bill would actually prove harmful, it claimed, by diverting

[45] Senate, *Clark Subcommittee GI Bill Hearings* (January 15, 1944), 27.
[46] Sullivan to Rankin, November 6, 1943; "The American Legion, 78th Cong." Folder, HR 78 A-F 39.2, Tray 17016, House Committee on World War Veterans' Legislation Records, Record Group 233, National Archives. Cited hereafter as Rankin Committee Records, RG 233, NA.
[47] The quarrel between the two organizations was patched up by February 22, 1944. Senate, *Clark Subcommittee GI Bill Hearings,* February 23, 1944, 160.

needed funds and facilities from the disabled. Millard Rice, national service director of DAV, said: "I do not believe the Veterans Administration should have any responsibility as to the postwar adjustments of able-bodied men." [48] This extreme position, which Rice continued to press, ultimately nettled the bill's supporters so much that an angry exchange took place during the otherwise placid Senate hearings:

SENATOR CLARK: There has never been a desire by anybody to put the rights of anybody ahead of the rights of the disabled veterans. It is the able-bodied veterans of the last war who made the fight to take care of the disabled veterans, and here you come on behalf of the disabled veterans protesting against rights for the able-bodied veterans.

MR. RICE: I am not protesting against the rights for the able-bodied veterans. I do not appreciate having my words twisted that way. I protested against submerging the activities on behalf of the disabled veterans of this country and probably jeopardizing those benefits. [49]

The DAV, VFW, Military Order of Purple Heart, and Regular Veterans Association joined in expressing doubts about the Legion's bill. In identical public letters dated February 16, 1944, to Clark and Rankin, representatives of the four organizations warned against acting in haste and repenting in leisure. [50] They preferred an adjusted compensation plan—a bonus—in lieu of the Legion's proposal. On March 6, 1944, they sponsored (with the Army and Navy Union as a new recruit) a bill to provide a king-size bonus, with a maximum amount of $5,000. Senator Robert Reynolds (D-N.C.), who introduced the bill into the Senate, estimated the plan would cost approximately $25 to $30 billion. [51] Coming on the heels of the Administration's success with mustering-out pay, and facing the stiff competition of the Legion's program, the bonus move went for naught. It indicated, however, that a cleavage existed among the veterans' organizations.

[48] House, *Rankin Committee GI Bill Hearings* (January 18, 1944), 138.
[49] Senate, *Clark Subcommittee GI Bill Hearings* (March 8, 1944), 205.
[50] The letter to Clark is reproduced as an attachment to Camelon, "GI Bill." The original letter to Rankin is in "D" Folder, HR 78 A-F 39.1, Tray 17011, Rankin Committee Records, RG 233, NA.
[51] *Cong. Rec.*, 78:2 (March 7, 1944), 2305.

This initial disunity among the veterans' organizations reflected some of the differing views concerning veterans' benefits. Everyone favored veterans' legislation; along with mothers, apple pie, and Old Glory, aid for veterans was accepted without dissent. On specific remedies and benefits, however, a wide range of views could be expected. The debates on the GI bill highlighted these differences. As in any comprehensive bill, moreover, other issues emerged in the push and pull process of legislative maneuvering. Traditional conflicts between supporters and opponents of the New Deal, partially submerged as a result of the war, broke to the surface at various points as the bill slowly progressed through the turbulent, and at times, murky, legislative stream. At other times division occurred over issues involving "states rights." These divergent views tended to crystallize around the two most significant and controversial titles of the Legion's omnibus bill: education and unemployment compensation benefits.

WHEN SENATOR CLARK'S Subcommittee on Veterans' Legislation completed its nine-session hearings on March 10, 1944, the measure went to the full Finance Committee.[52] In the process, the Senators had managed to change the original Legion bill's education and unemployment compensation titles. They substituted a revised Thomas' veterans' education bill for the Legion's proposal. The Senators made education and training benefits available to all veterans discharged under other than dishonorable conditions, with at least six months' service—rather than to just those whose education or training had been interrupted. They increased fee repayments to $500. Responding to the American Council on Education's advice, they added an advisory board that would assist the Veterans Administrator on education and training matters. The Senate bill allowed benefits (except subsistence allowances) to part-time students. But the Senators did bow to one of the Legion's cardinal principles by vesting considerable supervisory authority in the Veterans' Administrator.

The original Legion bill's unemployment compensation and em-

[52] A "clean" bill, S. 1767, 78:2 was introduced on March 15, 1944.

ployment sections disturbed members of Senator Clark's subcommittee. Senator Robert F. Wagner (D-N.Y.), a leading advocate and authority on unemployment compensation, appeared before his colleagues to urge that the Veterans' Employment Service be retained within the United States Employment Service.[53] Instead of moving it to the Veterans Administration, he suggested that Congress establish a Veterans' Placement Service Board—composed of the Veterans Administrator, the Chairman of the War Manpower Commission, and the director of the United States Employment Service. This board would set policies for the existing Veterans' Employment Service. The Clark subcommittee agreed.

Wagner then turned to unemployment compensation; the Legion's disqualification provisions were too harsh, he stated. The "double penalty" feature, he said, "really limits unduly the cherished American right to leave one job in order to take a better one—better for the veteran, for the community, and for the Nation." [54] Again the subcommittee members agreed; they restricted the maximum disqualification to four weeks (without the double penalty feature) for a non-repeat "violator" and eight weeks for multiple offenders. In addition the Solons struck out the ambiguous phrase "indirect participation" in a strike as a reason to curtail benefits. Finally, the Senators determined that beneficiaries of unemployment compensation—now dubbed "readjustment allowance"—would receive one week of benefits for each three weeks served in the armed forces.

The full Senate approved the revised bill unanimously.[55] This surprised no one. After all, seventy Senators had scrambled to add their names to those of the original eleven sponsors. In accord with the Legion's pragmatic attitude, the original sponsors did not resist publicly the Senate's revisions. The polite debate and the overwhelming vote in the upper house seemed to promise quick passage in the House of Representatives. Supporters could note that Rankin's com-

[53] Senate, *Clark Subcommittee GI Bill Hearings* (February 11, 1944), 105–15.

[54] *Ibid.,* 111.

[55] It passed on March 24, 1944, by a vote of 50 to 0, with 46 members absent. All of the absent members would have voted for the measure. *Cong. Rec.,* 78:2 (March 24, 1944), 3081.

mittee had been holding open hearings concurrently with the Senate's subcommittee. Witnesses had shuttled back and forth from one side of the Capitol to the other during the first two months of 1944. To be sure, the House committee technically had been barred from consideration of the original bill in its entirety until the committee jurisdictional question had been settled. But this did not hamper its deliberations. Committee members used mimeographed copies of the full bill, graciously provided by the Legion, from the first day of public hearings. It seemed, therefore, that House action could be brought about hard on the heels of the Senate's favorable vote.

ROSY EXPECTATIONS that the House of Representatives would emulate the Senate's rapid action proved premature. John E. Rankin now began to engage in dilatory tactics. Up to the time of the bill's passage by the Senate, Rankin had confined his observations in public hearings to general statements that indorsed centralization of responsibility for veterans' benefits under the Veterans Administration.[56] His criticisms centered on specific discharge practices employed by the military services.[57] His indignation knew no bounds at the thought of hapless servicemen allegedly signing away their rights for veterans' benefits in their urgent desire to be released from service. This issue took up an inordinate amount of time in the early House hearings. These almost endless forays into one specific phase of the bill should have warned the sponsors that Rankin had determined to go over the bill with a fine-tooth comb. When the Speaker referred the Senate version to Rankin's committee, the Mississippian expressed serious doubts about the bill.

First of all, Rankin was suspicious of the education title. Senator Thomas, strong New Deal adherent, had figured importantly in the drafting of that section. Rankin declared he would have nothing to

[56] At one point he said: "This is the agency most interested in the physical and mental welfare of these men who are veterans and more so than any other Government agency that I know of, and it is freer from isms." House, *Rankin Committee GI Bill Hearings* (March 28, 1944), 252.

[57] The bill provided for special procedures designed to prevent the long gap of time between discharge and commencement of benefits—the unfortunate case in 1943.

do with this social scheme—at least not in the form presented by the Senate. Had not Senator Thomas's bill been designed to invade the prerogatives of states in education by placing the United States Office of Education in charge of administration? He conveniently ignored the fact that the Senate version had shifted responsibility to the Veterans Administration. To him, the bill appeared a plot to channel the nation's heroes into colleges and there subject them to the tainted theories of sociologists. The result, he claimed, would be a continuation of the trend toward an "overeducated and under-trained" population. His preoccupation with the perils of higher education ("I would rather send my child to a red schoolhouse than to a red school teacher") characterized his dilatory tactics.[58]

But even this concern of Rankin paled beside his vehemence over the readjustment allowance section. The proposed title, he argued, rewarded the malingerer while it punished the virtuous:

There are two developments that I see in it. I see the most violent discrimination against that strong, virile, patriotic, determined man who goes into the Army to fight for his country and comes back and says 'I don't want anything. I am going back and go to work, and that is what the rest of you ought to do'. . . . At the same time I see a tremendous inducement to certain elements not to try to get employment. It is going to be very easy . . . to induce these people to get on Federal relief, which we call unemployment compensation, instead of getting back into active employment.[59]

Privately, the Congressmen from Tupelo wrote:

If every white ex-serviceman in Mississippi . . . could read this so-called "GI Bill," I don't believe there would be one in 20 who would approve it in its present form. . . .
We have 50,000 negroes in the service from our State, and in my opinion, if the bill should pass in its present form, a vast majority of them would remain unemployed for at least a year, and a great many white men would do the same thing.[60]

[58] House, *GI Bill Hearings* (February 24, 1944), 162–63.
[59] *Ibid.* (March 20, 1944), 387. The next day, the Legion's Harry Colmery countered: "The man who has served his country and comes back and wants a job does not want to live on his country. My God! he has fought to defend it." *Ibid.*, 445.
[60] Rankin to E. A. Hiller, April 25, 1944; "H" Folder, HR 78 A-F 38.1, Tray 17012, Rankin Committee Records, RG 233, NA.

The Mississippian's polemics and delays led Warren G. Atherton to comment:

This is not a half-baked bill, as Mr. Rankin says, but if it is I would like to ask how long it takes to bake a bill. Perhaps they need a new baker.

It is ridiculous to assume that every returning soldier and sailor will be a faker in order to get a pork and beans check once a week for a year or so. Such a suggestion is an insult to the men in service.[61]

Rankin's objections to the bill cannot be attributed solely to his alleged "hatred for the colored soldiers," as one radio announcer suggested.[62] He also hated labor unions. The Congressman agreed with correspondents who desired to exempt veterans from "payment of tribute" to labor organizations; he believed that failure to stop this "tribute" would mean "we have failed to maintain that very democracy for which [the GIs] . . . are fighting." [63] Rankin's version of democracy included staunch advocacy of states' rights; he wanted, for example, the Federal Government to return the United States Employment Service to individual state control when the war was finally ended. He must have been pleased to learn that Stanley Rector, Chairman of the Legislative Committee of the Interstate Conference on Unemployment Insurance, had worked with the Legion "in an effort to prevent the use of the Omnibus bill as an opening wedge for [permanent] federalization" of the United States Employment Service.[64] Finally, Rankin's persistent efforts to have adjusted service compensation included in the bill and, when that failed, to push for it strenuously later, indicates another area of his

[61] Quoted in *The Sun* (N.Y.), April 21, 1944. Clipping in "Atherton-Lucas and Guffey and Clark—re G.I. and Soldier Vote" Folder, HR 78 A-F 38.2, Tray 17017, *ibid.*

[62] Norman Jay to Rankin, May 1, 1944; "S. 1767, 78th Cong." Folder, HR 78 A-F 36, *ibid.*

[63] Frank M. Dixon to Rankin, April 6, 1944; and Rankin to Dixon, April 13, 1944; *ibid.* Dixon, a Birmingham lawyer and former Governor of Alabama (1939–43), also told Rankin he had written to the other "Southern members" of Rankin's committee expressing the same concern.

[64] Dixon to Rankin, March 29, 1944; *ibid.* Rankin answered Dixon on April 4, 1944, saying in part: "I am frank to say that I am apprehensive of the effect —which the provisions of Title V of this bill might have—as well as other provisions." *Ibid.*

dissatisfaction.[65] Undoubtedly, he shared Senator Burnet Maybank's
(D-S.C.) view that "many Southern and Western men . . . will not
desire educational benefits"; it would be necessary "to protect them"
by equalizing benefits. Adjusted service compensation would help
keep the balance.[66]

Rankin did not stand alone in his desire to move slowly. He found
support from a number of his committee colleagues, especially Paul
Cunningham (R-Iowa), Harry P. Jeffrey (R-Ohio), and Fred E.
Busbey (R-Ill.). The members of the Committee sincerely desired to
report a carefully deliberated bill. The novelty of the education, readjustment, and loan provisions must have concerned, perhaps even
frightened, some committee members. The committee members
listened patiently to witnesses during the sixteen public sessions of
the hearings. Then they met in executive session nineteen more
times between April 18 and May 3, 1944, hammering out their
differences. After all these meetings they had a new bill to offer—
one more closely in line with their chairman's views.[67]

The Committee reported a bill that narrowed eligibility for the
extended education benefits from all veterans to those whose education or training had been "impeded, delayed, interrupted, or interfered" by induction into the armed forces.[68] Moreover, the Senate's
modest loan provisions fared poorly at the House Committee's hands.
The Committee changed the maximum direct loan as contemplated

[65] Rankin had an adjusted compensation amendment to the GI Bill drafted
on May 1, 1944; *ibid.* His energetic espousal of adjusted service compensation
in 1945 is discussed below, chapter 7. Rankin's interest can be attributed in part
to his desire to expand his committee's jurisdiction, for the Ways and Means
Committee usually received adjusted compensation bills.

[66] Maybank to Corporal D. W. Fagg, November 10, 1943; "Legislation—
Veteran, 1944" Folder, Maybank Papers, South Carolina State Archives Dept.,
Columbia, S.C.

[67] Fred E. Busbey testified to the fact that the revised bill was the committee's, not just Rankin's. He said: "that politics at no time entered into our
discussions." Moreover, Rankin did not "attempt in the least way" to have
the committee adopt his "personal ideas"; Rankin had "always sat as the
Chairman . . . letting everyone in the Committee express their views freely."
Busbey to Rankin, May 23, 1944; "B" Folder, HR 78 A-F 38.1, Tray 17010,
Rankin Committee Records, RG 233, NA.

[68] This more closely approached the Legion's original provisions. The bill
also limited the duration of additional education to an amount equivalent to
time served since September 16, 1940, less the six months' qualifying period.

by the Senate, from $1,000 with a top interest rate of 3 per cent for farm, home, and business purposes, to a maximum $1,500 loan guaranteed by the Veterans Administration, with the high permissible interest of 6 per cent.[69] Once again Rankin's insistence on centralizing benefits found expression in this title, for the House version ignored the Senate's assignment of loan reviewing functions to agricultural, housing, and commerce experts. Instead, the entire function remained squarely with the Veterans Administration. In line with that principle, the House bill also jettisoned the upper house's decision to keep the veterans' employment placement functions within the United States Employment Service (USES). Not content merely to shift that responsibility to the Veterans Administration, the Rankin bill specifically called for the return of the wartime federalized USES to state control when hostilities ended. Finally, the Committee applied the scalpel to the fifty-two week duration of readjustment allowance benefits, limiting it to twenty-six weeks.

WHEN THE RANKIN COMMITTEE reported its bill to the House of Representatives for consideration, the question had become whether the Senate version, generally favored by the Administration, could be replaced in a floor fight. Under the House rule granted Rankin, his substitute version would be voted on first; if it won it would replace the Senate-passed S.1767. If it failed the House would then vote on the original S.1767. The Rankin bill, however, had the inside track since Rankin controlled the allocation of time for debate on the Democratic side and Mrs. Edith Nourse Rogers (R-Mass.), a staunch, if not unqualified, supporter of the House version, controlled the time for the other side of the aisle.

The debate in the House opened with an Administration spokesman, Adolph Sabath, Chairman of the Rules Committee. Sabath, a venerable (if an unheeded) liberal, scored the Rankin Committee's version for "reducing" the benefits provided in the Senate bill.[70]

[69] The significant shift here from "direct" to "guaranteed" loans represented the successful efforts of Rankin to keep the Federal Government participation at a minimum.

[70] *Cong. Rec.* 78:2 (May 11, 1944), 4323–25.

Rankin answered that he and his committee had refused "to be stampeded, excited, or dominated by any outside influence." [71] He commended his group for doing such a good job with "an awfully bad bill to start with." [72] The Mississippian had his usual disparaging comments about unidentified "flannel mouthed" politicians who had been critical of his bill. Ponderously, he played the "cost" theme, warning that if the House broadened benefits more than provided in his substitute, some sections of the country would not support the ensuing federal debt.[73]

Once the chairman started specific discussion of the bill, his opponents began to attack. Graham A. Barden (D-N.C.) led the charge. As chairman of the House Committee on Education, Barden had already explored the question of veterans' education benefits fully. He wanted the provisions of his bill, the so-called Barden bill, to be part of the omnibus legislation.[74] The Barden bill mirrored the views of many of the nation's educators. Fearful that the GI bill might center authority for education at the national capital, educators urged that the Veterans Administration be directed explicitly to use existing state educational agencies. Cloyd H. Marvin, chairman of the "Conference of Twenty-One," [75] thought that proponents of the Senate-passed S.1767 wanted "a uniform system, and one so set up that not only is it amenable but capable of being dominated." [76] The organization desired (and the Barden bill provided) that the state be left with:

the fundamental educational rights of establishing its own accrediting, setting up the curricula which it thought desirable and recommending the charges for such educational expenditures to the state and to the Administrator of the Veterans' Administration.[77]

[71] *Ibid.*, 4337.
[72] *Ibid.*, 4338.
[73] *Ibid.*, 4339.
[74] H. R. 3846, 78:2.
[75] Conference of Representatives of Educational Associations on Postwar Education. The Conference consisted, as its informal name implies, of 21 prominent educational organizations. Marvin was president of George Washington University.
[76] Mimeographed form letter, March 30, 1944; "S.1767, 78th Cong." Folder, HR 78 A-D 36, Rankin Committee Records, RG 233, NA.
[77] Marvin to Rankin, April 12, 1944; "M" Folder, HR 78 A-F 38.1, Tray 17013, *ibid.*

Despite the fact that Rankin's bill had eliminated the suspected advisory board features of the Senate version, some educators continued to prefer Barden's bill—on the grounds apparently that the latter more clearly protected states' rights.[78] More important, perhaps, the educators may have disliked the feature of both the Senate's and Rankin's bills granting to the Veterans Administrator the power to approve an educational institution not currently recognized by state agencies.[79]

Barden and his supporters focused their attack on specific education provisions of the Rankin bill. Their main assault was on the bill's allegedly restrictive nature. Barden preferred the more inclusive Senate bill (open to all veterans) to the Rankin Committee's bill, with its limits on supplemental benefits to veterans whose education had been interrupted. Under sharp questioning, the Rankin adherents seemed to think almost any veteran would be eligible under their wording. For example, Rankin assured critics that a veteran who had left school at the age of sixteen to work on a farm (but planned later to resume his schooling), and who had been farming up to the time of his military induction two years later, would qualify.[80]

This kind of casuistry failed to satisfy the discontented. Barden offered an amendment striking out the qualifying phrase concerning interrupted schooling. Supporters of Barden's amendment charged that Rankin's bill could be called a "rich man's son" bill; it did not give educational opportunities to the "poor" who had not had the advantage in the prewar period to taste the fruits of knowledge.[81] Intent on opening the schoolhouse doors to as many veterans as possible, the proponents of the Barden amendment seemed to be making headway.[82] Even two members of Rankin's own committee, A.

[78] See A. J. Cloud, President, San Francisco Junior College, and Lloyd D. Luckmann, President, Northern California Junior College Association, to Rankin, May 8, 1944; and Chancellor A. B. Butts, University of Mississippi, to Rankin, May 9, 1944; "S.1767, 78th Cong." Folder, HR 78 A-D 36, *ibid.*
[79] Representative Walter H. Judd (R-Minn.), an advocate of the Barden bill, did voice this objection. *Cong. Rec.*, 78:2 (May 11, 1944), 4344.
[80] *Ibid.*, 4341.
[81] See the remarks of Representative Ben Franklin Jensen (R-Iowa), *ibid.* (May 15, 1944), 4531.
[82] Twenty-four members spoke in favor of the amendment.

Leonard Allen (D-La.) and Mrs. Edith Nourse Rogers, the ranking majority and minority members, favored more liberal eligibility requirements.

Critics of Barden's amendment said it would lead to excessive costs, and would change the bill from a veterans' to an education measure. William J. Miller (R-Conn.)[83] questioned the justification of spending so much money "on a man who suffered no disability, incurred no handicap," but "who came back home with a broader vision." [84] Noah M. Mason (R-Ill.) harkened back to a theme broached by the Disabled Veterans of America representative, Millard Rice, before Senator Clark's subcommittee; every extra dollar spent on the able-bodied takes one away from the disabled.[85] Errett P. Scrivner (R-Kans.) broached the second theme: justice demanded that education benefits be extended only to those whose schooling had been interrupted, the mere fact of service alone not sufficing.[86] Despite this reasoning, the Barden amendment threatened to tap the support of a curious combination of interests. First, were those who wished to defeat Rankin's bill and pass the "purer" states' rights Barden bill. Second, were those who preferred the more liberal benefits of the Senate bill based on their concepts of equity, or on their belief that this would be a more direct route to achieve national influence in education, or in the understanding that this fell closer in line with the views of the Administration. And third, were those who on principle preferred to vote for the most generous veterans' provisions possible.

At this point Rankin, sensing the peril of the situation, quickly offered a substitute amendment. It provided that all individuals under twenty-four years of age at the time of their induction, and who had been in school within at least two years of that induction, would be presumed to have had their education or training interrupted and would be eligible for schooling above the one-year minimum. All

---

[83] Miller's views undoubtedly carried weight on questions of veterans' benefits. He had lost both legs as a result of an airplane crash in 1918; in addition, he had spent twelve years recovering in Veterans Administration hospitals.
[84] *Ibid.* (May 17, 1944), 4608.
[85] *Ibid.*, 4609.
[86] *Ibid* (May 15, 1944), 4551.

others would have to submit proof to qualify. The substitute amendment was a clever parliamentary stratagem. On the one hand it broadened eligibility enough to satisfy the marginal opponents; on the other, as a substitute motion, it would be voted on before Barden's. Still, the amendment passed with a narrow ten-vote margin (87–77).[87] The Barden brigade continued its opposition in vain, for the vote on eligibility proved decisive; the education title as defined by Rankin had weathered the debate in the House.

The loan provisions came next. Here the opposition to Rankin's bill resolved into two small factions. The first objected to the bill because, unlike the Senate bill, it did not provide the Agriculture Department with specific power to pass on farm loans.[88] Another group opposed what they considered the excessive interest rate of 6 per cent allowed in the bill.[89] The factions' combined opposition proved ineffective; their amendments successively went down to resounding defeats.[90] Rankin did, however, accept an amendment raising the maximum loan guarantee to $2,500.[91]

Moving quickly, House members then turned to the veterans' employment service section. They paid it scant attention. The Congressmen ignored appeals from state unemployment officials imploring them not to set up separate employment placement functions. The warning that duality of state and federal control would ultimately result in two employment services—a state service for citizens generally, and a federal service for veterans—was lost on the legislators.[92]

[87] *Ibid.* (May 17, 1944), 4619. A teller vote proved more favorable, 111–80.

[88] John W. Flannagan (D-Va.), Chairman of the Committee on Agriculture, led these critics.

[89] Jerry Voorhis (D-Calif.), an outspoken liberal, remained steadfastly opposed to this, as well as to other features of the bill.

[90] *Cong. Rec.*, 78:2 (May 18, 1944), 4657–70. They could muster, for example, only twenty-six votes in favor of the Flannagan amendment which proposed that farm loans be screened by the Agriculture Department.

[91] *Ibid.*, 4663. Here, perhaps, Rankin operated as a clever tactician. With a higher loan figure he now had a bargaining point to use in the joint conference with the Senate. He could "grudgingly" accept a lower figure in order to receive some concession on another point from the Senate.

[92] W. R. Curtis (Acting Chairman, North Carolina Unemployment Compensation Commission) to Rep. Robert L. Doughton (D-N.C.), May 8, 1944; "Folder 1199," Doughton Papers, U. of North Carolina; and telegrams

By the time the readjustment allowance section had been reached, Rankin's patience had worn thin. When Vito Marcantonio (ALP.-N.Y.) and Howard J. McMurray (D.-Wisc.) objected to what they considered anti-labor clauses (namely, disqualification from benefits while participating in a strike), Rankin subjected McMurray to a withering, sarcastic tongue-slashing for his alleged CIO inclinations.[93] But if the bill's disqualification provisions seemed anti-labor to Marcantonio, Howard W. Smith (D-Va.) thought them too mild. Smith offered an amendment providing a $1,000 fine for employers who made membership or nonmembership in any organization a condition for employment. This aroused Michael J. Bradley (D-Pa.). He observed that, "like Banquo's ghost, the gentleman from Virginia always appears when there seems to be an opportunity to do a little hatchet job on the workingmen of this country." [94] Obviously designed to limit the closed shop, Smith's proposal lost, 19–112.[95]

On this jarring note, debate ended. Rankin's substitute bill passed unanimously, 388 to 0, with 41 not voting.[96] The form of the House bill, and the final vote on it, reflected Rankin's skillful floor managership. He had been willing at numerous points to accept relatively minor changes; but at the crucial moment of the first serious amendment concerning eligibility for education benefits, he had offered a substitute motion that had effectively diverted the opposition's attacks. Could he match this parliamentary success in the joint conference with the Senate?

RANKIN CAME WITHIN an ace of achieving all he had wanted in the House-Senate conference.[97] Some House conferees had been willing

---

from the Chairmen of the Utah, New Mexico, and California commissions, May 8, 9, and 10, 1944; "S.1767, 78th Cong." Folder, HR 78 A-D 36, Rankin Committee Records, RG 233, NA.
[93] *Cong. Rec.,* 78:2 (May 18, 1955), 4674–75.
[94] *Ibid.,* 4675.
[95] *Ibid.,* 4676.
[96] *Ibid.,* 4677.
[97] The conferees for the House, in addition to Rankin, were: J. Hardin Peterson (D-Fla.), A. Leonard Allen, John S. Gibson (D-Ga.), Edith Nourse Rogers, Paul Cunningham, and B. W. Kearney (R-N.Y.). The Senate appointed J. Bennett "Champ" Clark, Walter George (D-Ga.), David I. Walsh (D-Mass.), Scott Lucas (D-Ill.), Robert La Follette (Prog.-Wisc.), John A. Danaher (R-Conn.), and Eugene Millikin (R-Col.).

to compromise with the Senators. Their chairman, however, stood firm in resisting efforts to replace the House's employment and read-justment titles with the Senate's. The House conferees divided evenly on these questions.[98] One member of the House team, John S. Gibson, had departed for his home because of illness. Rankin wired Gibson on June 5, 1944, asking for his proxy on the issues in dispute. Gibson complied the same day; he gave Rankin "full authority to cast such ballot as you think best." But two days later Gibson changed his mind; he instructed Rankin "to vote me in . . . favor of the Senate's" unemployment version.[99] When Rankin failed to do this the conference remained deadlocked; it looked as if the long period of debate and compromise would come to nought.[100]

Once again, however, the American Legion intervened. Learning in the late afternoon of June 9, 1944, that the conferees had agreed to take a final vote at ten o'clock the following morning, the legionnaires sprang into action. Alertly using their widespread organizational ties, they contacted Gibson at his home and begged him to return to Washington at once. They arranged to have the Congressman driven by a local legionnaire to the nearest Army base; there the Army provided him with transportation to a waiting commercial airliner that carried him to Washington. He arrived in time to cast his vote in person. With this dramatic flourish, the battle in favor of compromise was won.[101]

[98] *The National Tribune* (Washington, D.C.), a veterans' newspaper, reported on June 22, 1944, that Kearney, Allen, and Peterson supported the Senate version; and Rankin, Cunningham, and Rogers held fast for the House plan to move veterans' placement to the VA. The Legion, which had allegedly provided this information to the newspaper, disclaimed divulging that privileged data. Francis M. Sullivan to Rankin, June 21, 1944; "American Legion, 79th Cong. 1945" Folder, HR 79 A-F 38:2, Tray 17800, Rankin Committee Records, RG 233, NA.

[99] Rankin to Gibson, June 5, 1944, and Gibson to Rankin, June 7, 1944; "John Gibson & the GI Bill" Folder, HR 78 A-F 38.2, Tray 17017, *ibid.;* and Gibson to Rankin, June 5, 1944; "G" Folder, HR 78 A-F 38.1, Tray 17012, *ibid.*

[100] Gibson asserted that Rankin had gone back on his word. Camelon, "GI Bill." 50. One major difficulty remains: did Rankin have the power to exercise proxy votes in this situation? At least one of the conferees, recollecting later, thought not; it certainly was not the usual practice in Senate-House conferences. Scott W. Lucas to the author, February 1, 1965.

[101] See Camelon, "GI Bill," 50 ff. for an excited account of this storybook finish.

The Senate approved the new bill overwhelmingly on June 12, 1944; the next day the House followed suit. The revised measure featured such changes as increasing the cutoff age for presumptive proof of interrupted schooling from twenty-four to twenty-five years; substituting the Senate version on employment (veterans' placement remained with the USES) and readjustment allowances (fifty-two weeks maximum); and lowering the House-passed maximum loan guarantee amount from $2,500 to $2,000, with a reduction in interest from 6 to 4 per cent.

On June 22, 1944, the President signed the GI Bill at a typically pleasant ceremony.[102] The President noted with satisfaction that the bill "substantially" carried out his pleas made in the three addresses in 1943.[103] He added, however, that he hoped social security legislation would be forthcoming to aid the veterans. Finally, he reminded Congress that much needed to be done on the whole question of reconversion. With the traditional picture-taking, the ceremony ended: the GI Bill of Rights had become law.

WHO FATHERED the GI Bill of Rights? Samuel I. Rosenman has claimed the honor for President Roosevelt.[104] The chief executive did initiate the planning, provide the oratory, and place the Administration on record in favor of the various benefits incorporated in the act. Stated negatively, the President did not oppose or object to the GI Bill; if he had done that, the bill probably would have been delayed or even barred from passage.

Still, what specific role did the Administration play during the legislative development of the GI Bill? It does not appear that the President took more than a general interest in the fate of his program.

[102] Most of the Joint Senate-House conferees were present. Senator Clark's invitation had been underscored with the hope that his presence would enhance his reelection prospects. The Chairman of the Democratic National Committee, Robert Hannegan, had not overlooked this point. See Rosenman to "Pa" Watson, May 23, 1944; and Steve Early to "Pa" Watson, same date; OF 4675-R, GI Bill of Rights, Roosevelt Papers, FDRL. Representatives of the VFW and the American Legion also had been invited.
[103] "The President Signs the GI Bill of Rights," June 22, 1944; Rosenman, *Roosevelt Public Papers, 1944*, 180–83.
[104] See footnote 6, above, and Rosenman, *Roosevelt Public Papers, 1943*, 454.

Senator Clark, emerging from a meeting with FDR and Warren Atherton of the Legion, reported that the President favored "legislation of this nature . . . although he did not comment directly on the omnibus bill." [105] This noncommittal attitude matched his earlier tactics in regard to both the vocational rehabilitation and the mustering-out pay bills. Perhaps he had gauged congressional temper accurately; to indorse one specific veterans' bill might upset the sensitive legislators. Whatever the reason for his refusal to be more specific, the President at least could claim a general interest in veterans' welfare—an important consideration in an election year. On the other hand, his aloofness left his subordinates without a specific, positive program.

Without direction from the White House, departments and agencies demonstrated a greater interest in administrative jurisdiction than in presenting a unified front. Anxiety over the future of a particular administrative function dominated the attitude of some officials. The prospect of losing the chance to regain the United States Employment Service (USES) worried the Labor Department's James E. Dodson. Dodson thought that if the veterans' placement functions of USES were shifted to the Veterans Administration, as provided by the House bill, then the VA could not be counted on to support the return of USES to the Labor Department after the war.[106] The Selective Service System's (SSS) Benjamin M. Golder presented his analysis of the same situation: it would be desirable to separate veterans' and nonveterans' placement functions; but if that were done then "political pressure" would be exerted on the President to strip SSS of its reemployment functions as a "face-saving measure." [107] The bill hit other sensitive nerves: Agriculture feared duplication by the VA of its own farm loan information agencies; the National Housing Agency believed the bill should require home loan process-

[105] *The New York Times,* January 15, 1944.
[106] James E. Dodson to the Secretary of Labor, May 23, 1944; "Bills—Misc. (S.1767 or GI Bill) 1944" Folder, Secretary Frances Perkins General Subject File, 1940–44, Department of Labor Records, RG 174, NA.
[107] Major Benjamin M. Golder to Colonel Keesling, May 12, 1944; "113 Legislation, Jan.–June 1944" Folder, Central Files, Selective Service System Records, RG 147, NA.

ing only through its constituent agencies; and both War Department and War Production Board thought that to grant the VA equivalent priority for construction materials would hamper military programs.[108]

The GI Bill thus brought to the surface many administrative jealousies within the executive department. It also brought the Veterans Administration's (VA) role into clear relief. As mentioned above, the VA had received the Legion's draft bill on New Year's Eve, 1943. Edward E. Odom, the VA's Solicitor, thought the bill contained "numerous discrepancies and it's pretty broad." [109] Other staff members voiced more specific objections after the bill had been formally introduced. The VA's "administrative troubles" would be increased if it had to assume all these new functions; one adviser went so far as recommending an "adverse" report on the bill.[110]

Notwithstanding this initially cool reception, the VA provided both the Legion and Congress with valuable technical advice on the pending bill. Odom and Guy H. Birdsall (the VA's Legislative Counsel) stood on call to service the needs of the bill's promoters. On January 14, 1944, for example, the Legion called Birdsall at 8:30 A.M. to draft a new education section; Birdsall had it ready at the time desired: 2:00 P.M. that same day.[111] Odom not only wrote the House Committee's report for Rankin, but he also drafted the compromise bill for the House and Senate conferees.[112] After the middle of April, 1944, the VA stood not as a partisan of specific policies, but more as a highly skilled legal adviser to the real policymakers—the Legion and Congress.

[108] Claude R. Wickard to Rankin, May 11, 1944; "Legislation 1 (S.1767) Federal" Folder, Office of Secretary Files, Agriculture Department Records, RG 16, NA; John B. Blandford, Jr. to Rankin, April 18, 1944; and Donald M. Nelson to Rankin March 30, 1944; "S.1767, 78th Cong." Folder, HR 78 A-D 36, Rankin Committee Records, RG 233, NA.

[109] Odom to Guy H. Birdsall, January 1, 1944; "17 Servicemen's Readjustment Act—General, Part III" Folder, VA Records.

[110] Omer E. Clark to Odom, January 26, 1944; *ibid.*

[111] Birdsall, file memorandum, January 14, 1944; *ibid.*

[112] See Odom's draft of the report—printed as House Report 1418, 78th Cong., 2d Sess.—in "17 Servicemen's Readjustment Act, General, Part IVb" Folder, *ibid.;* Odom's role in respect to the conference bill is summarized in his note of June 19, 1944, "17 Servicemen's Readjustment Act, General, Part IVc" Folder, *ibid.*

This is not to say that VA officials had no ideas of their own. There had been one brief rebellion. Odom and Hines disliked unemployment compensation for veterans so much that they strongly urged adoption of adjusted compensation instead.[113] They had done this even though the Budget Committee on Veterans' Legislation had decided that the Administration would not even contemplate supporting adjusted compensation until after demobilization.[114] Events and ideas moved so rapidly during those hectic days that decisions made in January apparently seemed less binding in April. At any rate, after Rankin's committee members turned deaf ears to Odom's and Hines's pleas, the VA reverted to its more humble role as a service agency.

The American Legion also has claimed paternity for the GI Bill.[115] It is a solid claim. After the bill passed, legionnaire John Stelle tactfully reminded the President of the Legion's role:

> This achievement [the GI Bill], as you can well understand, means much to the American Legion because we feel that during the last six months we have not only had an active part in framing, but also in guiding its route through Congress. . . .[116]

Quietly and efficiently, men at the Legion's headquarters in Washington had directed a national "grass root" lobby campaign. Periodically, Legion posts throughout the country sent a freshet of telegrams and petitions to float the becalmed bill over delaying obstacles. A massive petition with the signatures of one million supporters

[113] Five days after Odom had prepared the VA's adjusted compensation bill (H.R. 4695, 78th Cong.), Hines wrote to James F. Byrnes, Director of the Office of War Mobilization, pointing out that many "forthright" veterans would "resent an unemployment dole as a reward for service"; also, once established, an unemployment system for veterans would be difficult to terminate. Hines to Byrnes, April 19, 1944; "Postwar & War Adjustment 4—Retraining & Reemployment Administration" Folder, General Classified File, Office of the Director, Office of War Mobilization and Reconversion Records, Record Group 250, National Archives.

[114] "Minutes of the Second Meeting, Monday, January 10, 1944 of Advisory Committee on Legislation for Veterans," in "O-2 Budget Committee on Veterans Legislation" Folder, VA Records.

[115] See Camelon, "GI Bill"; Jones, *The Legion,* pp. 217–21; and Moley, *The Legion,* pp. 270–78.

[116] John Stelle to James Barnes (Executive Secretary to FDR), June 24, 1944; OF 4675-R, GI Bill of Rights, Roosevelt Papers, FDRL.

testified to the Legion's organizing abilities. Again, as in the case of the Ohio department's thorough performance in the House jurisdictional battle, one state's legionnaires rose to dizzying heights of lobby enthusiasm. Tiny New Jersey chose Rankin as its target. From Pompton Lakes in the north to Cape May in the south, Legion posts competed in the unlikely hope of converting the intractable Mississippian. Vineland legionnaires, fearing perhaps that Rankin would overlook one telegram from their post, underscored their concern over his resistance by sending sixteen other wires with identical messages.[117]

Although New Jersey's legionnaires seemed to outdo their colleagues in other states, the Garden Staters couched their pleas in moderate tones. Not so one Forty-and-Eighter from Quincy, Illinois: this angry legionnaire curtly advised Rankin to resign his Legion membership or come back to his senses. Disdainfully he reflected on Rankin's right to obstruct passage of the Legion bill: "In all probability you have seven thousand poor white trash electing you year by year to Congress." [118]

Atherton's committee members in Washington supplemented the grass root appeals with their own telephone calls and meetings with individual Congressmen.[119] Legionnaire activity did not stop respectfully at the doors of the House of Representatives. No sergeant at arms could bar the most effective members of the Legion team: the Congressmen themselves.[120] John M. Vorys forthrightly and proudly told the Ohio department commander:

We members of the Legion were rather active on the floor in keeping the Bill in proper shape, particularly as regard, education, unemployment compensation and I feel the Legion will be satisfied with the results.[121]

The Legion's role, then, was crucial. Influential from drafting to final passage, legionnaires had a right to be satisfied.

[117] See wires in "S.1767, 78th Cong." Folder, HR 78 A-D 36, Rankin Committee Records, RG 233, NA.
[118] Thomas D. Hickey to Rankin, April 24, 1944; *ibid.*
[119] Camelon, "GI Bill" 32–34, explains the procedures followed.
[120] The Legion had 149 members in the House in 1944; Jones, *The Legion,* p. 59.
[121] Vorys to Rossiter Williams, June 1, 1944; "Veterans—GI Legislative 78th Cong." Folder, Vorys Papers, Ohio State Historical Society, Columbus, Ohio.

Again, who was the GI Bill's real father? The answer is clear, if nonbiological: both the President and the American Legion share the honor—with Congressmen like John E. Rankin affecting the measure's final form. The historical fact of the legislation, that is, its existence, depended upon the good graces of the President. Without his general blessing it could not have been achieved. The timing of the bill's passage remains the Legion's accomplishment; legionnaires provided the constant pressure to bring the bill through to enactment. It seems unlikely that the President's proposals in the autumn of 1943 would have been translated into law so soon without the energetic assumption of leadership by the Legion.

The final substance of the GI Bill demonstrated the intricacy of policymaking. The emery of the legislative process abraded the grand designs of the National Resources Planning Board, the Osborn Committee, and the President. One by one the New Deal attempts to link indissolubly veterans' benefits with general needs of the population failed: the GI Bill of Rights emerged as a veterans' measure, rather than a direct subsidy to education or home building. This was one of the fees paid to the Legion for its role. Looking back from the vantage point of almost a quarter century, the observer may speculate whether the "service fee" was too high. The Legion, after all, was so anxious to foster the GI Bill that conceivably it might have compromised on its basic principle of veterans' exclusiveness. During the negotiations over the GI Bill, the Legion often seemed to be saying: We'll accept almost anything, as long as we get a measure that will enhance our recruitment of new members from the ranks of World War II veterans.

The fact that the Legion was susceptible to bargaining seems to have eluded the Administration. For the first time, perhaps, the Legion might have listened to New Deal appeals to depart from the narrow perspective of veterans' exclusiveness. Conceivably, the Administration could have taken advantage of the opening to enlist the Legion as a close ally to further its New Deal tendencies—especially in light of the division among the veterans' organizations. But the Administration could not capitalize on its opportunity. War diversions and administrative differences within the executive branch nullified the chance to exert leadership.

Perhaps such speculation—like all "might have beens"—is mere academic musing. In any event, a unified Administration and a compliant Legion would have faced the same Congressional situation. Accommodations with a man like Rankin had to be made. The elimination of direct loans to veterans, the failure to gain an explicit indorsement of a Federal United States Employment Service's value for veterans' employment, and the scrapping of the United States Office of Education's primary position in regards to veterans' education, were the actual results. These were the fees extracted by conservatives in Congress. The Administration, apparently feeling in no position to balk, paid them all.

WHATEVER IT "cost" the Administration, the GI Bill of Rights was a substantial gain to the new Ulysseses. It would, to be sure, require modifications. In 1945, for example, the requirement that veterans have interrupted education or training was dropped, and loan provisions were clarified and made more liberal.[122] Ultimately, by the fall of 1955, approximately 7,800,000 veterans—about 50.6 per cent of all World War II veterans in civil life—embarked on education or training under the GI Bill. Large numbers, 5,322,000 and 3,782,000 respectively, partook of the readjustment allowance and home loan guaranty benefits. When queried, a decade after the GI Bill's passage, 73.7 per cent of approximately 16 million nondisabled veterans considered the readjustment benefits "adequate." [123] A major step, in brief, had been taken to insure that the new Ulysseses would find a welcome home.

[122] Public Law 268, December 1945.

[123] U.S., The President's Commission on Veterans' Pensions, *A Report on Veterans' Benefits in the United States, Staff Report No. IX, Part A: Readjustment Benefits General Survey and Appraisal,* printed as U.S., House of Representatives, 84th Cong., 2d Sess., *House Committee Print No. 289* (Washington, D.C., 1956), 90, 191, 232, and 240.

5

RECONVERSION, TRUMAN, AND HINES

THE FERMENT DURING autumn, 1943, brewed more than the GI Bill of Rights. While Republican "young Turks," Hearst editorial writers, and American Legionnaires clamored for rapid action to help the "neglected" veterans, the reconversion kettle also began to boil.[1] Although the GI Bill concerned veterans more directly, reconversion policies also affected them. Both the attempt to establish an administrative apparatus to coordinate veterans' affairs and the granting to veterans of rights to surplus war property, for example, stemmed from the more general planning for reconversion.[2] The GI Bill of Rights was not, in short, the last word on veterans' benefits.

Two events, moreover, altered the pattern of reconversion policies affecting veterans. The elevation of Harry S Truman to the presidency following Franklin D. Roosevelt's death on April 12, 1945,

[1] Good brief accounts of reconversion (the transformation of the economy from war to peace) policymaking may be found in Roland Young, *Congressional Politics in the Second World War* (New York, 1956), ch. viii; Stephen Kemp Bailey, *Congress Makes a Law* (New York, Vintage Paperback edition, 1964), pp. 28–36; and Herman Miles Somers, *Presidential Agency, OWMR, The Office of War Mobilization and Reconversion* (Cambridge, Mass., 1950), pp. 174–202.
[2] For an account of surplus war property disposal for veterans, see below, ch. vii.

eventually resulted in a key shift in personnel during the summer of 1945, when Omar N. Bradley replaced Frank T. Hines as Administrator of Veterans' Affairs. No less important, President Truman, a veteran himself, seemed to take a greater interest in veterans' policymaking than his predecessor.

The end of the war in Europe on May 8, 1945, and in the Pacific on August 14, 1945, also played a role in the story of continued policymaking for the new Ulysses. Victory intensified demands by the public, Congressmen, and some government officials for rapid relinquishment of wartime controls over the economy. By and large, these demands for diminution of the central government's control were fulfilled. The Truman Administration found itself on the defensive. Fighting a rear-guard action, it could not carry forward some of the more positive programs that involved veterans—such as a national health service. This desire to curb federal power was another factor in the general setting affecting veterans' programs.

PRESIDENT ROOSEVELT'S fireside chat of July, 1943, had lifted the question of reconversion policies out of the realm of confidential governmental discussion into the public arena. By October, 1943, reconversion had become an important topic of conversation. When victory came, how rapidly should war controls be lifted? What policy should be followed in terminating war contracts? When could industry begin to retool for peacetime production? What would happen to government-owned plants? What should the government do with the huge supplies of surplus war property? How soon could labor unions use their most potent weapon—the strike—without fear of being labeled traitorous? These and a cloud of related questions loomed up with increasing persistence during the fall and winter of 1943.

Not the least important task was to insure that the postwar manpower activities of the Federal Government would be coordinated effectively during the critical transformation period. The bureaucracy, some believed, needed a justice of the bureaucratic peace. James F. Byrnes, director of the Office of War Mobilization, must have perceived this after a meeting with federal agency chiefs in October,

1943, had disclosed how little had been done to coordinate veterans' policymaking.[3]

Other signs pointed to the need for closer attention to reconversion matters. Already Congress had begun to assert its claim to leadership of domestic reconversion. When House members killed the National Resources Planning Board, they had spoken gravely of Congress' duty to do its own planning. In the Senate, Walter F. George's (D-Ga.) hitherto moribund Special Committee on Postwar Economic Policy and Planning, set up in March, 1943, stirred to life in October. A provocative report that warned of potential war-created monopolies in industry had, one observer speculated, alerted George's committee.[4] Congress had begun to move.

Byrnes, perhaps sensing the threat to executive policymaking, hastened to the White House. Plan now for reconversion, the former Supreme Court Associate Justice urged. He repeated the litany of reconversion problems: war contract termination, surplus property and plant disposal, unemployment compensation, and development of job opportunities. Roosevelt needed little prompting; before leaving for Teheran and Cairo in November, he told Byrnes to form a staff to draw up a reconversion program.

Byrnes turned for aid to the man considered to be his mentor: Bernard Mannes Baruch. The choice was natural. Baruch, seventy-three years old in 1943, had earned an awesome national reputation for his industrial mobilization work during World War I as head of the War Industries Board. Known as the "adviser to Presidents," he had contributed ably to the solution of the critical rubber shortage in 1942. Son of a Confederate surgeon, baron of "Hobcaw" (a South Carolina plantation), Wall Street stock market speculator by profession, and park-bench sage by choice, Baruch enjoyed unmatched prestige.[5] Yet his political conservatism made liberals wary; it also

[3] See above, ch. iii, and James F. Byrnes, *All in One Lifetime* (New York, 1958), p. 207.
[4] Senator Joseph C. O'Mahoney (D-Wyo.)—"a glutton for facts—" wrote the report. TRB, "Post-War Planning at Last," *The New Republic,* CIX (October 25, 1943), 572.
[5] One columnist, Leslie Gould, averred that "Baruch today is without doubt the most respected individual in the country." *The New York Journal American,* May 26, 1944.

made Roosevelt reluctant to give Baruch real power within the Administration. Still, the President did consider him to be " 'an ever present help in time of trouble,' " not the least because of his close ties with influential Senators.[6]

Another member of Baruch's "team," John M. Hancock, joined the elder statesman in working on reconversion recommendations.[7] Hancock—Baruch's "old Diesel engine"[8]—matched his associate in his keen understanding of the American industrial economy. He had moved far in his sixty years: from boyhood days on his father's North Dakota wheat farm, to college at Grand Forks, followed by fifteen years in the Navy, and then, at the midpoint of his life, assignment to the War Industries Board; there he caught the attention of Baruch and Herbert Lehman. Following a brief trip to Europe after the Armistice with Roosevelt (then Assistant Secretary of the Navy) to help dispose of surplus naval property, Hancock cast aside the humdrum career in a peace navy in favor of affiliation with Lehman's extensive business interests. When Byrnes called in 1943, Hancock had built up an imposing twenty-four-year career as a financial expert and investment banker.[9]

The two men, assisted by Samuel Lubell—amanuensis, researcher, and brilliant analyst all rolled in one—began formal work on November 9, 1943.[10] Their casual methods concealed their realization that their task was second only to winning the war. With Baruch stretched out on a sofa, Hancock in an easy chair, and Lubell noting the flow

---

[6] Roosevelt to Baruch, July 29, 1942; Elliott Roosevelt, editor, *F.D.R., His Personal Letters, 1928–1945* (2 vols.; New York, 1950), II, 1334. For Roosevelt's attitude regarding Baruch, see Elting Morison, *Turmoil and Tradition: A Study of the Life and Times of Henry L. Stimson* (Boston, 1960), p. 512 note; and Samuel I. Rosenman, *Working With Roosevelt* (New York, 1952), pp. 335–37.

[7] The "team" consisted of individuals who had over the years worked with their "Chief" on various projects. They were loyal to Baruch personally; Hugh Johnson, Frederick Eberstat, William Jeffers, and John M. Hancock were among the more prominent.

[8] Margaret L. Coit, *Mr. Baruch* (Cambridge, Mass., 1957), p. 529.

[9] *Current Biography, 1949*, pp. 239–41.

[10] Walter Brown to Stephen T. Early, November 9, 1943; Official File 5330, White House Papers of Franklin D. Roosevelt, Franklin D. Roosevelt Library, Hyde Park. Cited hereafter as Roosevelt Papers, FDRL.

of conversation, their report began to take shape.[11] The division of labor cannot be made precisely.[12] It is certain that Hancock devoted his energies primarily to the knotty question of contract termination. Baruch's deep personal concern over the problems of the physically handicapped, however, determined the direction of his interest in reconversion.[13] From this empathy, perhaps inherited from Baruch's father who had pioneered in physical medicine, flowed one major emphasis of the combined Baruch-Hancock report: the stress on the "human side" of reconversion.

The authors urged Byrnes and Roosevelt to appoint a "Work Director" to coordinate and develop policies affecting military personnel demobilization, war workers' and veterans' job placement, physical and occupational therapy, resumption of education, and vocational training.[14] Baruch's sentiments appear in Biblical imagery: "a single, unforgetful mind" should insure that the Nation be just to its veterans. The work director, the authors concluded, "should be of such outstanding caliber as to command the immediate confidence of the country." [15]

The report came to the President as he convalesced from a cold (an illness that afflicted 17,000,000 other Americans that winter).[16] Yet the grippe had not left him slothful nor unaware of political timing. Within three days of the report's public unveiling on February 18, 1944, Roosevelt had appointed the work director; it took but three more days to promulgate the executive order setting up the

[11] Coit, *Mr. Baruch,* p. 529. The cozy scene portrayed by Coit refers to an earlier report on manpower; their working habits probably remained the same for these jobs. Hancock said later that they had worked from 7 in the morning to 11 at night for 4 months.

[12] Lubell did most of the actual writing; but each contributed to the various sections. Personal Interview with Samuel Lubell, January 20, 1967, New York City.

[13] His interest was more than verbal; shortly after agreeing to help Byrnes, Baruch announced a $1,100,000 gift for the support of physical medicine and rehabilitation. *The Washington Post,* April 27, 1944; and Bernard Baruch, *Baruch: The Public Years* (New York, 1960), 329–30.

[14] The American Council on Public Affairs reprinted the report as: Bernard Baruch and John M. Hancock, *War and Post-War Adjustment Policies* (Washington, D.C., 1944).

[15] *Ibid.,* 18–19.

[16] *The Washington Post,* January 8, 1944.

work director's agency—unpoetically styled the Retraining and Re-employment Administration.

The President had acted none too soon, for the Republicans had been fanning the embers of a potential political fire in this Presidential election year. Eric Johnston, United States Chamber of Commerce president (and potential political "timber" for high office), had already called for the creation of a new cabinet-level post to handle veterans' affairs.[17] Representative Hamilton Fish (R-N.Y.) had filed a bill to do just that three days after the business leader's appeal.[18] These rumblings eventually culminated in the gracious demagoguery of Representative Clare Boothe Luce (R-Conn.) in a speech before her party's Convention on June 27, 1944.[19] Her charm wowed the male delegates (who serenaded her with "Won't You Be My Sweetheart?" when she had finished). But she aimed her words straight for the hearts of Gold Star mothers. She dedicated her speech to "GI Jim"—GI Joe's buddy, who would not return from the war—the boy who had inherited heroically the "unheroic Roosevelt decade." The Republicans, she announced, did not view the veteran as a "terrific problem"; they did not desire to use his homecoming "as an economic club over the heads of the people." In a glorious peroration, and with what one uncritical admirer labeled "poetic insight," [20] she concluded: "We are Americans. We say, Joe, we welcome you. So hurry home, Joe, by way of Berlin and Tokyo. We need you to build this great America." [21]

WITH OPPOSITION POLITICIANS beginning to sniff hopefully for campaign issues, Roosevelt's rapid action in February appears understandable. Politics may also have determined his choice of the man

[17] *The New York Times,* January 16, 1944.

[18] *Ibid.,* January 19, 1944. Earlier, the Republican Governors of 11 western states had urged setting up of a veterans' cabinet post. *The Washington Post,* December 12, 1943. Not only Republicans desired this innovation; Representative James Herbert Fay (D.-N.Y.) introduced a similar bill two days before the Baruch-Hancock report was made public. *The New York Times,* February 17, 1944.

[19] *The Washington Post,* June 28, 1944.

[20] Mark Sullivan in *ibid.*

[21] Her speech is reprinted in *Vital Speeches,* X (July 15, 1944), 586–88.

to fill the potentially important post of "work director." If the President desired to select a noncontroversial man, he had made a perfect choice when he tapped his hardworking Veterans Administrator, Frank T. Hines.

The choice of Hines surprised official Washington. Paul V. McNutt, chairman of the War Manpower Commission, had seemed a likelier prospect.[22] Baruch himself had been Byrnes's selection, if not Roosevelt's. After two days of soul-searching, Baruch decided his age ruled him out; perhaps the President would choose Bill Jeffers, rubber "czar," president of the Union Pacific railroad, and another Baruch team member.[23] No, Roosevelt passed over these stellar and energetic figures to single out Hines, an exemplar of administrative caution.

If the appointment surprised some in Washington, it angered liberal journalists. *The New Republic* declared that Hines was "hostile" to the New Deal.[24] I. F. Stone, after gagging on the "social demagogy" and the "rich coating of applesauce" of the Baruch-Hancock report, could not stomach Hines's appointment:

The Work Director is supposed to be a man of "proven executive capacity . . . business sagacity . . . character . . . great courage." I can see no resemblance whatsoever between this portrait and the man chosen. . . . His appointment makes the job a kind of cruel joke.[25]

Other periodicals could do no more than stress Hines's qualities as a dedicated worker.[26] His appointment seemed as lusterless as his new agency's title.[27]

Hines soon revealed how he interpreted his new duties. He announced that he would coordinate and plan—not issue directives. If

[22] *The Washington Post,* February 23, 1944.

[23] *Ibid.,* February 22, 1944; Baruch, *Baruch,* p. 334; and Baruch to Marquis Childs, March 9, 1944; Correspondence "Childs" 1944, Baruch Papers, Princeton University Library.

[24] "The Baruch Plan," *The New Republic,* CX (March 6, 1944), 304.

[25] "Millionaires' Beveridge Plan," *The Nation,* CLVIII (March 25, 1944), 354–55. Stone confused the Baruch-Hancock recommendations concerning the Surplus Property Administrator and the Work Director.

[26] "Human Demobilizer," *Newsweek,* XXIII (April 3, 1944), 70.

[27] The Hearst press applauded Hines's appointment; joining veterans and civilians under one authority, however, raised suspicions. *The New York Journal American,* February 27, 1944.

squabbles emerged between federal agencies he would try to conciliate; if that failed, he would turn the entire matter over to Byrnes and Roosevelt.[28] Thus, Baruch's image of an "unforgetful mind," of a director, had been dispelled in a brief public announcement.

The ardor of the hopeful should have been chilled by that first announcement. One shrewd liberal, Mrs. Anna Rosenberg (New York regional director of the War Manpower Commission), perhaps sensing the false promise of the agency, declined to serve as Hines's chief deputy.[29] Others moved ahead less circumspectly; after all, they could reason, at least the General had spoken of "plans." The Office of War Mobilization and Reconversion's announcement referring to Hines's agency, moreover, listed eighty-six separate major problems to be worked on. Following these leads, Robert K. Burns and Frederick H. Harbison, two of Hines's consultants, charted an ambitious policy-coordinating and planning program for the Retraining and Reemployment Administration. Federal agencies would be canvassed, their postwar planning stimulated, and results coordinated to achieve "a comprehensive blueprint of programs for retraining and reemployment." Bustling with energy, Burns and Harbison spoke grandly of "integrated" patterns of planning, of the "active leadership and responsibility" the Retraining and Reemployment Administration should adopt.[30]

Hines did not like the consultants' plan. At that, Burns and Harbison quit. They could not work, they said, without Hines's full support.[31] The consultants' disillusionment with the agency found its counterpart in the declining zeal of the agency's policy board members. As early as May, 1944, two-thirds of the board members had lost interest and no longer attended meetings.[32]

[28] *The Washington Post,* February 23, 1944.
[29] *Ibid.,* March 3, 1944.
[30] See Robert K. Burns and Frederick H. Harbison to Hines, August 12, 1944; "3-Post X-Day and V-E Day Plans 1945" Folder, General Files, Series 1, Retraining and Reemployment Administration Records, Record Group 244, National Archives. Cited hereafter as RRA Records, RG 244, NA.
[31] Burns and Harbison to Hines, August 14, 1944; *ibid.*
[32] C. W. Bailey to Hines, June 3, 1944; "3c-Policy Board, Feb.–Sept." Folder, *ibid.* The Board, composed of representatives from twelve federal agencies interested in manpower policies during reconversion, was to advise Hines in his policymaking role.

Schooled for so many years to guard public purse strings so that no backlash reaction would harm veterans, Hines continued this cautious policy as head of the Retraining and Reemployment Administration. His advice to President Truman, just one week after V-E day, indicates his concern over the high costs of veterans' benefits. He urged first, that no more Waves, Wacs, Marine Corps Auxilliary, or Spars be inducted; second, that limited-service personnel should be retained; and third, that physical examinations of new draftees be rigorous. These measures, he believed, would keep the rising costs for veterans within the bounds of reason.[33] This caution may indeed have been wise for the head of the Veterans Administration; yet his Retraining and Reemployment job called for an energetic executive, not a pillar of conservatism.

But cautious or not, Hines had a more difficult task once Justice Byrnes had left office in April, 1945, as head of the Office of War Mobilization and Reconversion (OWMR); Hines lost one of his protectors. This left him exposed to the dissatisfaction of OWMR officials who believed he had muffed his chance to do an effective job. By June, 1945, William Haber, an OWMR member, had privately indicted the Retraining and Reemployment Administration; it had "signally failed to provide the kind of down-to-earth practical assistance which localities need." [34] Less than two months later, he confessed: "I have a genuine sense of hopelessness in regard to this whole problem, and . . . it is going to blow up in our faces unless we can take hold of it." [35] This kind of disillusionment among members of a superior agency cost Hines the confidence of fellow government officials. One year after the creation of the Retraining and Reemployment Administration, a loyal member noted the absence of her agency's prestige; she reported that "slowness in acting and get-

[33] Hines to Truman, May 15, 1945; "Retraining and Reemployment" Folder, Subject Numeric File II, Office of the Director, Office of War Mobilization and Reconversion Records, Record Group 250, National Archives. Cited hereafter as OWMR Records, RG 250, NA.

[34] Haber to Robert R. Nathan, June 27, 1945; *ibid.*

[35] Haber to Anna M. Rosenberg, August 7, 1945; *ibid.* Baruch wrote that Hines's agency was "not functioning." Baruch to Sen. Edwin C. Johnson (D-Colo.), August 8, 1945; Correspondence "Johnson" 1945, Baruch Papers, Princeton University Library.

ting organized, inability to retain staff, failure to follow through on projects, etc.," all had left her agency open to attack.[36]

The agency suffered also because Hines continued to wear two hats after February, 1944—one for the Veterans Administration and another for the new agency. He could not devote full attention or loyalty to the new job. His twenty-one years' tenure as VA chief had left him always conscious of veterans; but his job as Retraining and Reemployment Administrator, at least as projected by Baruch, demanded that he transcend his veterans' point of view. Furthermore, the VA itself required increased attention as servicemen began to return in sizeable numbers by 1944.

As a result, much of the Retraining and Reemployment Administration's affairs remained in the hands of C. W. Bailey, a trusted assistant recruited from the VA. Bailey tended to interpret the agency's powers very narrowly; in this he reflected faithfully Hines's views. For this and other reasons, Bailey stood at the center of a series of controversies that wracked the tiny agency all during Hines's one-and-a-half year term of office. The origins and courses of those intramural disputes defy unraveling—it suffices that the frequent exchanges of stiffly worded notes between Bailey and his colleagues demonstrate that the agency did not run smoothly.[37]

Why had Hines failed as Retraining and Reemployment chief? Hines's conservatism, his wearing-of-two-hats, and petty intraagency dissension give some clues. But there are at least two other reasons. First, Hines did not have the confidence of President Roosevelt's successor; and second, the fierce federal interagency competition during reconversion proved to be beyond Hines's control.

EVEN BEFORE President Truman assumed office in April, 1945, General Hines had been under public attack. As early as December,

---

[36] Irene G. Cooperman to C. W. Bailey, March 3, 1945; "10–13A NEA 1945" Folder, RRA Records, RG 244, NA.

[37] See Bailey to Richmond Harris, a consultant, October 5, 1944; and Harris's reply of October 6th. Harris closed his memo with the words: "In view of the fact that you refuse to talk to me I shall send you a copy of that memorandum, if you will have someone to notify me." "1–1 miscellaneous-F (1944)" Folder, *ibid.*

1944, Marquis Childs, a newspaper columnist, had been airing some of the criticism directed at the Administrator of Veterans' Affairs. Childs reported that although some observers in Washington thought Hines was "an excellent public servant," the VA head was getting old; he held a job that would tax a man half his age. Childs also wrote that the VA had become enmeshed in red tape: its hospital program was inefficient; the American Legion and other veterans' groups had obtained special hospital privileges for veterans of past wars, thereby cluttering up needed facilities; and finally, the medical men in the VA had been isolated from their profession.[38] In March, 1945, *The U.S. News* carried word that Hines was "under official fire on the inside" for failure to develop comprehensive plans dealing with reemployment of veterans.[39] A week later, Air Corps Colonel Thomas D. Campbell—an "unofficial" adviser to President Roosevelt—castigated Hines for being "unimaginative and timid to the point of inaction about doing anything outside of the routine to help veterans." [40]

But these criticisms paled in comparison to those Hines faced concerning treatment of veterans in existing VA hospitals. In March, April, and May, 1945, revelations about shocking conditions in some of those hospitals came to light. Representative Philip J. Philbin (D-Mass.) led the critics when, on March 7, 1945, he issued a press release that expressed his concern about medical treatment in government hospitals.[41] Two weeks later he amplified his remarks for the benefit of his colleagues.[42] Popular periodicals picked up the

[38] *The Washington Post,* December 16, 1944.
[39] XVII (March 23, 1945), 68.
[40] Unsigned File Memorandum, pencil-dated April 2, 1945; President's Personal File 2533, Roosevelt Papers, FDRL. Roosevelt by this time, a year after Hines's appointment, had asked Baruch to make a report on veterans' affairs. See "Addresses, Articles, and Special Memoranda" Files, March 1945, Baruch Papers, Princeton University Library.
[41] The release is reprinted in U.S., House of Representatives, Committee on World War Veterans' Legislation, 79th Cong., 1st Sess., *Hearings on Investigation of the Veterans' Administration With a Particular View to Determining the Efficiency of the Administration and Operation of Veterans' Administration Facilities* (Washington, D.C., 1945), Part I (May 17, 1945), 143–44. Cited hereafter as House, *VA Investigation.*
[42] U.S., *Congressional Record,* 79th Cong., 1st Sess. (March 24, 1945),

hue and cry. *Cosmopolitan, Reader's Digest,* and the New York newspaper *PM* each carried articles illustrating alleged inadequacies and maltreatment of veterans.[43]

The details of these disclosures were grim. A subsequent Congressional inquiry gave the particulars involving the Northport, L.I., VA hospital. There attendants had reportedly beaten veterans hospitalized due to mental illness. The reason for the maltreatment was clear, if inexcusable. The wartime acute shortage of trained medical attendants had forced the VA to call upon the Army for assistance. The War Department, reluctant to detail its best troops to such a task, had assigned those whom it needed least. As a result, Northport received a contingent of about three hundred and forty limited-service troops. Many of these men had physical and mental ailments of their own; sixty-four, for example, suffered from chronic back injuries, hernias, or leg impairments, while sixty more were sightless in one eye. These attendants, devoid of knowledge of how to handle neuropsychiatric patients, severely enforced the hospital discipline on their charges. Undoubtedly, the troops' fear of the patients made their acts of restraint all the more harsh.[44]

General Hines, the embodiment of the VA, became the object of sharp attack. The Northport and other incidents stripped him of his previous immunity. Even John E. Rankin, his loyal supporter in the House, could not prevent a full-scale inquiry into the VA's operations. To be sure, the Mississippian tried his utmost to divert attention. He attempted at first to brand the authors of the disclosures as communists. Although initially successful in obtaining a contempt citation against one of the writers, Albert Deutsch of *PM,* he had to drop that effort when his Committee on World War Veteran's

---

A1429–33. Cited hereafter as *Cong. Rec.,* followed by Congress and Session numbers, date, and page.

[43] Albert Q. Maisel, "Third-Rate Medicine for First-Rate Men" (Parts I and II), *Cosmopolitan* (March and April, 1945); *id.,* "The Veteran Betrayed," *Reader's Digest,* XLVI (April, 1945), 45–50; and Albert Deutsch in *PM,* May 18, 1945. The two *Cosmopolitan* articles are reprinted in House, *VA Investigation,* Part I (May 17, 1945), 145–51 and (May 24, 1945), 319–25; the *PM* column is in *ibid.* (May 18, 1945), 180–81.

[44] See House, *VA Investigation,* Part III (June 14, 1945), 1251–1360, for details on Northport.

Legislation broke out in an ill-concealed revolt against their chairman.[45] The committee's recalcitrance reflected a sound instinct for public relations; approximately 96 per cent of the mail received by the committee condemned Rankin's efforts to brand Deutsch a Red. Rankin, in the eyes of many correspondents, was a "fiend," "Satan," or a "little Gestapo chief from totalitarian Mississippi." [46]

Hines's response to criticism did not aid his cause. To be sure, his predicament was difficult; his repeated past assurances of the soundness of the VA hospitals had restricted his room for maneuvering in the face of these new charges. Only the year before, Hines had told Rotarians in Pennsylvania that sufficient hospital beds existed to meet any demands imposed by the returning servicemen of World War II. A month later, he had informed Congressmen that the VA's hospital program was adequate. When Philbin's resolution for an investigation appeared, the VA head declared that his hospitals were "on a par with any in the country." [47] When Hines did act, he invited more criticism. He requested the veterans' organizations to make their own investigation of existing facilities. Although this was a reasonable move—since those groups had widespread organizational ties that would permit quick coverage of the hospitals —the request was labeled by some as a whitewash attempt. The close relationship between the Legion and the VA did not seem to promise an unbiased investigation.

President Truman reacted to the criticism of his Veterans Administrator by firing Hines. Truman believed that his job called for the delegation of responsibility to trusted subordinates; as a result,

[45] *The New York Times,* May 19 and 30, 1945; House, *VA Investigation,* Part I (May 18 and 22), 182–365; *ibid.,* Part II (June 5, 1945), 586–661; and "Minutes of Committee Hearings-79th Cong." Folder, HR 79A-F38.2, Tray 17807, Records of the Committee on World War Veterans' Legislation, Record Group 233, National Archives. Cited hereafter as Rankin Committee Records, RG 233, NA.
[46] "Deutsch, Albert-1945" Folder, HR 79A-F38.2, Tray 17803, Rankin Committee Records, RG 233, NA.
[47] *The Washington Post,* April, 18, 1944; U.S., House of Representatives, Special Committee on Post-War Economic Policy and Planning, 78th Cong., 2d Sess., *Hearings on Post-War Economic Policy and Planning,* Part II, May 18, 1944 (Washington, D.C., 1944), 300–301; and *The Washington Post,* March 12, 1945.

he wanted to have men about him with whom he was familiar.[48] This explains his elevation of John W. Snyder, first to the post of Director of the Office of War Mobilization and Reconversion, and then to Secretary of the Treasury. Snyder, Truman's long-time friend, had served with the new President in the field artillery as a reservist from 1935 to 1940. Likewise, Truman wanted at his side another field artillery reservist, Harry Vaughan. These men Truman could trust.

But Frank T. Hines was another matter. For, in addition to the accumulation of grievances against the VA chief, another element blocked good working relations between the two. Harry S Truman had come to office committed to carry out the New Deal policies of his former chief.[49] Within five months of his Presidential accession, he had laid down a bold plan of action that smacked of the New Deal. On September 6, 1945—four days after Japan's official surrender—Truman issued his reconversion message, the "21-point" program.[50] He asked Congress for legislation that would liberalize unemployment compensation; set more fair labor standards; permit orderly termination of wartime controls; set up on a permanent basis the Fair Employment Practices Committee; continue the no-strike, no-lock-out policies; extend federal control of the United States Employment Service; support agriculture; continue the Selective Service System's draft powers; provide housing; stimulate research; revise the tax structure; dispose of war surplus property; foster small business; provide veterans with social security coverage for time spent in military service, and give them greater job rights; foster public work projects; facilitate Lend-Lease and postwar reconstruction; adjust Congressional salaries; set guidelines for disposal of surplus

[48] Richard F. Fenno, Jr., *The President's Cabinet* (Cambridge, Mass., 1959), p. 43; and Harry S Truman, *Memoirs by Harry S. Truman* (2 vols., Garden City, L.I., 1955), I, 226–7. Cited hereafter as Truman, *Memoirs.*

[49] Truman, *Memoirs,* I, 12 and 149–55; and Richard E. Neustadt, "Congress and the Fair Deal: A Legislative Balance Sheet," in Richard M. Abrams and Lawrence W. Levine, editors, *The Shaping of Twentieth-Century America* (Boston and Toronto, 1965), pp. 566–67

[50] Harry S Truman, *Public Papers of the Presidents of the United States: Harry S. Truman, 1945* (Washington, D.C., 1961), pp. 263–309. Cited hereafter as Truman, *Public Papers, 1945.* See also Richard E. Neustadt, cited in footnote 49, above.

ships; and permit stockpiling of strategic materials. The comprehensiveness of these requests testifies to Truman's desire to continue on the high road of the New Deal.

Thus, one thrust of the Truman Administration was liberal. At the same time, conservatives held key posts—Snyder in the Treasury, John D. Small in the War Production Board's successor, the Civilian Production Administration, and Frank T. Hines as head of the VA. Clashes between the implications of the September speech and the inclinations of Truman's conservatives were bound to happen. If the personal ties between the President and his advisers were strong enough, conservatives could weather the storms of liberal criticism. Hence John Snyder's durability. But Frank T. Hines had only the tenuous common bond of Veterans of Foreign Wars membership with his chief. That was not enough; the VA hospital disclosures provided the opportunity for easing him out.

President Truman announced on May 15, 1945, that the VA was being "modernized." [51] On June 7, 1945, he told the press that Hines had resigned. He explained:

[The Veterans Administration will be] for World War II. That was the setup for World War I, and has been very adequately handled for World War I. But as a World War I soldier, I wouldn't have been happy to have had the Spanish-American War veterans running the Veterans' Administration, and I don't think—[laughter]—the new veterans would. I think they would much rather have a general of their own war in the place.
And General Hines thought so, too—after we discussed it.
Are there any questions? [laughter][52]

The World War II soldier he had in mind was General Omar N. Bradley. Born in Missouri in 1893, Bradley had graduated from West Point in 1915 along with his military commander in Europe, Dwight D. Eisenhower. Although credited with being able to "throw a [baseball] farther than any man who ever attended the Academy," he had more impressive credentials.[53] At the time of his selection to head the VA, he commanded the Twelfth Army Group, the largest field mili-

[51] Truman, *Public Papers, 1945,* pp. 56.
[52] *Ibid.,* pp. 108–109.
[53] *The Washington Post,* June 8, 1944.

tary force ever headed by one man. No showman, Bradley nonetheless was considered the "GI's General." [54]

The VA appointment came as a complete surprise to Bradley. General Eisenhower, in Paris, had left a message for Bradley to come to the headquarters from Germany; at the time, Bradley was talking with Soviet Marshal Ivan S. Konev. After Konev had left, Bradley flew to Paris and went straight to Eisenhower's billet. When he entered, he was told to pour himself a "good drink" before he read President Truman's telegram about the VA. Thus fortified, Bradley learned the news—to him a disappointment, for he preferred military command. Bradley assumed his new task dutifully.[55] He could not take up his job, however, until August; in the interim, General Hines ran a caretaker operation in the VA.

General Bradley, however, was not given Hines's Retraining and Reemployment Administration (RRA) job, a post which remained vacant for two months after Hines's promotion to Ambassador to Panama in September, 1945. The fact that President Truman waited until November 8, 1945, before appointing Marine Major General Graves Blanchard Erskine, underscores the low-level priority enjoyed by the RRA. Erskine, who had seen action in France in 1917, had participated in the Kiska landings in the Aleutian Islands in 1943, and later had commanded the 3d Marine Division at Iwo Jima.[56]

Like Bradley, Erskine brought to his new job considerable staff experience; he infused the RRA with a new sense of purpose—not at the stratospheric heights envisioned by Bernard Baruch in 1944, but on a more modest level. Just how modest a level that RRA had been reduced to can be seen in General Erskine's complaint (shortly after embarking on his new duties) that "the supervisory staff of RRA has been limited to six persons . . . whose work has been

[54] See Bill Davidson, "Veterans' New Dealer," *Collier's,* CXVI (November 24, 1945), 24 ff.; *The New York Times,* June 8 and October 21, 1945; Ernest K. Lindley, "Bradley and the Veterans," *Newsweek,* XXV (June 18, 1945), 35; and "People of the Week," *The United States News,* XIX (September 21, 1945), 78–80.
[55] Interview with Omar N. Bradley, May 6, 1965, New York City.
[56] *Current Biography, 1946,* 182–84; and Sutherland Denlinger, "The Vets' Best Bet," *Collier's,* CXVII (April 27, 1946), 34 ff.

carried on independently, with little effort at coordination or integration into a specific program." [57]

General Erskine thus had the unenviable task of presiding over a discredited agency. Under Hines it had failed twice—once in regard to veterans' information centers, and once concerning a dispute over veterans' job seniority rights. These two controversies demonstrate how Bernard Baruch's concept of a work director to coordinate postwar manpower policies actually worked in practice. They also provided what must have appeared to Hines as an unfitting epitaph to a long career of public service.

SHORTLY AFTER taking up his new duties as Retraining and Reemployment Administrator in February, 1944, Frank T. Hines had to settle an administrative question. Which Federal Government agency or agencies should direct the dissemination of information about veterans' benefits in the man's own home town or nearest urban center? Also, should "information centers" do more than dispense information—for example, process claims? No one of the competing agencies could be expected to answer these questions without understandable bias. Logic, Congressional intent, and Executive desires pointed unhesitatingly to the Retraining and Reemployment Administration as the most likely agency to answer the questions.

The questions were not academic. No one could predict how many veterans would suffer unnecessarily because they had no place to go to find help. Nor, on the other hand, could it be estimated how many veterans would not use legal benefits merely because red tape discouraged them. Men who could courageously face the hail of the enemy's steel were known to blanch at the prospect of being enmeshed in the coils of red tape. Washington had to act well in advance of final victory so that the administrative structure on the local level could withstand the expected shock wave of returning troops.

General Hines, following the suggestions outlined in the Baruch-Hancock report (and Byrnes's wishes), dutifully issued instructions

---

[57] Erskine to the Secretary of Labor; November 27, 1945; "Administrative Budget" Folder, General Files, Series 2, RRA Records, RG 244, NA.

on May 17, 1944, to set up the Federal Government's information centers.[58] He decreed that the state and local committees be formed to coordinate the dissemination of information about federally bestowed rights and benefits for veterans. The committees would be composed of representatives from the Selective Service System (with its duty to insure that the veterans' pre-induction jobs be restored), the Veterans Administration, and the War Manpower Commission (with its constituent agency—the United States Employment Service—charged with the task of finding new jobs for discharged servicemen).[59] In theory, these agencies would blend their efforts harmoniously and follow the benign direction of General Hines in serving veterans' interests.

The Retraining and Reemployment Administration, however, had to deal with prima donnas among the federal agencies. The War Manpower Commission had pioneered in December, 1943, when it had set up seven "experimental" centers in United States Employment Service offices to meet veterans' needs.[60] Impelled by the dual motivation of assisting returning servicemen and preempting veterans' coordinating responsibilities among federal field offices, the War Manpower Commission did not relish relinquishing its lead role to join the chorus.[61] The Veterans Administration's field locations simply ignored other agencies.[62] The veteran ultimately would find his way

[58] "When he [the veteran] returns to his home community, *there should be one place to which he can go in dignity and where he can be told of his rights and how he can get them.*" Bernard Baruch and John Hancock, *War and Post-War Adjustment Policies,* 17 [their emphasis]. For Byrnes's statements see *The Washington Post,* April 13, 1944, and May 21, 1944.

[59] Retraining and Reemployment Order No. 1, May 17, 1944; U.S., *Federal Register,* IX (May 20, 1944), 5391–2.

[60] See Rilla Schroeder to Arthur W. Motley, December 23, 1943; File 1 B.4.h, Records of the War Manpower Commission, Record Group 211, National Archives. In March, 1944, WMC reported that its centers had not lived up to all expectations as "one-stop" offices. *The Washington Post,* March 31, 1944.

[61] "Paul V. McNutt [Chairman of the War Manpower Commission] staked a claim yesterday to the many-sided job of absorbing millions of soldiers and sailors back into civilian life. . . . McNutt told a press conference he anticipates no jurisdictional struggle in handling demobilization." *The Washington Post,* December 21, 1943.

[62] See, for example, "Interagency Relations in Veterans' Matters: Chicago," excerpts from Bureau of the Budget Field Memorandum, August 20, 1945; copy in General Files, Series 1, RRA Records, RG 244, NA.

to the indispensable Veterans Administration; why join in advertising other agencies' "competitive" services? Moreover, long accustomed to the solo part, the Veterans Administration had had no experience of close cooperation with these other offices.

The Selective Service System, deeply jealous of its veterans' reemployment duties, would be the last to share the center stage gracefully with others. The System's staff members had consistently guarded their prerogatives. When, for example, preliminary planning for the Postwar Manpower Conference was underway, one Selective Service System official had seemed aggrieved that so much had been done by the National Resources Planning Board before his own agency had been contacted. After all, he had reasoned, Congress had charged his agency to set up a Personnel Division to deal with reemployment problems. The information that the National Resources Planning Board acted under Presidential orders seemed barely to mollify him.[63]

Hines's coordinative efforts, furthermore, conflicted with the Selective Service System's own expansionist aims. From Dallas came the report of the Selective Service System's "sporadic attempts to start an Employment Service of its own." [64] More significantly, not long after President Roosevelt's death, Truman had received—apparently from Selective Service System sources—the plea that the draft boards' functions be broadened to include all phases of the returning veterans' problems. The quality of its voluntary staff, the accumulated experience of handling the draft, its existing statutory responsibilities, and the hint that President Roosevelt had desired it, all pointed logically, it was argued, to expansion of the Selective Service System.[65]

By the summer of 1945, no one could argue that Hines's information center decree had been carried out. In Chicago, for example,

[63] Col. Parker to Lewis B. Hershey, June 30, 1942; "002.34 National Resources Planning Board, 1942" Folder, Central Files, Records of the Selective Service System, RG 147, NA.

[64] Report, dated July 26, 1945, from Dallas Field Office of the Bureau of the Budget; attachment to Irving H. Siegel to Frank T. Hines, September 6, 1945; "10–12 P" Folder, General Files, Series 1, RRA Records, RG 244, NA.

[65] Report, "Veterans' Assistance Program," July 16, 1945; Official File 190, White House Papers of Harry S Truman, Harry S. Truman Library, Independence, Mo. Cited hereafter as OF . . . , Truman Papers, HSTL.

anarchy existed among federal agencies. As a result, the regional branch of the Office of Price Administration led the way in setting up an ad hoc committee to coordinate local veterans' affairs. That an agency with functions relating to wartime economic controls (such as rules to check hoarding, rent gouging, and inflation) took the initiative at Chicago, shows the lack of direction coming from Hines's office in Washington. More to the point, with the Chicago committee boasting of representation from twelve separate federal agencies, the magnitude of the coordinating job in the Windy City can be seen. Denver was no better off. In Dallas, the undercurrent of agency bickering, combined with the competition of state and municipal programs, threatened to doom the federal information center plan for veterans to hopeless confusion.[66] Something had to be done.

Two alternatives seemed possible to observers in Washington. First, the entire program could be revamped. Instead of having the centers merely dispense information, as they were currently doing, convert them into "one-stop" offices where veterans could have readjustment allowance claims processed, job referrals made, and answers provided to perplexing loan guaranty questions. The second solution differed radically from the first. Turn over the entire information service function to state, county, and municipal organizations. Would it not be better to have community control over what everyone agreed was essentially a community duty?

Proponents of a streamlined system made one major effort to convert the centers. In June, 1945, the War Department's Major General William F. Tompkins suggested that the information centers be transformed into "One-Stop Service Centers." The Navy and Labor Departments, the Federal Works Agency, and the War Shipping Administration agreed with the Army's proposal. The Federal Security Agency, the War Production Board, and the War Manpower Commission were noncommittal; and the Department of

[66] Material relating to Chicago is based on "Inter-Agency Relations in Veterans' Matters: Chicago," excerpts from Bureau of the Budget Field Memoranda, July 5 and August 20, 1945; copies in "10–12 P" Folder, General Files, Series 1, RRA Records, RG 244, NA. For Denver, see Paul Lawrence to Hines, August 28, 1945; *ibid.* For Dallas, see report cited in footnote 64, above.

Agriculture, Veterans Administration, Civil Service Commission, Selective Service System, as well as General Hines (as Retraining and Reemployment Administrator), all opposed the plan.[67]

The military establishments probably liked the idea because it would have relieved them of the necessity of looking after so many officials from so many agencies at the discharge centers. The Labor Department, along with officials of the Office of War Mobilization and Reconversion, ever sensitive to possible "blow ups," believed one-stop centers would improve an already chaotic system.

Those who opposed the plan exhibited the usual concerns about their own agencies' functions. The Agriculture Department, for instance, clung tenaciously to its own highly specialized field system; any attempt to alter it was viewed with suspicion. The Veterans Administration, without whose cooperation the venture would fail, did not believe all the agencies who would be interested could be housed in one building.

Five agencies for the one-stop idea, five against, and two on the fence; surely, not enough to change an existing program. The one-stop proposal, moreover, would have affected the 8,000 information centers already set up; since the very number of offices could be cited as proof of the government's concern about veterans' welfare—regardless of whether they did anything or not—the proposal failed.[68] A Federal Security Agency official summed up the feeling of discontent about the centers:

These centers should have something made out of them or quit; if they are just information centers one could pick up a telephone book or go to the American Legion and get plenty of service—there's some point between full service and just information centers.[69]

With the defeat of the one-stop plan, the move to adopt the second alternative—that of turning the centers over to state control—gained impetus.

[67] See memoranda and letters, June 4, 1945 to July 14, 1945; "1–4 Information Centers—General 1945" Folder No. 1, *ibid.*

[68] Since each local Selective Service System Board was counted as an "information center," the total was high.

[69] Summary of Retraining and Reemployment Technical Inter-Agency Committee on Information Centers Meeting, August 3, 1945; "1–4 Information Centers—General 1945" Folder, General Files, Series 1, *ibid.*

Liquidation of federal control, however, was delayed until February, 1946. General Hines's replacement did not begin his duties until November, 1945; until he had become familiar with his job no switch to state control could be pressed. Graves B. Erskine, once acquainted with the controversy, sided with state control adherents; he argued: "I don't believe that any Government agency or group of . . . agencies can possibly operate these community advisory centers. The problem of readjusting a man back into the community is a problem for that community." [70]

Erskine's appointment ended one reason for the delay; the President, however, barred quick action. Truman at first objected to ending federal control. Engaged in a bitter Congressional fight over a similar move to return control over the United States Employment Service to the states, Truman questioned the timing of Erskine's proposed order to shift responsibility for the centers: "It is my opinion, due to the fight we are having with the employment service, that this order ought not to go out. I suggest that you have it held up." [71] The President's opposition lasted briefly; perhaps prospects of settling the employment service controversy seemed too remote to hold up the information center transfer any longer. At any rate, less than a week after Truman's "stop order," Erskine called a meeting of his advisory board. The Board agreed then to Erskine's plan by an eight to two vote.[72] The transfer was announced on February 13, 1946.[73] Hence, the short-lived experiment of federal information centers, á la Baruch, came to an end.

The veterans' information center imbroglio had tested General Frank T. Hines's ability to settle a controversy that had remained

[70] Verbatim Minutes of RRA Advisory Council Meeting, January 21, 1946; "Advisory Council" Folder, General Files, Series 2, *ibid.*

[71] Truman to Lewis B. Schwellenbach, Secretary of Labor, January 15, 1946; "White House-General 1946" Folder, Secretary of Labor Files, Records of the Department of Labor, Record Group 174, National Archives. Cited hereafter as Labor Department Records, RG 174, NA.

[72] Verbatim Minutes of RRA Advisory Council Meeting, January 21, 1946; "Advisory Council" Folder, General Files, Series 2, RRA Records, RG 244, NA. Only the Selective Service System and the Civilian Production Administration opposed the transfer among those who voted. The Office of War Mobilization and Reconversion observer also disliked the move.

[73] *The New York Times,* February 14, 1946.

intramural and unpublicized. He had, at most, merely held the question up to debate for members of his Advisory Council. In a sense, Hines seemed more interested in sampling opinion than acting. His successor, however, did not let differences of opinion halt him. Erskine proceeded with his plan vigorously; undoubtedly his forceful statement of his position helped clarify the policy decision that had to be made. Erskine, of course, enjoyed one advantage over Hines. He had Hines's failure as an example to indorse his own plan.

General Erskine's executive vigor, however, had another consequence. Through him, the Truman Administration had renounced the Federal Government's responsibility to control all administrative arrangements affecting veterans locally. Bradley's continuation and expansion of regional Veterans' Administration facilities stood in sharp contrast to Erskine's renunciation of real control over the information centers. To have set up local one-stop centers, the Federal Government would have had to begin its effort early in 1944. Such an expansion needed unity among federal agencies as well as more commitment and energy than General Hines possessed. When the plan received serious consideration in the summer of 1945, it was too late. By then, the conservative swing away from enlarged central government activity was gaining momentum. It proved to be easier to shrug off the information centers, than to devote time and energy to fight the tide.

Erskine's decision, although significant in regards to the Federal Government's role, may not have affected the veterans adversely. Local volunteers throughout the nation's urban centers spread out the welcome mats for returning servicemen. Some of their efforts were outstanding. The Bridgeport, Connecticut, center, for one, earned praise for its sympathetic and efficient service to veterans. Local American Legion and Veterans of Foreign Wars posts stood ready to guide World War II veterans in their search for information. Newspapers, popular magazines, and radio networks ran series on veterans' benefits. Civic organizations, fraternal lodges, and other groups added their voices. Americans at home by and large informed their returning heroes of the largess that awaited them.

DURING 1945, while the information center issue perked, yet another boiled over, resulting in a major public dispute that involved government agencies, labor unions, veterans' organizations, and businesses. Frank T. Hines, as chief of the Retraining and Reemployment Administration, faced the unpleasant task of settling this conflict.

The struggle over veterans' seniority or (as friends of labor unions liked to dub them) superseniority rights had an innocuous origin. Congress, when it passed the Selective Training and Service Act of 1940, had granted to inductees who had left their jobs certain reemployment privileges.[74] The argument that emerged in 1944 and reached its climax in 1946, began in earnest when the Selective Service System's director, Major General Lewis B. Hershey, issued clarifying instructions on May 20, 1944, to local draft boards concerning application of Section 8 of the 1940 law. The instructions, known as Local Board Memorandum 190-A, defined veterans' rights to reemployment.[75] Hershey's memo decreed that qualified returning veterans had an absolute claim to their old positions; if necessary, a nonveteran with greater seniority must be discharged to make room for the veteran. In addition, the one-year immunity from discharge, other than for cause, protected veterans from layoffs as well —unless, of course, the entire plant shut down. Once rehired, furthermore, the veteran could not be "bumped" by another veteran with greater senority who applied for reinstatement after the first. Congress intended, Colonel Paul H. Griffith of the Selective Service Sys-

[74] See above, chapter 2.
[75] *The Washington Post*, May 26, 1944. The periodical literature on veterans' reemployment is vast. In addition to articles cited later in this section, see Walter J. Couper, "The Re-employment Rights of Veterans," *The Annals of the American Academy of Political and Social Science*, CCXXXVIII (March, 1945), 112–21; Charles Hurd in *The New York Times*, April 7 and 8, 1945; " 'Superseniority' for Veterans?", *The United States News* (September 1, 1944), 38 ff.; Jack Schuyler, "Veterans and Union Rules," *The American Mercury*, LXI (December, 1945), 666–71; "An Old Riddle Crops Up Again," *Newsweek*, XXV (May 21, 1945), 76 ff.; DeWitt Gilpin, "Bread and Butter Front," *Salute*, I (April, 1946), 28 ff.; and Leopold Lippman, "When the Veterans Come Home," *The New Republic*, CXI (September 4, 1944), 272–74. In addition, see Joel I. Seidman, *American Labor From Defense to Reconversion* (Chicago, 1953), pp. 230–32.

tem thought, "to give a man his job when he returned"—with no ifs, ands, or buts.[76]

Union officials disliked Hershey's ruling.[77] They muted their cries, however, for the time being. For one thing, both the American Federation of Labor (AFL) and the Congress of Industrial Organizations (CIO)—although bitterly at odds on other matters—had joined with the Veterans of Foreign Wars (VFW) in an attempt to carve out a general employment policy for all veterans, not just those who had jobs before their military service.[78] Union officials hoped that the AFL-CIO-VFW statement of principles of July 25, 1944, would prove more attractive and beneficial for veterans than Hershey's May ruling. But the AFL-CIO-VFW agreement rested on shaky ground. The union leaders could only recommend, not order, that their local unions give all veterans seniority credit for time spent in the service. This flaw soon caught the eyes of both the press and supporters of the Selective Service System's interpretation.[79] The agreement, unfortunately for labor, did not earn wide support.

Yet another reason may have delayed labor's more strenuous outcry during the summer of 1944. The Presidential election campaign probably did not seem to be a propitious moment to launch a debate about such controversial matters. Once President Roosevelt had been safely reelected, however, opponents of Hershey's ruling swung into action. They argued that Memorandum 190-A subverted traditional and bitterly won seniority rights; it encouraged clashes between veterans and labor; it was grossly unfair to those veterans who, al-

[76] Griffith in large part fashioned the interpretation. For this outspoken American Legionnaire's (he became the Legion's National Commander in 1947) views, see especially his memorandum to Colonel C. S. Dargusch, March 21, 1944; "700. Employment & Reemployment, General-1944" Folder, General Files, SSS Records, RG 147, NA.

[77] The Congress of Industrial Organizations (CIO) protested as early as July, 1944. *The Washington Post,* July 28, 1944.

[78] See "Veterans, Unions, Jobs," *American Federationist,* LI (August, 1944), 3.

[79] "Behind Union-Veteran Deal," *The United States News* (August 4, 1944), 38; and Colonel Paul H. Griffith to Frank T. Hines, November 11, 1944; "Veterans Reemployment Rights" Folder, General Subject Files, Deputy Director for Reconversion, Manpower and Veterans' Affairs Division, OWMR Records, RG 250, NA.

though with greater seniority and military service, through the vagaries of the discharge system would return later than their more fortunate colleagues; it violated constitutional safeguards of labor-management contracts; and it introduced uncertainty into industrial relations.[80] Defenders of labor's view hinted at a plot to ruin labor organizations by inflaming veterans against unions.[81] Old memories of the use of World War I veterans as strike-breakers, as in the Boston Police strike in 1919, haunted observers in 1944 and 1945.

Labor's supporters believed that Congress had intended to restore to veterans the same civilian occupational benefits they would have possessed had they not gone to war. Their argument may be summarized as follows:[82] Above all, the hallowed seniority system had to be left intact. No veteran had an absolute right to reemployment. Conceivably, the work force of an employer might have contracted during the veteran's absence; in the process of that contraction employees with lowest seniority would be laid off, including—again hypothetically—individuals with greater seniority than the departed veteran. If the veteran had not been inducted, he too would have been laid off. Was it just, advocates of the unions' view queried, for the returning veteran to force the discharge of an employee with greater seniority? Would it not be fairer to place the veteran on a waiting list for reemployment, ranked according to his accrued seniority?

Union leaders also disliked the allegedly furtive manner in which the Selective Service System had issued its memorandum. Hershey's failure to consult responsible labor and management groups prior to the directive's issuance, the CIO charged, created an unnecessary and dangerous dispute. It put the unions in a bad position; they did not relish the prospect of seeming to be anti-veteran at the very mo-

[80] Walter J. Couper to William Haber, January 23, 1945; *ibid.;* see also Boris Shishkin, "Organized Labor and the Veteran," *The Annals of the American Academy of Political and Social Science,* CCXXXVIII (March, 1945), 146–57.

[81] Aaron Levenstein, "Superseniority—Postwar Pitfall," *The Antioch Review,* IV (Winter, 1944–45), 531; and, earlier, "Veterans and Workers," *The Commonweal,* XLII (July 27, 1945), 349.

[82] J. Donald Kingsley, "Veterans, Unions, and Jobs," *The New Republic,* CXI (October 23, 1944 and November 13, 1944), 513–14 and 621–23.

ment their image with servicemen suffered due to scattered wartime strikes. By attacking the Selective Service System's superseniority ruling, the unions believed they would provide "a Roman holiday for the anti-union press of the nation." [83]

But labor could count on the support of the liberal press and, as it developed, even some businessmen and a leading business journal.[84] It will be recalled that during the war years many columnists and government planners had dark apprehensions about the economic crisis predicted for the early postwar years.[85] No wonder that the Selective Service System's ruling upset these observers. In a period of declining employment the reemployment rights of veterans would take on major significance. For the advocates of a full employment policy, Hershey's ruling symbolized the tendency of some government officials to see their task as one of separating veterans as a class from others, rather than enthusiastically embracing programs to help all to gainful employment. Liberals and union leaders asserted that "it is impossible to build an island of security for the veterans in the midst of depression. . . . The basic solution is full employment—for civilian and veteran alike." [86]

Unable to make headway with Hershey, labor appealed to the White House for aid. Significantly, labor leaders bypassed General Hines, even though he was in charge of coordinating policymaking and interpretation for veterans' affairs. Hines apparently had displeased organized labor when he appointed Colonel Griffith as his

[83] Philip Murray to Lewis D. Hershey, February 21, 1945; "Veterans' Reemployment Rights" Folder, General Subject File, Deputy Director for Reconversion, Manpower and Veterans' Affairs Division, OWMR Records, RG 250, NA. Quote is from "Statement of the CIO. Veterans Committee to President Murray and the Executive Board, by Clinton S. Golden, Chairman, April 12, 1945." Mimeographed copy in *ibid.*

[84] An Armstrong Cork Company personnel official stated at an American Management Association meeting in April, 1945, that business would lose "the battle of publicity" when it had to engage in litigation over veterans' reemployment rights. *The New York Times,* April 13, 1945; see also "Veterans' Job Showdown Near," *Business Week* (May 19, 1945), 100–102. For outright opposition to Hershey's ruling see "What Price Superseniority?," *Fortune,* XXXI (January, 1945), 111.

[85] See chapter 2, above.

[86] Aaron Levenstein, "Superseniority—Postwar Pitfall," *The Antioch Review,* IV (Winter, 1944–45), 542.

deputy.[87] Lee Pressman, the CIO's General Counsel, asked Samuel I. Rosenman, the President's Special Counsel, to request the Attorney General to rule on the disputed issue. But Rosenman, with a fine sense of bureaucratic niceties, forwarded labor's importunities to General Hines for "coordination." [88] No less alert than the President's speechwriter in recognizing "hot potatoes," Hines referred the matter to General Hershey—on the grounds that Congress had made the latter responsible for the Act's interpretation.[89] Having come full circle, labor's cause seemed frustrated. Hines's game of "hot potatoes," however, soon came to an end. By the end of the year, the Department of Labor had entered the fray, siding (not unnaturally) with labor against Hershey.[90] Now the issue involved not merely the Selective Service System and unions, but brought two agencies of government in more or less direct conflict.

At this point Hines turned the matter over to a committee of his agency's Advisory Board. This committee—with Donald Tracy, Assistant Secretary of Labor as Chairman, and General Hershey of Selective Service and John K. Collins of the War Manpower Commission as members—met during the early months of 1945. The dispute continued, because the committee members could not agree on a recommendation for a unified national policy. Hershey and Collins presented a majority report that upheld the Selective Service System's position; Tracy, in a closely reasoned minority report, supported labor.[91] Tracy thought that any policies adopted had to meet three requirements: "are the policies workable?" "do they accord with the reasonable expectations of the veterans?," and "do they further, and not endanger national unity?" In light of these questions,

---

[87] J. Luhrsen, executive secretary of the Railway Labor Executives Association, telephoned his objection to Griffith's appointment to a White House staff member. Unsigned memo to Samuel I. Rosenman, November 3, 1944; OF 5584-D, Roosevelt Papers, FDRL.
[88] Rosenman to Hines, November 20, 1944; "10–12 Training Act, Labor Interpretations" Folder, Series 1, RRA Records, RG 244, NA.
[89] Hines to Rosenman, November 25, 1944; *ibid.*
[90] Douglas Maggs to Frances Perkins, December 28, 1944; "Veterans—Misc." Folder, Secretary of Labor Files, Labor Department Records, RG 174, NA.
[91] Mimeographed copies of both reports, dated March 5, 1945, attached to William Haber to Lucius D. Clay, March 7, 1945; "Retraining and Reemployment" Folder, General Classified Files, OWMR Records, RG 250, NA.

Tracy believed that Hershey's policies fell short; a policy that interfered with established seniority systems, he argued, obviously would endanger national unity. Tracy's superior, Frances Perkins, the Secretary of Labor, agreed with him. Upon the request of James F. Byrnes, Director of the Office of War Mobilization and Reconversion, she requested Attorney General Francis Biddle to issue a definitive ruling to guide executive department agencies.[92]

The Attorney General, like Hines before him, was not eager to act. For one thing, shortly after submission of Secretary Perkins's request, a decision made in the field by a federal labor arbitrator, Herman A. Gray, had upheld labor's position. Gray had decided in a case where a veteran "bumped" a nonveteran with greater seniority that nothing in the statute gave a veteran benefits above those that he would have had if he had not been inducted.[93] In addition, Biddle probably did not wish to antagonize either the veterans or labor by leaning one way or the other.[94] As a result, he instructed all United States District Attorneys not only to follow Hershey's ruling of "superseniority," but also to present labor's side, since Hershey's "interpretation is not free from doubt under the Act." [95]

Meanwhile, General Hines, having met with no success with his advisory committee, arranged for a conference with representatives of labor, management, and veterans' organizations.[96] The conferees

[92] Perkins to Byrnes, March 7, 1945; "Office of War Mobilization—Retraining & Reemployment Policy Board 1945" Folder, Labor Department Records, RG 174, NA; William Haber to Byrnes, March 8, 1945, and copy, Perkins to Biddle, March 10, 1945 in "Postwar and War Adjustment 9—Legislation & Planning for Demobilization . . ." Folder, Office of the Director, OWMR Records, RG 250, NA.

[93] Mimeographed copy of Gray's decision (United Steelworkers of America, Arbitration Information Bulletin No. 143, covering case No. 778—Timken Roller Bearing Co., Canton, Ohio plant—March 13, 1945) in "Veterans' Employment-Decisions" Folder, General Subject Files, Deputy Director for Reconversion, Manpower and Veterans' Affairs' Division, OWMR Records, RG 250, NA.

[94] See "Washington Whispers," *The United States News,* XVIII (March 23, 1945), 68.

[95] Department of Justice Circular Number 3851, Supplement No. 3, May 10, 1945. Copy in "Records re . . . the Retraining and Reemployment Policy Board, 1944–46, Asst. Secretary Daniel M. Tracy" Folder, Labor Department Records, RG 174, NA.

[96] This conference had been suggested to Retraining and Reemployment Ad-

met at Washington, and predictably, ended once again in a stalemate over the basic element of the controversy. Labor remained steadfast—particularly since it now had the support of the Labor Department and the National War Labor Board.[97] But from the wreckage Hines salvaged a possible answer to the vexing problem. Section 8, he proposed, should be rewritten; instead of absolute reinstatement rights for veterans, some modification would be introduced. A veteran, he suggested, could not bump a nonveteran employee with greater seniority if the latter's seniority commenced prior to the passage of the Selective Training and Service Act, September 16, 1940. Thus, long-time employees who had remained loyal to their employers would be protected, and some of the bitter feeling possibly could be avoided.[98]

By the summer of 1945 there existed three major views: first, that of labor unions, with the Labor Department and the National War Labor Board in support, advocating reinstatement within the framework of existing seniority systems; second, that of the Selective Service System pressing for absolute reinstatement rights; and third, an intermediate position advanced by General Hines and indorsed by members of the Office of War Mobilization and Reconversion.[99] This last view admitted the validity of Hershey's interpretation; yet to require "a single individual—the person thrown out of work to make a place for the returning veteran—to bear the cost of the debt which the Nation as a whole owes to the veteran" was unjust. The answer lay in requesting Congress to rewrite that part of the statute, perhaps along the lines suggested by General Hines.[100]

---

ministration officials as early as January 1945. Millard Rice to Paul H. Griffith, January 22, 1945; "10–12 Seniority" Folder, RRA Records, RG 244, NA.

[97] George Meany, Matthew Woll, and Robert J. Watt for the American Federation of Labor; Philip Murray and Clinton S. Golden for the CIO to Hines, March 20, 1945; "1–3d Advisory Council" Folder, *ibid.*

[98] "The Employment Status of Veterans During the Reconversion Period," May 26, 1945; "Reemployment-Decisions" Folder, General Subject Files, Dep. Dir. for Reconversion, Manpower and Veterans' Affairs Div., OWMR Records, RG 250, NA.

[99] It was rumored that both President Truman and his newly appointed Attorney General were about ready to side with the Selective Service System's ruling against labor. "Washington Whispers," *The United States News*, XIX (August 17, 1943), 80.

[100] William Haber to Frederick Vinson, June 21, 1945; "Reemployment-

But the rush of events of V-J Day, the return of Congress from summer recess, Hines's promotion to ambassador to Panama, and the preparation of more pressing material for inclusion in President Truman's notable "twenty-one point" address of September 6, 1945, diverted attention. By the time the OWMR chief, John W. Snyder, returned to the question at the turn of the year, the matter had been taken out of the executive department's hands.[101] Fittingly enough, the Nation's highest tribunal had now entered the dispute by agreeing to hear a case on appeal involving the superseniority interpretation of the Selective Service System.

Two years and one week after General Hershey issued his ruling, the Supreme Court cast it aside by a seven to one vote in the case of *Fishgold v. Sullivan Drydock & Repair Corporation et al.*[102] Abraham Fishgold, a reemployed veteran, had been laid off for nine days in the spring of 1945—even though several nonveterans with greater seniority stayed on the job. The company followed the provisions of a collective bargaining agreement with the union. Claiming that Section 8 gave him immunity from layoffs within one year of reemployment, Fishgold (upon the advice of New York City Selective Service System officials) brought suit before a Federal District Court.[103] The Court ruled in his favor and ordered that he be paid

---

Decisions" Folder, General Subject Files, Deputy Director for Reconversion, Manpower and Veterans' Affairs Division, OWMR Records, RG 250, NA. See also Hines to John W. Snyder, August 28, 1945; and Haber to Snyder, September 5, 1945; "Retraining and Reemployment" Folder, Office of the Director, *ibid.*

[101] Snyder had turned to the new Secretary of Labor, Lewis Schwellenbach, for an answer on January 17, 1946. Schwellenbach, in turn, had been advised by General Hines's successor, Major General Graves B. Erskine, that the whole question had "been ballooned far out of its proper perspective." Snyder to Schwellenbach, January 17, 1946; "Retraining & Reemployment" Folder, General Classified Files, OWMR Records, RG 250, NA; Schwellenbach to Erskine, February 14, 1946; Retraining and Reemployment Administration, 1946" Folder, Labor Department Records, RG 174, NA.

[102] 328 U.S. 275, decided May 27, 1946. The decision is reprinted in Senate, Committee on Military Affairs, 79th Cong., 2d Sess., *Hearing on Superseniority Rights of Veterans,* July 12, 1946 (Washington, D.C., 1946), 10–16. The whole legal background can be found in "Veterans' Reemployment Litigation," *Harvard Law Review,* LIX (April, 1946), 593–604.

[103] *The New York Times,* June 5, 1945.

$86.40 for the nine days' layoff.[104] The Circuit Court of Appeals on March 5, 1946, reversed the judgment.[105] Two months later the Supreme Court upheld the appeals court's decision.[106]

Associate Justice William O. Douglas, arguing for the majority, maintained:

> There is indeed no suggestion that Congress sought to sweep aside the seniority system. What it undertook to do was to give the veteran protection within the framework of the seniority system plus a guarantee against demotion or termination of the employment relationship without cause for a year.[107]

Since the layoff did not "terminate" Fishgold's employment, he could not claim protection under the statute. Justice Douglas denied that Hershey's ruling had any more than advisory effect. In addition, the fact that Congress had amended Section 8 of the law ithout clarifying its basic intent did not mean that it tacitly accepted Hershey's ruling.[108] Policymaking for the reemployment of veterans thus concluded decisively, affirming labor's position.

The record of achievement on seniority by the executive department seems meager in retrospect. The Selective Service System blundered when it failed to confer adequately with other agencies of government, let alone with labor, before issuing its fateful order. Responsibility for the two-year-long stalemate in public policy that followed must be shared by President Truman, General Hines of the Retraining and Reemployment Administration, and by the various chiefs of the Office of War Mobilization and Reconversion. The controversy seemed to be tailor-made for settlement by either RRA or OWMR. Both agencies enjoyed administrative powers involving policy coordination over other agencies. If General Hines of RRA, or James F. Byrnes, Frederick Vinson, or John W. Snyder of OWMR believed they lacked authority to settle the dispute themselves, then they had an obligation to present the entire matter to the President, with their recommendations. Yet these officials shilly-shallied; they hoped, it would appear, that someone else would resolve the matter

---

[104] "Veterans: Senior to Whom?" *Newsweek,* XXVII (April 15, 1946), 37.
[105] *The New York Times,* March 6, 1946.
[106] "Unsuper Seniority," *Newsweek,* XXVII (June 3, 1946), 26.
[107] 66 S. Ct. 1113.
[108] *Ibid.* Justice Hugo Black was the lone dissenter.

for them.[109] If the question were essentially a judicial one, then the executive branch could have pressed for a Supreme Court decision before it finally did in the spring of 1946. Or, if the matter needed legislative clarification, then Congress could have been approached. But these officials followed a policy of drift instead.

As it turned out, the lack of leadership in policymaking within the executive department did not have serious consequences. Employment conditions remained sufficiently good to ward off bitter confrontations between labor and veterans on the question. General Erskine had been accurate in saying that the question had ballooned out of proportion to its importance. Reemployment rights were, after all, applicable only to a relatively small group of veterans.[110] Furthermore, most employers needed little persuasion to be just to veterans; good public relations demanded careful treatment of the returning veterans. Yet the issue carried the possibility—dormant as the event proved—of great political significance.[111] The Supreme Court, fortunately for the politicians, acted in time.

SEVERAL CONCLUSIONS can be made about the reconversion experience as it affected veterans' policymaking. The clarion call of Bernard Baruch and John A. Hancock exhorting the Federal Govern-

[109] The repeated appeals to the Attorney General exemplify this. In July, 1945, not long after Tom C. Clark took over that function from Francis Biddle, the questions had been resubmitted to the Justice Department. Clark, like Biddle, remained silent.

[110] One poll showed, for example, that only about one-third of the veterans who had had jobs before the service had returned to their old positions. "Work Choice of GI's," *The U.S. News* (February 15, 1946), 32. A Selective Service System official, testifying in July, 1946, said that only 22 cases were filed with the courts to restore veterans to jobs—out of 5,000,000 servicemen with seniority rights. Senate, Committee on Military Affairs, 79th Cong., 2d Sess., *Hearing on Superseniority Rights of Veterans,* July 12, 1946 (Washington, D.C., 1946), 9. The Attorney General claimed that during the period July 1, 1944, to July 1, 1946, only 4,531 men out of an estimated 4,000,000 with job rights, applied to the Justice Department for aid. "Veterans Being Placed," *Business Week* (August 17, 1946), 83–85.

[111] At least one Congressman and a federal judge tried to regain seniority and reemployment privileges through Section 8. The Judge, William Clark of the Third Circuit Court of Appeals, tried unsuccessfully to get back the post he left in 1942 for military service. See *The New York Times,* January 11 and 12, 1946. Congressman James E. Van Zandt (R-Pa.) had hoped in vain to regain the seniority he gave up by entering the Navy in 1943. One of his colleagues, Representative Daniel A. Reed (R-N.Y.), grumbled: "This con-

ment to act decisively received a weak answer. President Roosevelt, to be sure, gave formal recognition to the imperatives of the Baruch-Hancock recommendations. But that was about all he did. In 1944 he saw clearly the political implications; but his response remained on a "treaty of peace" level—a diplomatic move designed to meet Congressional and political restiveness, form rather than substance.[112] For over a year he kept Frank T. Hines in office, despite Hines's inactivity. Instinctively, perhaps, the President wanted to maintain a noncontroversial position on domestic affairs so he could push forward on more important international fronts. Walter Lippmann's analysis early in 1944 sums up the situation well:

> It is silly to suppose that the President can have much strength and energy left to form the right views on domestic issues. His fault, and it is a grievous one, is that he does not admit it, and reorganize his cabinet, and turn over to others authority he cannot possibly exercise himself.[113]

One of President Truman's more significant actions concerning reconversion and veterans' affairs was the removal of Frank T. Hines. Hines, after years of valuable public service, certainly was no man for the task of a "work director." His laudable devotion to economy and to veterans generally did not equip him with the positive executive attitude essential to transform the Baruch-Hancock written recommendations into reality. His long isolation from interagency activities rendered him impotent to act boldly in settling disputes. Hines had learned for twenty-two years how to take orders—from Congress, veterans' organizations, and Presidents. This conditioning, perhaps, had made him into a good follower; it certainly had not prepared him to be a "czar."

Ironically, the one controversy which seemed to elicit greater imag-

---

stitutes a rank discrimination against the man who is serving as a Representative . . . , but of course in the eyes of certain radical elements the mere fact that he is a Member of Congress should subject him to the firing squad or a concentration camp." Reed to Franklyn S. Richardson, February 27, 1947; "H.R. 1457 [80:1] "Folder, Box 51, Reed Papers, Cornell University.
[112] The "Peace Treaty" analogy is from Samuel Lubell, *The Future of American Politics* (rev. ed.; New York, 1956), p. 20.
[113] *The Washington Post*, March 9, 1944.

ination on Hines's part—the superseniority fight—demonstrated still another reconversion lesson. For where Roosevelt had allowed Hines not to act, Truman and Hines's superiors in the Office of War Mobilization and Reconversion had not helped Hines when he did want to act. After all, the Retraining and Reemployment chief had come up with a reasonable solution to the veterans' seniority question. Yet his advice did not receive support. Part of the reason for this lay in the fact that Hines had been discredited by his past inaction. More important, however, Hines's political superiors themselves shrank from the thought of acting positively. Hines was not, in brief, the only "shrinking violet" within the Truman Administration.

These criticisms must be put into perspective. War and international diplomacy left Presidents Roosevelt and Truman with little time for less important domestic affairs. Moreover, the constant and inevitable interagency competition had been intensified by reconversion itself. That is, the federal agencies' functions and powers had been swollen by the needs of war; the Selective Service System and War Manpower Commission, to name two agencies, had to fight strenuously either to keep functions or find new ones during the transformation of the Administration from war to peace. A stronger man than Hines might also have foundered on the reefs of such agencies' ambitions. Coordination of veterans' affairs during reconversion, in short, called for superior talents. That Hines did not possess those requisites is certain; that another official might have succeeded can only be conjectured—and then only if he had greater support from the Chief Executive than Hines himself enjoyed.

Finally, what impact did the poor showing of the Executive have on veterans? No one can answer this with assurance. Relatively few veterans, probably, cared very much about the Federal Government's inefficiency in handling the information center or seniority matters. Some may have been annoyed at the bureaucratic confusion; but by and large the missteps in the reconversion process were offset by more positive notes: the bountiful harvest of the GI Bill of Rights, the plenitude of jobs in postwar America, and the sympathetic efforts of volunteers and staff of local, county, and state "welcome home" offices.

6

THE RETURN OF ULYSSES

EVEN AS SEAMEN lit the battleship *Missouri*'s fires for the triumphant mission to Tokyo Harbor, enormous pressures were building up at home to return American GIs to their hearthsides. Less than two weeks after Japanese leaders had signed the articles of surrender, the wife of an American soldier stationed in India wrote:

For 27 months I have kept my silence, and endured all I've had to, without a word. But now I'm empty of patience—tolerance—patriotism—I'm emptied of everything but an awful bitterness! [1]

Hard words indeed, yet they typified civilians' and, shortly, servicemen's attitudes concerning demobilization. Most Americans agreed in principle that sacrifices still had to be made. But when specific cases arose, wives, mothers, fathers, and sweethearts each thought that their soldier had done more than his duty. Bring home, they pleaded, their Ulysses "pining on a lonely island far away in the middle of the sea." They believed vehemently that the "shirkers"—those who, for a variety of reasons, had not seen military service—should be rushed to replace those who had done the fighting.[2]

---

[1] Mrs. L. Keele to Senator Elbert D. Thomas (D-Utah), September 18, 1945; "Legislation-Demobilization, October" Folder, Box 113, Thomas Papers, Franklin D. Roosevelt Library. Cited hereafter as FDRL.

[2] One example of this view: "Continue the draft. Take a lot of these cowardly farm boys and so called essential workers into the army and release the boys who did the real fighting." H.D.F. to Truman, August 6,

This massive, and at times hysterical, public demand to bring back the boys had not been foreseen by all of President Roosevelt's wartime planners. The National Resources Planning Board, for example, had been more concerned with the attitude of the GI. In 1943 the Postwar Manpower Conference, operating under National Resources Planning Board aegis, completed recommendations for military personnel demobilization.[3] The conferees had believed that servicemen would be patient over unavoidable delays in the demobilization process.[4]

The conferees spent less time with the equally important task of gauging the reasonableness of the American public. Perhaps it appeared incomprehensible to the planners that a nation, deeply engaged in a war to preserve liberty, would so soon refuse to listen to the pleas of reason. In effect, the planners had committed themselves to the expectation that the war had sounded the death knell for prewar isolationism. For officials in Washington at least, the war had taught a lesson, at a huge cost in lost lives and mangled bodies— Americans could not return to their now-destroyed illusions. In specific terms this meant commitment of American occupation forces abroad.

Yet the war had been an imperfect teacher; for in the immediate postwar period a new mood seized the nation. Having defeated military dictatorships abroad, many now feared a similar despotism at home.[5] They did not have far to look, they thought, for proof or militarism; how else explain the urgent appeals by military experts for compulsory military training during the autumn of 1945?[6] And

1945, Official File 245-Misc. "F", White House Papers of Harry S Truman, Harry S. Truman Library. Cited hereafter as OF . . . , Truman Papers, HSTL.

[3] See above, ch. ii. National Resources Planning Board, *Demobilization and Readjustment* (Washington, D.C., 1943).

[4] *PMC Report,* 37.

[5] See, for example, the petition that reads, in part: "Peacetime compulsory military training might lead to militarism and regimentation as it did in Japan and Germany." Citizens of Erlanger, Ft. Thomas, Southgate, Newport, Covington, Mitchell, and Park Hills, Kentucky to Representative Brent Spence (D-Ky.), n.d.; "Legislation-Selective Service, Demobilization, etc., 1945–1946" Folder, Spence Papers, University of Kentucky.

[6] One correspondent castigated plans for continuance of the Selective Serv-

what about all those generals with temporary ranks of lieutenant colonel, or major, or captain? Anti-militarists suspected that the "brass" trumped up artificial reasons for slowing down the armed force's discharge rate in order to avoid their own demotion or retirement.[7] Other citizens, convinced that the dark years of strife had proved the folly of war, urged disarmament, joining the chorus chanting for the rapid return of servicemen. Even staunch liberal supporters of the Democratic Administration at times disagreed with their leaders' reasoning for a moderate demobilization rate. Senator Harley M. Kilgore (D-W. VA.), for example, observed:

It has been said that our commitments in the field of foreign policy require a large army. . . . Such a policy constitutes not only an injustice to the GI who is kept in the Army or Navy unnecessarily, but it prevents the development of mutual confidence among nations so essential to the building of a secure peace.[8]

Furthermore, renascent isolationists—individuals and groups that opposed America's assumption of its newly expanded international commitments—also obected to the retention of draftees in the armed forces. They criticized not only American occupation duties in conquered enemy territory,[9] but in addition they complained about the diversion of troopships to carry foodstuffs to famine-ridden nations —both allied and former enemy countries.[10] Others shared the isola-

---

ice System's induction powers: "The drafting of men for a standing Army is un-American and un-Christian and a crime against civilization." Louis L. Akin to Truman, n.d. (probably September, 1945); OF 245-Misc. "A," HSTL.

[7] See comments of Representatives John Taber (R-N.Y.) and Joseph P. O'Hara (R-Minn.), U.S., *Congressional Record*, 79th Cong., 1st Sess. (October, 19, 1945), 9831. Cited hereafter as *Cong. Rec.*, followed by Congress and Session numbers, date, and page.

[8] Statement of the Senator's position, n.d. (probably September or October, 1946); "Kilgore-1946 Campaign Material" Folder, Box 1, Kilgore Papers, FDRL.

[9] See petitions from the House of Representatives, 63d General Assembly of Missouri, October 3, 1945; from 554 citizens of President Truman's home town of Independence, Missouri, October 15, 1945; and from the City Council of New Bedford, Massachusetts, October 25, 1945; OF 190-R, Truman Papers, HSTL.

[10] President Truman defended U.S. food shipments in his message to Congress on September 6, 1945: "Our own enlightened self-interest tells us that hungry people are rarely advocates of democracy. The rehabilitation of these countries, and indeed the removal of American occupational troops, may be

tionists' concern about diversion of shipping. Rumors that American troopships transported soldiers of other countries on "imperialist" missions, for example, incurred the wrath of such diverse individuals as Senator Wayne Morse (R-Ore.) and Joseph Curran, President of the National Maritime Union.[11] Morse said bluntly: "I am not interested in using American ships to preserve the Dutch Empire." [12] Curran, at that time hewing a close line with American communists, wired the President:

Have just returned from abroad where I spoke with hundreds of American troops. Am shocked that American ships are being diverted from all important task of bringing our boys home speedily. . . . We demand immediate cessation of all transfers of American ships to foreign powers.[13]

Another left-wing labor union official, Saul Mills, Secretary of the Greater New York Industrial Union Council (CIO), argued that "so long as a single G.I. is stranded in a foreign port sick for the sight of his family, no shipping demand has greater urgency or priority." [14]

unnecessarily delayed if we fail to meet those responsibilities during the next few months." *Public Papers of the Presidents of the United States, Harry S. Truman, 1945* (Washington, D.C., 1961), 273. Cited hereafter as *Truman Public Papers.*

[11] One editorial charged the U.S. with spending funds to "underwrite white imperialism in the Orient." "Warning from the Ranks," *The Christian Century,* LXIII (January 23, 1946), 104. American ships moved Chinese Nationalists to North China and transported Japanese prisoners from China to their homeland. The War Department denied that these diversions delayed American troop transportation. U.S., House of Representatives, Committee on Naval Affairs, 79th Cong., 2d Sess., *Hearing No. 177,* February 5, 1946 (Washington, D.C., 1946), 2520–22. See also *The New York Times,* November 1 and December 27, 1945.

[12] U.S., Senate, Committee on Naval Affairs, 79th Cong., 1st Sess., *Hearings on Demobilization and Transportation of Military Personnel,* November 15, 1945 (Washington, D.C., 1945), 56. Morse referred to the supposed use of U.S. ships to bring Dutch and English troops to the strife-torn Netherlands East Indies to put down rebellious Indonesians. The War Shipping Administration in the summer of 1942 had leased Dutch vessels for use in the Pacific theater. Three years later Dutch authorities anxiously inquired about these ships; they wished to have vessels for "transportation of military personnel" and for members of the Netherlands East Indies Civil Affairs to the Far East. See Netherlands Ambassador to Acting Secy. of State James Grew, June 6, 1945 (and attachments); WSA Original Action, 3W2, R88, Box 63, Records of the War Shipping Administration, Record Group 248, National Archives.

[13] Curran to Truman, October 30, 1945; OF 190-R, Truman Papers, HSTL.

[14] Mills to Truman, November 2, 1945; *ibid.*

AT FIRST, LEADERS in the Truman Administration responded firmly to these general pressures. They stated that America's continued occupation duties required a large number of men; unlike World War I, when only a small number of Americans served as occupation forces, the Army and the Navy could not be disbanded overnight. Also, they reasoned, unlike earlier experiences, the wide dispersion of men and material over the face of the globe would slow demobilization down. Finally, they argued that the war had made the United States the unchallenged leader of the free world. This committed American armed power to new responsibilities—all of which restricted the rate of military demobilization. As the Army's Chief of Staff, General Dwight D. Eisenhower, observed: "My sole purpose . . . is that the Army which did so much to win the victory will be left fit to preserve it." [15]

These arguments of broad national interest headed the list used by the Truman Administration's spokesmen to explain delays in disbanding the armed forces. They pointed out also how the requirements of a two-front war had complicated the demobilization process. After all, the fight did not end on May 8, 1945, with victory in Europe. Indeed, military strategists had believed that to defeat Japan a long and bitter struggle would be necessary in the Pacific. Experiences at Iwo Jima and Okinawa had reinforced this estimate. The conquest of these two bastions of Japanese insular defense consumed time and, more important, lives. The engagement at Iwo Jima began with intensive aerial bombardment in August, 1944, and did not end until after the island had been secured on March 16, 1945. Almost 7,000 Americans lost their lives in seizing their objective—symbolized by the climactic raising of the stars and stripes on Mt. Suribachi—in the face of the fanatically stubborn resistance of the defenders. The attack on Okinawa began on October 10, 1944; on Easter Sunday, 1945, the American forces began landings on the beaches. By June 22, 1945, the battle had been won. But American losses were high; the navy lost 30 ships, with 368 others

[15] Statement, dated January 15, 1946, reprinted in U.S., Senate, Committee on Military Affairs, 79th Cong., 2d Sess., *Hearings on Demobilization of the Armed Forces,* January 17, 1946 (Washington, D.C., 1946), Part III, 353. Cited hereafter as Senate, *Army Demobilization Hearings.*

damaged. Over 12,000 Americans had died (including the famed war correspondent Ernie Pyle and the Army commander Lieutenant General Simon B. Buckner, Jr.) and 36,000 more had been wounded. The immense Japanese losses amounting to more than 100,000 killed—many by their own hand by hara-kari or in suicidal Kamikaze flights—testifying to the enemy's will to resist.[16]

In addition, the unexpected last ditch counter-offensive of the Germans on December 16, 1944, at the Bulge, had made planners more wary.[17] This sudden, albeit temporary, reverse stood as a lesson of the ability of an enemy fighting on or near his native land. As a result, most military planners had assumed that the earliest probable defeat of Japan would occur in the autumn of 1946.[18] As it turned out, knowing nothing of the Manhattan project, they greatly over-estimated the task. V-J Day occurred over a year earlier, on August 14, 1945.

That the planners had strayed far from the mark had important consequences on military demobilization. The Army and Navy, envisaging a long war, had arranged for the large-scale shipment, or redeployment, of men and supplies from the European to the Pacific theater after V-E day.[19] Military needs in the Far East contributed

[16] For a brief account of these campaigns see A. Russell Buchanan, *The United States and World War II* (New York, Evanston, and London, 1964), II, ch. xxvi.

[17] See *ibid.,* ch. xx.

[18] Air Force planners, however, perhaps convinced of the total effectiveness of air strikes, seemed more optimistic. Lieutenant General Ira C. Eaker, Deputy Commander of the Army Air Forces, stated in September, 1945, that air planning had assumed that "the fall of Japan would occur August 31, 1945." U.S., House of Representatives, Committee on Military Affairs, 79th Cong., 1st Sess., *Hearings on Demobilization of Material and Personnel,* September 19, 1945 (Washington, D.C., 1946), 23. Cited hereafter as House, *Army Demobilization Hearings.* Yet this was a minority view. The Joint Chiefs of Staff used October, 1946, as the planning date. The British and American Chiefs of Staff, moreover, as late as July 24, 1945 (during the Potsdam Conference), agreed upon November 15, 1946. See John C. Sparrow, *History of Personnel Demobilization in the United States* (Washington, D.C., 1952), pp. 49–51 and 112; and Harry S Truman, *Memoirs by Harry S. Truman* (Garden City, N.Y., 1955), I, 382. Cited hereafter as Sparrow, *Personnel Demobilization* and Truman, *Memoirs,* respectively.

[19] For an account of this process see Bell I. Wiley, "Reorganizing for Redeployment," in Kent Roberts Greenfield, *et al., The Army Ground Forces: The Organization of Ground Combat Troops,* Vol. I of *The History of the*

to inequities that later developed in the demobilization process. As President Truman explained to an inquiring Senator: "Redeployment has caused us to take those Divisions which had seen the least action in Europe and bring them here and prepare for redeployment in Asia—leaving in Europe the men who had been there longest." [20] Hence, after the collapse of Japan reduced Far Eastern manpower needs, some men became civilians before their former European comrades—angering the latter. Furthermore, the high estimates of men and supplies needed to defeat Japan led to the routing and stockpiling of men and goods in the Pacific far in excess of actual requirements. The mountains of supplies accumulated, particularly in the Philippines, after V-J Day in turn created a need for men to handle and maintain them. All this, of course, slowed the War Department's demobilization rate.[21]

THE INACCURACY of the V-J Day estimate also affected the instrument of demobilization, the "point system." Military planners had worked out this program for partial demobilization to be used between V-E and V-J days.[22] During the early stages of planning in the spring of 1943, the Army leaned toward the idea of demobilizing entire organizational units, rather than releasing soldiers as individuals. Unit separation had been followed after both the Civil War and World War I; it lent itself to flexibility and rapidity of operation, as well as interfering less with redeployment. Although militarily desirable, the unit system had at least one major flaw: individuals with no combat experience within units containing battle veterans would

---

United States Army in World War II (Washington, D.C., 1947), 496–504. Cited hereafter as Greenfield, *The AGF.*

[20] Truman to Senator Walter F. George (D-Ga.), August 25, 1945; OF 190-Y, Truman Papers, HSTL.

[21] See statement of Kenneth C. Royall, Under Secretary of War; Senate, *Army Demobilization Hearings,* January 16, 1946, 268.

[22] For the genesis of the point system see Samuel Stouffer, "The Point System . . ." in Stouffer, *et al., The American Soldier: Combat and Its Aftermath,* Vol. II of *Studies in Social Psychology in World War II* (Princeton, N.J., 1949), pp. 520–48. Cited hereafter as Stouffer, *Point System.* See also, U.S., House of Representatives, Committee on Military Affairs, 79th Cong., 1st Sess., *Hearings on the Operation of the Army Personnel Readjustment Plan,* June 19, 1945 (Washington, D.C., 1945).

be discharged at the same time as their buddies, thereby unjustly reaping the benefits of their arbitrary unit assignments.[23]

The most "democratic" solution—"first in, first out"—did not receive serious consideration by either military or civilian planners. Although indorsed later (shortly before V-E Day) by Senator Edwin C. Johnson (D-Colo.) and welcomed by many GIs, this suggestion fit neither military nor economic planning objectives. In the former case, such a policy would have stripped the armed forces of their most experienced men at the very moment the assault on Japan was underway. As for the economic planning goal, the men who entered the services first frequently had not held "key" jobs or possessed special occupational skills; to release them first hardly met the civilian planners' objectives. The issue resolved itself into a competition of values: should military convenience and needs outweigh democratic and national economic planning considerations?

On September 28, 1943, the Joint Chiefs of Staff agreed to go along with the individual release procedure.[24] The PMC report apparently had convinced military leaders to shift from unit to individual release.[25] This is not to say they accepted the PMC's economic planning motives. In the ensuing months, War Department officials frantically attempted to dissociate their decision from the civilian planners' objectives. Forgetting his energetic promise made in January, 1943, that the Army would not muster men out of "the ranks into a breadline," [26] Robert P. Patterson, Under Secretary of War, ten months later denied charges that the military wished to retain servicemen until jobs became available. Forgetfully, but firmly, he informed Senators:

I know of no responsible War Department representative who has proposed any such plans. . . . We have no intention of retaining soldiers in the Army when they are no longer needed and can be returned to civilian life. . . . Neither I nor anyone else representing the War De-

[23] A discussion of the debate in the War Department may be found in Greenfield, *The AGF*, 440–41.
[24] Samuel Lubell to Bernard Baruch, December 4, 1943; "Agency Reports: War" section, Miscellaneous Binder, John M. Hancock Papers, University of North Dakota.
[25] Greenfield, *The AGF*, 441.
[26] *The New York Times,* January 26, 1943.

partment . . . has advocated delaying military service, until it is believed that industry will provide them with jobs.[27]

The vehemence and timing of the War Department's denials came at a significant domestic political moment—the Presidential campaign of 1944. Republicans, seeking issues to exploit, pounced on a comment made by Major General Lewis D. Hershey, head of the Selective Service System, at a press conference in Denver on August 21, 1944.[28] Since Hershey had echoed PMC views about retaining men in the service, Governor Thomas E. Dewey of New York, the Republican presidential candidate, scored the Democrats for their heartless policy.[29] This incensed Hershey's subordinates. How could anyone misconstrue their superior's motives? Hadn't he "banged his fist and spread sulphuric English all over the office" when anyone suggested relaxing efforts in behalf of veterans? [30] Rather than rage silently against political "calumny," President Roosevelt turned the incident to his own advantage. Speaking before members of the Teamsters Union on September 23, 1944, he answered Dewey's "fantastic" charges:

I learned—much to my amazement—that the policy of this Administration was to keep men in the Army when the war was over, because there might be no jobs for them in civil life. . . . This callous and brazen falsehood . . . did . . . a very simple thing; it was an effort to stimulate fear among American mothers and wives and sweethearts. And,

[27] Patterson to Samuel I. Rosenman, October 18, 1944 (quoting Patterson's statement in executive session of the Senate's Special Committee Investigating the National Defense Program—the Truman Committee—on November 10, 1943), "Post-war & War Adjustment 9-Legislation & Planning for Demobilization" Folder, Subject Numeric Folder, Subject Numeric File II, Office of the Director, Records of the Office of War Mobilization and Reconversion, Record Group 250, National Archives. Cited hereafter as OWMR Records, RG 250, NA.

[28] Hershey had said virtually the same thing on January 11, 1944; but this had not attracted notice. *The Washington Post,* January 12, 1944.

[29] See text of Dewey's speech at Philadelphia's Convention Hall, September 7, 1944; *The Washington Post,* September 8, 1944. Republicans also used the slogan "Bring the Boys Home Quicker, with Dewey and Bricker"; "Lying to Get Elected," *The New Republic,* CXI (October 16, 1944), 580.

[30] John Dulles Langston, Head of the Presidential Appeals and Advisory Board in the Selective Service System, to Col. O'Kelliher, September 16, 1944; "Stayback of Colonel John D. Langston, 1/44 to 12/44," Langston Papers, Duke University.

incidently, it was hardly calculated to bolster the morale of our soldiers and sailors and airmen who are fighting our battles over the world.[31]

With political cannonading resounding in their ears, the military planners had already turned from the basic decision of individual release to their next task—the delicate construction of an equitable and simple priority release plan that would meet the widest possible approval.

Emboldened by the novelty of the basic decision, War Department officials implemented it in an equally novel manner. The GIs themselves would determine the basis for priority of discharge. The Army polled soldiers stationed throughout the world in a series of surveys held from November, 1943, to August, 1944.[32] The majority of servicemen believed that combat, parenthood, overseas duty, and service longevity, in that order, should be given most weight in determining priority of discharge.[33] On the basis of this expression of opinion, the War Department constructed the point system and, in September, 1944, publicized its basic principles—omitting actual value assigned to the factors.[34] After V-E Day (May 8, 1945), the Army released the computation:

Combat   = 5 points per campaign star or combat decoration, including the Purple Heart

Parenthood   = 12 points per child under 18, with 36 points as the maximum

Overseas Service = 1 point per month

Total Army Service = 1 point per month.[35]

[31] Samuel I. Rosenman, compiler, *The Public Papers and Addresses of Franklin D. Roosevelt*, Vol. XIII, *1944–1945 Victory and the Threshold of Peace* (New York, 1950), 289–90.

[32] Later surveys were made periodically to check and refine data already accumulated. Stouffer, *Point System,* 648–51.

[33] See Table 3, *ibid.,* p. 526.

[34] War Department Press Release, September 6, 1944; reprinted as Appendix IV; Sparrow, *Personnel Demobilization,* pp. 302–305.

[35] Stouffer, *Point System,* p. 529; and War Department Press Release, May 10, 1945, Sparrow, *Personnel Demobilization,* Appendix VI, pp. 311–16.

The point system covered all personnel and served as the basis for priority of discharge in 1945–1946. Certain classes of individuals were exempted: those claiming hardship, the mentally and physically disabled, Congressional Medal of Honor recipients, and those considered over-age. Enlisted men who

Thus, military planners had devised a uniquely democratic plan—embodying the spirit of individual merit and resting on the seemingly unimpeachable fact that the GIs themselves had chosen it.

Yet the War Department intended to apply the point system solely to the period between V-E and V-J days. Officials planned to release only two million soldiers in that "one year" interim.[36] In a way, the point system was "experimental"; following V-J Day, it would be replaced with another plan, once the flaws of the first had been demonstrated.[37] But when Japanese resistance collapsed on August 14, 1945, a scant three months after V-E Day, the military had not had time to formulate a new plan. For good or ill, they were wedded to the unreformed point system.

FAULT LINES IN the point system emerged rapidly. Although reasonable men anticipated that mistakes would be made in such an immense operation, it proved difficult for troops to withstand the infectious feeling "that we have done our part, now get us home." Not aware of the sophisticated sampling technique used by the War Department, many servicemen (since they personally had not been polled) doubted whether the Army had asked any of their colleagues. One Congressman, casting himself in the role of a GI spokesman, claimed to have talked with over one hundred servicemen, none of whom had ever heard of the point system before its publication.[38] An Army Corporal observed in disgust: "When you read that old

possessed "critical skills" could be retained in the service regardless of point totals. Officers also accumulated points; but their discharge priority was determined in the first instance by the requirements of the service, and then by point totals.

After V-E day the War Department announced that personnel with eighty-five points as of that date would be eligible for discharge. After V-J day, the War Department progressively lowered this "critical" score. V-E day became the cutoff date for the accumulation of points, but this was later extended to V-J day.

The Navy's system, although similar to the Army's, substituted age for combat, and computed the points for dependents differently. The Coast Guard followed the Navy's pattern; the Marines used the Army formula.

[36] War Department Press Release, May 5, 1945; in Sparrow, *Personnel Demobilization,* p. 307.

[37] *Ibid.,* p. 85.

[38] Representative George B. Schwabe (D-Okla.) to Truman, September 12, 1945; OF 190-R, Truman Papers, HSTL.

baloney about it is the way the GI's wanted it, then it burns you up, as I have not yet run into a GI that was ever asked before the point system was put into effect." [39] One group of soldiers stationed in Europe, skeptics all, queried: "We would like to communicate with just one EM in Europe who was interviewed." [40]

Whether polled or not, servicemen filed the inevitable complaints about the plan's injustices. Bachelors were aggrieved: "I suggest that single men be given more points than married men. . . . After all, they ought to be given some time to go out and 'cherchez la femme' so that they too can start a family." [41] Childless married men complained that "it's a fine state of affairs when a man gets credit for a child and not for his wife! How do they think a man gets a kid anyway, by inoculation?" [42] Combat infantrymen protested that their important contributions to victory had been put on the same level with those who had never seen the front line. This led to bitter observations:

Some romantic fool called the infantry the "Queen of Battles." We say he is a liar. She's just an old whore who is . . . tossed a few pennies for her body, but is blithely . . . set aside when her duties are no longer required.[43]

When the armed forces' newspapers reported that the American press viewed the point system favorably, an angry GI warned:

Stand back, because I'm blowing my top! . . . Why in hell do you print such tripe? Are you trying to sell us the idea that the point system is fair? We know we've been shafted, so don't rub it in! [44]

These initial reactions to the plan had been expected. Not everyone could be pleased, for as President Truman said irritably: "It wouldn't make any difference what sort of plan they had, somebody wouldn't like it." [45]

[39] Quoted in Sparrow, *Personnel Demobilization,* p. 127.
[40] "23 Doubting Thomases," *The Stars and Stripes,* London edition, V (May 24, 1945), 2.
[41] "Lt. (JG) McG.," *ibid.,* V (May 4, 1945), 2.
[42] "83 Pointer," *ibid.,* V (June 6, 1945), 2.
[43] Pvt. Fred H. Glass and ten others, "Dear Yank," *Yank; The Army Weekly,* IV (July 13, 1945), 19.
[44] "Shafted," *The Stars and Stripes,* London edition, V (June 4, 1945), 2.
[45] "The President's News Conference of August 23, 1945," *Truman Public Papers, 1945,* 233.

The fissures developing in the soldiers' confidence widened in the early autumn of 1945 as the point system began to operate. Quite naturally, the manner of awarding points proved to be one of the most persistent objects of complaints. At Air Corps locations, for example, where bomb and service groups worked side by side, the awarding of campaign stars (at five points a star) to all members of the flying unit and none to the service organization created bitter feelings. Who could answer the angry question: "Is it right for a latrine orderly with a fighter squadron to receive four battle stars?" [46] With little else to do, the servicemen could render this gripe poetically:

> Twinkle, twinkle little star,
> Sometimes we wonder where you are,
> Maybe we as service groups,
> Are considered lonely gooks.
> And as for stars . . . we'll not be blest
> All stars adorn bomb group chests.[47]

These inequities could not be avoided. The military could not assume the enormous administrative task of distinguishing latrine orderlies from combat soldiers in each unit throughout the world. Nor could the geographical reality of distance be shortened. The plight of Air Force personnel stationed on Iwo Jima illustrated that fact. Shipments for home did not begin from that island until almost three weeks after V-J Day and, more important, not until after similar evacuation had already begun in the Marianas. The relatively remote location of Iwo Jima delayed the arrival of troop transports. Moreover, authorities arranged for removal of high-point men (those with more than eighty-five points) "in order of score priority" within flight echelons. Thus, conceivably an individual with one hundred points in the third echelon would depart as much as one month after fellow airmen with ninety points in the first echelon.[48]

More protests came from "stranded" GIs who watched vessels

---

[46] S/Sgt. J. H. Watkinson, *The Stars and Stripes,* London edition, V (May 25, 1945), 2.
[47] Anonymous, *ibid.,* Middle Pacific edition, I (August 18, 1945), 2.
[48] Colonel Thayer S. Olds to Brigadier General Harry H. Vaughan, October 26, 1945; OF 190-R, Truman Papers, HSTL.

leaving Pacific ports after V-J day with empty berths.[49] The constant reminder of the large number of ships seemingly becalmed in those ports added to the frustration.[50] When the Army pointed out that the "empty" vessels were unconverted cargo ships too dangerous for transporting troops, intrepid servicemen, following the ancient example of Ulysses, offered to convert the ships themselves. In one instance, in the Philippines, the War Department reluctantly acceded to this unusual request. The result confirmed the Army's fears; one of the converted ships, buffeted by strong winds on its first trip, suffered heavy damage.[51]

In the early months of demobilization, poor coordination between agencies also caused difficulties. The Office of Defense Transportation (ODT), responsible for providing rail transportation to meet incoming troopships, claimed that the War Department did not warn them of fluctuations in shipping schedules. Since ODT officials believed they had to provide servicemen with a modicum of comfortable transportation, such as pullman cars for overnight journeys, they needed time to arrange for the proper cars. The War Department, however, thought almost any type of rail coach would be adequate —until public clamor against sending men from New York to San Francisco by coach led them to blame ODT for not providing pullman cars.[52] At times, especially near holidays, rail shipping became

[49] One vessel reportedly sailed from the Philippines with 620 empty spaces —to the anguish of homesick GIs. *Daily Pacifican; Army Newspaper in the Western Pacific,* I (January 5, 1946), 1, clipping attached to Sgt. J. F. Herman to Senator Hugh B. Mitchell, January 5, 1946; "Army-General Demobilization," Box 11; Mitchell Papers, University of Washington.

[50] This was a constant problem for the military services. Demobilization intensified the expected confusion following V-J Day. The Army and Navy protested, not without justice, that the rapid discharge of personnel by the point system siphoned off experienced men required for loading and unloading operations, therefore delaying shipping still more. For typical statements by officials concerning this problem, see U.S., Senate, Special Committee Investigating the National Defense Program, 79th Cong., 1st Sess., *Hearings,* December 12, 1945 (Washington, D.C., 1945), Part XXXII, 16211–12 and 16237–38; and *ibid.,* 79th Cong., 2nd Sess., *Hearings,* January 1, 1946 (Washington, D.C., 1946), Part XXVI, 19622–23 and 19655–56. Cited hereafter as Senate, *Mead Committee Hearings.*

[51] "On Bringing 'Em Home Alive," *Newsweek,* XXVI (December 3, 1945), 56.

[52] See Senate, 79th Cong., 1st Sess., *Mead Committee Hearings,* July 23, 1945, Part XXXI, 14879, *et seq.*

so snarled that servicemen resorted to Yankee ingenuity.[53] Five sailors, for example, hired a cab at $55 per man to drive them from San Pedro, California, to Atlanta, Georgia, so that they could arrive home in time for Christmas.[54] The entire problem of transportation led the ODT chief, Colonel J. M. Johnson, to explain:

Nobody knows what is going to happen. You can't look deep into this redeployment. It is too complicated and too big for the human mind. We are getting it done better and better as we go along. We will make a lot of mistakes. Doing things as fast as we are doing, you can't hit all the balls.[55]

One "strike"—although not with ODT at bat—occurred in the shipment of seventy-three GIs from Naples. They boarded a vessel, ultimately destined (they thought) for the United States, carrying Brazilian troops to Rio de Janiero. When the ship arrived at Rio, the dispatchers changed its orders so that it could return to Marseilles for a full load of American troops. While in the balmy South American port the servicemen complained to their Congressmen; the War Department finally sent an airplane to pick them up. But it arrived too late; the ship had sailed back to France.[56]

Transportation problems did not exhaust the list of grievances. Since the War Department had not planned to release men in the Zone of Interior with less than eighty points until after December 1, 1945,[57] many men languished at posts even though they had sufficient points for release.[58] Combat veterans took basic training courses over again or attended classes on, for example, the operation and

---

[53] "Colossal Rail Snafu Holds Up GIs in Christmas Rush Toward Home," *Newsweek*, XXVI (December 24, 1945), 27–8.

[54] *The New York Times*, December 23, 1945. With a stop in Dallas, the sailors made it home in three days. Another group of six marines traveled from San Diego to Pittsburgh in four days—arriving the day after Christmas; *ibid.*, December 27, 1945.

[55] Senate, 79th Cong., 1st Sess., *Mead Committee Hearings*, July 23, 1945, Part XXXI, 14889.

[56] *The New York Times*, September 20 and 21, 1945.

[57] Returnees from overseas would keep separation centers filled until that date. General Brehon Somervell to the Chief of Staff, September, 1945; WDGAP 370.01 (19 May 45) File, War Department Records, Record Group 319, World War II Records Branch, National Archives.

[58] The press reported that one enlisted man at the Santa Ana Army Air Base in California had 150 points. "Army Proposes, Fate Disposes and GI's Long for Boats to U.S.," *Newsweek*, XXVI (October 22, 1945), 56.

maintenance of the M-1 rifle.[59] Those "make work" details to keep the men occupied led one Senator to charge:

We have more than the 3,000,000 men in the Army for which there is no need and who should be released, but they cannot be released because there are 100,000 men with higher priority who cannot be brought home, so the point system . . . is not a device for getting men out of the Army but a device for keeping the men in the Army.[60]

Surplus soldiers disturbed the War Department as much as it did Congressmen and GIs. The situation worried Robert P. Patterson, Under Secretary of War:

I can think of no situation more calculated to destroy the confidence of the soldiers, the public and Congress in the integrity of our merit system for discharge. . . . I do not underestimate the many serious problems involved in finding replacements for those men who are genuinely essential, but the description must not be applied to men cutting grass, washing windows . . . or doing other relatively unimportant jobs.[61]

COMPLAINTS FROM SOLDIERS, at least during the autumn of 1945, constituted only one source of pressure being exerted upon officials in Washington. Relatives of servicemen urged priority of discharge for special groups with even greater insistence than the GIs. Appeals for the release of fathers, eighteen-year-olds, miners, railroad workers, scientists, doctors, policemen, and teachers, headed the almost endless list of individuals who deserved preferential treatment without regard to the point system. In the face of these demands the Administration did not falter officially in its support of the basic plan until January, 1946.[62] Up to that time President Truman and his advisers constantly repeated that the plan was the fairest way

[59] Senate, *Army Demobilization Hearings,* September 19, 1945, Part I, 164–72.
[60] Sen. Edwin C. Johnson, *ibid.,* September 19, 1945, 185.
[61] Patterson to the Deputy Chief of Staff, July 24, 1945, quoted in Sparrow, *Personnel Demobilization,* pp. 131–32.
[62] The Army had, to be sure, furloughed approximately 4,000 railway workers in the summer of 1945, but only with considerable reluctance. See Paul V. McNutt, Chairman of the War Manpower Commission, to the Secretary of War, Henry L. Stimson, June 23, 1945, and Stimson to McNutt, July 7, 1945; reprinted as Exhibits 1489 and 1490, Senate, *Mead Committee Hearings,* 79th Cong., 1st Sess., Part XXXI, 15491–92.

to deal with the partial liquidation of the armed forces.[63] To give special groups preferential treatment would "effect a complete breakdown of the present demobilization program." [64]

Pious repetitions, however, did not quiet the swelling public demand that married men and fathers be released regardless of the point system.[65] In the summer and fall of 1945, opinion began to be felt in that most sensitive arena, Congress. One after another, Congressmen began to urge a change in Administration policy. Representative John W. McCormack (D-Mass.), then Majority Floor Leader, wired the President:

While I appreciate the difficulties in satisfying everyone who is seeking an early discharge from our armed forces I feel very strongly that without regard to points, married men should be discharged as soon as possible. As we know the family is the basis of society and it is only natural and proper that husband and wife should be together. . . . The early reuniting of families is important to society as I see it.[66]

Representative James C. Auchincloss (R-N.J.) put it more forcefully in asserting "that a generation of fatherless children would make our country a second rate power and everything should be done to prevent such a tragedy." [67]

Supporting these Congressmen's requests, soldiers' wives formed "Bring Back Daddy" Clubs. Clubs sprouted up in such widely scattered cities and towns as LaFayette, Ind.; Pittsburg, Kansas; Baltimore, Md.; East Syracuse, N.Y.; Seattle, Wash.; and Oshkosh, Wisc. Soon baby shoes weighted down the legislators' mail—all bearing

[63] See, for example, Truman to Governor Charles G. Gossett (R-Idaho), September 4, 1945; OF 190-R, Truman Papers, HSTL.

[64] Matthew J. Connelly, the President's Secretary, to Rep. James C. Auchincloss (R-N.J.), January 8, 1946; and Presidential Press Releases, January 8 and 9, 1946, *ibid.*

[65] As early as 1943, James F. Byrnes, then Director of the Office of War Mobilization, contemplated urging President Roosevelt to make a statement "that when the time comes for demobilization . . . preference will be given fathers, so far as practicable." Byrnes to Roosevelt, October 2, 1943 [file copy marked: "Not Used—File"], White House Papers of Franklin D. Roosevelt, Official File 5404, FDRL. In the summer of 1944 Byrnes expressed this view publicly; *The Washington Post,* June 13, 1944.

[66] McCormack to Truman, September 1, 1945, OF 190-R Truman Papers, HSTL.

[67] Auchincloss to Truman, December 21, 1945, *ibid.*

tags reading "bring daddy home." Concurrently, the mothers started a post-card campaign with queries like: "Do they believe some kind of fairy is taking care of the service man's family?" [68] The heavy weight in the point system (a maximum of thirty-six points) given for parenthood did not satisfy these spouses.

As the beginning of the school year approached in the early fall of 1945, agitation increased for the release of GIs who had had their education interrupted by the call of the draft. "Why in the hell don't they release immediately any boy who wants to go back to college this fall?" [69] a Kansan inquired. One mother whose son's education had been disrupted asked rhetorically: "Are not these boys our future citizens [and] . . . leaders just as much as those [be]coming eighteen that some Congressmen are trying to protect from induction and military training?" [70] Rumors that President Truman seriously considered special treatment for prospective students prompted Robert P. Patterson to react sternly. Such a policy would, he argued, "do violence to the Army's merit system of discharge." Brigadier General Harry H. Vaughan, one of the President's confidants, beat a hasty and equivocal retreat:

The President agrees with the points you make. He holds that the point system must be maintained at all costs. He merely held that any soldier with sufficient points for discharge who desires to enter college, should if possible be discharged in September and enter school rather than in October or November and be forced to miss a school year.[71]

The demand for the release of the younger members of the armed forces in advance of their normal discharge dates could not be di-

---

[68] Mrs. Gus Harrison to Sen. J. W. Elmer Thomas (D-Okla.), December 14, 1945; "Bring Back Daddy" Folder, Legislation-Correspondence and Papers, 79th Cong., Thomas Papers, University of Oklahoma. The Senate Military Affairs Committee donated the shoes to the Foreign Relief Society for distribution to needy children in Europe. Thomas to Mrs. John Duffy, January 18, 1946, *ibid.*

[69] Harry Tidd to Representative Clifford R. Hope (R-Kans.), September 5, 1945; "Veterans—Legislative (79th Cong.)" Folder, Hope Papers, Kansas State Historical Society.

[70] Mrs. J. E. Keiffer to Truman, October 24, 1945; "Armed Forces 2" Folder, General Classified File, Part 1, OWMR Records, RG 250, NA.

[71] Patterson to Truman, August 20, 1945; Vaughan to Patterson, August 21, 1945; OF 190-R, Truman Papers, HSTL.

vorced from the current controversy concerning American postwar conscription policy. Almost from the very end of hostilities, as it grew apparent that the draft must be continued, the demand mounted for draft exemption for the eighteen-year-olds not yet in service. Advocates of this policy believed that it was unnecessary and, some also thought, unwise to make the nation's youth perform occupation duties. Military manpower needs, it was argued, could be met with volunteers and reenlistees by making military service more attractive; pay raises and increased provisions for material comforts would create a "buyer's market" for the military services. Thus, it was claimed, there would be no need to draft eighteen-year-olds. After all, the future of the nation depended upon the proper development of the country's youth. To draft eighteen-year-olds would interrupt their education at a most critical juncture. Finally, the argument concluded, to subject these immature youths to occupation duty in foreign lands would lead them inevitably to vice and degradation; with little to occupy their time the young men would naturally go astray.[72]

This argument, however, cut two ways. It opened up new avenues for attack for those who urged more rapid release of the younger, unmarried servicemen. All the arguments advanced by the opponents of drafting eighteen-year-olds could be applied with equal merit for the discharge, irrespective of accumulated points, of the eighteen-year-olds already in the service. Moreover, proponents of rapid release argued that logically one could not limit the rightful demand for discharge to eighteen-year-old men in the service since 1945. What of the youths drafted or who volunteered early in the war and who were now twenty-two or twenty-three years old? Did they not also deserve the solicitude of society?[73] Furthermore, GIs did not relish the prospect of being held in the armed forces because

[72] For a full expression of anti-draft sentiment see testimony in Senate, Committee on Military Affairs, 78th Cong., 2nd Sess., *Hearings on Selective Service Extension* (Washington, D.C., 1945).

[73] For a sampling of opinion on both sides of the question see correspondence in OF 245 Miscellaneous-Con-Folders A–Z (1945–1946) Truman Papers, HSTL. Truman's decision to continue the draft and retain the integrity of the point system pleased neither side. See Press Release, August 27, 1945, OF 190-T, *ibid.*

of lack of replacements. Speaking for men in the Pacific, *The Stars and Stripes* editorialized: "They're pretty angry. They can see no excuse for discontinuing the draft until enough men have been inducted to occupy Japan and Germany." [74]

Many others claimed preferential treatment. These pleas for special handling ran the gamut from releases for older personnel [75] to the discharge of a craftsman of artificial teeth.[76] Arguing that the War Department should release coal miners, Secretary of the Interior Harold L. Ickes painted a dark picture for both home and abroad if his advice went unheeded: "Next winter will be the coldest of the war for the people of the United States." Further, if we failed to send bituminous coal to Europe: "We must expect rioting, bloodshed, and the destruction of nearly all semblance of orderly government" there.[77] The "critical" shortage of professional personnel—scientists, doctors, and teachers—received heavy publicity in the campaign for early release. America needed doctors to take care of the backlog of medical cases accumulated during the war; the atomic age ushered in a new era requiring all types of scientists; and finally, advantages under the GI Bill of Rights would be curtailed by a lack of teachers. As might be expected, agencies within the Government also joined the clamor for exceptions to the discharge policy—usually, however, not publicly (Secretary Ickes was an outstanding exception). Thus, while the President and the War Department maintained the policy's integrity, the Office of War Mobilization and Reconversion, for one, urged that scientists receive special treatment in

---

[74] Middle Pacific edition, I (August 17, 1945), 2. Earlier during the war one airman indignantly asked: "Why in hell not put 18-year-olds into uniform? For God's sake, man, if they're good enough to live in our grand and glorious country they're good enough to serve it." Sgt. Irving Weinberg, *ibid.,* London edition, V (January 4, 1945), 2.

[75] "The thought of losing my chance to have kids is pretty heavy on my mind." T/S Arnold Burger, *ibid.,* Middle Pacific edition, I (August 6, 1945), 2.

[76] Martin Myerson, vice president, Ideal Tooth, Inc. to Office of War Mobilization and Reconversion, March 20, 1946; "Manpower 6–3" Folder, General Classified File, Part 1, OWMR Records, RG 250.

[77] Senate, *Mead Committee Hearings,* 79th Cong., 1st Sess., July 31, 1945, Part XXXI, 14983 and 14985; see also, Ickes to Frederick M. Vinson, OWMR Director, July 16, 1945; "Shipping 5—Coal for Europe" Folder, Subject Numeric File II, Office of the Director, OWMR Records, RG 250, NA.

order to alleviate the shortage.[78] Not all observers, however, shared OWMR's concern. Representative James W. Wadsworth (R-N.Y.), commenting on a bill that would release scientists from service, wrote:

Can you imagine what would happen to the morale of the men in the Army and Navy if they should see thirty-five thousand men picked out of the ranks and sent home as the result of a special act of Congress? Believe me, the protest would be deafening. . . . The people devoted to science, and I respect them, must be patient. The country is not going to the dogs.[79]

Agreeing with Representative Wadsworth, the President remained adamant in the face of these and other importunities. He summed up his response to the requests for special treatment advanced by Congressmen, especially in a letter to Representative Edward E. Cox (D-Ga.): Congressmen would "have to take the heat in order to keep an injustice from being done to the men who really did the fighting." [80]

BY THE WINTER OF 1945 the accumulation of grievances, real and imagined, set the stage for the dramatic climax of demobilization.[81] The obvious inability of the military to inform each man when he would return home created an air of uncertainty.[82] Furthermore, any change in shipping schedules, however justified, sapped the GIs' good will. Conflicting rumors and reports, the boredom of enforced idleness, and the overwhelming desire to get home, all contributed to a dangerous state of morale as 1945 closed.[83]

[78] See, for example, the exchanges between Artemus Gates, Under Secretary of the Navy, and OWMR chief, John Snyder, September 29, 1945 to December 1, 1945; "Armed Forces 2" Folder, General Classified File, Part 1, OWMR Records, RG 250, NA.

[79] Wadsworth to Joseph T. Anderson, June 14, 1945; "Conduct of World War II" Folder, House of Representatives Files, Wadsworth Papers, Library of Congress.

[80] September 12, 1945; OF 190-R, Truman Papers, HSTL.

[81] See R. Alton Lee, "The Army 'Mutiny' of 1946," *The Journal of American History,* LIII (December, 1966), 555–71. Cited hereafter as Lee, "Army Mutiny."

[82] Pfc. S.S., stationed at Cochran Field, Georgia, complained: "Doesn't each man in the services have a right to know what is going to happen to him?" *The New Republic,* CXIII (September 24, 1945), 375.

[83] See Sparrow, *Personnel Demobilization,* pp. 295–97.

All of these complaints led to a series of "amiable mutinies" by GIs during the first two weeks of January, 1946.[84] Three War Department statements triggered these spontaneous worldwide outbursts. The first statement had been made on September 20, 1945, when the Army's Chief of Staff, General George C. Marshall, announced that the point system would be "relaxed" by the "late winter" and men with two years of service would be eligible for demobilization.[85] The General's impromptu announcement stunned his advisers; in an earlier briefing session they had told him the transition could probably be made in the summer of 1946. Later, Army spokesmen tried to make the best of this situation by lamely explaining that "late winter" meant the last day of that season: March 20, 1946. But for the GI, whose hopes had been buoyed by Marshall's *faux pas,* winter probably ended in December, 1945.

The War Department's second announcement, on January 4, 1946, informing servicemen that the demobilization rate would be slackened, came as a bruising blow to the burgeoning hopes of servicemen.[86] Because they had been reducing the armed forces at an incredible and increasing rate during the latter half of 1945, military leaders had to "slow down" in 1946. Since there were less servicemen abroad, and replacing those still there performing essential tasks required extra time, the demobilization rate quite naturally declined. The so-called slow down announcement, coming in the wake of Marshall's promise concerning the transition from the point system to a duration of service policy, set the stage for the third and most dramatic aspect of the War Department's public relations.

Secretary of War Robert P. Patterson,[87] embarking on an official trip to the Far East, fanned smouldering GI discontent into flames

---

[84] "The GI Revolt," *The Commonweal,* XLIII (January 25, 1946), 372. Servicemen had demonstrated earlier than January 1946, as in Manila on Christmas Day 1945, when an officer reportedly informed the 4,000 discontented soldiers: "You men forget you're not working for General Motors. You're still in the Army." *The Stars and Stripes,* Middle Pacific edition, I (December 26, 1945), 1.

[85] Marshall made the statement while testifying before Congress. See Sparrow, *Personnel Demobilization,* pp. 234–35, for a discussion of the background of the announcement.

[86] *Ibid.,* p. 320.

[87] He succeeded Henry L. Stimson, who resigned September 21, 1945.

when he allegedly said that soldiers had been accumulating points past V-J Day.[88] The GIs despaired.[89] Did an incompetent control their destiny? Many thought so; despair turned to unalloyed anger. Countless letters and telegrams flooded the War Department, Congress, and the White House—all vilifying Patterson. One message to the President from the Philippines summed up the reaction: "The only action I deem for this member of your Cabinet is to kick him out of office by the seat of his pants." [90]

Indignant servicemen did more than write critical letters. At Guam, soldiers burned Secretary Patterson in effigy, threatened a hunger strike, and, at a meeting held by authorities to explain policy, booed the commanding General off the stage.[91] In Yokohama, an irritated provost marshal, breaking up what he called a "near mutiny," allegedly told the unruly GIs that they were "acting like a lot of goddamn babies." [92] During the tumultuous early days of January, servicemen staged demonstrations at Frankfurt; at Paris; at Hickam Field, Hawaii; at Seoul; at Calcutta; at London; and even in the United States at Andrews Air Base near Washington, D.C., at Wright Field, Dayton, Ohio, and at Fort Shafter, California.[93]

[88] Patterson denied that he did not know that point accumulation had ceased on V-J Day; but he did admit that it was possible that a reporter could have misinterpreted his remarks.

[89] "If the Secretary of War doesn't know the facts, how can we ever hope to find out what is going on?" *The Deadeye Dispatch* (the 96th Division's newspaper), V (January 5, 1946), 1.

[90] T/S Louis Schley and 5 others to Truman, January 5, 1946; OF 25-Misc., Truman Papers, HSTL. One bit of doggerel advised:

> Shed a tear for RP
> We all know he ain't no sharpy
> He don't know the present score
> The why or the wherefore
> We think its so much malarky.

Three enlisted men stationed at Salzburg, Austria, to Truman, January 13, 1946; *ibid.*

[91] Sparrow, *Personnel Demobilization,* p, 163; *The Stars and Stripes,* Southern Germany edition, II (January 10, 1946), 1; and O. F. Beasley (enclosing a letter from his son stationed on Guam, dated January 9, 1946) to Representative George B. Schwabe (D-Okla.), January 17, 1946; Legislative Correspondence File, 79th Congress, "Legislation—Servicemen" Folder, Schwabe Papers, University of Oklahoma.

[92] *The Stars and Stripes,* Southern Germany edition, II (January 10, 1946), 1.

[93] See telegrams from servicemen at those locations, January 6 to 13, 1946;

Soldiers at Manila outdid their buddies at other posts. On January 7, 1946, a crowd (variously estimated to be from 8,000 to 25,000 in number) massed to protest the demobilization "slow-down." Milling about before the city hall, the GIs bore placards reading: "Japs Go Home, How About Us?"; "Service Yes, But Serfdom Never"; and "Lincoln Freed the Slaves, Who Will Free Us?" In an "orderly though wildly enthusiastic" [94] manner, the troops exercised their democratic, if not military, right to gripe.[95] That these demonstrations proved, as *The New Republic* conjectured, that the servicemen were "fed up with an antiquated, undemocratic, unworkable system of caste and officer privilege," [96] may be questioned; but no one doubted that the GIs wanted to go home.

The War Department, upon learning of the break in discipline, chose not to label these outbursts as "mutinies." General Douglas MacArthur magnanimously reported that the discontent had been "primarily caused by acute homesickness aggravated by the termination of hostilities. These men are good men who have performed magnificently under campaign conditions and inherently are not challenging . . . authority." [97] No reprisals would be made, the Army told Congress; further high jinks, however, would not be allowed. After noting that demobilization would be speeded up, General Eisenhower observed: "There is no further useful purpose to be served by those mass meetings. I have told all commanders that the time for them is past." [98]

OF 190-R, Truman Papers, HSTL; *The Washington Post,* January 7 to 13, 194; and *Time,* XLVII (January 21, 1946), 21–22. By the third day of demonstrations in London, soldier interest had lagged so much that only six men showed for a meeting covered by ten reporters and seven military policemen. *The Washington Post,* January 13, 1946.

[94] *The New York Times,* January 8 and 11, 1946.

[95] See also "Eligible or Not, GI's Whoop It Up Against Slowdown in Getting Out," *Newsweek,* XXVII (January 21, 1946), 59–60; "Unrest of Veteran Troops," *The United States News,* XX (January 25, 1946), 19–21; and Senate, *Mead Committee Hearings,* 79th Cong., 2d Sess., January 13, 1946, Pt. XXXVI, 19917–21.

[96] "Why the GI's Demonstrate," *The New Republic,* CXIV (January 21, 1946), 73.

[97] Quoted in General Dwight D. Eisenhower's report to the President, issued as a press release, January 9, 1946; OF 190-R, Truman Papers, HSTL.

[98] Senate, *Army Demobilization Hearings,* January 17, 1946, Pt. III, 361.

THE CHIEF OF STAFF was right; the demonstrations had driven the soldier's message home. Their complaints would now be heeded. The President's cabinet made discharge policy the main topic of its meeting on January 11, 1946.[99] No less sensitive, General Eisenhower, still suffering from the traumatic experience of being trapped in a corridor by irate wives and mothers and then chased into Representative Andrew J. May's office, lost no time in ordering the return to the United States of high-point men and individuals with long service.[100] The order, providing that personnel with two or more years of service be in "pipe line" for discharge by June 30, 1946, finally signified the partial abandonment of the point system. After this capitulation, demobilization proceeded rapidly; pressure consequently became less extreme by the summer of 1946.

Perhaps "politics" explains this surrender to GI and public opinion. Practically without exception the servicemen in their public relations campaign indicated that, unless the Administration acted promptly, they would resort to political reprisals. As one punster wired from Osaka, Japan: "Give us our independence or go back to yours." [101] Another group cabled their Senator: "Thanks for Christmas in 29th Replacement mud hole. Waiting 20 days, no boats, no votes. 25 Returning Tennessians." [102] Admonishments such as "we shall never forget" underscored references to possible political retaliation.[103]

The other services followed suit; six marine non-coms stationed at Ewa Air Station, Hawaii, were broken to privates for circulating petitions criticizing the discharge policy. "Broken Leathernecks," *Newsweek,* XXVII (March 4, 1946), 34.

[99] Walter Millis, ed., *The Forrestal Diaries* (New York, 1951), p. 129. Cited hereafter as Millis, *Forrestal Diaries*

[100] For the General's uncomfortable experience, see "Bring Back Daddy," *Newsweek,* XXVII (February 4, 1946), 55–57. The War Department order may be found in Senate, *Army Demobilization Hearings,* January 17, 1946, Pt. III, 353–54.

[101] Sgt. Don Connor to Truman, January 9, 1946; OF 190-R, Truman Papers, HSTL.

[102] John Whiteside, *et al.* to Senator Kenneth McKellar (D-Tenn.), December 26, 1945; "Military—Misc." Folder, Box 315, McKellar Papers, Memphis Public Library.

[103] Members of the 331st Ordnance Company to Truman, January 10, 1946; OF 190-R, Truman Papers, HSTL. GIs adopted effective slogans to express their feelings. One eye-catching sticker, to be placed on envelopes, read:

No $\dfrac{\text{Boats}}{\text{Votes}}$

Few persons ignored the political side of demobilization. Shortly after V-J day, Representative Chet Holifield (D-Calif.) advised President Truman to act in order to prevent the Republicans from making political gains by "partisan charges." [104] Advisers reminded the Chief Executive that midterm elections were in the offing; and like Shelley's "Spring," the 1948 presidential campaign lagged not far behind. One agitated Congressman urged the President to appoint a "civilian demobilization czar" to handle the whole problem. The man to be appointed, however, "must not be a Democrat. He might fail; that would be fatal in 1946. This man must not be a Republican. He might succeed; that would be fatal in 1946." [105]

Yet the fears of the President's more nervous advisers did not materialize. This may be attributed, perhaps, to one inescapable fact: from a technical point of view demobilization succeeded magnificently. From a wartime strength of over twelve million in 1945, military leaders reduced the armed forces to a little over three million one year later—and by the summer of 1948 had lowered the figure to a postwar nadir of somewhat less than one-and-one-half million.[106] The Army alone underwent a net reduction of more than six million men—over two-thirds of its 1945 strength—in the first year of demobilization. The number of individuals demobilized from the Army in the one-year period July 1, 1945, to June 30, 1946, exceeded by 31 per cent the greatest number of persons mobilized during the war in any single year (Fiscal Year 1943).[107]

The conclusion that "never before had so many troops been moved so far and so fast" applies not only to the redeployment, but also to the demobilization of the armed forces.[108] The successful

[104] Holifield to Truman, September 25, 1945; *ibid.*

[105] Representative Daniel J. Flood (D-Pa.) to Matthew J. Connelly, September 27, 1945; *ibid.* The Congressman thought that Fiorello H. LaGuardia would fit the qualifications he had in mind. Nothing came of this proposal. As it happened, it is questionable whether demobilization policy played a major role in the 1946 elections; the Democrats already had enough "fatal" issues for that year.

[106] U.S. Bureau of the Census, *Historical Statistics of the United States, Colonial Times to 1957* (Washington, D.C., 1960), 736.

[107] Computed from figures in tables 15–17, and 19–22, U.S., Department of Defense, *Annual Report of the Secretary of the Army, 1948* (Washington, D.C., 1949), 303–305 and 307–312.

[108] Joseph Bykofsky and Harold Larson, *The Technical Services; The Trans-*

achievement of this stupendous task testified to the technical efficiency of the military commands. To be sure, they made mistakes; to expect otherwise would have been pure utopianism. Some caviled at the rigidity of the point system's operation. Others found fault with the lack of foresight on the part of the Administration in not anticipating the rapid collapse of the Japanese. But the important point remains as stated by Representative James W. Wadsworth in January, 1946: "I think when this thing is all over the historian will say that for speed and thoroughness this demobilization beats all records." [109]

AFTER AGREEING WITH Wadsworth, the historian has the less happy task of questioning the wisdom of demobilizing so efficiently. By disarming itself far too rapidly, the United States may have weakened its diplomatic negotiating bases.[110] With the Soviet Union's armies standing poised in Eastern Europe, the United States moved in reckless haste to disarm. This presented Joseph Stalin, a man who understood force, with a golden opportunity to ignore the pledges he made at Yalta and Potsdam to insure self-expression in the "liberated" areas east of what Winston S. Churchill dubbed the Iron Curtain.

There may be a simple answer to the question: why did it happen? Those who advised moderation had weak voices before the strident and nearly universal GI and public demands. General Eisenhower admitted: "I am frank to say that I had never anticipated this emotional wave [to get men out of the Army] would reach proportions of

portation Corps: Operations Overseas, Vol. IX of *The History of the United States Army in World War II* (Washington, D.C., 1957), 373.

[109] Wadsworth to Mrs. Clarence Graff, January 10, 1946; House of Representatives Files, "Demobilization" Folder, Wadsworth Papers, Library of Congress.

[110] See W. W. Rostow, *The United States in the World Arena* (New York, 1960), pp. 166, 172–73, 179, and 517. Some historians have disputed this view. Their arguments are too extensive for review at this point. Generally speaking, these "revisionist" historians cast the United States in the role of expansionist in the early Cold War years and the Soviet Union as being forced to react to that expansion. For a general sense of this viewpoint see William Appleman Williams, *The Tragedy of American Diplomacy* (rev. ed., New York: 1962), pp. 204–76.

near-hysteria." [111] As frequently happens, hysteria overcame all prudent counsel. Individuals in authority in Washington had dark forebodings about the rapid demobilization of the armed forces, yet only a few publicly voiced their dismay. Admiral Chester Nimitz, speaking amidst the din that followed the soldier demonstrations, told the nation:

After every war the United States has thoughtfully and deliberately done what no enemy could do, and that is reduce its Navy almost to impotency. . . . At the present moment [January 10, 1946], less than five months after the defeat of Japan, your Navy has not the strength in ships and personnel to carry on a major military operation.[112]

But no one listened.

All during the autumn of 1945, with the Soviet Union growing increasingly intransigent and demonstrating expansionist tendencies, officials held worried meetings.[113] The Secretaries of State and War, James F. Byrnes and Robert P. Patterson, viewed the crumbling American military capacity with mounting concern during the periodic State-War-Navy meetings.[114] The President, of course, shared their worries. He confided to one Congressman:

Now the settlement of the results of the [two world wars] is not in any sense of the word near completion—the only language those people understand is the language of force. At the rate we are demobilizing troops, in a very short time we will have no means with which to enforce our demands—a just and fair peace—and unless we have that means we are heading directly for a third world war.[115]

Yet in face of this danger and despite limited attempts to educate the American public, the "disintegration" [116] of the armed forces

[111] Statement made January 15, 1946; reprinted in Senate, *Army Demobilization Hearings,* January 17, 1946, 340.

[112] "Bluejacket Ranks Thin So Fast New Ships Couldn't Fight a War," *Newsweek,* XXVII (March 4, 1946), 30.

[113] The cabinet discussed demobilization rates at meetings held on August 31, October 5, and November 2, 1945, in addition to the January 11, 1946, session referred to above. See "Cabinet Folder 1945," Schwellenbach General Subject File, Records of the Department of Labor, Record Group 174, NA.

[114] Millis, *Forrestal Diaries,* pp. 102, 107, and 110.

[115] Truman to Representative John M. Folger (D-N.C.), November 16, 1945; OF 190-R, Truman Papers, HSTL.

[116] As President Truman has characterized demobilization. Truman, *Memoirs,* I, 509.

continued unchecked. As a result, the United States by 1947 found itself, as one air force officer had predicted earlier, "right behind the 8 ball." [117]

Who was responsible? President Truman later castigated the press and Congress for opposing the moderate rate of demobilization that he and his advisers thought necessary.[118] No doubt the President was partly correct. As one Congressman wrote at the time: "There is no question but what pressure from Congress has resulted in a complete revision of the demobilization program." [119] Among other forms of persuasion the Congressional threat to cut military appropriations for personnel (thereby forcing the Army and Navy to quicken demobilization) could hardly be ignored.[120] Yet, the Administration did have supporters on Capitol Hill; Congress did not pass legislation to force a more rapid release rate.[121]

The Secretary of the Navy, James V. Forrestal, assigned responsibility, in part, to left-wing groups.[122] Others agreed with him. Paul V. McNutt, American High Commissioner to the Philippines, reported the presence of "considerable communistic influence" in the leadership of the Manila disorders.[123] One Congressman thought

[117] Brigadier General W. E. Hall; House, *Army Demobilization Hearings,* October 8, 1945, 105. The impact of rapid demobilization on the effectiveness of a particular Army division is recounted by Major General Frank A. Keating in "Redeployment Jitters," *The Infantry Journal,* LIX (Sepetmber, 1946), 38–40. For the effect of demobilization on the Navy's ability to hold peacetime maneuvers, see Millis, *Forrestal Diaries,* p. 196.

[118] Truman, *Memoirs,* II, 345. On the other hand, a careful military historian has concluded that "the majority of the objective newspapers . . . were farther ahead than any other group" in support of the President's program. Sparrow, *Personnel Demobilization,* p. 296.

[119] Clifford R. Hope to Lloyd Benefiel, October 12, 1945; "Veterans-Legislative (79th Cong.)" Folder, Hope Papers, Kansas State Historical Society.

[120] See Representative John Taber's remarks, *Cong. Rec.,* 79:1 (October 19, 1945), 9831.

[121] Congress did go so far as to tack a policy statement on the War Mobilization and Reconversion Act, approved Oct. 3, 1944: "The War and Navy Departments shall not retain persons in the Armed forces for the purpose of preventing unemployment or awaiting opportunities for employment." 58 *Stat.* 787.

[122] Arnold A. Rogow, *James Forrestal: A Study of Personality, Politics, and Policy* (New York, 1963), pp. 126 and 128.

[123] House of Representatives, 80th Cong., 1st Sess., *House Document No. 389,* "Seventh and Final Report of the High Commissioner to the Philippines" (Washington, D.C., 1947), 58.

that "leftwingers" who formed "Mothers and Sweethearts Clubs" to help generate pressure for the return of the troops had been influential.[124] A union official observed that "the most rabid in the C.I.O. [for rapid return of troops] . . . , the most articulate, were the Communist sympathizers." [125] These observers, of course, were right. Communists did want to "bring the boys back home." Party opposition to "American interference in Chinese internal affairs," for example, prompted a modest Times Square demonstration in December, 1945.[126]

Nevertheless, it is clear that the American communists were but one voice among many in the cacophonous roar of 1945 and early 1946.[127] Responsibility rests with the American people. As an attempt to avoid the mistakes of World War I, the adoption of the point system stands as a real accomplishment of democratic individualism. Passing this test, the nation then failed—because it was not yet ready—to meet the responsibilities of world power.

Rapid demobilization had other consequences. Men were brought back so fast that veterans' officials could hardly keep up with the pace. The Veterans Administration was overwhelmed with claims and inquiries—at the very time it was being modernized by General Omar N. Bradley. An acute housing shortage was made more severe by the sharp rise in veterans' demands for homes. The nation's schools and colleges could not expand rapidly enough to meet the requests of ex-servicemen to study under the GI Bill of Rights. Finally, although the new Ulysses found jobs more numerous than had been predicted, many veterans probably were delayed in entering employment.

[124] Reminiscences of Representative Eugene J. Keough (D-N.Y.), 75; Oral History Project, Columbia University.
[125] Reminiscences of John Brophy, 943; *ibid.*
[126] *The New York Times,* December 9, 1945.
[127] Lee, "The Army Mutiny," 570.

7

THE WINNOWING FAN

BLOWING TRUMPETS and banging brasses met the new Ulysseses streaming back in 1945 and 1946 from distant hardships. In New York harbor, for example, as the first troopships to leave Europe after V-E Day hove into the Narrows, the Army's Welcome Home Boat Q-200 chugged out into the rain to meet the four big vessels. The Q-200 bore a twenty-eight piece all-female band led by Warrant Officer Marybelle Nissly; as the troopships moved toward berths on Staten Island, Q-200 bobbed along with them. The ladies serenaded the troops with such current tunes as "One Meatball" and "The Pennsylvania Polka." The GIs cheered lustily, particularly when a sharp breeze scattered the musical scores into the harbor. At other ports official welcomers at pierside blew kisses to the men jammed along the gunwales. Often the veterans could not debark fast enough. At Boston, a captain and a lieutenant, not content with airy gestures, leapt fifteen feet to the dock to collect a kiss. Chance indorsed rank: the captain won his embrace; the lieutenant broke his ankle. No matter, it was great to be home.[1]

But the euphoria of homecoming did not linger long. Old clothes, old friends—even relatives—no longer "fit." Other buddies who had gone off to war did not return, for "Troy was the end of many another man." Not all sweethearts or wives had resisted suitors'

[1] *The New York Times,* May 20, 1945; and *ibid.,* August 12, 1945.

blandishments as firmly as Penelope. Factories now blossomed where fields of loose strife once had beckoned vagrant youth. Former acquaintances who had escaped the martial call looked sleek and fat. And soon vivid stories of homefront sacrifices competed all too well with drab tales of guard duty at Sitka. Yes, it was great to be home —but Ithaca, Ulysses, Penelope, and Telemachus, all had changed.

One thing remained the same. As in ancient times, a man still needed to work for a living. In the *Odyssey,* Homer hints at the course of Ulysses' life after his return to Ithaca. The hero, it will be recalled, had to embark on another journey; this trip would take him far from the sea. So far, in fact, that inhabitants of that interior region would mistake Ulysses' ship's oar for a "winnowing fan," an implement used to separate the chaff from the wheat. When that occurred, Ulysses would have to plant his oar, make ceremonial offerings to Poseidon, king of the sea, and return home once again —presumably to enjoy his remaining years, "surrounded by a prosperous people."

Homer's parable may mean that Ulysses' stormy wanderings would continue until he had lost his martial identity. Clothed in battle dress, he could not settle with ease once again among his native Ithacans. To be sure, he could destroy the suitors and their relatives. He could be master by sheer force. But peace could not be his or Ithaca's until husbandry or agriculture succeeded war. The winnowing fan, not the nautical oar, would be the tool that would fashion the prosperity and happiness of Ulysses' declining years.

The new Ulysses, too, needed winnowing fans. That the returning GIs would need jobs—a simple, undeniable, and compelling fact— had dominated the thinking of the architects of the Federal Government's policy for veterans. Employment benefits had become the keystone in the arch designed to carry the returning soldiers and sailors from military to civilian life. Basic blueprints called for restoring men to old jobs, training others for new ones, and providing collateral services to tide still more over the transitional period. Naturally, the desire to repay in part the national debt to the veteran moved government planners to build a sturdy arch of benefits. Yet, building the bridge alone did not end the task; the road over the bridge had to lead to postwar prosperity. For, in a period of general unemployment, government guarantees to old jobs that no longer existed and elaborate training programs to give men unneeded skills would be a mockery. But planners feared the future road would meander; distress would precede stability. Hence, veterans' policy formulation (particularly within the executive branch) also was directed by the desire to make Ulysses' plight less grim as he traveled the road looking for a job.

From 1940 to 1946 an almost bewildering variety of employment benefits flowed from a bounteous nation to its heroes.[2] Some of the benefits shattered precedents, others were cast in familiar molds; yet all had been shaped, to repeat, by the hope that no veteran of World War II would walk the streets vending apples.[3] Government officials desired, in brief, to insure that the "winnowing fan" be as shapely as the "nautical oar" had been.

Parts of the winnowing fan already have been discussed: mustering-out pay, as a cash benefit to assist the veteran's wardrobe change from khakis and blues to mufti; legal rights to reinstatement to old jobs; job training for the able-bodied; loan guarantees for setting up new businesses and farms; special administrative arrangements to guide the new Ulysses through the bureaucratic maze; and finally, in the event all else failed, unemployment compensation payments during periods of enforced idleness.[4]

The remainder, outgrowths of programs developed for World War I doughboys and new responses, included: preference rights to Federal Government civil service positions; privileged access to public homestead lands for settlement; prior claims to surplus property for use in commercial and agricultural ventures; terminal leave payments, which augmented mustering-out pay; and finally, attempts to facilitate the process of job seeking for veterans.

[2] The term "employment benefits" is used in a broad sense: any benefit that had as its basic purpose the easing of the process of finding, training for, or maintaining a job.

[3] To cite a typical example: Lieutenant General Brehon Somervell, chief of the Army Service Forces, vowed in 1944 that " 'there aren't going to be any apple sellers on the street corners after this war if we can prevent it.' " Quoted in *The Washington Post*, April 22, 1944.

[4] See chs. ii through v above.

FEDERAL CIVIL SERVICE preference rights came easily for veterans, since this form of aid was deeply entrenched.[5] With veterans forming by 1944 approximately 15 per cent of the total civilian employment of the Federal Government, policymakers could hardly deny this privilege to the World War II veterans.[6] The shortage of labor to staff war agencies, moreover, gave an added indorsement to the move to attract veterans to government jobs. Almost 750,000 World War II veterans already had returned to civilian life by the end of 1944;[7] many of these men and women, it was thought, would be eager to embark on civil service careers.

In February, 1944, President Roosevelt told the heads of all federal departments and agencies to give preference to veterans referred to them by the Civil Service Commission. He asked also that these officials use the Civil Service Commission as their recruiting agent; this would, he believed; encourage the hiring of veterans.[8] At the same time, the President requested Congress to enact legislation to provide preference to returning servicemen:

It is impossible to take millions of our young men out of their normal pursuits for the purpose of fighting to preserve the Nation, and then expect them to resume their normal activities without having any special consideration shown them.[9]

Congress agreed with the President. Only the generosity of a House member, Charles N. LaFollette (R-Ind.) delayed legislative action. LaFollette believed that the Administration bill (drawn up

[5] See Samuel H. Ordway, Jr., "The Veteran in the Civil Service," *The Annals of the American Academy of Political and Social Science,* CCXXXVIII (March, 1945), 133–39.

[6] U.S., The President's Commission on Veterans' Pensions, *Veterans' Benefits Administered by Departments and Agencies of the Federal Government: Digests of Laws and Basic Statutes, Staff Report No. II* (Washington, D.C., 1946), Table 113, p. 328. Cited hereafter as President's Commission on Veterans' Pensions, *Staff Report II.*

[7] U.S., The President's Commission on Veterans' Pensions, *Readjustment Benefits: Education and Training, and Employment and Unemployment, Staff Report No. IX, Part B* (Washington, D.C., 1956), Table 2, p. 145. Cited hereafter as President's Commission on Veterans' Pensions, *Staff Report IX B.*

[8] Roosevelt to Harry B. Mitchell (U.S. Civil Service Commissioner), February 26, 1944; Official File 4675-J, Franklin D. Roosevelt Papers, Franklin D. Roosevelt Library, Hyde Park. Cited hereafter as Roosevelt Papers, FDRL.

[9] Roosevelt to Rep. Robert Ramspeck (D-Ga.), February 26, 1944; *ibid.*

by Representative Joe Starnes [D-Ala.] and officials of the American Legion, Veterans of Foreign Wars, Disabled American Veterans, and Civil Service Commission) was restrictive. He was particularly disturbed by one provision. The measure proposed to grant to wives of disabled veterans their husbands' preference rights to federal jobs. LaFollette wanted to give the same benefit to the husbands of disabled servicewomen. He explained: "I have heard it said, suppose a woman comes home and she marries some fellow, a bad fellow, and [*sic*] IV-F who did not serve in the war, and yet he would get preference." [10] Actually, LaFollette observed, the wife was the only one to be helped—no alternative existed. He went on:

Can we presuppose that every girl that a soldier marries necessarily on the home front makes any real contribution to the war effort? We know, as a matter of fact, that unfortunately some women who have married soldiers are little strumpets. I think most of the wives of these soldiers are grand. But, for us to object to whom a woman might marry is to presuppose that every girl that an ex-serviceman marries is a perfect woman and runs to the blood donor station every month and is tremendously interested.[11]

LaFollette's logic ran up against the nervous response of representatives of the veterans' organizations. Millard W. Rice, of the Disabled American Veterans, feared the possible ridicule that LaFollette's amendment would bring upon the whole bill.[12] George D. Riley, another veterans' representative, echoed Rice's anxiety. Already he could hear the snickering "on the side lines"; the bill, he said, was even then being called "a form of Government-paid alimony." Just this sort of thing could lead to another "whirlwind economy act." [13] The caution of the veterans' organizations prevailed; LaFollette's amendment failed.

With that diversion out of the way, Congress passed the sweeping

[10] U.S., Senate, Committee on Civil Service, 78th Cong., 2d Sess., *Hearings on S. 1762 and HR 4115 . . . Preference in Employment of Honorably Discharged Veterans Where Federal Funds Are Disbursed,* May 19, 1944 (Washington, D.C., 1944), 13.
[11] *Ibid.*
[12] Rice to Senator Sheridan Downey (D-Calif.), April 18, 1944; reprinted in *ibid.,* 35.
[13] *Ibid.* (May 23, 1944), 37.

measure.[14] All qualified veterans and wives of physically disabled veterans unable to perform the job's functions had their scores on competitive civil service examinations boosted five points for the nondisabled, and ten for the disabled. Unremarried widows of servicemen killed in action also received preference. Among other provisions, the law stated that the names of "five point" veterans would be placed ahead of all others with the same score on the civil service registers; the names of disabled veterans—"ten pointers"—would be placed at the top of the list for some positions regardless of examination score. This extra preference for the disabled did not apply, however, to professional and scientific positions in which the starting salary exceeded $3,000 per year. Since the statute required appointing officials to consider the top three eligible persons, as well as to explain in writing to the Civil Service Commission the reasons for passing over a veteran in favor of a nonveteran, it can be appreciated how extensively the preference worked. In fact, some positions (elevator operators, messengers, guards, and custodians) could be filled only by veterans during the war and for five years thereafter. Finally, once appointed to a position and having received a "good" rating, the veteran could not be laid off before any other nonveteran employee.[15]

The law completed veterans' preference policy for civil service; during the period 1944–1946, no major pressures from discontented organizations developed to liberalize this benefit. Of course, a few persons had objected to Congress' generosity and quick action. The editors of *The Washington Post,* for example, opposed the principle of veterans' preference. Before the law had passed, the newspaper's editors proclaimed that "it would be a national misfortune if, in our zeal to place veterans in congenial jobs, further liberalization of veterans' preferences were to be approved." [16] When their advice

[14] Public Law 359, 78:2, June 27, 1944. The vote in the House was 312 to 1, with 116 not voting. Only Howard W. Smith (D-Va.) opposed the bill; he did not explain why. The Senate passed the measure without debate.
[15] Harold D. Smith to M. C. Latta, June 26, 1944; "V79 (2) Veterans' Preference" Folder, Series 39.1, Legislative and Reference Division Files, Records of the Bureau of the Budget, Record Group 51, National Archives. Cited hereafter as Budget Records, RG 51, NA.
[16] June 8, 1944.

went unheeded, the editors poked fun at Congress. They queried: "Why not give veterans' preference benefits to former servicemen who might want to run for election in the national legislature?" They went on to observe:

The status of these men can only be debased by treating them as inferiors incapable of securing jobs through free competition with their fellow citizens. And the Government of the United States can only be debased if it selects its personnel on a basis of sentiment rather than merit.[17]

But voices of protest were lost as Congress and Administration hastened to remove any possible barrier to Ulysses' peacetime employment. They succeeded almost too well; by 1954, 49.5 per cent of all federal civilian employees were veterans—62.8 per cent of male employees had seen military service.[18]

LAND SETTLEMENT remained a persistent and attractive solution of what to do with the returning Ulysses. After each war this had been an important benefit for the homecoming hero.[19] Despite the traditional use of this bounty, however, government planners during World War II with few exceptions hardened their countenances to the bucolic image of happy homesteads peopled by yeomen veterans. The familiar and seemingly all-pervasive fear of postwar unemployment led some planners to warn nervously against "dumping" the industrial unemployed on vacant farm lands.[20] Other experts wished

[17] July 11, 1944. Another critic concluded two weeks later that veterans' preference did not seem to differ from the old spoils system; she claimed that "the man who rang doorbells the day before election may be as well qualified to sit behind a government desk as the man who practiced digging slit trenches in some Army encampment." Miriam Roher, "Veterans and the Civil Service," *The American Mercury,* LXII (December, 1946), 689.

[18] President's Commission on Veterans' Pensions, *Staff Report II,* Table 113, p. 328.

[19] See an interesting discussion of World War I land schemes, Bill G. Reid, "Proposals for Soldier Settlement during World War I," *Mid-America,* XLVI (July, 1964), 172–86; and for a more general account of settlements, U.S., Department of the Interior, *Government Aid to Land Acquisition of War Veterans, 1796–1944* (Washington, D.C., 1944).

[20] See U.S., National Resources Planning Board, *Demobilization and Readjustment* (Washington, D.C., 1943), 95; and testimony of Carl C. Taylor, an Agriculture Department official; U.S., Senate, Special Committee on Postwar Economic Policy and Planning, 78th Cong., 2d Sess., *Hearings . . . Part 3, The Problem of Unemployment and Reemployment After the War,* May 11, 1944 (Washington, D.C.), 684.

to impress the unwary that farm work was arduous; moreover, veterans needed to be reminded that they—as a class—often had been the object of unscrupulous land speculators.[21] Still others desired to prevent the establishment of all-veteran communities; they thought it more desirable to encourage the absorption of the veteran into society, rather than promote his isolation.[22] The fear that veterans might be enticed into an occupation that, for some, promised to be filled, animated other observers.[23] Concern ran high; in 1944, the Department of Agriculture decided to dampen unwarranted enthusiasm about agricultural opportunities by issuing a pamphlet entitled "Shall I Be a Farmer" for distribution to soldiers and sailors. The pamphlet stressed the rigor of farm life. In short, no back to the land movement could be expected nor would it be desirable.

Despite these convictions, the basic desire to provide preferential treatment to qualified veterans for access to public lands remained. An early law testified to this. On September 27, 1944, Congress granted World War II veterans benefits as homesteaders. The law authorized veterans to apply the time they spent in military service against the normal residential requirements under homestead legislation.[24]

Another outward manifestation, at least, of this concern to aid veterans came during that same year. In May, 1944, the House of Representatives was considering a bill involving the Central Valley reclamation project (CVP) in California. Representative Carl Elliott

[21] Seth B. Sims, Asst. to the Secretary of Agriculture, to Harry J. Johnson, February 9, 1944; "Economic 6–1 Post Defense, 1944" Folder, Office of the Secretary, Records of the Agriculture Department, National Archives.

[22] Charles Brannan to Harold D. Smith, August 11, 1944; "V80 (1) Veterans Preference—Soldier Settlement" Folder, Budget Records, RG 51, NA. See also General Frank T. Hines's testimony; U.S., House of Representatives, Special Committee on Post-War Economic Policy and Planning, 78th Cong., 2d Sess., *Hearings on Post-War Economic Policy and Planning*, Part. 2, May 18, 1944 (Washington, D.C., 1944), 309. Cited hereafter as *Colmer Committee Hearings*.

[23] See questions directed to, and testimony of, Claude Wickard, Secretary of Agriculture; U.S., House of Representatives, Committee on Expenditures in the Executive Department, 78th Cong., 2d Sess., *Hearings on . . . Disposal of Surplus Government Property and Plants*, August 8, 1944 (Washington, D.C., 1944), 116–18. Cited hereafter as House, *Manasco Committee Surplus Property Hearings, 78:2*.

[24] Public Law 434, 78th Cong., 2d Sess.

(D-Calif.) proposed an amendment that would exempt the project from the customary federal reclamation land limit of 160 acres per farming unit.[25] Apparently chances seemed good for the amendment's passage. Because of this, Harold L. Ickes, Secretary of the Interior, thought it was necessary to work quickly to frustrate Elliott's amendment. He had to "save" the CVP by conforming it to other reclamation projects.

Ickes hit upon the shrewd device of proposing, as a countermeasure, a plan whereby the "excess" land of the CVP would be made available to veterans on a preferential basis.[26] Ickes's brainstorm displeased his colleagues in the Bureau of the Budget, the Veterans Administration, and the Agriculture Department. F. J. Bailey, head of Budget Legislative and Reference Division, observed gloomily:

This is, to me, the kind of legislation that provides a hand-out for returning soldiers, which would cost the Government a lot of unreimbursable money and not do the soldier much good. We tried it on a reclamation project or two after the last war with dismal results. A good soldier does not become thereby a good farmer. And yet, I suppose there isn't much we can do to stop this surfeit of impractical benefits with which Congress seems prepared to smother our returning soldiers.[27]

Frank T. Hines disliked the bill because, among other things, it did not provide immediate benefits for veterans; the "pre-project" owners would not have to rid themselves of "excess" lands until at least four years after the war's end.[28]

Interior's main opponent, however, was the Agriculture Department. Acting Secretary of Agriculture Charles Brannan was distressed at the alleged aggrandizement of his Department's functions by Interior's Bureau of Reclamation.[29] The major point in contention

[25] Some Californians justified this amendment by noting that CVP had been superimposed on an already flourishing agricultural economy; thus it would be unfair to require "pre-project" owners to divest themselves of their "excess" lands.

[26] For details of the plan see H.R. 4947, 78:2, June 3, 1944; for reasoning behind it, see Abe Fortas to Harold D. Smith, May 22, 1944; "V80 (1) Veterans Preference-Soldier Settlement" Folder, Budget Records, RG 51, NA.

[27] Bailey to Messrs. Curran, Dodd, and Geoffrey May, May 23, 1944; *ibid.*

[28] Hines to Harold D. Smith, July 31, 1944; *ibid.*

[29] Brannan to Harold D. Smith, August 11, 1944; *ibid.*

involved Agriculture's insistence that Interior's responsibilities ended with the construction and maintenance of reclamation dams; Agriculture then selected settlers and established agricultural projects. Interior obviously thought the entire reclamation project, dam and all, belonged in its bailiwick.

At this point, with both the Veterans Administration and the Agriculture Department to back it up, the Budget Bureau informed Interior that veterans' preference for reclamation lands should be separated from the specific CVP measure; the two should stand on their respective merits.[30] Perhaps due to the division within the Executive Branch, Congress produced no legislation during the 78th Congress to grant preference to veterans for settlement on reclamation land. Ickes, however, refused to remain at rest. He obtained the support of President Roosevelt for his scheme to make reclamation land available to veterans. Ickes drafted a letter—designed for public consumption—for Roosevelt's signature that read, in part:

One of the things we must do is to make a place on the land for large numbers of returning servicemen, without whose protection many of us today might have been working as slaves upon rich farms that we now own and operate as free men.[31]

The President's general views apparently had little effect upon the Department of Agriculture. By January, 1945—with the beginning of the 79th Congress' first session—the rift between the Departments had widened. Conferences had failed; communication between the two threatened to break down on the issue.[32] The Secretary of Agriculture expressed pained surprise upon learning that Interior had proceeded to introduce legislation that contained provisions that still were in controversy.[33] The Interior Department, on the other hand, steadfastly maintained that it had given Agriculture ample opportunity to propose specific legislation as an alternative to Interior's

[30] Harold D. Smith to Harold L. Ickes, August 23, 1944; *ibid.*
[31] Roosevelt to Oliver S. Warden, President of the National Reclamation Association, November 11, 1944; President's Personal File 993, Roosevelt Papers, FDRL.
[32] See F. J. Bailey intraagency memorandum, February 23, 1945; "V80 (1) Veterans Preference-Soldier Settlement" Folder, Budget Records, RG 51, NA.
[33] Wickard to Harold D. Smith, April 4, 1945; *ibid.*

—to no avail. Meanwhile, according to Michael W. Straus, Assistant Secretary of the Interior, the House of Representatives' Committee on Irrigation and Reclamation would not tolerate further delay.[34] This jurisdictional question threatened to sidetrack veterans' preference to reclamation lands, with which, ironically, it had little to do. Even a Presidential appeal to Congress to pass Interior's controversial bill (H.R. 520) for veterans' preference failed.[35]

The situation, however, called for directives to the quarreling agencies, not to Congress. For, following President Roosevelt's death, the internecine battle continued. Agriculture worked behind the scenes in Congress to have H.R. 520 amended to bring it in line with their own views. They succeeded all too well, according to Ickes. Unconsciously demonstrating that Interior, like Agriculture, cared less for veterans' preference than for obtaining the responsibility of handling reclamation projects, Ickes made one last, desperate appeal for Administration support for his bill. He asked President Harry S Truman to instruct Agriculture officials that if they "feel that they cannot support the bill . . . at least [they should] do nothing, say nothing, or write nothing in opposition." [36]

But significantly, Congress failed to pass a general statute for all reclamation projects as originally envisioned by Ickes. The long administrative wrangle had made that impossible. Wrangle or no, neither issues of homestead nor reclamation lands affected many veterans. Yet the former benefit, limited as it was, formed a part of Ulysses' winnowing fan.

OF THE FOUR legislative portions of the reconversion program (war contract termination, surplus property disposal, creation of the Office of War Mobilization and Reconversion, and unemployment compensation), only the second contained specific provisions for veterans. For, among the myriad considerations that formed Congressional opinion in 1944 about how to dispose of surplus war property,

[34] Straus to Harold D. Smith, April 10, 1945; *ibid.*

[35] Roosevelt to Rep. John R. Murdock (D-Ariz.), April 10, 1945; Official File 402, Roosevelt Papers, FDRL.

[36] Ickes to Harold D. Smith, January 22, 1946; "V80 (1) Veterans Preference-Soldier Settlement" Folder, Budget Records, RG 51, NA.

the claims of exservicemen remained ever-present. On the most general level, all the legislators desired a surplus property program that would not interfere with employment opportunities for veterans. More specifically, some Congressmen believed that individual GIs should be permitted to buy single surplus items direct from Uncle Sam.[37]

The tangled legislative history of the Surplus Property Act of 1944 cannot be told here. Yet, the many concerns that pressed upon the minds of Congressmen during the debates over the original bill merit brief review. The very number of conflicting sentiments contributed to the difficulties experienced later as the program moved into operation. On one thing, however, the legislators agreed. The sorry experiences following World War I had to be averted. Those memories included visions of a depression caused, in part, by the untimely dumping of surplus war property with a consequent rise in business failures and a drop in job openings. Rather than releasing goods in large amounts in 1919 while the war-deferred consumer demands were at their zenith, the Government did not bring appreciable quantities onto the market until 1920—just in time to compete with industry.[38]

The more specific apprehensions of Congressmen in 1944 may be grouped into at least seven separate, sometimes related and overlapping, yet more often conflicting, categories.[39] First, some legislators believed that surplus war property should be sold rapidly at the highest cash return to the government. Do not give away surplus goods, proponents of the view argued, no matter how worthy the cause; the taxpayer must be protected, and favoritism barred. Dis-

[37] Public Law 457, 78th Cong., approved October 3, 1944. See Roland Young, *Congressional Politics in the Second World War* (New York, 1956), pp. 202–6, for an overall sketch of the legislative maneuvering. Allen Drury's *A Senate Journal, 1943–1945* (New York, 1963), pp. 246–54, contains interesting comments about both Senate and House debates. Cited hereafter as Drury, *Senate Journal*. For a good two-part summary of surplus property, see "Guidebook to Surplus Disposal," *Business Week*, May 26 and June 2, 1945, 43–75 and 43–70.
[38] A. D. H. Kaplan, "Liquidating War Production," in *Economic Reconstruction*, edited by Seymour E. Harris (1st ed. New York and London, 1945), pp. 139–40.
[39] These categories are based on House and Senate debates during August and September, 1944.

position of surplus property, in short, was a business function that must follow sound business principles. The preservation of American small business enterprise animated adherents of a second category. These men thought that monopolies (or large businesses, which sometimes were regarded as the same thing) should in no event be assisted. Surplus goods should be made available instead in small lots, with small purchasers given preference. They proposed to bar speculators by banning excessive markups. The war had helped the large businesses; reconversion should aid the small. Protection of American national interests formed a third area of apprehension. The argument took several forms; but it reflected a basic fear that improper disposition of surplus property might affect adversely the Nation—economically, or militarily. A fourth concern—that relationships within the economy would be upset—plagued some Congressmen. Specifically, they insisted that existing channels of trade should be used to distribute surplus goods. The government should refrain from setting up retail outlets to compete with established companies; in brief, Uncle Sam should not sell directly to individuals. A fifth consideration involved familiar district or local interests: schools should be given discounts on sale of surplus war goods; soil conservation projects should receive preference to surplus dirt-moving machinery; surplus food should not be dumped because of the adverse affect upon farm communities, and so forth. A sixth concern reflected current Congressional-Executive department tensions. A sizeable minority group feared that Congressional control over reconversion would be harmed by creation of a "dictatorial" single administrative head. A board would be more "democratic."

The seventh and last specific concern, over veterans, cropped up infrequently during debates on the Surplus Property bill in 1944. Only Representative William J. Miller (R-Conn.) spoke at length in an attempt to secure tangible rights for veterans. Miller desired to allow veterans to purchase goods directly from the government, perhaps through the Army's Post Exchanges. The House adopted his amendment designed to achieve this; but the House-Senate Conference, made necessary by the two chambers' different versions of the bill, discarded Miller's proviso. Instead of Miller's concrete suggestion, Congress merely stated that the Surplus Property Board should "aid veterans to establish their own small business, professional or agricultural enterprises, by affording veterans suitable preferences . . . in the acquisition of the type of surplus property useful in such enterprises."

Whatever the precise nature of the tugs and pushes that determined the outcome, the resultant Surplus Property Act granted veterans "preferential" rights to surplus property immediately following the "priority" claims of federal governmental agencies, states and local governments, and public nonprofit institutions supported by taxes. Veterans who needed surplus property for their farms or businesses thus stood fourth in line. Clearly, Congress had not written a veterans' benefit measure.

The law's twenty more-or-less diffuse objectives made it an ungainly creature.[40] Its shape led to charges later that it had been drawn hastily, implying that more sober consideration would have led to the elimination of the act's more awkward features.[41] In retrospect, it does not seem likely that more time would have resulted in a clearer bill. The Senate and House had held a combined total of eleven public hearings on it and previous plans during 1943–1944. The debate itself had been conducted at a reasonable pace; in fact, it had proceeded beyond the limits set by the bill's managers.[42] Indeed, time may well have contributed to the bill's deformities—each day seemed to bring a new purpose that had to be met by tacking another objective onto the bill.

Confusion in surplus property disposal objectives extended beyond the confines of the Capitol. The Executive Department also had its divisions. Secretary of the Interior Ickes, for example, foresaw a new generation of speculators patterned after "the inspired looters of the past"; he feared repetition of the mistakes of World War I.[43] Ickes presented an unorthodox plan in April, 1944. He

[40] See Young, *Congressional Politics,* pp. 202–203.
[41] See extension of Representative Carl T. Curtis's (R-Neb.) remarks in U.S., *Congressional Record,* 79:2 (February 7, 1946), A-627; and Blair Bolles, *How to Get Rich in Washington* (New York, 1952), pp. 80–81.
[42] Drury, *Senate Journal,* p. 521.
[43] Ickes to Carter Manasco, August 10, 1944; reprinted in Senate, Committee

suggested that government-owned war plants be turned over to veterans after the war. The Federal Government could, he thought, set up a corporation with the plants as its assets. The veterans would receive stockholder shares in the corporation; what the government built and owned, he reasoned, should remain in the hands of the people.[44]

The plan met almost universal obloquy. *The Washington Post* editors proclaimed that "the whole plan is obviously fantastic." [45] The Hearst press writers flagellated Ickes for his "gold brick . . . bonus" to veterans. One Hearst editorial asserted: Ickes, a leader of the "bonehead school of New Deal economics," had proposed "a diabolic scheme for leading worthy war veterans to their economic slaughter. . . . [They] would be crucified by the Ickes formula on a cross of demagogy. . . . Let us hope that the screwball thinkers will soon be eliminated from the national scene." [46] Although some believed Ickes's plan merited calmer examination, it could not make headway against orthodoxy.[47]

Orthodoxy in 1944 within the Executive Department rested in the person of Will Clayton, who, before the Surplus Property Act had passed, had been appointed by President Roosevelt in 1944 in response to the Baruch-Hancock reconversion report's recommendations. Clayton reputedly was the nation's most successful cotton broker. He enjoyed the wide admiration of the business community and of a large number of Congressmen. Allen Drury has given a good thumbnail sketch: "Will Clayton is a big, tall, well-built Texan in his 60s, with gray hair, a handsome, rather rugged face, and the smoothest manner imaginable when it comes to handling recalcitrant committees." [48] Clayton wanted a statute that would give him—or

on Military Affairs, Subcommittee on War Contracts, 78th Cong., 2d Sess., *Hearings on . . . Mobilization and Demobilization Problems* (Washington, D.C., 1944), Part 13, 942–3. Cited hereafter as *Murray Subcommittee Hearings.*

[44] *The Washington Post,* April 15, 1944.
[45] *Ibid.,* April 16, 1944.
[46] *The New York Journal American,* May 1, 1944.
[47] "A Stake in the Future," *The Christian Century,* LXI (May 10, 1944), 582–83; and Max Lerner (writing on April 29, 1944), in *Public Journal: Marginal Notes on Wartime America* (New York, 1945), pp. 366–69.
[48] *Senate Journal,* p. 247.

his successors—room for meeting unexpected situations. He opposed including statutory preference requirements. He argued: "Now, I want to say I just do not yield to anybody in a feeling of responsibility . . . to these returning veterans. I have that feeling very deeply"; yet to write that feeling into law would create enormous administrative difficulties.[49] Not even the Smaller War Plants Corporation's monitory slogan ("LITTLES MUST BE PROTECTED, OR THE BIGS AND SPECULATORS WILL MUSCLE IN AND GET IT ALL")[50] affected Clayton. His leadership in drafting the legislation that appeared as the House bill presented the Administration's position clearly. The measure that emerged, however, strayed far from Clayton's expectations; he resigned while the bill was in conference.[51]

The bill's administrative provisions also made Harold D. Smith, the Director of the Bureau of the Budget, unhappy. Smith, while commenting later on the Office of War Mobilization and Reconversion (OWMR) bill, grumbled about the surplus property bill as well:

It is with reluctance that I recommend approval because I feel that this [OWMR bill] and the surplus property bill represent about the worst legislation from the point of view of policy and administration that I have ever seen. Both will plague us for a long time.[52]

Smith's gloomy premonition stemmed from the awkward three-member Surplus Property Board set up by the act. The board, according to Congressional theory, would set the policies which the disposal agencies would follow.[53]

[49] House, *Manasco Committee Surplus Property Hearings, 78:2* (August 8, 1944), 52; and Senate, *Murray Subcommittee Hearings,* Part 15 (August 16, 1944), 1042.
[50] House, *Colmer Committee Hearings, 78:2,* Part 3 (June 13, 1944), 540.
[51] Bernard Baruch shared Clayton's distaste for the Surplus Property bill. He told Sen. Edwin C. Johnson (D-Colo.) that the proposed board was "hydraheaded, spineless." Baruch to Johnson, August 8, 1945; Correspondence "Johnson" 1945, Baruch Papers, Princeton University Library.
[52] Smith's notation to Roosevelt on Smith to F. C. Latta, September 21, 1944; "D44 Demobilization and Reconversion—General #1" Folder, Budget Records, RG 51, NA.
[53] There were many changes in the program, but by the time of the statute's passage in October, 1944, seven agencies were disposing of surplus goods: Procurement Division of the Treasury Department (consumer goods), Reconstruction Finance Corporation (capital and producer goods), War Food Admin-

Smith's foreboding proved to be accurate. The troika, pulled by men who were not appointed until after New Year's 1945, just did not move.[54] The board's chairman, Guy M. Gillette, remained only until the summer.[55] President Truman then asked W. Stuart Symington—head of Emerson Electric Manufacturing Company of St. Louis —to fill the vacancy. Truman told Symington (according to the latter's doting campaign biographer): " 'I'm going to drop a load of coal on you.' " [56] It was only a slight exaggeration. For, although Symington succeeded in persuading Congress to eliminate the troika and set up a one-man administration, that was about all he was able to do.[57]

Symington took the oath of office on October 1, 1945, as the sole head of the Surplus Property Administration. From that point forward his efforts were dogged with failure to solve the veterans' preference question. Since the preceding May, veterans as business men had been permitted to use the Smaller War Plants Corporation (SWPC) as their purchasing agent. This in effect gave the veteran a priority equal to that of federal agencies. The veteran's enthusiasm was dimmed, however, by the facts that regulations limited him to $2,500 worth of goods and, more significantly, that the SWPC acted as purchasing agent for nonveteran small businessmen as well.[58]

---

istration (food), Maritime Commission (ships), Foreign Economic Administration (all surplus in foreign countries), National Housing Agency (housing) and Federal Works Agency (community facilities financed by FWA and all nonindustrial real property other than that handled by RFC or NHA).

[54] Roosevelt appointed Guy M. Gillette who had been defeated in his bid for reelection to the Senate in 1944, Edward H. Heller, and Robert A. Hurley. James F. Byrnes had wanted David Lilienthal of TVA as chairman, but FDR disappointed him. See Byrnes, *All in One Lifetime* (New York, 1958), pp. 240–41. Ironically, Gillette had been a prime object of Roosevelt's ill-fated "purge" of 1938.

[55] *Business Week* reported that Gillette quit because he was "scared of the job." *Ibid.*, June 9, 1945, 5.

[56] Paul I. Wellman, *Stuart Symington* (Garden City, N.Y., 1960), p. 116.

[57] See *ibid.*, p. 128, for an unusually bald account of Symington's tenure: "A few months of continuous effort, and the big job was done."

[58] For a discussion of the veteran's preference, see Symington's testimony in U.S., Senate, Committee on Military Affairs, Subcommittee on Surplus Property, 79th Cong., 1st Sess., *Hearings . . . on Veterans' Priority for Surplus Property*, December 12, 1945 (Washington, D.C., 1946), 5–6. Cited hereafter as Senate, *O'Mahoney Subcommittee Surplus Property Hearings.*

Thus, to choose a hypothetical example, a veteran who desired to buy a surplus refrigeration unit for his butcher shop had three options. He could request the SWPC, acting as his agent and enjoying a top priority status as a federal agency, to buy the unit for him. If the loss of control over his own purchasing disturbed the butcher, he could ask the SWPC to certify him as a veteran with a bona fide small business; in that case he would then be able to buy any refrigeration machinery remaining after federal agencies, state and local governments, and public nonprofit institutions supported by taxes had exercised their prior claims. If the number of forms and delays involved in the SWPC certification process seemed too formidable for the butcher, he could say the hell with it, and take his chances along with his fellow citizens, claiming neither priority nor preference.

By December, 1945, the harassed Surplus Property Administrator wanted to scrap the provision that only veterans with business interests be given privileged access to surplus goods. He also hoped that a plan could be devised whereby the Veterans Administration (VA) would certify the veteran and give him coupons. The veterans could then use these coupons as scrip to buy surplus goods at wholesale houses. Obviously, Symington believed that the Government had to permit wholesalers (with their perfected marketing devices) to buy large lots of surplus goods.[59]

Symington's plan died a-borning. The Veterans Administration viewed it suspiciously. It seemed to Edward E. Odom, the VA's solicitor, that the VA's image might be affected adversely by becoming involved with this white elephant. Odom asked: "What are the repercussions going to be to us when those fellows find the coupons are not worth anything?" [60] No one had to answer that. Everyone— Symington, the VA, the Budget Bureau, Congress—wanted to get rid of the beast.

Things were destined to become worse before they improved. Indeed, the days prior to the massive demobilization of men in the winter of 1945–1946 seemed halcyon in contrast to those that fol-

[59] *Ibid.*, 19–27.
[60] *Ibid.*, 53.

lowed. For, as veterans came back by the hundreds of thousands, they all seemed to want a car, a jeep, or a truck. Their desires appeared to be exceeded only by their impatience. The war was over; the Army had millions of unneeded vehicles; why not let the former servicemen jump right into the drivers' seats?

Cold reality, however, met hot desire. Government officials had the unhappy duty to explain that only veterans with small businesses or farms could obtain the veterans' preference. This, of course, had been no secret; but secret or not, many GIs saw little reason for the distinction. They tended to view surplus property disposal as a veterans' benefit, not as a general reconversion measure. This misunderstanding contributed to the increasing ill repute of the whole program.

Still another misunderstanding can be traced to the early days of surplus property disposal. John M. Hancock had told the House's Special Committee on Post-War Economic Policy and Planning: "I think you are going to have so much material of the kind you are talking about [consumer goods for farmers and veterans] that nobody need worry about getting priorities." [61] Hancock was irrepressible: "There will be plenty for all." [62] As late as June, 1945, Charles Hurd, *The New York Times*'s expert on veterans' benefits,[63] quoted the Surplus Property Board:

The demobilization of men and material will be concurrent and ample surpluses of all kinds are expected to be on hand to fulfill the needs of all veterans as they return to civilian life.[64]

It would be difficult to imagine more injudicious statements. As a matter of fact, by October, 1945, 7,500 passenger automobile requests had been filed with the New York regional SWPC office; less than 50 vehicles had been declared surplus.[65] In February, 1946,

[61] House, *Colmer Committee Hearings, 78:2,* Part 1 (March 16, 1944), 40.

[62] *Ibid.,* 41. He said the same thing a week later. U.S., House of Representatives, Committee on Banking and Currency, 78th Cong., 2d Sess., *Hearings on . . . a Bill to amend the Reconstruction Finance Corporation Act . . . ,* March 22, 1944 (Washington, D.C., 1944), 220.

[63] Hurd later wrote a handy and authoritative book, *The Veterans' Program: A Complete Guide to its Benefits and Options* (New York and London, 1946).

[64] *The New York Times,* June 24, 1945.

[65] *Ibid.,* October 12, 1945.

a disposal official estimated that over 500,000 requests had been filed nationally for cars; he believed that only 11,000 more cars would be forthcoming from military sources.[66] Despite the enormous amounts of surplus goods, many items, such as vehicles, cameras, dental and medical supplies, and electronic equipment, were in short supply. Unfortunately, the early ill-considered statements, once issued, proved difficult to retract. As a result, when government officials trooped to witness stands to answer irate Congressmen during 1946, they had to emphasize invariably that the demand for some items far exceeded the supply.

The sheer magnitude of the job indicates another reason for the difficulties experienced in surplus property disposal. Lieutenant General Edmund B. Gregory, Chairman of the War Assets Administration (the Surplus Property Board's ultimate successor), reported that up to August, 1945, $1,420 millions worth (based on initial cost to government) of property had been declared surplus by government agencies. During September, 1945, another $828 millions were added; October's accretion exceeded the entire amount accumulated through August, 1945, by $234 millions. At least $1,000 millions were added for each of the succeeding months during fall and winter 1945–1946.[67] The armed forces, under public pressure, dumped their surpluses into the hands of overworked disposal officials. Here was the load of coal.

The job of sifting, identifying, labeling, pricing, posting records, and advertising this mountain of material was arduous. It had been made more difficult, moreover, by differences in record-keeping. When soldiers on the line needed screwdrivers, for example, they did not care about the tool's description; Army records usually identified items only by numbers. Yet the disposal agency needed more than a number to sell the surplus. As a result, almost every piece of equipment had to have its military jargon translated into

[66] House, *Manasco Committee Hearings, 79:2* (February 14, 1946), 14.
[67] U.S., House of Representatives, Committee on Appropriations, Subcommittee on Deficiency Appropriations, 79th Cong., 2d Sess., *Hearings on Third Deficiency Appropriation Bill for 1946,* June 18, 1946 (Washington, D.C., 1946), 528.

sales jargon.[68] That was not all. How much could you ask a buyer to pay for a used screwdriver? Or a gas-driven refrigeration unit? Or 50,000 tank grousers? Or a ten-wheeled truck? Or a roll of concertina wire, wound under tension, and designed for prison camp use? Experts in Washington set many of the prices; but their expertise did not always insure accuracy. One item, for example, described as an eight-inch auger, was priced at twenty-three cents by experts who thought the dimension referred to the length of the tool's shank. It turned out that the eight inches referred to the diameter of the hole which the auger could drill; the error amounted to twelve dollars and twenty-seven cents per auger.[69]

It took time to declare an item surplus and ready it for sale. Under favorable conditions the process required one to two months. Many people could not understand why it often took longer. Representative Alfred J. Elliott, for one, told of his difficulties with the War Assets Administration in attempting to procure a building for a local municipality's use:

That thing has been passed back and forth so far that every time I get another letter on it I just get so I start to run my hands through my hair. I will be barking like a dog in another week on that one building.[70]

In any circumstance the sale of public property generates suspicions. The disposal of surplus war goods, of course, did not escape unscathed in this regard. Some of the dark thoughts about the program probably had partisan origins; a Republican Congressman from Missouri, Marion T. Bennett, observed that "the surplus property deal is being handled in a typical New Deal fashion with plenty of graft, corruption, special privilege and bungling." [71] Other suspicions had been aroused by circumstantial evidence. Senator Kenneth C. Wherry (R-Neb.), like others, got hot around the collar be-

[68] See statement of Kenneth C. Royall, Asst. Secy. of War; U.S., House, *Manasco Committee Hearings, 79:2* (February 21, 1946), 193.

[69] U.S., House of Representatives, Select Committee to Investigate Disposition of Surplus Property, 79th Cong., 2d Sess., *Hearings . . .* Part 1, July 15, 1946 (Washington, D.C., 1946), 76.

[70] *Ibid.*, 74.

[71] Bennett to George P. Maris, November 17, 1945; Folder 1308, Surplus Property File, Bennett Papers, Univ. of Missouri.

cause some surplus trucks wound up for sale at Gimbels department store in New York City, rather than distributed to dairy farmers in Nebraska. The vehicles actually were uneconomical to operate; Gimbels had difficulty selling them. Wherry obviously had charged rashly into print.[72]

The major source of questions about surplus property came, however, from veterans. Many simply refused to believe statements made by disposal officials. A persistent skepticism concerned overseas surplus property. Veterans returning from the Pacific insisted that they had seen acres of trucks, mountains of lumber, tons of steel, and row upon endless row of airplanes. Tropical sun and rain, salt spray, teredo worms, and the ever-encroaching, creeping jungle—all worked to help eat away valuable property. Why did the Army and Navy abandon these things that could be brought back to the States in empty vessels?

Many veterans could accept philosophically the "dust into dust" process of Nature; they could not remain silent about what they termed wanton destruction of good property by military officials. Servicemen bombarded their Congressmen with tales of trucks pushed off cliffs, of bulldozers crushing planes, of lumber going up in bonfires, of power shovels burying tons of corrugated metal, of carbines being dumped into pits, and of clothes, blankets, ropes, and canvas put to the torch. Servicemen brought back more than memories; some even had taken pictures—a notable one showing a Navy vehicle stranded in a lagoon as the tide came in.

Congress proved to be a perfect sounding board for these and other complaints. Members could be as wrathful as any soldier or sailor. Senator Alexander Wiley (R-Wisc.) thundered:

It is my belief . . . that WAA's administration of this program is a national disgrace and is crying to high heaven for full exposure in the broad daylight and . . . a worse scandal than Teapot Dome is involved in WAA's flagrant violation of the law with respect to priorities for veterans.[73]

---

[72] See U.S., Senate, Special Committee Investigating the National Defense Program, 79th Cong., 2d Sess., *Hearings . . . Part 33*, May 14 and 15, 1946 (Washington, D.C., 1946), 17131–210 for details of the Gimbels truck sale.
[73] Senate, *Stewart Sub-Committee Hearings, Part 97*, June 18, 1946, 10860–1.

More to the point, Representative Clare E. Hoffman (R-Mich.) summed up the main problem for Congressmen:

You see . . . here is our trouble. We got on the hot spot about this thing. These boys come back . . . in the district, and the old folks write us. I can never make the old man believe that his kid is lying about this thing; and I can't make the kid believe it, because he saw the thing. What am I to do? I am running for re-election.[74]

Government officials attempted to answer the charges hurled at them. They argued that Congress had decreed that goods be sold at highest reasonable prices, according to a complicated sales priority schedule. These conditions made a difficult task more burdensome. Military officers pointed out, somewhat meekly, that one reason so much overseas property had been abandoned or destroyed was that rapid demobilization stripped the Army and Navy of the men needed to handle the goods. The force of this argument, however, was vitiated by the disclosure that prior to February, 1946, neither the Army nor Navy had attempted even to return surplus goods to the United States, other than to fill their own needs.[75]

Veterans demanded that Congressmen do more than hold hearings —although the latter did a creditable job on that score, conducting seven open committee inquiries after the act had been passed until its amendment in 1946. The Veterans of Foreign Wars (VFW), the American Legion, American Veterans of World War II (AmVets), and Disabled Veterans of America all demanded that something be done. The organizations vied with one another for Congress' attention. The Legion demonstrated again the effectiveness of its dispersed organization. Legionnaires from Punxsutawney, Pa., Indian Orchard, Mass., and Alliance, Nebraska, repeated the charge summed up later by their National Commander, John Stelle, that the surplus property program had collapsed.[76] The AmVets of Massachusetts insisted that the Government sell directly to veterans.[77] The VFW

[74] House, *Manasco Committee Hearings,* February 21, 1946, 215.
[75] *Ibid.,* 100, 189–90.
[76] *Cong. Rec.,* 79:2, Appendix (January 22 and 23, 1946), A 160–1, A 175 and A 184. Stelle's open letter to Congressmen is reprinted in *ibid.* (March 28 and 29, 1946) at three places: A 1735, A 1756, and A 1777.
[77] *Ibid.,* (February 4, 1946), A 477–8.

urged that Congress give veterans priority second only to federal agencies, and permit them to use that priority for personal as well as for business purposes.[78]

The pressures exerted by the veterans' groups received added weight from an unexpected source—the War Assets Administration (WAA)—at the beginning of April, 1946. The WAA had advertised that scarce photographic equipment would be sold in Baltimore. Word spread wide; veterans came from New England, Atlanta, Pittsburgh, and Los Angeles. Some journeyed all night, arriving early in the morning to join the waiting crowd of fellow veterans. Expectancy charged the air; some grumbling could be heard when it was rumored that the keys to the door had been mislaid. Soon, however, the doors were opened; the veterans rushed in, eager to share in the bonanza. What did they find? Almost nothing of value. All the prime items had been gobbled up by higher priority groups during an earlier portion of the sale. Some items remained: "Look, here's the locknut off a Mitchell movie camera. The eye piece from a Speed Graphic. . . ." [79] And who had been these privileged buyers? Federal agencies, of course; but the rest of the list of purchasers made veterans snort with disgust. The Young Men's Christian Association, the Boy Scouts of America, the Maine Seacoast Missionary Society, and the Board of Foreign Missions of the Presbyterian Churches had been reported as among the privileged buyers.[80] Worthy institutions all; yet they preempted veterans—leading early birds among the latter to greet latecomers with: "Hello Sucker! How far did you come?"

The Baltimore nonsale dramatized the veterans' grievances. War Assets officials had erred seriously by improperly advertising the sale. A better procedure by far (given the restrictions of the original statute) would have been to announce the sale for top priority groups; hold that portion of the sale—and then send out circulars to veterans based on new inventories taken after the priority groups

[78] See testimony of VFW representative before Senate, *O'Mahoney Subcommittee Surplus Property Hearings, 79:1* (December 14, 1945).

[79] Marvin Richmond, one of the disgruntled veterans, in the *Worcester Telegram*, reprinted in *Cong. Rec.*, 79:2 (April 17, 1946), A 2250.

[80] *The Washington Post*, April 3, 1946.

had combed through the surplus. Although a slower technique, it might have prevented the hopes of veterans from soaring to stratospheric heights, only to be deflated so sharply when the cupboard was found bare. The long treks veterans frequently had to take irritated them also. False promises, arduous travel, WAA incompetence, and worthless goods seemed to veterans their only rewards.

When news about the Baltimore fiasco broke, Senators rose to vow unceasing vigor in procuring justice for veterans. Senators Carl Hatch (D-N.Mex.), Robert La Follette (Prog.-Wisc.), and Burnet Maybank (D-S.C.) led the outcry.[81] That, apparently, was all that was needed. With scant debate, both House and Senate rushed through a bill giving veterans priority second only to federal agencies. The bill also permitted the War Assets Administrator to "set aside" select goods for exclusive use by veterans. Moreover, veterans could now purchase items for their personal use.

These new principles did not please some government officials. John Snyder, Chief of the Office of War Mobilization and Reconversion (OWMR), thought that the new veterans' priority would prove difficult to administer; more veterans' hopes would be bruised. But the rush of sentiment was too great to withstand. Although OWMR, the Treasury Department, and Veterans Administration all had objections to the bill, they recommended that President Truman sign it. It became law on May 3, 1946. By the law, the United Nations Relief and Recovery Administration (UNRRA) lost its privilege of using the Treasury Department as a priority purchasing agent of surplus goods; educational institutions slipped back one notch on the totem pole of surplus preference; and the Veterans Administration had to worry about goods—such as medical supplies—being placed out of its reach onto the set-aside list for veterans. No matter; action had to be taken to ease criticism of the whole program. In an election year those other considerations had to be ignored.[82]

President Truman uttered a warning as he signed the bill on May

[81] *Cong. Rec.,* 79:2 (April 14, 1946), 3075–76.
[82] See Harold Smith to M. C. Latta, May 2, 1946, with attachments; "S.1747, approved May 4, [*sic*], 1946," The President's Bill File, Harry S Truman Papers, Harry S. Truman Library, Independence, Missouri. Cited hereafter as Truman Papers, HSTL.

3, 1946. No miracles could be expected: "Veterans will have the chance to take *all* of these surplus items [on the set-aside list]. But individual veterans may not get certain items they want, or the quantities they want." [83] After signing the bill the President probably settled back in relief; he already had told Senator John D. McClellan (D-Ark.): "I have been having a world of trouble with that [surplus property] situation but I believe I am on top of it now." [84]

The worst was indeed over, although Congress continued its probing.[85] Some veterans still griped, but others obviously had taken advantage of the amended law. Former GIs bought $501,133,000 worth of personal property during the period July, 1946, through January, 1947—approximately 22 per cent of all surplus property sales during the period. War Assets Administration staff members estimated that only about 10 per cent of all World War II veterans bought surplus property. From that, they deduced that about all the needs of veterans entering businesses, professions, or farms had been met.[86]

Despite WAA's self-congratulation, the surplus property program for veterans had not worked out well. The basic statute had too many conflicting purposes, and too few specific administrative instructions, to permit government officials to operate efficiently. Crucial months passed before Congress and Executive corrected some of the more glaring weaknesses of the law. The demand to "bring the boys home" in 1945 and 1946 had its corollary in the importunities to get rid of the materials of war just as rapidly. As a result, the War Assets Administration faced an almost impossible task—compounded, once again, by confusion about the purposes of the overall surplus property program.

The greatest flaw of the whole program lay in improper "public relations." Priorities—and their consequences—might have been

[83] Harry S Truman, *Public Papers of Harry S. Truman, 1946* (Washington, D.C., 1961), 230–231. Cited hereafter as *Truman Public Papers, 1946.*
[84] Truman to McClellan, April 20, 1946; Official File 345, Truman Papers, HSTL.
[85] Three more public hearings were held during 1946.
[86] War Assets Administration, "A Study on Priorities," April, 1947; OF 345, Truman Papers, HSTL.

accepted more widely if a major campaign had been instituted early to impress upon Americans two important facts: the law was not primarily a veterans' measure, nor was it the golden key to abundance. Neither one of these considerations became the central, undeviating theme of surplus property disposal for veterans. As a result many a false dream naturally went unfulfilled.

THE MUSTERING-OUT PAY ACT and the GI Bill of Rights, both passed in 1944, had failed to silence demands for greater cash benefits for World War II veterans. Representative John Cochran (D-Mo.), for one, told his colleagues: "We are going to have an adjusted-compensation bill. Every one of you know we are going to have that." [87] In January, 1945, John E. Rankin, however, was not so sure. He said:

In all the history of the world there has never been a time when servicemen have been cared for better than they are being cared for now. . . . Agitation for additional benefits for veterans is . . . not coming from the servicemen themselves. . . . They don't want government handouts, because they know they and their children must foot the tax bill.[88]

But five months later, Rankin had changed his tune. A scant month after President Roosevelt's death, Rankin confronted the new chief executive with the "1945 model" of adjusted service compensation, or bonus.[89] Rankin professed that he had remained dissatisfied that only unemployed veterans could get readjustment allowance benefits under the GI Bill. He wished to extend eligibility to all veterans (unemployed or not) who had served more than ninety days.[90]

Rankin's proposal received a cold shoulder from the advisers in the executive department. The Bureau of the Budget had strong

[87] U.S., *Cong. Rec.*, 78:2 (August 16, 1944), 7000.
[88] Washington, D.C., January 3, 1945; Clipping in "Bonus" Folder, HR 79 A-F 38.2, Tray 1780, Records of Committee on World War Veterans' Legislation, Record Group 233, National Archives. Cited hereafter as Rankin Committee Records, RG 233, NA.
[89] Rankin to Harry S Truman, May 26, 1945; OF 190-V, Truman Papers, HSTL.
[90] His bill was H.R. 3103, 79:1, May 2, 1945. Rankin threatened to delay the summer recess unless some veterans' legislation passed.

fiscal reservations about the bill.[91] The Bureau canvassed other interested agencies (War Manpower Commission, Office of War Mobilization and Reconversion, and Veterans Administration). The agencies' replies (coached by Budget's Geoffrey May) brought forth formidable arguments against Rankin's plan. Paul McNutt of WMC thought the bill was "inequitable and wasteful"; actually, he argued, it would retard the entry of veterans into essential war industries work by providing them with an incentive to stay home and receive readjustment benefits.[92] Judge Frederick M. Vinson, OWMR Director, added that Rankin's bill gave an "easily expendable bounty"; as such, it did not accord with established public policy. The GI Bill, Vinson averred, laid down the principle of speedily reintegrating veterans into civilian life; Rankin's bill failed to do this. Finally, Vinson could not resist a not-too-subtle jab at the Congressman. He advised, in effect, that rather than proposing unsound legislation, Rankin might better support President Truman's request for an increase in the weekly amount of readjustment allowances, and consider legislation to improve the standards of the Veterans Administration's medical program.[93] General Hines also disliked the proposed bill, particularly in light of the enormous cost of the program.[94] Hines said that the VA had, in 1940 and again in 1943, advocated an adjusted compensation bill in lieu of the benefits of both the mustering-out bill and the GI Bill of Rights. Now, with these programs already in effect, Rankin's plan came too late. The President went along with these negative reports; Rankin's challenge to the government's cash benefits policy had been frustrated.[95]

Rankin had equal difficulty in mustering support outside the executive branch. Some veterans, to be sure, probably agreed with Sergeant A. P. Levine, who wrote in a service newspaper: "We don't know what mental process it is that prompts men, who in

[91] Geoffrey May to F. J. Bailey, May 28, 1945; "B48 (5) Bonus—Service Men, Number 4" Folder, Budget Records, RG 51, NA.
[92] McNutt to Bailey, June 12, 1945; *ibid.*
[93] Vinson to Harold D. Smith, June 13, 1945; *ibid.*
[94] Draft, Hines to Rankin, n.d., attachment to Hines to Harold D. Smith, June 25, 1945; *ibid.*
[95] Harry S Truman notation of approval on Harold D. Smith to Matthew Connelly, July 3, 1945; and Smith to Rankin, July 5, 1945; *ibid.*

other matters exhibit such reckless financial abandon, to become suddenly transformed into pillars of parsimony when confronted by the legitimate demands of the country's defenders."[96] Others, however, may have indorsed the simply stated view of Corporal Jean M. Kenlipp: "In my opinion the 'G.I. Bill of Rights' plus the present mustering out pay is sufficient"; it would be "foolhardy," the Corporal continued, to have a bonus.[97] In addition to the conflicting views of individual veterans, Rankin also faced a cool response from their organizations. The Veterans of Foreign Wars, for example, wanted a bonus differential imposed for men who saw combat or served overseas. One VFW local post adjutant told the Mississippian that his group had pledged "100 per cent" opposition to Rankin's bill.[98] Equally as important, Rankin's own House committee refused to vote his measure out.[99] Rankin had run into a blank wall.

The next challenge to the cash benefits policy for veterans was more potent. It emerged as a result of the War Department's terminal leave policy. The Army paid officers—but not enlisted men— for unused accumulated leave or furlough time. Complaints about this had been aired as early as September, 1944.[100] Sporadic criticisms appeared during 1945.[101] The full outcry for "justice" for enlisted men did not begin, however, until January, 1946. The soldier demonstrations of that month generated considerable comment about the "undemocratic" nature of military service. Some observers thought the roots of soldier discontent could be found in the fertile soil of the military "caste" system. The "amiable mutinies" may

[96] *The Stars and Stripes,* Middle Pacific edition, I (July 28, 1945), 2.
[97] Kenlipp to Rankin, January 11, 1945; HR 79 A-F 38.1, Tray 17793, Rankin Committee Records, RG 233, NA.
[98] Telegram, Roy Ogden to Rankin, June 30, 1945; "Bonus" Folder, HR 79 A-F 38.2, Tray 17802, *ibid.* For a similar objection voiced a year later, see Max Novack, "About That Bonus," *Salute,* I (April, 1946), 12–13.
[99] "Minutes of Committee Hearings, 79th Congress" Folder, HR 79 A-F 38.2, Tray 17807, Rankin Committee Records, RG 233, NA.
[100] See Drew Pearson's "Washington Merry-Go-Round," *The Washington Post,* September 13, 1944.
[101] See "Two Sergeants" letter to the editor, *ibid.,* March 14, 1945; also see a petition for leave pay signed by 1,530 enlisted men of the Army, Navy, and Seabees aboard the *USS Beckham* enroute to the United States from the Pacific, dated November 26, 1945; OF 190-AA, Truman Papers, HSTL.

have made enlisted men more sensitive to the alleged preferential treatment of officers.

Some Congressmen doubted the propriety of making terminal-leave payments to anyone; since the War Department had already made payments to officers, however, elemental justice called for equal treatment of enlisted men.[102] More than elemental justice was at stake for one Representative. Alvin E. O'Konski (R-Wisc.) worried about Congress' virility:

Wake up Members of Congress. Let us take the bull by the horns and remedy this rotten deal. . . . Members of Congress, are we men or are we mice? Where is our manhood—when we permit this to continue. . . . It is one of the most disgraceful and dishonorable acts perpetrated on all mankind.[103]

"Dirty deal . . . crude deal . . . rotten deal . . . raw deal." O'Konski's vocabulary almost failed him; but his indignation made up for any verbal deficiency. His anger had been caused, in part, by the dilatory attitude of the House's Military Affairs Committee. That group did not seem inclined to report out any of the several bills designed to rectify the injustice. One member called the committee's failure to act "the great congressional mystery" of the 79th Congress.[104]

Still, there was no real mystery. The enormous sums involved and the consequent threat of inflation had convinced Administration leaders and others that they should proceed slowly. For example, W. Sterling Cole (R-N.Y.), a conservative, responded to a correspondent who had expressed concern about possible inflation and wanted to "stop this spending spree sometime": "You are entirely right in your attitude toward the payment of terminal pay to all enlisted men. To do so would involve an expenditure of several billions of dollars and the way to correct it is to discontinue terminal leave to officers." [105]

[102] Clifford Hope to James M. Starkey, April 26, 1946; "Terminal Leave-Legislative 79th Cong." Folder, Hope Papers, Kansas State Historical Society, Topeka.
[103] *Cong. Rec.*, 79:1 (November 21, 1945), Appendix, A 5047.
[104] Joseph R. Bryson (D-S.C.), *ibid.*, 79:2 (June 7, 1946), 6471.
[105] Harry M. Savacool to Cole, April 1, 1946; and Cole to Savacool, April 4,

The Military Affairs Committee's procrastination may have pleased Cole, but a majority of his colleagues chafed at the delay. When (seven months after the terminal leave bill had been introduced) nothing had been done, 218 Congressmen forced the issue by discharging the Military Affairs Committee from further consideration.[106] When the House began formal debate the only serious question centered on why terminal-leave payments had to be made. Some Congressmen emphasized that a blow was being struck for democracy: "Democracy is getting around to the armed forces, and it is about time." [107] Others stressed that a mistake had been made; Congress should uphold its honor by redressing the wrong. Their logic was ingenious. When Congress passed the mustering-out payment act, they reasoned, it included individuals up to and including the rank of captain. But unknown to the legislators, those officers received terminal leave pay as well as the mustering-out payment. Because these junior officers enjoyed the double benefit, all who received mustering-out pay should also get terminal-leave pay. A simple matter of adjusting an error.[108] The cost? A simple matter of three to six billion dollars.[109] Undaunted by the price tag, the House handsomely passed the measure unanimously.[110]

In the Senate the bill experienced heavier sledding. The President and his advisers opposed the House's proposal to pay the accrued leaves in lump sum amounts. In addition to the traditional fear that

1946; "Terminal Pay-Enlisted" Envelope, 79th Cong. Files, Box 30, Cole Papers, Cornell University.

[106] The bill selected (H.R. 4051, 79th Cong.) had been introduced by Dwight L. Rogers (D-Fla.) on September 13, 1945; Rogers drummed up the requisite number of signatures by April 17, 1946. To the chagrin of those desiring rapid action, the Military Affairs Committee reported the bill formally on May 9, 1946 making it necessary to go through the regular process of obtaining a rule for its consideration. Hence the House could not commence its debate until June 7, 1946.

[107] Thomas J. Lane (D-Mass.), Cong. Rec., 79:2 (June 7, 1946), 6481.

[108] Walter G. Andrews (R-N.Y.), ibid., 6485–86.

[109] Robert L. F. Sikes (D-Fla.), ibid., 6487. By the time the measure passed Congress, the Budget Bureau estimated the cost would run to $2,679,493,000. James C. Webb to M. C. Latta, August 2, 1946; "HR 4051, approved August 9, 1946," Bill File, Truman Papers, HSTL.

[110] Cong. Rec., 79:2 (June 11, 1946), 6665. James J. Wadsworth (R-N.Y.), unable to vote either for or against the bill sounded a lonely "present" when the clerk bade him vote.

veterans would spend the windfall recklessly, government officials had nightmares over the inflationary threats of cash payments. The American Veterans Committee (AVC), a newly organized World War II veterans' organization, offered a solution. The AVC suggested that non-negotiable, five-year maturity bonds be issued at 2½ per cent interest to veterans for terminal-leave payment amounts that exceeded fifty dollars.[111] The Senate's bill incorporated this feature. Senator Edwin C. Johnson, the bill's floor manager, told his colleagues that if they refused to accept the deferred payment plan and supported the House's lump sum proposal the President surely would veto it. Once vetoed, he explained, there would be no time to override it, due to plans for an imminent adjournment.[112]

For the first time, however, serious public misgivings on the part of other than Administration spokesmen about the bill began to emerge. Senator Joseph Ball (R-Minn.) opposed key features of the House bill. It changed the terms of an employment contract, he argued, by making it retroactive to cover all who served during the war. Most soldiers, he thought, would claim the full amount to which their service entitled them, regardless of whether they had taken any furlough at all. He observed philosophically that war brought many inequities; the proposal seemed to be an expensive way to correct an error. The "caste system" argument, moreover, exaggerated the true story. He said: "It is part of a campaign to prove that all the officers in the Army and in the Navy were heels who had special privileges while all the enlisted men had hearts of gold and fought the war all by themselves." [113] He pointed out that enlisted men enjoyed many benefits (free food and clothing, greater dependence allowances) denied to officers. Ball concluded his criticism by observing that there was no need for a "concealed bonus" at the time—except that 1946 was a political campaign year.[114] To prove his devotion to

[111] AVC's Role is mentioned by J. Donald Kingsley to John R. Steelman, July 26, 1946; "Retraining and Reemployment" Folder, Office of the Director Files, OWMR Records, RG 250, NA. See also remarks of R. Ewing Thomason (D-Tex.), *Cong. Rec.,* 79:2 (July 31, 1946), 10581.
[112] *Cong. Rec.,* 79:2 (July 23, 1946), 9731–32.
[113] *Ibid.,* 9719.
[114] *Ibid.,* 9719–20. His colleague, Robert A. Taft (R-Ohio), echoed Ball: "Because we perhaps made a mistake and were too generous with captains

economy, Ball offered an amendment to authorize the subtraction of mustering-out pay from terminal-leave payments. Only eleven others joined him; and, after a series of futile efforts by Claude D. Pepper to restore the immediate payment features, the upper house passed the bill. The House-Senate conference brought about only one relatively minor change.[115] The House reluctantly accepted their conferees' arguments that "it is just this or nothing at the present time as we view it." [116] The President signed the bill on August 9, 1946.

But the Armed Forces Leave Act of 1946, unfortunately for the Administration, did not satisfy the veterans who expected ready cash: "I think this G.I. Bill for terminal leave pay . . . is one of the worst things Congress has ever passed. . . . If an [officer] rates cash pay, so should the men who had to give blood and guts for these unworthy people's freedom." [117] As long as the President had an important influence over the legislative situation, these protests had little effect. But January, 1947, brought a Republican Congress to Washington. Would this change the situation? At first, the change in control apparently did not matter. In May, 1947, Representative John Taber passed on to an inquirer the news that "the Armed Services Committee . . . advises me that no hearings have been scheduled on the bill [providing cash redemption of terminal-leave bonds] and it is very unlikely that it will be taken up this session." [118]

A month later, however, the new Speaker of the House, Joseph Martin (R-Mass.), reportedly predicted passage of legislation to permit cashing the bonds.[119] This was disturbing news to government officials. Despite suggestions that it would be advantageous

---

and lieutenants, five hundred thousand of them, it is now contended we must extend that to 11,000,000 men; I think it is an utterly fantastic and illogical and unjustifiable argument."

[115] Instead of making the bonds completely non-negotiable, the conference bill permitted use of the bonds for payment of government life insurance premiums.

[116] R. Ewing Thomason, *ibid.* (July 31, 1946), 10582.

[117] Bill L. Crowley to Truman, August 3, 1946; OF 190-AA, Truman Papers, HSTL.

[118] Taber to Howard M. Hance, May 22, 1947; "Veterans Affairs 1947" Folder, Box 161, Taber Papers, Cornell University.

[119] John L. Thurston to John R. Steelman, June 20, 1947; OF 190-AA, Truman Papers, HSTL.

politically to change their policy, officials continued to believe this would threaten the economy.[120] It would inject over two billion dollars into consumer spending and remove "an admirable tool which may be sorely needed later to combat deflationary pressures." [121] They recognized that some veterans did need aid; yet most did not require it at that moment.

Congressmen had tumbled over themselves in their haste to put a cash redemption proposal into the Speaker's hopper. Throughout the spring Democrats needled the Republican leadership in the House to expedite the terminal-leave measure. Finally, in June, a bill emerged from committee. It was passed without dissent.[122] The Senate sped it to the President for signature, with a unanimous vote on July 19, 1947.[123] By this time political momentum had overcome the reluctance of the Administration to approve bond redemption. The President, with little alternative, signed the bill on July 26, 1947. He asked veterans to use restraint in employing their option to cash the bonds, futilely hoping that most would hold the bonds to maturity.[124]

But if the Administration had not seen its views on terminal leave followed, it had one important consolation: terminal-leave pay, along with mustering-out payments and readjustment allowances, had emasculated demands for a bonus. Representative John E. Lyle (D-Tex.) during the 1946 debate noted that he had not enthusiastically indorsed terminal leave because it promised to kill a future bonus; his foreboding turned out to be correct.[125] World War II veterans would not receive a bonus. Although the principle of noncash benefits to assist veterans in the transition from military to civilian life remained in-

[120] President Truman's adviser on veterans' affairs, Major General Harry H. Vaughan, received the opinion that a "great many families . . . would be very grateful to the present administration" for the ability to cash the bonds. Lieutenant Colonel W. R. Livingston to Vaughan, May 8, 1947; ibid.
[121] Thurston to Steelman, June 20, 1947; ibid.
[122] H. R. 4017, 80th Cong., Cong. Rec., 80:1 (July 7, 1947), 8385. Characteristically, John E. Rankin asserted: "I am much more in favor of this kind of legislation than I am of legislation to send American money to feed and clothe every lazy lout from Tokyo to Timbuktu." Ibid. (July 7, 1947), 8380.
[123] Ibid. (July 19, 1947), 9377.
[124] "Statement by the President Upon Signing Bill Authorizing Redemption of Veterans' Terminal Leave Bonds," July 26, 1947, in Truman Public Papers, 1947, 358.
[125] Cong. Rec., 79:2 (June 7, 1946), 6502.

tact, the cost was high: by 1955, payments to veterans for terminal-leave, mustering-out, and readjustment allowances alone amounted to $10.2 billion.[126] No one could doubt that part of the fervor behind terminal-leave payments represented support for a bonus. The lid on the boiling pot of bonus demands imposed by Presidents Roosevelt and Truman had been only partially successful in containing pressures. The lid was still on; but a good deal of the steam had escaped.

MAKING CASH PAYMENTS to veterans seeking work was but one facet of the government's efforts; guiding this new Ulysses to a new job was another. The effort by the Federal Government to bring together veteran and employer during 1945 and 1946 turned out to be as storm-tossed as the quarrel over "superseniority." Erupting in December, 1945, the controversy centered on the status of the United States Employment Service (USES). The question was: When, if ever, should USES be returned to State control? The argument that ensued contained many of the divisive issues of the day: States' rights versus federal control, rapid reconversion versus slower relinquishment of controls, anti-labor versus pro-labor, Congress versus Executive, bureaucrat versus bureaucrat, conservatism versus the New Deal, Republican versus Democrat, and rural versus urban.

The United States Employment Service's history set the framework for the debate in 1945 and 1946.[127] Since 1933, USES had functioned as a national clearing house for job counseling and referrals. Theoretically, it matched, on a nationwide basis, the man to the job. In principle, an employer would contact his state's employment service office when he needed new workers; the USES office would search its list of individuals seeking work for persons possessing the

[126] President's Commission on Veterans' Pensions, *Staff Report IX-B*, and *id., Staff Report II*, 323.
[127] The summary in this and the five following paragraphs is based on William Haber and Daniel H. Kruger, *The Role of the United States Employment Service in a Changing Economy* (Kalamazoo, Mich., 1964), pp. 26–35; Harold W. Metz, *Labor Policy of the Federal Government* (Washington, D.C., 1945), pp. 128–41; The President's Commission on Veterans' Pensions, *Report No. IX, Part B*, 269–71 and 277–87; and on Congressional Hearings and Debates, cited in footnotes below.

needed skills; if employment officials succeeded in their survey, they referred the workers to the prospective employer; if the search proved unproductive, the USES office would send the employer's request to USES offices in other states for their handling. Similarly, when an individual sought work, he would register at the USES office, see a counselor, receive advice, and wait until a suitable job opened up. USES had long argued that a complex industrial society with a national (rather than local or regional) economy required a national employment service.

In practice, however, the United States Employment Service prior to World War II had not functioned as theory would have it. There were many reasons for this. During the depression, the USES served a restricted market—it concentrated on placing unemployed persons in government-sponsored public works jobs. As a result, the job-counseling and job-matching functions had to be subordinated to the immediate need to get people back to employment rapidly; any work would do. Most of its referrals were to unskilled or semiskilled posts. Private employers seeking more skilled labor frequently shunned USES. The agency, moreover, earned the enmity of some businessmen because it refused to refer workers to a struck plant, or to businesses which USES believed paid "substandard" wages. In short, it had a "pro-labor" reputation.

In 1933 the so-called Wagner-Peyser Act had provided for a voluntary federal-state matching grant system to finance USES; the Federal Government put up four million dollars (apportioned to the states according to population), and the states, if they desired, matched the amount. By June, 1935, twenty-four states had cooperated. Congress passed the Social Security Act, which, among other provisions, set up an unemployment compensation system, with compensation to be paid through an USES office. If that were done, the Federal Government would pay the major portion (as it turned out, 90 per cent) of the administrative expenses for the employment service offices. Hence, in order to receive unemployment compensation benefits, states had to set up USES offices. Once established, these offices were controlled by state governors.

The linking of employment service offices with unemployment

compensation functions tended to hobble the USES. Most states set up one office to oversee the activity of both jobs. The unemployment operation tended to obscure the employment service functions; that is, it became more important to get a man a job, no matter how unsuitable, instead of insuring that the "man-match-job" principle remained intact. Rather than send requests for labor to other states, for example, most USES officials ransacked their own state, ignoring in the process the "national" character of USES. In short, to keep their own unemployed lists down, state officials made referrals from those lists almost exclusively.

On December 19, 1941, President Roosevelt requested each state governor to relinquish his control over the local USES group. The President and his advisers deemed this move essential in order to procure and allocate labor for war industries' work. By early January, 1942, the governors had complied; Roosevelt's argument seemed compelling. During the war, the volume of employment activity handled by USES understandably increased; moreover, members of the organization entered military service. To fill these vacancies, the USES staff was augmented. When the war ended, the state governors wanted to regain control of the system. Part of the furor that resulted stemmed from differing ideas of what to do with the USES employees hired after January, 1942.

The issue involved, moreover, the status of special functions performed by USES for veterans. The Wagner-Peyser Act also had provided for a Veterans' Employment Service (VES) to operate within the United States Employment Service. As its name implies, this unit was to insure that veterans received special employment counseling and referral treatment. Among other duties, VES was to promote employment of veterans, and to accord the former servicemen preferential referral to job openings. In 1944 the GI Bill of Rights superimposed on VES the Veterans' Placement Service Board (VPSB) to set the policies for veterans' employment. The new board (composed of the Veterans Administrator as chairman, the Selective Service System's director, and the head of the Federal Security Agency) operated independently of USES; but it did control the policies of VES, one of USES' units. Hence, the proposal to "defederalize" USES directly affected the fate of VES.

Critics of the proposal to return USES to state control were quick to point out the alleged bad effect upon veterans' employment chances if the transfer were made in the midst of the reconversion period. "Save the veterans" provided a persistent theme. Some individuals who used this plea, however, really did not support the existing VES and VPSB system. At the time of the GI Bill's passage, for instance, Douglas B. Maggs of the Labor Department expressed a typical New Deal sentiment about veterans' policy:

Veterans are morally entitled to initial preferential treatment because they have been exposed to the hazards of war and their opportunities for economic advancement have been prejudiced by removal from the sphere of civilian activities. . . . But that initial preference should be temporary. The recognition of veterans as a special group in the national society entitled to indefinite preferential and special treatment is an extremely hazardous policy to adopt.[128]

Five months later, Harold D. Smith exhibited another side of this antipathy:

In my opinion, the overlapping responsibilities in this field can only lead to confusion. I believe that contacts with private industry and with veterans will be duplicated by the two organizations [VES and USES] and will inevitably lead to dissatisfaction on the part of the veterans whose needs are being serviced and on the part of the general public.[129]

Mrs. Roosevelt added her note of concern about potential duplication. James F. Byrnes told her he knew about the situation; he comforted her with the thought that General Hines was keeping an eye on it.[130]

[128] Maggs to Frances Perkins, June 2, 1944; "Bills-Misc. (S.1767 or G.I. Bill) 1944" Folder, Secretary Frances Perkins General Subject File, 1940–44. Records of the Department of Labor, Record Group 174, National Archives. Cited hereafter as Labor Department Records, RG 174, NA.

[129] Smith to Hines, November 1, 1944; "1–1 Bureau of Budget" Folder, Series I, General Files, RRA Records, RG 244, NA.

[130] Byrnes to Eleanor Roosevelt, January 11, 1945; Retraining and Reemployment" Folder, General Classified File, Records of the Office of War Mobilization and Reconversion, Record Group 250, National Archives. Cited hereafter as OWMR Records, RG 250, NA.

If some New Dealers used the "save the veterans" plea to obtain their primary objective—to retain a federal USES—other Administration members probably valued the veterans' special needs more highly. President Truman may have belonged to this second group. In his twenty-one point message on September 6, 1945, Truman asserted that "placing demobilized veterans and misplaced war workers in new peacetime jobs is the major human problem of our country's reconversion to a peacetime economy." [131] He went on to urge the continued federal operation of the USES, at least until June 30, 1947. He repeated this theme in his message conveying the reasons for the veto on December 22, 1945, of the rescission act,[132] in his State of the Union address on January 21, 1946,[133] and in a special message on March 14, 1946.[134] In May, the President told his budget chief:

I have always been very much interested in the Veterans Employment Service and I understand that a tremendous slash has been made in its budget by your office. I'd like very much to talk with you about this situation.[135]

In brief, Harry S Truman, the former field artillery officer, in addition to his New Deal inclinations, genuinely believed veterans' employment chances would be impaired by quick transfer of USES.

The President had other reasons to oppose the move. The tactics of the "defederalizers," particularly a stratagem devised by Representative Everett M. Dirksen (R-Ill.), angered him. Dirksen had chafed over the President's delay in returning USES to state control. The Roosevelt-Truman Administration repeatedly had blocked legislative efforts to bring this about.[136] Dirksen had an idea. Why, he thought, if President Roosevelt had federalized USES by executive

[131] Truman, *Public Papers*, 1945, 283.
[132] *Ibid.*, 579–83.
[133] Truman, *Public Papers*, 1946, 40.
[134] *Ibid.*, 159–60.
[135] Truman to Harold D. Smith, May 4, 1946; OF 552-B, Truman Papers, HSTL.
[136] John E. Rankin and others had tried in vain to get the idea of rapid return incorporated in the GI Bill of Rights. But Sen. Scott Lucas had greater success on September 19, 1945, when the Upper House voted (56 to 23) to return USES in 90 days. That measure died in the House.

action, was legislation necessary to defederalize it? Dirksen's logic continued: "It occurred to me that it was a question of money. So as I began to speculate on it, I thought we could contrive language that would put . . . [USES] back in the hands of the States." [137]

So, Dirksen looked about for a handy "money" device. This appeared in the form of the awesomely titled "First Supplemental Surplus Appropriation Rescission Bill of 1946." This rescission bill proposed to reclaim funds amounting to about fifty-two-and-a-half billion dollars previously appropriated for fiscal year 1946 (July 1, 1945 to June 30, 1946). Dirksen engineered a provision that rescinded funds for the continued federal operation of USES, on the one hand, and, on the other, appropriated money to the states to take over the system. He called the measure a "weapon" to return the nation to "free enterprise [to achieve] . . . reasonably full employment." [138] A substitute amendment designed to replace Dirksen's lost on a teller vote, 101–162.[139] After the House passed the bill containing Dirksen's measure, the "pro-Federal-USES" Senators attempted in vain to alter the bill to insure a modicum of central control. The bill then went to test its fate at President Truman's hands.

Truman vetoed the bill. It would create, he said: "A disrupted and inefficient employment service at the very time when efficient operation is most vitally needed by veterans, workers and employers." [140] Urging that transfer be delayed until June, 1947, he closed the veto message with forceful words:

While I object to the specific measure which this bill proposes to carry out with respect to our employment service, I object even more strongly to the legislative method employed for its enactment. To attach a legislative rider to an appropriation bill restricts the President's exercise of his functions and is contrary to good government.[141]

The pocket veto merely prolonged the fight. John Taber (R-N.Y.), one year shy of assuming the chair of the powerful House Appropria-

[137] U.S., Senate, Committee on Appropriations, 79th Cong., 1st Sess., *Hearings on . . . Supplemental Surplus Appropriation Rescission Bill, 1946*, November 1, 1945 (Washington, D.C., 1945), 343.
[138] *Cong. Rec.*, 79:1 (October 19, 1945), 9840.
[139] *Ibid.*, 9859.
[140] Truman, *Public Papers, 1945*, 580.
[141] *Ibid.*, 583.

tions Committee, told a constituent that despite the veto: "I think we will be able to prevent appropriations to carry [USES] on in the Federal Security [Agency]." [142]

While Taber and others laid their plans, Administration officials busied themselves with their own schemes. The "save-the-veterans" theme became the lead-off argument. Secretary of Labor Lewis Schwellenbach on January 17, 1946, informed a House committee that a national USES could take care of veterans because they suffered "temporary but serious readjustment problems, requiring access to job opportunities throughout the Nation." [143] Other witnesses echoed Schwellenbach. James B. Carey, the Congress of Industrial Organization's (CIO) Secretary-treasurer, an ardent proponent of a federal USES, stated the position more vigorously:

In the case of veterans, vast numbers will be entering the labor force for the first time—mature as individuals but beginners in the world of work. . . . The GI bill of rights should not be misstated or garbled by those eager to trade on the veteran for justification of their position. The veteran can best be served, as the whole people can best be served, by national administration.[144]

General Omar N. Bradley, Veterans Administrator, followed Carey; he repeatedly assured skeptics that it would be better for the Veterans Placement Service Board if USES remained federal.[145]

When debate began in the House on a new Administration bill (HR 4437) to transfer USES to modified state control on June 30, 1947, the bill's proponents continued to "trade on" the "save-the-veteran" idea.[146] Jennings Randolph (D-W.Va.), John J. Rooney

[142] Taber to N. G. Gould, January 4, 1946; "Appr.—Labor-Fed. Security" Folder, Box 77, Taber Papers, Cornell University.
[143] U.S., House of Representatives, Committee on Labor, 79th Cong., 2d Sess., *Hearings on . . . United States Employment Service*, January 17, 1946 (Washington, D.C., 1946), 10. Cited hereafter as House, *Randolph Committee USES Hearings, 79:2.*
[144] *Ibid.*, 29 and 30.
[145] *Ibid.*, 36–42.
[146] Prominent Administration officials who desired permanent federal retention of USES (such as Paul McNutt and Lewis Schwellenbach) reluctantly had to agree to the inevitable concerning transfer. They attempted, however, to place in the various USES bills "recapture" clauses; these sections permitted the Secretary of Labor to take over a state USES system when the state failed to provide an adequate program. For McNutt's views on USES's permanent

(D-N.Y.), and Augustine B. Kelley (D-Pa.), all emphasized the necessity to keep USES federal, at least during reconversion, to help the veteran.[147] That theme began to annoy the bill's opponents. Charles Vursell (R-Ill.) observed:

With all honor to General Bradley as a military strategist and a great commander, but since when did he become also . . . an expert on the . . . writing of unemployment compensation. . . . Do not drag the soldiers into this. In every piece of legislation for the last number of years . . . there are those who have sought to bring in the American flag or the soldiers.[148]

Apparently, most House members heeded Vursell's admonition. Overwhelmingly, the House amended HR 4437 by moving the date up one year to June 30, 1946.[149] The bill was sent to the Senate on January 30, 1946.

Administration supporters in the Senate stalled for time. James M. Tunnell (D-Dela.) held hearings in February and March on the bill during which, he later claimed, "witnesses representing all sections of our economy were invited to present their views." [150] This was somewhat disingenuous; twenty-seven witnesses appeared, only four of whom supported HR 4437.[151] Perhaps because of the weight of opinion, Tunnell's subcommittee provided for December 31, 1946, as a compromise date of return. Although the bill was reported on April 30, 1946, Senate leaders delayed debate on the measure until June.

Meanwhile, the Administration leaders continued to struggle to enhance USES's prestige. They had already decided in September,

---

status, see U.S., House of Representatives, Committee on Appropriations, Subcommittee on Labor Department and Federal Security Appropriations, 79th Cong., 1st Sess., *Hearings on . . . War Manpower Commission,* April 26, 1945 (Washington, D.C., 1945), 26; for Schwellenbach's see U.S., Senate, Committee on Education and Labor, Subcommittee on S.1456 and S.1510, 79th Cong., 1st Sess., *Hearings . . . on . . . United States Employment Service,* November 13, 1945 (Washington, D.C., 1946), 18. Cited hereafter as Senate, *Tunnell Subcommittee USES Hearings, 79:1.*

[147] *Cong. Rec.,* 79:2 (January 23, 1946), 471, 481, and 485.

[148] *Ibid.,* 481, see also Dirksen's and Hatton Sumners's (D-Tex.) remarks, *ibid.* (January 29, 1946), 531 and 539.

[149] *Ibid.,* 546.

[150] *Ibid.* (June 24, 1946), 7369.

[151] See Senate, *Tunnell Subcommittee USES Hearings, 79:2* (February 18 through March 25, 1946), 85–333.

1945, to center all veterans' employment activity in USES. But that decision had been imperiled by the activities of General Lewis B. Hershey of the Selective Service System (SSS). Hershey continued to agitate for more funds for his agency; part of his clamor stemmed from the desire to provide better employment counseling services at local SSS boards for veterans. Hershey's noise prompted Harold D. Smith to suggest to President Truman that the SSS Chief needed a reminder. Truman (in a letter drafted by Smith) then informed Hershey, in effect, to keep his hands off veterans' employment: "I am sure you will not wish to propose any program . . . involving expanded veteran services contrary to my program." [152]

Hershey refused, however, to let the matter rest. In January, 1946, he decided to appeal to Office of War Mobilization and Reconversion (OWMR) director, John W. Snyder, for aid. Hershey charged that the Federal Government currently was not meeting its responsibilities to veterans in the fields of housing, employment, and education. He insisted that emergency measures were needed; specifically, all government agencies who could help veterans should be allowed to do so. The Selective Service System had a network of local boards that served thousands of communities. Utilize them, he urged; do not throttle their effectiveness by budget slashes.[153] Hershey's advice fell on deaf ears. Snyder told him that USES had the primary duty to help veterans find new jobs. Piously, he told Hershey that no duplication of services could be allowed.[154]

Snyder may not have had deaf ears, but the SSS's continued obduracy probably made Harold Smith wonder about Hershey's. For Hershey would not let matters remain settled. Impatient over the delay in getting a reply from Snyder, Hershey turned again to the President. Could not, he pleaded, the Administration permit him to ask Congress for more funds for the rest of the year? [155] Smith, who had been asked to comment on Hershey's new request, repeated his view that USES, and only USES, should provide employment ser-

[152] November 2, 1945; OF 440, Truman Papers, HSTL.
[153] Hershey to Snyder, January 17, 1946; "Retraining and Reemployment" Folder, General Classified Files, OWMR Records, RG 250, NA.
[154] Snyder to Hershey, February 6, 1946; *ibid.*
[155] Hershey to Truman, February 2, 1946; OF 440, Truman Papers, HSTL.

vices for veterans seeking new jobs. He scrawled on his letter to the President: "This is another evidence of a lack of discipline that is creeping into the government." [156] The President agreed apparently. Again the cold admonition from the White House to the unruly Hershey: "I am sure you will not present to the Congress material and views contrary to the recommendations I have made." [157] Two weeks later, the irrepressible general made a last plea to the President: "It would be a catastrophe for the veteran and the Nation of the abilities of Selective Service are curtailed." [158]

Hershey's troubles extended to functions concerning veterans' reemployment, as well as to new employment. While he argued with Snyder and Smith, a bill to transfer SSS's reemployment duties to the embattled USES was introduced by Senator Edwin C. Johnson (D-Colo.). Hershey excoriated the bill:

I believe it is detrimental to the best interest of the veterans and dangerous to the security of this Nation. . . . It will lose advantages for which a quarter of a million fighting men gave their lives, thousands gave their blood, and millions gave years of their lives.[159]

Hershey viewed the proposed move as a slight to the services of the thousands of unpaid volunteers who staffed SSS. Three weeks later he added a more specific objection; all other federal agencies, he said, had been overburdened with functions—it would be foolhardy to add one more to USES.[160]

Meanwhile, the legislative situation had thickened by the time the Senate began its debate on HR 4437 on June 24, 1946. The House of Representatives continued its upsetting role. On June 11, 1946, the House debated and passed the "Labor-Federal Security Agency" appropriation bill for 1947. That measure proposed to end federal control of USES on October 6, 1946. Hence, when the Senators proceeded to debate HR 4437 they knew about the House's superior

[156] Smith to Truman, February 12, 1946; *ibid.*
[157] Truman to Hershey, February 13, 1946; *ibid.*
[158] Hershey to Truman, February 23, 1946; *ibid.*
[159] U.S., Senate, Committee on Military Affairs, 79th Cong., 1st Sess., *Hearings on Selective Service Extension,* March 5, 1946 (Washington, D.C., 1946), 2.
[160] *Ibid.* (March 28, 1946), 25.

strategic position. Nonetheless, the Senate adhered to Tunnell's amended version; viz., December 31, 1946, remained the transfer date. But the House refused to confer with the Senate over the amended HR 4437. The Senate, not to be outdone, inserted the amended HR 4437 as an amendment to the Labor-FSA appropriation bill. As a final gesture, the House changed the date to November 15, 1946. That is where it stayed.

After all the legislative wrangling had ended, Everett Dirksen provided an epilogue:

One might say that when a public function or an agency falls into the hands of the Federal Government and becomes centralized, it is about as difficult to get it back into State hands by means of a legislative transfer as it is to push a spirited bull calf through a barn door.[161]

Other conclusions seem just as pertinent. The long struggle over control of USES sapped the morale of its employees. Uncertainty about their own future may have made interviewers and other staff members less sympathetic to problems of veterans. No less important, the frequently adverse publicity that accompanied debate on USES hardly helped the agency. Its close identification with labor unions (fostered both by its own actions and the zeal of its defenders in labor's ranks) was particularly strong. At a time when unions had begun to resume use of the strike weapon, such an identity may not have been beneficial. Its opponents saw this. Representative Harold Knutson (R-Minn.) had told the House during debate in October, 1945, that "when you vote for the McCormack amendment [to alter Dirksen's desire for a rapid return of USES] you are voting the way the CIO wants you to vote and the way many have been ordered to vote." [162] Clay Williams, a representative of the Texas Trade Association Executives, told a House committee that "the CIO-PAC [Congress of Industrial Organizations' Political Action Committee] is probably the most tainted, as well as tinted, political organization in America today." [163] USES was hurt more by its friends than its enemies.

[161] *Cong. Rec.*, 79:2 (July 11, 1946), 8661.
[162] *Ibid.*, 79:1 (October 18, 1945), 9856.
[163] House, *Randolph Committee USES Hearings*, 79:2 (January 18, 1946), 81.

Still another conclusion may be reached. The promoters of USES used the "save-the-veterans" theme; the opponents of federal control used the "states' rights" tool. The latter won. On the surface this may be surprising; given a situation where both values compete (and others are absent) the veterans' appeal would be assumed to be the stronger. After all, there were more veterans than states. But the USES battle demonstrated the limits of "trading on" the veterans. Proponents of USES could not show conclusively that veterans in fact would have been injured if transfer were made. Why not? For one thing, hypothetical arguments do not always convince skeptics.

More compelling, however, USES had not been serving the veteran that well. This had been predicted, even by Administration officials, as early as October, 1944. Richmond Harris, a Retraining and Reemployment Administration counsultant, had told Frank T. Hines: "After exhaustive research and interviewing over 300 persons, . . . the consensus . . . definitely points out that the U.S. Employment Service will be inadequate when thrown into reverse to provide counseling, guidance, referral and replacement." [164] Harris had predicted that USES, geared for the mass placing of war workers for employers who were not highly selective, would be unable to give the veteran the individual treatment he needed.

The actual record of USES was better than Harris had forecast. Robert Goodwin, USES's director, pointed out that his agency had received 941,392 veterans' applications in January, 1946, alone; moreover, 744,000 veterans (out of 847,000 referred) had been placed in jobs from July, 1945, through January, 1946.[165] The story for the whole of 1946 was not so impressive; USES placed only 28 veterans per 100 applications.[166] This did not compare favorably with USES's performance with nonveterans. In fiscal year 1947 (July 1, 1946 to June 30, 1947), for example, USES placed 81 nonveterans per 100 applications; the placement ratio for veterans 63.[167] Still,

[164] Harris to Hines, October 24, 1944; "1–1–U.S. Employment Service" Folder, Series I, General Files, RRA Records, RG 244, NA.
[165] Senate, *Tunnell Subcommittee USES Hearings,* 79:2 (March 25, 1946), 302.
[166] President's Commission on Veterans' Pensions, *Staff Report No. IX, Part B,* 273.
[167] *Ibid.,* 295.

from 1944 through fiscal year 1946, USES did manage to place 4,598,900 out of a total of 9,769,400 new applicants.[168] That was no mean accomplishment.

But statistics revealed only one side of the coin. Charles Hurd, *The New York Time*'s expert on veterans' affairs, reported: "One of the worst complaints this column has heard repeatedly about USES is that for the most part it offers to veterans only the lowest paid and the most undesirable jobs in industry." [169] In two ways the Administration itself confessed USES's weaknesses. Each time President Truman indorsed USES, he included a plea to employers to use the agency. The recognition that many did not, of course, reflected the Administration's view of USES's effectiveness. The second self-indictment came in September, 1946, when the Veterans' Placement Service Board (VPSB) appointed a special committee to investigate the relationship of the Veterans' Employment Service (VES) and USES. The committee concluded that the VPSB-VES-USES triangle had "created endless confusion and can only lead to administrative chaos." [170] The report observed that differences of opinions about routine procedures and competition between VES and USES had "developed into active antagonism in some places." The committee report continued:

In some instances . . . [VES] personnel have been expending their energies in "policing" with excessive zeal, the operations of the . . . [USES], whereas their time might better be utilized in selling the . . . [USES] to employers and the public, including the veterans themselves.[171]

The committee recommended that VPSB be abolished; but this, given the VPSB's position as a darling of veterans' organizations, could not be brought about.

The Administration had only bought time. The forces for decontrol, and rapid return to prewar arrangements, had triumphed in a long, bitter fight. The Administration had been weakened by its continued proclamation of intent to return USES to the states. But

---

[168] *Ibid.*

[169] *The New York Times,* February 24, 1946.

[170] "(VPSB-1946)" Folder, Office of the Secretary, Labor Department Records, RG 174, NA.

[171] *Ibid.*

the real reason for its failure to prolong central governmental supervision lay in its lack of votes in Congress. President Truman, by a quirk of fate, could rely only on organized labor as an effective pressure group to side with him; this ironically, at the very moment he was assailing unions bitterly for their alleged promotion of industrial disharmony in 1946. Moreover, there is little evidence that veterans suffered the dire effects of defederalization of USES. Approximately 70 per cent of nondisabled veterans had found regular employment within 6 months of discharge, 8.8 per cent within 6 to 11 months, 8.8 per cent within 1 to 2 years, 7.7 per cent waited more than 2 years, and 5 per cent had no regular job since service.[172] The Administration, in brief, suffered a setback; but the new Ulysses nonetheless managed to find a job. And that, after all, was all that really counted.

TAKEN SEPARATELY, each of the benefits discussed would appear unimpressive. But viewing these programs as a unit enhances their collective significance—despite the imperfections that marred some of them. A pattern had emerged out of the seemingly unrelated veterans' policymaking of the GI Bill of Rights and those affecting civil service preference, homestead lands, access to surplus war property, terminal-leave payments, and the United States Employment Service. The Federal Government had fashioned successfully, on the whole, a series of benefits that anticipated the job needs of its Ulysses. Farmer, baker, apprentice, clerk, laborer—employed or unemployed—all could find aid from Uncle Sam.

The complex process of decisionmaking had not failed the World War II veteran. Legislators and administrators—made wise by the memories of failures with doughboys, made fearful by the Great Depression, and made confident by the successes of the New Deal—had enshrined the principle that the Federal Government's responsibility extended beyond the granting of pensions to its wounded; able-bodied men needed help too. In brief, the "winnowing fan" had been completed.

[172] The President's Commission on Veterans' Pensions, *Staff Report IX, Part A,* 216. These percentages include both World War II and Korean War veterans. Thus, of the 16,048,000 veterans, 12,423,000 were of World War II vintage.

8

EUMAEUS'S HUT

WHEN ULYSSES returned to Ithaca he could not go at once to his palace. It had been preempted by Penelope's suitors. Instead he spent his first days at the humble abode of his swineherd, Eumaeus. This crude hut served him well; but it was a far cry from the accommodations that he had longed for during his nineteen years' absence. The Ulysses of 1945 and 1946 may have fared worse than his classical Greek prototype. He too had expected to return to friendly hearthsides. He too was disappointed.

But the new Ulysses was not alone in his distress. The postwar housing shortage affected all Americans. Tales of extreme hardship during 1945 to 1947 abounded. One magazine reported: "In Norwood, Ohio, within twenty-four hours after the arrest of a man who strangled his wife, police received five telephone calls from people who wanted his house." [1] In Washington, D.C., a man leapt from the Taft Bridge to his death because he could not find an apartment.[2] Of course, some believed that the crisis would shortly "work itself out." John M. Mowbray, a National Association of Real Estate Boards' official, thought that Americans overemphasized their current

---

[1] "Mr. Wyatt's Shortage," *Fortune*, XXXIII (April 1946), 105.
[2] John Ihlder to Harry S Truman, June 25, 1947; Official File 63, White House Papers of Harry S Truman, Harry S. Truman Library, Independence, Mo. Cited hereafter as OF . . . Truman Papers, HSTL.

housing difficulties.[3] But this was a minority view, for Americans suffered from a chronic dearth of homes.

By Pearl Harbor, the home building industry had not fully recovered from the debilitating impact of the Great Depression. To be sure, the 1941 total of 706,100 permanent dwelling units started stood in dramatic contrast with the 1933 nadir of 93,000; yet the formidable housing production figures of the "boom" years 1923 to 1928 where the annual average of starts reached approximately 852,000, served as a reminder of the production capacity of the industry.[4] More to the point, perhaps, Americans in 1940 occupied 95 per cent of all available living quarters, with approximately 1,700,000 families "doubled up," that is, without separate domiciles.[5]

The war affected the building field in much the same manner as had the depression. Permanent housing starts fell to a wartime low of 141,800 in 1944.[6] The diversion to war uses of raw materials ordinarily utilized in residential construction and the consequent lowering of inventory levels of these materials contributed to the postwar crisis in housing. The immediate needs of war properly took precedence over the less essential requirements of permanent housing. Although nearly a million temporary defense and public low-rent housing units erected during 1941–1945 added to the housing "stock," the additions could hardly be considered an adequate response to basic housing needs. These units helped to meet immediate war demands, but masked fundamental long-term needs.

Wartime social and demographic changes magnified the intensity of the emergency in 1945–1946. Movements from rural to urban areas, a pattern observed in the prewar period, accelerated as a result of the war. High wages in defense factories enhanced the at-

[3] U.S., House of Representatives, Committee on Banking and Currency, 79th Cong., 1st Sess., *Hearings, 1945 Housing Stabilization Act,* December 7, 1945 (Washington, D.C., 1946), 122. Cited hereafter as House, *Patman Bill Hearings.*

[4] U.S., Bureau of the Census, *Historical Statistics of the United States, Colonial Times to 1957* (Washington, D.C., 1960), Series N 106, 383. Cited hereafter as *Historical Statistics.*

[5] "The Housing Situation," a report by the Bureau of the Budget, May 1947; "Housing Administration" Folder No. 1, Clark Clifford Files, Truman Papers, HSTL.

[6] *Historical Statistics,* Series N 106, 393.

tractiveness of the cities. As one St. Louis observer noted, farmers and small-town residents who migrated to his city did not want to leave after "having a taste of metropolitan atmosphere and higher wages." [7] Workers moved to centers of war industry in states like California, swelling the population and placing additional burdens on existing housing facilities. Governor Earl Warren estimated that by 1946 California's population had increased by two million over its seven million total in 1940, while the state's housing supply remained relatively stable.[8]

Other phenomena of the war years added to the subsequent housing problem. Marriages increased and remained at a higher rate, except for 1943 and 1944, than for any year of the prewar decade.[9] A baby boom accompanied this expanded marriage rate. The numerical increase of births dramatized the change: more births occurred in 1943 than in any previous year since 1909, the first year for which reliable statistics are available.[10] Birth rates for the early years of the war actually went up. As a result of wartime population movements, of marriage and birth rate growth, and of the decrease in housing production, the need for more and larger living quarters after hostilities ended became increasingly apparent.

The end of the war created new stresses in the clamor for homes. The rapid mass demobilization of servicemen broke like a tidal wave, washing ashore, as it were, anxious consumers in the search for homes.[11] Many had deferred marriage because of the uncertainty of their futures; others "came of age" during the war and eagerly looked forward to begin "normal" life as adult members of society. The

[7] Bernard F. Dickmann to Harry S Truman, November 30, 1945; OF 63, Truman Papers, HSTL.

[8] Warren to Harry S Truman, June 13, 1946; *ibid.*

[9] The rate climbed from 12.7 (per 1,000 unmarried females) in 1941 to 13.2 in 1942; the level dropped for 1943 and 1944 (11.1 and 10.9 respectively), but rose again to 12.1 in 1945. *Historical Statistics,* Series B 176, 30.

[10] Based on estimated total live births per 1,000 population, the rates for the years 1941–1945 were: 20.3, 22.2, 22.7, 21.1, and 20.4. *Historical Statistics,* Series B 19 and B 6, 22–23.

[11] The Army estimated that 41 per cent of its force—approximately 2,870,000 men—would be seeking housing after demobilization. See House, *Patman Bill Hearings* (December 3, 1945), 5.

marriage rate, already high, reached an astronomical level in 1946.[12] Thus, many veterans who otherwise might have returned to their pre-war households did not wish to do so now.

Yet, without some form of government aid the veterans could not count on monopolizing the buyer's market. Despite his need he had to compete with other people for the inadequate supply of dwellings. War workers, with accumulated savings and generally high earnings, could vie favorably with the returning heroes for homes. But even they did not represent the most formidable of the veterans' potential competitors. Speculative builders, held in check during the war, rushed to siphon off the depleted stock of construction supplies. The promise of a more attractive profit led some builders to erect office buildings, roadside stands, race track grandstands, and bowling alleys, to cite some examples; these threatened to elbow home construction from the field.

Labor difficulties added to the crisis of 1945–1946. A rash of work stoppages in the autumn of 1945 in construction materials industries (most noticeably in lumbering) slowed down production significantly at that critical time. The population movements which created shifting geographic patterns of demand also affected adversely some building materials producers. Workers who formerly labored in brick factories, for example, readily forsook their relatively poorly paid and physically onerous work for easier jobs. Whatever the cause, shortage of labor contributed to the inadequacy of supplies in the immediate postwar period.[13]

As a result of this classic combination of scarce supply and heavy demand, inflation, reined in during the war years, threatened to gallop away following V-J Day in September 1945. During late 1945 and early 1946, appeals to patriotism and the need for continuing "equality of sacrifice" became less effective.[14] President Truman

[12] 16.4 per thousand unmarried females. *Historical Statistics,* Series B 176, 30.

[13] For an elaboration of these labor difficulties, see the testimony of John D. Small, Civilian Production Administrator, before U.S. House, *Patman Bill Hearings* (January 28, 1946), 359–409.

[14] See Roland Young, *Congressional Politics in the Second World War* N.Y., 1955), 6–7.

complained that "there is no incentive to cooperate like there is in war. . . . It's just as hard as hell for the President to get any help." [15] Others also complained: "Six months ago I was piloting a B-29 against the Japs. Now I am trying to build a home in my own home town. The first fight was easier. . . . A simple concrete unfurnished house of 3 rooms and bath would cost $8,500." [16] One indication of inflation in housing may be found in the rapid increase of the median asking price for existing houses in Washington, D.C. Prices rocketed from $8,649 in 1944 to $10,131 in 1945, and to $12,638 in 1946.[17]

If inflation seemed apparent to all, no unanimity occurred in the prescriptions for its cure. If the shortage of materials (the basic cause of the inflation) could be attributed to labor difficulties, for example, a course of action focusing on the latter would be in order. Thus, once labor difficulties had been "settled" by controls over wages and work stoppages, the materials supply would flow once again and ultimately match demand. An obvious corollary to this policy called for the early abandonment of wartime controls over materials: specifically the War Production Board's Conservation Order L-41 and the Office of Price Administration's regulations on prices.[18] But if the problem lay in a basic inadequacy of production capacity to meet all immediate residential and nonresidential de-

[15] Response to a question posed at a press conference in April, 1946. Harry S Truman, *Public Papers of the Presidents of the United States, Harry S. Truman, 1946* . . . (Washington, D.C., 1962), 210. Hereafter referred to as Truman, *Public Papers-1945.*

[16] G. O. Hathaway and seven others to Harry S Truman, December 8, 1945, "Housing" Folder, General Classified File, Office of the Director, Records of the Office of War Mobilization and Reconversion, Record Group 250, National Archives. Hereafter referred to as OWMR Records, RG 250, NA.

[17] *Historical Statistics,* Series N 149, 395. For some national figures see U.S., Senate, Subcommittee of the Committee on Banking and Currency, 79th Cong., 2d Sess., *Hearings on HR 4761, Veterans' Emergency Housing Act of 1946* (Washington, D.C., 1946), 91–92. Cited hereafter as Senate, *Patman Bill Hearings.*

[18] Promulgated in April, 1942, Order L-41 restricted construction of "nonessential" facilities. Only necessary maintenance and repair could be undertaken without special permission from the War Production Board. See Marshall R. Colberg, "Federal Control of Construction Following World War II" (unpublished Ph.D. dissertation, U. of Mich., 1950), 31 ff.

mands, regardless of labor supply, then continuance of wartime controls on materials would be in order.

Hence, a basic question of reconversion policy became: should the controls, especially L-41, be lifted as soon as hostilities ceased, or continued for an indeterminate period? Before V-J Day the official consensus seemed to be for retention of controls until at least the end of 1945, and, in the opinion of some, perhaps well into 1946.[19] But soon pressures from within and outside the government for the elimination of controls grew, forcing the Administration to decide quickly, and possibly rashly. The natural upsurge of demand for return to "business as usual" proved irresistible to the President and his chief advisers; the Administration revoked L-41 effective October 15, 1945. The Federal Government thus embarked on its program of aid to the veteran inauspiciously.

THE REVOCATION of the L-41 Order was a group decision.[20] The President apparently did not participate actively in the process, although he approved the immediate result.[21] John W. Snyder, the Director of the Office of War Mobilization and Reconversion (OWMR) and Julius Krug, head of the War Production Board, led the advocates for lifting controls on building materials. On a lower staff level, OWMR's Hugh Potter (a former official of the National Association of Real Estate Boards and a recent Snyder recruit to the agency), Miles Colean, and Alvin Brown worked diligently to convince skeptical government officials that decontrol would produce more homes for veterans and others.[22] Allied with them were the National Housing Agency and the Federal Works Agency, the latter

[19] See "Notes of Meeting of August 10, 1945 . . . of the Inter-Agency Committee for Construction," "Inter-Agency Committee for Construction" Folder, Files of the Deputy Director for Reconversion (Construction Division), OWMR Records, RG 250, NA.
[20] See an excellent article on the struggle within the Truman Administration over wartime controls: Barton J. Bernstein, "The Removal of War Production Board Controls on Business, 1944–1946," Business History Review, XXXIX (Summer 1965), 243–60. Cited hereafter as Bernstein, "WPB Controls."
[21] Interview with John W. Snyder, April 13, 1965, New York City.
[22] See "Intra-Agency Committee for Construction" Folder, Files of the Deputy Director for Reconversion (Construction Division), OWMR Records, RG 250, NA.

because the L–41 Order hindered construction of nonmilitary public works.[23]

National Housing Agency (NHA) officials viewed the war as an interruption in New Deal programs; NHA's position had evolved from the impetus given to public housing programs by President Roosevelt's second inaugural address in 1937. It desired to return as quickly as possible to permanent housing plans. These involved expansion of housing facilities for all Americans, undertaken by private industry, with the Federal Government providing the initiative and the guidance.[24] Hence, during the war, NHA officials had averred repeatedly that the central government was equipped to meet national housing requirements. John B. Blandford, Jr., NHA chief, for example, had claimed in 1943 that his agency had a "well-stocked statutory arsenal" to stimulate private housing construction; his agency looked upon home building as "primarily a job for private industrial expansion rather than public works." [25]

The agency, furthermore, did not find merit in special housing programs for veterans. Blandford had told James F. Byrnes that such a move would possibly "obstruct or complicate" more comprehensive plans for the public.[26] Specifically, the NHA feared that the government would be forced to build countless temporary structures for veterans, thus derailing the permanent housing program.[27] As a result, Blandford and his subordinates were willing to gamble that revocation of L-41 would stimulate home building sufficiently to meet the crisis.

Chester Bowles, head of the Office of Price Administration, stood

[23] Philip B. Fleming, Administrator of the FWA, to William E. Davis, Director of the Office of Economic Stabilization, September 17, 1945; "Restrictions 7" Folder, Files of the Director, *ibid.*

[24] John B. Blandford, Jr., to Holmes Green, November 9, 1945; OF 63, Truman Papers, HSTL.

[25] Samuel Lubell summarizing Blandford's response to Bernard Baruch's memo asking what agencies were doing in the way of postwar planning. Lubell to Baruch, November 30, 1943; "Agency Reports—Housing" Section, "Miscellaneous" Binder, John M. Hancock Papers, University of North Dakota Library, Grand Forks, N.D.

[26] Blandford to Byrnes, October 7, 1943; "Postwar and War Adjustment, 6-Programs for Aiding Discharged Veterans" Folder, Files of the Director, OWMR Records, RG 250, NA.

[27] House, *Patman Bill Hearings* (December 4, 1945), 41 and 51.

as the lonely advocate of continued restrictions on nonresidential construction. Bowles argued that revocation of L-41 so rapidly "would be a disastrous mistake. . . . It would result in something very close to chaos in the building field, with consequent discredit to the entire administration." [28] He believed that only if the supply of materials for housing balanced adequately with demand could L-41 be immediately revoked. If demand greatly exceeded supply, inflation would result. In his view the War Production Board's estimates of the materials available to meet demand failed to take into consideration the paucity of supplies then in "pipeline" (that is, in varying stages of transit from producers to suppliers) or in inventory. This, coupled with what he considered an erroneous prognosis concerning demand itself, rendered the War Production Board's advocacy for revocation untenable, he believed. The abandonment of L-41, and the failure to replace it with a modified equivalent, he contended, would retard, not stimulate building, especially "in the field of low and medium-price housing, where our greatest shortages exist." [29]

Conservation Order L. 41, in the words of an OWMR staff member, died "hard." [30] Early rumors had indicated that Chester Bowles's position was winning out.[31] Then, the National Association of Real Estate Boards (NAREB) began to act; the editor of its publication carried a strong message to NAREB members: "I ask that every Realtor personally and individually go to work on this matter of [revoking L-41]. Drop everything you are doing for a day or two in order to save the future of your business." [32] During the first days following formal conclusion of the war, Bowles's contentions seemed to predominate. One Congressman, keeping a close eye on the situa-

[28] Bowles to William E. Davis, September 17, 1945; "Restrictions 7" Folder, Files of the Director, OWMR Records, RG 250, NA.

[29] *Ibid.*

[30] Miles Colean to Hugh Potter, August 22, 1945; "Intra-Agency Committee for Construction" Folder, Files of the Deputy Director for Reconversion (Construction Division), OWMR Records, RG 250, NA.

[31] "Washington Whispers," *The United States News,* XIX (August 24, 1945), 96.

[32] *Headlines,* XII (September 3, 1945), 1. Attached as enclosure, Nate Block to Representative William G. Cole (R-Mo.), September 19, 1945; Folder 646, A.C. 47, Housing, Cole Papers, U. of Missouri, Columbia, Mo.

tion, gloomily informed interested correspondents that "the chances of having Order L-41 abolished soon seem rather discouraging." [33] But soon the balance swung in favor of revocation. Snyder (who had been on a trip to Europe concerning surplus property) returned to Washington on September 16, 1945, to add his personal emphasis. As he explained later: "It has been our policy when the issues are finely drawn to resolve these questions in favor of revocation if it appeared that production would be speeded up by such action." [34] Two days after his return, Snyder told the public that L-41 would be lifted, effective October 15, 1945.

When the dust had settled after this administrative brawl, one fact emerged with embarrassing clarity. The returning veterans still needed houses. Activity in residential construction did not appreciably increase as a result of the lifting of L-41. Actually, prices increased an estimated 32 per cent in the five months following that decision.[35] Instead of building houses, moreover, constructors erected " 'race tracks, mansions, summer resorts, bowling alleys, stores, and cocktail bars.' " [36]

In the hope of meeting the crisis, John W. Snyder announced a new housing program of six objectives: increasing building materials supply; strengthening inventory controls to prevent hoarding; buttressing price controls over building materials; discouraging unsound lending practices; fostering industry support for the program; and providing information and advice for people buying homes.[37] The new program typified the Administration's dilemma during the fall

[33] John M. Vorys (R-Ohio) to Earl K. Drumm, September 6, 1945, and identical messages to Edgar R. Johnson, and to Francis M. Thompson, on September 10, and 15, 1945. "L-41 Building Materials" Folder, 79th Cong., Vorys Papers, Ohio State Historical Society, Columbus, Ohio.
[34] U.S., House of Representatives, Special Committee on Postwar Economic Policy and Planning, 79th Cong., 1st Sess., *Hearings on the Use of Wartime Controls During the Transitional Period*, November 8, 1945 (Washington, D.C., 1946), 2189.
[35] Senate, *Patman Bill Hearings*, 92.
[36] Wilson W. Wyatt on October 3, 1946; quoted by Richard O. Davies, *Housing Reform During the Truman Administration* (Columbia, Mo., 1966), 43. Cited hereafter as Davies, *Truman Housing Program*.
[37] Snyder's program is summarized in his "Report on Housing, Memorandum for the President," December 8, 1945; OF 122-I, Truman Papers, HSTL.

of 1945. On the one hand, Truman in his message to Congress on September 6, 1945, had committed himself to a general New Deal program, including housing measures. On the other, he had delegated responsibility on a key reconversion decision to perhaps his most conservative adviser, John W. Snyder. As long as Snyder made the important housing decisions, the New Deal goals of the twenty-one point address would not be fulfilled. Veterans still needed homes, and Snyder's program was passive. It may have been true that President Truman had, as one scholar has suggested, "insight into the problems of the dislocation of postwar adjustment"—an insight that "undoubtedly had influenced his determination to aid the veterans of the Second World War." [38] But the President's tendency to delegate responsibility, along with the pressures of more important global matters, added to the delays in responding more directly to the veterans' housing difficulties. In short, the wind blew the ship of state along its troubled course, with New Deal pennants flying, but with a conservative sheet anchor dragging in its wake.

IF THE REVOCATION of L-41 had temporarily quieted advocates of decontrol, the Administration now faced potentially a far more frightening reaction. The assurance that officials considered "the housing of veterans as the primary emergency housing task in this country," had not allayed criticism.[39] Even before the lifting of L-41, some veterans' groups vociferously decried the government's failure to step in and aid the new Ulysses, shivering, as it were, in Eumaeus's hut. Jack W. Hardy, National Commander of American Veterans of World War II (AmVets), warned the President that unless he acted: "It is likely that a desperation born of unmerited privation, inexcusable in this country, may create an acute and dangerous rift between veterans and the political management that makes such conditions possible." [40] The Commander-in-Chief of the Veterans of Foreign Wars (VFW), Joseph Stack, echoed the AmVets leader:

[38] Davies, *Truman Housing Program,* p. 30.
[39] John B. Blandford, Jr. to Holmes Green, November 9, 1945; OF 63, Truman Papers, HSTL.
[40] Hardy to Harry S Truman, September 7, 1945; *ibid.*

the situation "is one that borders on a National Calamity. . . . The prestige of the whole Government is at stake." [41]

By December, 1945, the President (perhaps beginning to reflect the strain of this pressure) testily informed a Congressman who had urged greater executive initiative:

You must remember that there isn't any possible way of waiving [sic] a wand and getting houses to spring up. . . . There just isn't any solution that can be accomplished in ten days and the Congress is going to have to share the burden because eventually we will require some legislation. Making speeches and blaming somebody for something which can't be helped is not going to meet the shortage.[42]

The President was somewhat unjust to the legislature; as a matter of fact, Congress had begun to "share the burden." Hearings by the House Committee on Banking and Currency had commenced on December 3, 1945, on a bill introduced by Wright Patman (D-Tex.). The measure, HR 4761, originally provided for the establishment of a housing "czar," and included among its provisions the return of powers formerly associated with the L-41 Order. Two other controversial features of the bill provided for subsidies to encourage production of scarce building materials and for fixing sales price limits on new and "used" dwellings.

Congress' misgivings about the revocation of L-41 had its parallel within the executive branch, despite Snyder's success in September. As early as October 9, 1945, the War Production Board's "Order Clearance Committee" had recommended review of the decision.[43] Chester Bowles had continued his guerilla action; the Patman bill had been drawn up with Office of Price Administration assistance.[44] More important, President Truman himself, along with staff members of the Office of War Mobilization and Reconversion, had become convinced by December, 1945, that revocation of L-41 had been an error.[45]

[41] Stack to Harry S Truman, December 14, 1945; ibid.
[42] Truman to Rep. Jerry Voorhis (D-Calif.) December 5, 1945; ibid.
[43] L. Z. Foster to Lincoln Gordon, October 9, 1945; "410.5 C Construction-Orders, 1944–March 1946" Folder, WPB Policy Documentation File, Records of the War Production Board, Record Group 179, NA.
[44] The New York Times, September 20, 1945.
[45] Bernstein, "WPB Controls," 258.

As a result of this shift, the Administration announced a speed-up in the release of surplus temporary war housing units and building materials for use in constructing veterans' homes.[46] Moreover, a regulation (to appear later) would channel certain scarce materials into construction of dwellings designed to sell at $10,000 or less, or with a shelter rental of $80.00 per month or less per unit. Dutifully, the Civilian Production Administration (the War Production Board's successor) issued the regulation as PR-33 on January 11, 1946. During the two weeks that followed, several "Directions" to the basic order appeared. The order set aside varying percentages of eleven items in short supply so that veterans and builders constructing homes for former servicemen would receive priority in their use. The original list of materials included common and face brick, clay, sewer pipe, structural clay tile, gypsum board, gypsum lath, cast iron soil pipe and fittings, cast iron radiation, bathtubs, lumber, millwork, and concrete blocks.[47]

Veterans, in addition, would receive preference on the sale of homes built utilizing the priority regulation. To insure that the new program would be directed effectively, President Truman appointed a "Housing Expediter." This official's task would be to "break bottlenecks" in housing production. Finally, the Truman Administration had begun to act.

To FILL the newly created post of Housing Expediter, the President chose Wilson Watkins Wyatt, a lawyer and wartime mayor of Louisville, Kentucky.[48] Wyatt, born in 1906, had earned a distinguished reputation in Louisville. As mayor, he had battled with the major private electric power company that served his city, although he had been the company's attorney before taking office; he also had the Ohio River dikes rebuilt to avert recurrence of the 1937 flood disaster. Perhaps his major contribution came when he revitalized Louisville and helped to make it a center for war industries. Hard work was a trademark of his city hall tenure; he often put in twelve to

[46] John W. Snyder, "Report on Housing, Memorandum for the President," December 8, 1945, OF 122-I, Truman Papers, HSTL.
[47] See U.S. House, *Patman Bill Hearings*, 367–75, for copies of the orders.
[48] Truman to Wyatt, December 12, 1945, Truman, *Public Papers-1945*, 539.

fifteen hours a day at his desk.[49] He brought this habit with him to Washington.

Wyatt threw himself into his task energetically. He held an exhausting round of conferences with business, labor, veterans, and local and federal agencies; frequently, he worked eighteen hours a day.[50] He hoped not only to design a program, but also to forestall further criticism of the Government. Yet, despite this display of furious activity, complaints still poured in: "the influx of 'aliens and refugees' preempted scarce housing space in New York City; seal off this flow of immigration so that 'our heroes' may be housed!" Red tape held up veterans from occupying vacant units in a Booth Bay Harbor, Maine, Federal Public Housing Authority project; "situation desperate . . . can you not do something for these men?" Military authorities in California held surplus building materials that could be used for immediate relief of veterans; "could not this material be released?" [51]

By February, 1946, Wyatt had his answer for the critics: "Only by bringing to bear the same daring, determination, and hard-hitting teamwork with which we tackled the emergency job of building the world's most powerful war machine four years ago" could the urgent crisis be met.[52] Wyatt envisioned the erection of at least 90

[49] For an illuminating sketch of Wyatt, see John Gunther, *Inside U.S.A.* (New York and London, 1947), pp. 650–52; and *The U.S. News* (February 15, 1946), 72.

[50] Press Release, Office of War Mobilization and Reconversion, January 5, 1946; OF 63, Truman Papers, HSTL.

[51] Mrs. M. Julia Mulhaney to Truman, January 17, 1946; F. L. Littlefield to Truman, January 18, 1946; and J. A. Beek transmitting Joint Resolution of the California Senate and Assembly, January 21, 1946; *ibid.*

[52] "The Veterans' Emergency Housing Program; A Report to the President from the Housing Expediter," February 7, 1946, *ibid.* The description of the program in this and succeeding paragraphs is based on this document. See also Barton J. Bernstein, "Reluctance and Resistance: Wilson Wyatt and Veterans Housing in the Truman Administration," *The Register, Kentucky Historical Society*, LXV (January, 1967), 47–66. Earlier Truman and Wyatt had indorsed a "Share Your Home" plan; a policy by which the scarcity would be alleviated by neighborly action. See Truman, *Public Papers-1946*, 136; and Wyatt, Press Release, January 31, 1946, OF 63, Truman Papers, HSTL. This idea received the somewhat impertinent suggestion from one correspondent that the President set an example by "making a part of the White House available to one or more veterans' families." Oscar W. Cooley to Truman, March 2, 1946, *ibid.*

per cent of the estimated 3,000,000 dwelling units required by the end of 1947. Specifically, he called for the construction starts of 1,200,000 homes in 1946 and 1,500,000 in 1947. Veterans would receive preference for these homes. The new plan—the Veterans' Emergency Housing Program—began the second phase of the Federal Government's response to the veterans' housing needs. Indorsed by President Truman, it repudiated the more passive attitude that had characterized Snyder's Six-Point Program; it also gave official recognition that the revocation of L-41 might have been hasty.

The new plan called for greatly increased production of conventional and new building materials, utilizing a combination of techniques. These included: premium payments to reward producers; guaranteed markets for new and untried products; wage-price adjustments (where noninflationary); priorities and allocations of scarce equipment for producers; use of war plants and new facilities; rapid tax amortization of new plants and equipment; and absorption by the government of undue risks in developmental work on new materials.

Wyatt acknowledged the need for an intensive recruiting and training program; he hoped that the construction industry could attract many of the rapidly returning servicemen. They would be needed, for this program called for an additional 1,500,000 workers. Inasmuch as this would represent a threefold increase in labor supply —whereas the planned production called for a seven-and-a-half times increase—Wyatt obviously counted on a dramatic "breakthrough" in output per worker.

The answer of how to achieve this breakthrough lay partially in the successful development of the prefabricated house. Wyatt hoped labor needs could be reduced considerably through use of the techniques of mass production. In some respects he seemed to share the dreams of many Americans that a "house of the future" (perhaps the "Dymaxion" house[53]) could be achieved through prefabri-

[53] Constructed entirely of metals and plastics, the circular "Dymaxion" house (designed by Richard Buckminster Fuller, Jr.) received considerable publicity in 1946. In an issue devoted entirely to housing, *Fortune* magazine depicted the Fuller house in all its attractive colors. See "Fuller's House," *Fortune* XXXIII (April 1946), 167–79. The *Fortune* editors thought that if Fuller's

cation. Since almost a third of the total housing goal consisted of "prefabs" [54] Wyatt devoted a good portion of his report to the special problems involved. He carefully pointed out that market guarantees, developmental loans, premium payments, and special materials and equipment allocation permits would be granted only after prudent investigation demonstrated the product's soundness.

If Wyatt's emphasis on stimulating production of the industrial house bothered some observers, his advocacy of the pending Wagner-Ellender-Taft bill proved his willingness to engage in other controversial matters. This measure (hereafter referred to as the W.E.T. bill) called for a permanent long-range housing program including, among other provisions, low-rent public housing—a *bête noire* for many conservatives of both political parties. By urging its passage, Wyatt dutifully reflected the continuing view of the Administration that the pressing requirements of the veteran should not obscure the nation's overall housing needs. Perhaps hoping for support for a long-term housing plan by associating the needs of veterans with it, Wyatt included reference to W.E.T. in the veterans' program. He felt that the temporary nature (two years) of the Veterans' Emergency Housing Program made necessary a permanent policy to continue the work already commenced. The tactical position adopted by the Administration leaders concerning W.E.T., however, forced them to neglect one major need of the veterans: construction of low-rent housing, since that belonged to the province of the W.E.T. Bill.[55]

At least one feature of a permanent housing plan found its way into Wyatt's program. He urged extension of the Federal Housing

---

venture succeeded, the house "is likely to produce greater social consequences than the introduction of the automobile." *Ibid.,* 167.

[54] Miss Jessie Sumner (R-Ill.) irreverently termed prefabs "glorified garbage cans." U.S., *Congressional Record,* 79th Cong., 2d Sess., February 26, 1946, XCII, Part ii, 1655. Cited hereafter as *Cong. Rec.,* followed by Congress and Session numbers, date and page reference.

[55] Thus, when the 79th Congress failed to pass the W.E.T. bill, the rental provisions that Wyatt counted on to supplement the veterans' program met a similar fate. Ironically, Wyatt received criticism later for failing to emphasize rental housing in 1946 when, in fact, he merely followed a general Administration policy of supporting W.E.T.

Administration's insured mortgage system so that low-cost homes could be insured up to 90 per cent of value (based on "necessary current costs").[56] The success of the mortgage insurance system in the past, as well as its popularity with many Congressmen regardless of philosophic commitment, insured that this portion of the program at least would not be seriously challenged.

Wyatt's emphasis on community action also helped disarm would-be opponents. Recognizing that the Federal Government alone could not possibly accomplish the gargantuan task set forth, Wyatt commended the establishment of community housing committees to provide initiative on the local level. To be composed of representatives from local government, veterans, labor, builders, building materials producers, financing institutions, chambers of commerce, and other interested groups, the committees, it was hoped, would act as "gadflies" to ensure action. Not the least of their functions would be to secure extension of emergency building codes and modernization of existing regulations.[57]

The Veterans' Emergency Housing Program, to summarize, required that the Federal Government expedite the large-scale construction of dwellings for the veteran.[58] A variety of methods—subsidies, materials allocation, wage-price control, mortgage insurance, and tax revision—used singly or in combination, would help reach the goal of 2,700,000 units by the end of 1947. In brief, the program called for the Federal Government to take action just short of actually becoming a builder.

Wyatt and his supporters felt that the principle of the government not entering the construction field represented a strong selling point. Later, whenever opposition seemed to require special persuasion, ad-

[56] This corresponded to Title VI of the Lanham Act which had provided insurance for financing of war housing.

[57] See H. Dewayne Kreager, "Community Action for Veterans' Housing," *Public Administration Review,* VIII (Winter 1948), 29–33.

[58] Other features of the program included: postponement of all deferrable and nonessential construction for the balance of 1946; federal cooperation and assistance where necessary in the development of home sites; the channeling of the largest portion of materials into low-cost homes and low-rental housing; continued reliance on OPA controls to curb inflation; and increased conversion of military housing for temporary re-use to provide emergency shelter.

herents would remark that if the plan failed to receive enough support, public opinion would force Uncle Sam to pick up the hammer and saw. Conveniently, the American Communist Party (although indorsing the Wyatt program generally) went further than the Expediter by indorsing direct building by the Federal Government.[59]

Thus, the "liberals" found themselves for once on the side of the angels in recommending a program that would forestall a solution recommended by communists.[60] Yet, that latter political group did not stand alone as advocates of an even more forceful program than Wyatt's. A *Fortune* survey in the spring of 1946 demonstrated that a large proportion (48.1 per cent) of veterans queried thought the Federal Government should itself be a builder.[61]

FOR THESE OBSERVERS, the program did not range widely enough because Wyatt had formulated the plan with one eye on possible Congressional opposition. He needed funds for premium payments to stimulate production and for research on new materials and methods. In addition, the insured mortgage system required Congressional extension. It would be necessary to revise the tax laws, moreover, to permit rapid tax amortization. Finally, Wyatt needed legislation extending authority to December 31, 1947, for determining priorities and allocations.[62]

Some of the statutory requirements requested by Wyatt coincided with those provided for in the Patman bill, debates on which began in the House of Representatives shortly after Wyatt's program appeared.[63] The Patman bill, however, as reported to the House

[59] Henry Schubart, "The Housing Crisis," *Political Affairs,* XXV (March, 1946), 244.
[60] Not all the angels sided with Wyatt. Miss Jessie Sumner (R-Ill.) thought that the qualified communist support revealed the true nature of the Wyatt program. *Cong. Rec.,* 79:2 (May 13, 1946), 4937.
[61] 42.1 per cent opposed such action; 9.8 per cent did not know. "The Fortune Survey (the Housing Situation)" *Fortune,* XXXIII (April, 1946), 268.
[62] The Civilian Production Administration's PR 33 had been issued under a delegation of authority through the Second War Powers Act by the President. This act, however, expired on June 30, 1946; Wyatt needed the power for the additional one-and-a-half-year period.
[63] Debate commenced on February 26, 1946, and continued intermittently until the bill's enactment as Public Law 388, 79th Cong., on May 22, 1946.

by the Committee on Banking and Currency, did not contain all the provisions Wyatt wanted. The Republican minority of that committee, along with some of the Democratic members, had pruned the original bill of its most controversial features; most noticeably, premium payments and sales price limits on new and existing houses had been eliminated.[64] Alarmed by indications of growing opposition as the debate progressed in the House, Wyatt wrote to Brent Spence (D-Ky.), chairman of the committee, urging adoption of amendments to restore the missing features.[65]

When the House decisively registered its unwillingness to heed Wyatt or his supporters on the floor, bigger guns were brought to train. The President informed the Speaker, Sam Rayburn (D-Tex.), of the importance especially of the premium payment plan: "The defeat of this . . . would defeat the hopes and transgress the rights of ever-increasing hundreds of thousands of veterans and their families whose housing conditions are now deplorable and are becoming increasingly acute." [66] Two days later, Robert E. Hannegan, Postmaster General and Democratic National Chairman, translated this general appeal into a warning to each party member that the Democrats, not the Republicans, would receive the blame for inaction. "It is essential to the entire Administration's program," Hannegan wired Democrats, "that this legislation be passed at the earliest possible moment." [67]

Debate in the House reflected the importance of the struggle.[68] The Democratic leadership complained about the immense pressure

---

[64] The House bill did go farther on one point than Wyatt had specified. It granted him broad power to direct other federal agencies to act if he felt the veterans' program required it. As one wit put it: "One tyrant [could] compel another to take certain action." (Senator Kenneth Wherry (R-Neb.), *Cong. Rec.*, 79:2, April 8, 1946, 3270.) This turned out to be his major administrative tool; also, perhaps, the source of most of his later worries.

[65] Wyatt to Spence, February 26, 1946; reprinted in *ibid.*, 1659–60.

[66] Truman to Rayburn, March 1, 1946; OF 63, Truman Papers, HSTL.

[67] *The New York Times,* March 4, 1946, 38; Hannegan to Spence, February 26, 1946; Wyatt to Spence, February 28, 1946; and Hannegan to Spence, March 3, 1946; "Housing-1946" Folder, Spence Papers; U. of Kentucky Library, Lexington, Ky.

[68] For the House debate see *Cong. Rec.,* 79:2 (February 26, 1946), 1658 *passim.*

being put on Congress by the "real estate" lobby.[69] This "intrusion" on the legislative process could not be countenanced, said Adolph Sabath (D-Ill.)[70] Throughout the ensuing debate, the bill's supporters echoed the President's words on the "deplorable" housing conditions. Failure to support the original Patman bill acted as presumptive evidence of an uncharitable feeling toward the plight of the veteran. Lyndon B. Johnson (D-Tex.) displayed a tendency toward periodic phrases as he stated the veterans' view as he understood it: "Our returning heroes want rooms, not reasons. They want enclosures, not excuses. They want houses, not just hopes." [71] The familiar charge that Republicans resorted to politics, while the Democrats acted only in the national interest, filled the air each time Wright Patman took the floor.

Yet, on the substance of the bill the Democrats remained relatively silent. For them, it seemed above debate; if the main problem involved the scarcity of materials, then the Housing Expediter must be granted the tools he requested. No one, they reasoned, liked the continuation of controls and priorities or the payment of premiums. But the opposition, they argued, had no way to provide the needed housing other than by permitting the free play of market forces to inflate prices beyond the reach of the average veteran.

The "opposition" (conservative Republicans and Democrats) did not in fact have a substitute plan. They admitted that inflation would undoubtedly occur with the lifting of controls; but inflation could not be prevented at any rate. Not even Chester Bowles, the "boy wonder" of the Office of Economic Stabilization, could stop the natural rise of prices. Their argument rested on the premise that further red tape and controls would merely antagonize the very elements of the business community whose cooperation would be essential for the success of an effective housing program.

The debate against the bill ranged from the harangue of Frederick

[69] NAREB, for example, urged that its members contact their Congressmen to defeat the Patman bill. "Act now if you want to save your business" Herbert U. Nelson, NAREB's Executive Director, advised. *Headlines,* XIII (February 25, 1946), Copy in OF 63, Truman Papers, HSTL.

[70] *Cong. Rec.,* 79:2 (February 26, 1946), 1652.

[71] *Ibid.* (March 4, 1946), 1875.

C. Smith (R-Ohio) that "the main purpose of the Patman Bill is not to provide homes for veterans but to set up a dictatorial Government agency to seize power and promote the totalitarian state" [72] to the dulcet literary references of Everett M. Dirksen (R-Ill.) about the impracticality of both the Patman bill and the Wyatt program. Urging a more moderate approach, Dirksen asked portentously: "Do you want to foist upon an ex-serviceman a house built with green lumber . . . only to find two years later he will be able to put a brawny fist through the side . . . ?" [73]

John S. Gibson (D-Ga.) shared Dirksen's concern about the "unworkable" nature of the proposed bill; he cried: "God, pity the veterans, if from this effort, their roofs must come." [74] The reasoned strictures of Dirksen, Jesse P. Wolcott (R-Mich.), and Fred L. Crawford (R-Mich.) that the proposed legislation would only impede housing production further were moderate complaints. Others, agreeing with Dr. Smith's dim view of the implications of creating a powerful government agency, displayed vigorous distrust of this "communistic Patman-Wyatt" program.[75] "All the perfumes of Arabia would not sweeten it in its present form," asserted John E. Rankin.[76]

When debate ended on March 7, 1946, however, the bill seemed "sweet" enough for Rankin; he, with 358 colleagues, voted for the bill. Only twenty-four opposed it.[77] But the House bill disappointed the Administration. The premium payment amendment had lost; and although HR 4761 authorized sales price limits for homes constructed after the bill's enactment, it omitted the same restrictions on

[72] *Ibid.,* 1683.
[73] *Ibid.* (February 27, 1946), 1744. Dirksen's fears came to fruition in at least one instance: "I think the prize horror case concerns a new house built in Sacramento of such inferior construction that a nine year old boy threw a baseball through the solid wall." Tighe E. Woods to John R. Steelman, January 6, 1948; OF 63, Truman Papers, HSTL.
[74] *Cong. Rec.,* 79:2 (February 27, 1946), 1735.
[75] Miss Jessie Sumner, *ibid.* (February 26, 1946), 1655. Dewey Short (R-Mo.) warned: "Veterans, beware of these Greeks bearing gifts. You fought too long . . . in a war to destroy Communism for you to accept it now." *Ibid.* (March 5, 1946), 1949.
[76] *Ibid.* (February 28, 1946), 1773.
[77] The vote on recommitting the bill provides a better idea of the actual division of opinion; that motion lost 76–304. *Ibid.* (March 7, 1946), 2000–2001.

existing structures. But perhaps a little more pressure would prove the Senate more tractable. Apparently thinking so, President Truman went to work at the Jackson Day Dinner held on March 23 at the Mayflower Hotel. Speaking over a nationwide radio hookup, he hammered away at the inflationary theme:

The veterans returning from battlefronts all over the world deserve the opportunity to obtain homes—and at reasonable prices. They must not become the victims of speculators. . . . My friends in Congress have . . . got to make up their minds whether they are for the veterans' rights, or whether they are going to bow to the real estate lobby! [78]

The Senate proved responsive to the challenge hurled by the President. Surprisingly, few partisan charges found their way into the decorous debate in the upper house. Confining their energies to an orderly discussion, the Senators completed their deliberations in two days. After brief debate, they restored the premium payment feature that the House had defeated; they also added the guaranteed market plan for prefabricated houses. As a final move to meet the Administration's demands, they extended the life of the bill to December 31, 1947. A large majority voted for the amended bill on April 10, 1946. Some sixty-three of the seventy-seven members who voted sped the bill to a House-Senate conference committee.[79]

There the measure threatened to run out of steam. For almost a month the conferees remained deadlocked over the premium payment or "subsidy" plan: the Senate members continued to insist on authorizing $600 million for that purpose; the House conferees just as steadfastly held that they had no authority to agree to this demand. An influential Republican, John Taber, for instance, averred: "The subsidy program that has been proposed is absolutely ridiculous and will not speed up anything. It will just involve the whole picture and result in more delays." [80] Another GOP member, Clifford Hope from Kansas, explained his opposition to a critic: "My vote against subsidies in this particular instance was not directed altogether against the [housing premium payments] . . . but be-

[78] Truman, *Public Papers-1945*, 168.
[79] *Cong. Rec.*, 79:2 (April 9, 1946), 3433.
[80] Taber to Wyatt, April 3, 1946; "Fed. Housing Administration" Folder, Box 116, Taber Papers, Cornell U., Ithaca, N.Y.

cause I think it is essential to stop the subsidy habit before it gets any worse." [81]

On May 9, the House conferees returned to their chamber for further instructions. Again the various Congressmen aired their positions; finally, by a 187–158 vote, the House agreed to the Senate's version—but with $400 million as the allowable amount.[82] This compromise removed the last obstacle to the bill's passage. Four days later the Senate approved the measure in its final form; the House followed suit the same day.[83]

FOR SOME THE Patman bill represented a victory for the veteran; for others it meant only that the lower chamber had showed "the yellow feather in response to . . . hysteria." [84] Few could dispute the fact that another six months had passed (from the time of the bill's introduction in the House). The loss of such precious time could only mean that the Housing Expediter's job, already difficult, would be that much harder.

This proved to be the case; new challenges presented themselves with the bill's passage. In the process of receiving Presidential approval for the Patman bill an administrative squabble developed—symptomatic of ones to follow later. Reviewing the bill, the Veterans Administration expressed reservations to the Budget Bureau and to the President. General Omar N. Bradley, the Veterans Administrator, believed that the veterans' hospital construction program (which formerly shared top priority rights for building materials with the military services) should not be placed in a secondary position to veterans' housing. He pointed out that earlier requests to the Civilian Production Administration and to the Housing Expediter for continuation of this preference had been to no avail. Bradley maintained that these agencies should be directed to comply with his request at the time the President approved the proposed law. Wyatt thought otherwise. He rejoined that the Patman bill vested in

[81] Hope to Helen Hostetter, April 12, 1946; "Housing-Legislative (79th Cong.)" Folder, Hope Papers, Kansas State Historical Society, Topeka, Kans.
[82] *Cong. Rec.,* 79:2 (May 9, 1946), 4765.
[83] *Ibid.* (May 13, 1946), 4915 and 4939.
[84] Rep. Jesse P. Wolcott, *ibid.* (May 9, 1946), 4753.

the Housing Expediter sole authority in determining priorities; to dilute that authority at the outset would run counter to Congressional intent. Wyatt concluded somewhat sharply that it would be "preferable for the President to watch allocation of materials . . . in operation before coming to a predetermination that materials will not be properly and soundly allocated under the law." [85] His view prevailed; he did have sole responsibility—at least as long as he could produce results.

This skirmish, to be repeated with varying casts of characters over other issues, did provide a lesson other than who had "sole responsibility." It highlighted the inescapable fact that an official vested with directive authority over other agencies would be in an unenviable position. As long as the directives did not interfere with the basic functions and aims of the other agency concerned, such an arrangement promised to work relatively smoothly. Yet as soon as the goals of the housing program impinged upon other Administration policies the frequency of internal strife would increase. This appeared to be the case as the autumn of 1946 drew near and it became abundantly clear that the announced goal of the preceding February could not be met.

A difference of opinion arose, for example, between the National Housing Agency and the War Assets Administration.[86] This latter agency had been charged with the liquidation of surplus war property located within the continental limits of the United States. To the displeasure of the War Assets Administrator, Robert M. Littlejohn, the Housing Expediter frequently required the disposition of property in cases where, in his judgment, the veterans' housing program would be materially aided. These directives cut across the established procedures of the War Assets Administration; also, since that agency handled surplus property disposal to veterans, occasionally former servicemen (enjoying presumed preference under the

[85] See Bradley to Truman, May 16, 1946; Wyatt to F. J. Bailey, May 20, 1946; and Bailey to M. C. Latta, May 21, 1946; HR 4761, approved May 22, 1946, Bill File, Truman Papers, HSTL.

[86] Upon John B. Blandford, Jr.'s resignation as National Housing Administrator on February 1, 1946, Wyatt assumed that position as well as that of Housing Expediter.

Surplus Property Act of 1944) would lose their opportunities for equipment because of National Housing Administration preemption.[87] Thus, as in the case of the Veterans Administration, the interests of one group of veterans (those desiring houses) were deemed more important than another group (those desiring surplus property).

Wyatt consistently upheld the absolute priority of veterans' housing over competing veterans' programs. Nowhere can this be seen better than in his refusal to provide housing facilities for nonveterans, even though this would benefit large groups of former servicemen. Specifically, during the spring and summer of 1946 the special problems facing colleges in preparing for the coming autumn semester when the first wave of GIs would flood in received full discussion within Administration circles.[88] The University of Kansas provided a typical illustration of the housing problems at colleges: "We have converted one floor of Spooner Thayer Museum for 80 men. We are building housing under the stadium for 64." Kansas's difficulty in getting priorities stood in dramatic contrast to the physical evidence of a bowling alley under construction a few blocks away.[89]

A special facet of the general problem bothered some observers; educators predicted that their capacity to handle the huge increase in enrollment would be hampered if housing facilities could not be found for the nonveteran faculty members. Under the veterans' program, temporary quarters and building materials provided to educational institutions could not be diverted to other uses; all Wyatt

[87] Littlejohn to Wyatt, September 5, 1946, "Housing" Folder, Central Classified File, Office of the Director, OWMR Records, RG 250, NA. See also U.S., Senate, Special Committee to Study and Survey Problems of Small Business Enterprises, Subcommittee on Surplus War Property, 79th Cong., 2d Sess., *Hearings, Part 97*, June 18, 1946 (Washington, D.C., 1946), 10913–15.

[88] A *New York Times* report on February 27, 1946, showed that 70 per cent of 500 colleges surveyed would have a housing shortage in the fall. The head of the University of Chicago, Robert M. Hutchins, concluded that "the crisis in education about which the country is now hearing is a housing crisis." *The New York Times* (June 9, 1946), section VI, 11.

[89] Irvin E. Youngberg, Director of Housing, University of Kansas, to Senator Clyde Reed, with copy to Senator Arthur Capper, June 21, 1946; "Federal Housing" Folder, Capper Papers, Kansas State Historical Society, Topeka, Kansas.

need do, the educators urged, would be to make an exception in order to help out the hapless veteran who could not be admitted unless trained instructors could be recruited.[90]

The educators' pleas for more veterans' and nonveterans' housing did not go unheeded among the staff in the Expediter's office. Judson Hannegan, a Wyatt aide, informed his superior that he felt the problem "of AAA importance to you and to the President." [91] Others agreed with him. The President's former tailor and best man at his wedding, for example, attempted to convince his friend of the interrelationship of veterans' housing and education.[92] At the same time, John W. Snyder suggested that Wyatt provide for an increase in building material set-asides to help alleviate the crisis experienced by, among others, educational institutions.[93]

The Housing Expediter bridled at this advice. He would have none of it:

Present H.H. set-asides are wholly inadequate to cover the needs of [veterans' housing]. If the set-asides are to mean anything, we cannot add new claims against them. H.H. is a purely housing rating, and to deviate from its classifications by adding college facilities, hospitals and clinics, would invite other service facilities to demand to be admitted to this classification. The result would be no homes for veterans.[94]

Wyatt, although sympathetic to this special problem, did not believe that his responsibilities should be stretched any further without Congressional approval.[95] The Veterans' Housing Advisory Council initially sustained the Expediter's position.[96] But even that group soon deserted the Expediter. As pressure during the summer mounted,

[90] See correspondence for April through August, 1946; Folder 2–01–8(1), Central Files, Records of the Office of the Housing Expediter, Record Group 252, National Archives. Hereafter cited as OHE Records, RG 252, NA.

[91] Hannegan to Wyatt, April 29, 1946; ibid.

[92] Theodore Marks to Truman, April 15, 1946; OF 63, Truman Papers, HSTL.

[93] Snyder to Wyatt, April 26, 1946; Folder 2–01–8(3), Central Files, OHE Records, RG 252, NA.

[94] Wyatt to Snyder, May 1, 1946; ibid.

[95] Wyatt to Matthew Connelly, April 25, 1946; OF 63, Truman Papers, HSTL.

[96] Composed of representatives from the leading veterans' organizations, the council had been established by Wyatt in February, 1946. See Telegrams,

members of the Council had second thoughts.[97] On August 21, 1946, they recommended to Wyatt that a new plan be promulgated to help distressed colleges. Wyatt, having no other support, acquiesced; nonveteran faculty members would be entitled to receive priority assistance.[98] But the reaction of one college official to this loosening of policy provided a fitting epitaph to the episode: "I am afraid the priority assistance for nonveteran faculty members who want to build comes too late to do us any good." [99]

If that ominous and almost ungrateful note were not enough, reports of widespread black market activities in lumber and other building materials added to Wyatt's woe. One story, perhaps apocryphal, related how a New England trucker handling lumber got around OPA price limitations. He always sold his load at the authorized levels, but insisted that the dealer purchase his dog at the same time at the special rate of $500. After the deal had been completed the faithful hound returned dutifully to his former master; this procedure could be repeated indefinitely.[100] The impact of the black market could be insidious; the morale of veterans who stood by and watched dwellings erected with that material could not fail to drop. One former Air Corps sergeant observed:

If you're a veteran . . . you can't get materials for a little $4,000 three roomer. That's all I can afford. But if you're a banker or slot-machine operator, you can put up an eight-room house at the beach to live in three months out of the year. I don't think that's what I flew the Hump for. In fact, I know it isn't.[101]

Judson Hannegan to various college officials, June 13, 1946; 2–01–8(1) Folder, Central Files, OHE Records, RG 252, NA.

[97] See, for example, Jack W. Hardy, National Commander, AmVets, to Francis J. Brown, Secretary to American Council on Education, August 15, 1946; 2–01–8(2) Folder, *ibid.*

[98] Judson Hannegan to Virgil M. Hancher, Secretary-Treasurer, National Association of State Universities, August 21, 1946; 2–01–8(3) Folder, *ibid.*

[99] Arthur A. Haucke to Hannegan, August 26, 1946; *ibid.*

[100] H. R. Northrup, "Where's the Lumber?", *The American Magazine,* CXLII (December 1946), 27. This device apparently found use in black market deals involving automobiles also. See Eric Goldman, *The Crucial Decade —and After* (New York, 1960), p. 27.

[101] Quoted by Richard L. Neuberger, "This Is a World I Never Fought For," *The New York Times* (July 28, 1946), VI, 9.

October and November must have seemed a time of troubles for Wyatt. His support in the Administration had already begun to wane. His program had become a political liability in face of the approaching Congressional elections. The growing impatience with controls, combined with an exasperation over the failure of the Administration to obtain passage of the Wagner-Ellender-Taft bill, had provoked angry remonstrances from politically sensitive observers. Later criticized for delaying passage of W.E.T. by placing his emergency legislative needs ahead of the long-term program, Wyatt could not be accused of not trying hard enough. He had drafted a vigorous message urging House action on the controversial legislation during the summer of 1946. In fact, Raymond B. Keech, an Administrative Assistant to the President, thought he pushed too hard. Keech thought Wyatt's proposed message would "be construed as a chastisement of Congress," particularly in light of that body's determination for an early adjournment. Yet Wyatt's position found considerable support once Congress did adjourn on August 2, 1946. A flood of telegrams and letters from Congressmen, organizations, and outraged citizens inundated the White House with demands that the President call a special session to enact the needed legislation. The city of Detroit's Housing Commission stated that Detroit faced the "worst housing crisis in its history. . . . Many of our citizens will be homeless and forced to sleep in parks this winter." But to these importunities Truman replied: "It is my opinion that it would do no good now to call a special session of the Congress to pass the Wagner-Ellender-Taft Bill." [102]

Despite Wyatt's advocacy of W.E.T., protests from party members continued. Joseph R. Smith, a Texan friend of the Administration (although a member of NAREB), sharply criticized the failure to

[102] See Coleman Woodbury, "Objectives and Accomplishments of the Veterans' Emergency Housing Program," Supplement *The American Economic Review*, XXXVIII (May 1947), 518 for criticism of Wyatt. The proposed draft message of Wyatt is dated July 22, 1946; Keech's memo to the President bears the same date. Detroit sent its plea for the special session on August 3, 1946; and the President's decision may be found in his letter to Rep. Thomas S. Gordon (D-Ill.), October 21, 1946. See OF 63, Truman Papers, HSTL. Davies, *Truman Housing Program*, p. 49, agrees that Wyatt "had devoted much time in support of the [W.E.T.] bill."

provide adequate rental dwellings. It boded ill for the "future success of the Democratic Party" in the coming election.[103] Other "failures" of the program also carried political overtones. The alleged red tape and noncooperative attitude of the Federal Public Housing Authority in handling veterans' emergency temporary housing disturbed Mayor Edward J. Kelly of Chicago—a figure to be reckoned with in party councils. Kelly felt that these delays were "important enough for Mr. Hannegan to bring it personally to the attention of the President." [104]

The Administration could not overlook warnings from influential party members; nor could it ignore symptoms of discontent among veterans. As long as the apartments-wanted advertisements contained items such as: "Parents joyously welcomed us from overseas seven long months ago; their smiles dimming; veteran, wife, baby need apartment; Manhattan to $65. Is there any such thing?" [105] the political implications had to be considered. At the very worst the dire predictions of one veterans' magazine could turn out to be right: "An ungrateful nation has rewarded the victors by throwing them back into the foxholes. . . . The vets are not taking this lying down. If Congress will not back the vet instead of the profiteer, the veteran will find other Congressmen at this Fall's elections." [106]

The Republicans, ignoring the fact that most of the gibes at Congress were directed at their expense, seized upon the veterans' housing plight with glee. Stories of veterans living with their families in automobiles, chicken sheds, railroad terminals, garages, and even jails, provided grist for the political mill. As the campaign progressed in 1946, the Wyatt program inevitably became another issue to exploit. To the billboard slogan of "Have You Had Enough? Then Vote Republican," could be added "Under Truman: Two

[103] Joseph R. Smith to R. R. Zimmerman, October 17, 1946; "Housing" Folder, General File, Office of the Director, OWMR Records, RG 250, NA.
[104] Paul V. Betters, Executive Director, U.S. Conference of Mayors, to Gael Sullivan, 2d Assistant Postmaster General, June 3, 1946, attached to copy of Wyatt to Sullivan, June 13, 1946; 2–01–8(1) Folder, Central Files, OHE Records, RG 252, NA.
[105] *The New York Times* (August 11, 1946), Section VIII, 10.
[106] "Get Back in That Foxhole!" *Salute,* I (September, 1946), 14.

Families in Every Garage." The political skies had brightened for the Republicans.[107]

Wyatt's position within the Administration mirrored this political situation. Thus, as prospects of a Republican victory in November improved, Wyatt's program became politically less desirable. Expecting a reverse, the Administration almost intuitively looked for ways in which it could mend its fences in time for the Presidential election in 1948. This necessitated the overhaul of controversial programs then underway.

A ready-made controversial program could be found in Wyatt's emphasis on the development of the "industrial" house. By October, 1946, the results of the program impelled members of the Administration to urge Wyatt to look more realistically at what could be done in 1947.[108] Wyatt responded to this pressure by stepping up the tempo of his own demands for support on priority controls, so that prefab manufacturers would receive the materials necessary. Despite John D. Small's warnings about possible metal shortages in 1947, the Housing Expediter continued to publicize an expanded prefab program. This evoked a nettled response from Small, who, in addition to repeating his warnings to Wyatt, appealed to the new Office of War Mobilization and Reconversion chief, John R. Steelman, for support in "preventing any government commitments involving the use of large quantities of steel and aluminum sheet before a thorough study has been made of their impact on the rest of the economy." [109] Not one to accept suggestions that he refrain from issuing his directives without prior approval of others, Wyatt

[107] Arthur Krock, "Confident GOP Knows It Must Win Out in '46," *The New York Times* (October 16, 1946), Section IV, 3.

[108] Only 25,000 factory-built prefabs had been developed through September, 1946; the goal had been 100,000 by the end of the year. (John D. Small to Wyatt, October 21, 1946; Housing Folder, Central Classified Files, Office of the Director, Records of OWMR, RG 250, NA.) Experts in OWMR had also become increasingly critical of Wyatt and his "unrealistic" goals. See especially Joseph E. Loftus to Harold Stein, September 10, 1946, *ibid.* Loftus criticized what he termed the tendency of the National Housing Administration to fix goals that bore no relation to actual possibilities. He felt that "on housing items we have so far step by step mimicked the war experience with priorities and allocations in just the same fumbling, stumbling fashion."

[109] Small to Steelman, October 28, 1946; *ibid.*

reasserted his independence: "Congress has charged the Housing Expediter with responsibility for these matters and I intend to exercise that responsibility in full." [110]

Seeming to thrive on adversity, Wyatt fought tenaciously for another part of his program: continuation of price controls on building materials. He informed John R. Steelman that controls had to be retained; "without them," he warned, "the Veterans' Emergency Housing Program would be in serious jeopardy." [111] A week later, corresponding with John D. Small, the Housing Expediter contended that controls must be continued for "the next six months, at least." [112]

But even this was not to be. The death knell sounded for price controls on election day, November 5, 1946. The Republicans won a whopping victory.[113] Jubilantly pouring back into Washington following the election, the GOP readied for the final assault on the Administration's bastion of price supports. But to their chagrin they met no real opposition. Four days after the election the President announced the lifting of all controls except those on rent. He made it clear that even though housing needs continued to be acute "other considerations" required his action. He explained that "price controls over building materials alone, with no price controls on products competing for the same raw materials, would drive these materials away from housing and defeat the objectives of the program." [114]

CONCURRENT WITH this struggle on price controls, Wyatt had been tilting lances with another, and as it happened, final "foe"—the Reconstruction Finance Corporation (RFC). His struggle with the Civilian Production Administration over metals requirements only

[110] Wyatt to Small, November 1, 1946; *ibid.*
[111] October 24, 1946; "Housing" Folder, General File, *ibid.*
[112] November 1, 1946; Central Classified File, *ibid.*
[113] The election is discussed briefly in Alfred Steinberg, *The Man From Missouri* (New York, 1962), pp. 286–89. The Republicans won control of both houses; their margin stood at 246–188 in the House, and at 51–45 in the Senate.
[114] "Statement by the President Upon Terminating Price and Wage Controls," November 9, 1946, Truman, *Public Papers-1946*, 477. See Davies, *Truman Housing Program*, pp. 54–57, for a different view of the election's impact.

presaged the conflict with the RFC over the same "industrialized" housing program. The Expediter not only needed materials for allotment to manufacturers; above all he required the financial cooperation of RFC so these producers could begin their work. But the RFC did not seem eager to use its funds in the fashion that Wyatt thought the situation demanded. By October, 1946, after a long period of attracting firms to develop mass-produced houses, Wyatt decided to force the issue with the government's lending agency. He appealed to the Office of War Mobilization and Reconversion for support; after a conference with RFC officials seemingly had settled the question to Wyatt's satisfaction, he arranged for the formal filing of applications for loans aggregating $54,460,000 for eleven companies.[115]

To Wyatt's dismay the RFC turned down the majority of the loans. More significantly, the Board refused the application of the largest of the individual requests, that of the Lustron Corporation. This company had desired to manufacture a metal home; it had its eye on the huge Dodge-Chrysler war plant in Chicago. To complicate matters, Preston Tucker, a putative automobile producer, had already reached an agreement with the War Assets Administration (WAA) to use that plant. Wyatt strove mightily with WAA, using maximum directive authority. He succeeded in obtaining a revision, so that Tucker and Lustron could share the facility.[116]

But Wyatt could not budge the adamantine George Allen of the RFC. Allen, a friend of the President, had been appointed to the RFC as a watchdog to guard against scandals involving the lending agency.[117] He followed his directions to the letter; he rejected Lustron's application. He did not heed admonitions from Senators like Hugh B. Mitchell (D-Wash). that "veterans desperately in need of

[115] This dispute was aired fairly frankly before U.S., Senate, Special Committee Investigating the National Defense Program, 79th Cong., 2d Sess., *Hearings on Emergency Housing Program* (Washington, D.C., 1946) part xxxix. Hereafter referred to as Senate, *Kilgore Committee Housing Hearings.* The applications were filed on October 22, 1946.

[116] See *ibid.,* 23025 ff.; and Davies, *Truman Housing Program,* pp. 52–54, for discussions of the Tucker-Lustron affair.

[117] George E. Allen, *Presidents Who Have Known Me* (New York, 1950), pp. 195–209.

housing, and looking to their government for forthright action, bear the brunt of this delay. They suffer while the Reconstruction Finance Corporation leisurely goes its own way." [118] Instead, Allen mantained that the company's equity in its proposal was foolishly small. No one would lose if the venture failed except the Federal Government; at the same time, if the Lustron house sold according to its sponsors' expectation the return on the investment would amount to approximately 14,000 per cent. Allen considered it a bad loan; he also indicated that even if Wyatt directed that the loan be made he would receive only minimal cooperation from the RFC.[119]

Wyatt, for his part, had never asserted that the proposed loans could be viewed as "good" business risks; but he had believed that the emergency nature of the crisis required the abandonment of the "business as usual" philosophy. He asserted that "even in banking there are other values than the dollar. . . . This country can afford to risk losing dollars, but it cannot afford to risk losing the faith of millions of its young men." [120]

At an impasse with Allen, Wyatt could only appeal to the President for support. He already had given Truman his 1947 housing program; that plan proposed an expansion of prefabs. Wyatt had based his whole approach on the necessity for the government to commit its entire energies to meet the housing crisis. Thus, at the beginning of December, 1946, he presented an ultimatum to Truman: accept my 1947 housing program and order Allen to approve the Lustron loan, he said in effect, or I resign.[121]

The President had a difficult decision to make. He could heed the importunities of his energetic Housing Expediter and, in the face of certain Congressional opposition, continue the ambitious "New Deal" type of program Wyatt had formulated. The President knew that the more vocal and "liberal" veterans' organizations would sustain his continued indorsement of Wyatt. Ray Sawyer, National Com-

[118] Mitchell to Charles B. Henderson of the RFC, October 29, 1946; "Veterans' Housing Correspondence" Folder, Box 3, Mitchell Papers, U. of Washington Library, Seattle, Wash.
[119] Senate, *Kilgore Committee Housing Hearings*, 23248.
[120] *Ibid.*, 23225.
[121] See memo, M. L. Houck to Clark Clifford, December 3, 1946; "Housing Administration Folder #2" Clark Clifford Files, Truman Papers, HSTL.

mander of AmVets, summed up the views of impatient veterans:

The time has come for your Administration to decide whether to carry out this program or to abdicate in favor of the real estate lobby, many of whose members seem to be primarily interested in constructing conventional houses, by handcraft methods at high prices. . . . The issue is between 17th century handcraft building methods and 20th century mass production methods.[122]

Furthermore, Wyatt had not failed totally; he had fulfilled by the end of 1946 approximately 83 per cent of the planned starts for that year.[123]

On the other hand, notwithstanding the support of the new veterans' organizations like AmVets and the American Veterans' Committee, Wyatt's plan had few proponents left within the government. Those closest to the President opposed continuation of the prefabricated housing program. George Allen's position had been made abundantly clear before the Kilgore Committee. In addition, Clark Clifford and John R. Steelman, two important Presidential aides, were reported in opposition.[124] The Civilian Production Administration, as well as an important housing expert, Mrs. Dorothy I. Rosenman—who had been influential in the choice of Wyatt the year before—thought the Lustron plan unsound.[125]

The President sided with Wyatt's critics. He told Wyatt that the time had come for cooperation among agencies, rather than continuation of directives. Unable to persuade Truman to indorse his program, Wyatt resigned on December 4, 1946. Truman accepted the Expediter's terse note.[126] The President was probably relieved to have the stormy petrel out of Washington; he told John H. Fahey, Commissioner of the Federal Home Loan Board, that he "sincerely"

[122] Sawyer to Truman, December 2, 1946; OF 63, Truman Papers, HSTL.

[123] He had called for 1,200,000 starts for 1946; 996,700 were actually achieved. Nat Rogg, "A History of the Veterans Emergency Program," (Washington, D.C., n.d.), 28.

[124] The New York Times, December 1, 1946.

[125] M. L. Houck to Clark Clifford, December 3, 1946; and Mrs. Samuel I. Rosenman, Chairman, National Committee on Housing, to Clifford, January 22, 1947; "Housing Administration Folder #1," Clifford Files, Truman Papers, HSTL.

[126] Press Release, December 4, 1946; OF 63, Truman Papers, HSTL.

hoped "that the housing situation will be more satisfactorily handled from now on." [127]

The President tried to save the veterans' program by shifting the emphasis from prefabricated to rental housing.[128] The latter emphasis had been urged with vehemence ever since the 79th Congress failed to pass the W.E.T. bill. Mrs. Samuel I. Rosenman had argued: "The solution to Joe's plight, and that of the whole home-hungry American people, is more *rental* housing." [129] Yet, the Administration's 1947 program signified the end of veterans' housing per se; in its place increasingly the orientation would be on public low-rent housing for all who needed it. In short, after being diverted first by the war, and second by veterans, the New Deal focus on public housing had been restored.[130] It also meant that (in the words of a contemporary observer): "The problems of providing urgently needed dwellings for homeless veterans and their families ceased this week to be a responsibility of the Government and became a responsibility of free enterprise." [131] For, despite its belated approval of the Lustron loan seven months after Wyatt's resignation, the Administration had decided no longer to commit itself to energetic espousal of novel techniques to break the housing bottleneck.[132]

The only continuing element of veterans' housing could be found, ironically, in a program that had preceded Wyatt's: the mortgage insurance system provided under the GI Bill of Rights in 1944.[133] Not subject to the buffeting of political winds, the guaranteed loan

[127] Truman to Fahey, December 6, 1946; *ibid.*

[128] "Statement by the President Outlining the Housing Program for 1947," December 14, 1956; Truman, *Public Papers-1946,* 495–98.

[129] "The Racket in Veterans' Housing," *The American Magazine,* CXLII (September, 1946), 117. [Her emphasis.]

[130] During the first few months of 1947 the program was pushed "energetically." See reports of Raymond M. Foley to John R. Steelman, January 24, February 11, and March 10, 1947; OF 63, Truman Papers, HSTL.

[131] Samuel A. Tower, "Housing Returned to Private Hands," *The New York Times* (December 8, 1946), Section IV, 12.

[132] Seen enclosure to memo, Tighe E. Woods to John R. Steelman, December 4, 1948; OF 1930, Truman Papers, HSTL. Truman directed that the RFC lend Lustron the $15.5 million in 1947; a year later the company received an additional $10 million. The whole venture failed ultimately; Lustron turned the plant over to the Navy for aircraft production—and, in March, 1951, the building was torn down by the government.

[133] Ch. V, Title III, Public Law 346, 78th Cong., June 22, 1944.

provisions of that act proved to be a long-lasting bulwark of aid to veterans desiring to purchase homes. Initially guaranteeing mortgage loans of 50 per cent value up to a maximum of $2,000, Congress liberalized benefits so that, by 1950, World War II veterans could receive insurance on mortgages up to $7,500.[134] The guaranteed loan provisions helped former servicemen receive mortgages with lower down payments and longer terms than those offered to non-veterans by financial institutions. Approximately 3,782,000 World War II veterans, 26 per cent of those in civil life at the end of 1955, used the home-loan benefits of the GI Bill of Rights. Thus, many individuals could enter the home buying market under relatively favorable financing conditions.[135]

But even this "successful" program did not escape criticism. Students of housing complained that the Federal Government encouraged people who could not handle the economic responsibilities of mortgages into home ownership.[136] The government should "do more than just grease the path to ownership," the critics maintained.[137] When the government, however, did attempt something more ambitious (as in the Wyatt program) it "flopped on its first postwar assignment." [138]

THE TRUMAN ADMINISTRATION had "flopped"; but 1946 had been an exciting year for Wyatt at least. In later years when builders had asked Wyatt how long he had been in Washington, Wyatt would reply "One year." The response frequently would be "Oh, I thought

[134] Major revisions were made by Public Law 268, 79th Cong., December 28, 1945, and by Public Law 475, 81st Cong., April 20, 1950.

[135] For an excellent evaluation and detailed description of the mortgage program, see U.S., President's Commission on Veterans' Pensions, *A Report on Veterans' Benefits in the United States, Staff Report No. IX-C* (Washington, D.C., 1956). Figures are from Table 4.31, p. 90.

[136] An early and persistent critic of this "ballyhooing" policy was Charles Abrams. See his "Government and Housing," *The Nation*, CLIX (October 21, 1944), 498; and the more comprehensive *The Future of Housing* (New York, 1946), pp. 51–53.

[137] Lloyd Rodwin, *Housing and Economic Progress* (Cambridge, Mass., 1961), p. 47.

[138] Franklin D. Roosevelt, Jr., "Sick and Tired of Doubling Up," *The New Republic*, CXV (December 23, 1946), 852.

it was much longer than that," leading Wyatt to say, "Well, I had the accelerated course." [139]

Wyatt's "accelerated course" had illustrated many handicaps. He had appeared on the scene after false starts had impaired the government's quick response to the new Ulysses' plight. Little had been done during the war to prepare for the inevitable postwar housing shortage. The hasty revocation of L-41 had been an unnecessary blunder for it encouraged nonresidential construction at the expense of homes for veterans. The conservatism of John W. Snyder and the timidity of Harry S Truman in the face of articulate pressure for decontrol made them less sensitive to the less organized, yet valid, cries of homeless veterans. As a result, for three crucial months following V-J Day, the government floundered on the housing problem.

Once in Washington, moreover, Wyatt learned that his directive powers fell far short of the plenary. His orders repeatedly proved unavailing with unsympathetic officials like John D. Small and George E. Allen. Thus, he not only had to contend with the durable resistance of builders and hostile critics within Congress, but he also had little cooperation from the cadre of government housing officials, who desired a long-term permanent housing program; their resentment of the high statutory priority of the veterans' temporary plan rendered Wyatt's job more difficult. And not least important, President Truman's lack of commitment, evidenced by his response to the November 1946 election, deprived Wyatt of essential support.

Finally, Wyatt himself did not display understanding of the difficult administrative and political positions of his colleagues. He misunderstood the realities of the postwar era. The American people were fed up with wartime controls and measures; the 1946 elections reflected this. Yet Wyatt continued to force upon his more politically aware chief programs that may have promised some houses for veterans, but also more votes for Republicans. Wyatt's enthusiasm, a desirable attribute for leadership, affected his judgment; the Lustron case demonstrated that he had unwisely placed too great an emphasis on prefab-housing in light of the realities of the home building in-

[139] Wilson Wyatt to the author, February 20, 1965.

dustry and consumers' tastes. Once emphasized, the program could not be scrapped until Wyatt himself had left the scene.

In any event, by 1946 the number of Americans "doubled up" had reached 2,500,000.[140] As the Truman Administration embarked on its second full year of reconversion it had a formidable job before it. Its efforts had not proved successful in 1945 and 1946 for the veterans. The new Ulysses was destined to remain in Eumaeus's hut for some time to come.

[140] "The Housing Situation," a report by the Bureau of the Budget, May 1947; "Housing Administration" Folder No. 1, Clark Clifford Files, Truman Papers, HSTL.

CONCLUSION

THE NEW ULYSSES of 1945 and 1946, unlike his classical ancestor, had not been forsaken nor forgotten by his Ithaca. No hostility met him. Thousands of years had brought progress; man had learned at least some lessons from his past. In January, 1947, President Harry S Truman proclaimed in his State of the Union Message that policymaking for the new veterans had ended. The job was done. Only summary questions remain: What roles did Presidents, their Administrations, Congress, and interest groups like veterans' organizations, play? What principles were indorsed or discarded in the complicated process of veterans' policymaking? Finally, what was the overall shape and significance of the many benefits that emerged during 1940 to 1946?

How EFFECTIVELY did Presidents Roosevelt and Truman lead in preparing for the return of Ulysses? In the case of Franklin D. Roosevelt the answer is complex. Basically, he viewed able-bodied veterans as part of the whole American people; they should not receive benefits that would perpetuate distinctions between veterans and citizens. Able-bodied veterans' claims on the government, in short, were no more legitimate than demands of other groups with similar needs. Or, to state it positively, he linked veterans' benefits with broader public welfare programs. His position on the bonus and the GI Bill of Rights exemplified this side of his approach to nondisabled veterans. Yet he was willing, as in the case of civil service and reclamation land settlement proposals, to contradict this principle—perhaps due to the strong traditions that indorsed separate preferential treatment for veterans in these areas.

Other considerations forced him to compromise his basic approach. The bitter bonus fight during 1934–1936 had demonstrated the political strength of veterans' organizations; these groups proved to be potent forces in opposition to his ideas. Once burned, he may have been reluctant to press the hot plate again. In addition, his tendency to diffuse administrative responsibility may have deprived him of an efficient tool by which plans could be given force in confrontations with Congress. At no time was he willing to invest a single agency or individual within the Executive branch with broad powers over veterans' policymaking; perhaps this is best illustrated by the case of General Frank T. Hines and the Retraining and Reemployment Administration.

Politics, of course, impinged on his freedom to achieve basic New Deal goals. He had faced since 1937 an anti-New Deal coalition of Democratic and Republican conservatives in Congress; that coalition made itself felt during the war, most noticeably from 1943 to 1945.[1] The coalition had control of the purse strings and the backing of veterans' organizations. Moreover, political campaigns came on schedule during the war. The 1942 Congressional election results whittled Roosevelt's margin in both chambers—at one point in 1944 during the fashioning of the surplus property bill, the Democrats' edge was narrowed to two, 215–213. Voters in 1944 improved the Roosevelt count somewhat; but this was offset in part by the conservative coalition. Roosevelt, even if he had decided to engage in a battle with Congress on veterans' affairs, probably could have reaped little more than a bitter harvest of recriminations and bad feelings.

Finally, the war and international diplomacy made it impossible

---

[1] For an analysis of the early activities of this coalition, see James T. Patterson, "A Conservative Coalition Forms in Congress, 1933–1939," *The Journal of American History*, LII (March, 1966), 757–73.

for President Roosevelt to spend much time personally on veterans' policymaking. Such a subject properly took a subordinate position. That he did initiate many of the broad programs for veterans brings him deserved praise. It may be unjust to President Woodrow Wilson, whose war lasted but eighteen months, to compare him with his first Democratic successor; yet Roosevelt did far more planning for veterans in the face of equally pressing global distractions. Roosevelt, in summary, had to accept modifications of his proposals; but his leadership of planning stands out as an important and lasting contribution to veterans' policymaking.

President Harry S Truman inherited Roosevelt's problems. Yet the situation he confronted differed. The spadework on veterans' policymaking had been done; but he had to put the finishing touches on the rest of the foundation. He had to do this during reconversion, a period of great pressure. He responded firmly, after understandable delays compounded by his early reliance on conservative advisers. Circumstances may have forced him to play a more direct part in veterans' affairs than Roosevelt. His own status as a veteran also may have prompted him to act, especially in regards to housing and the fight over the United States Employment Service. Once in action, of course, Truman had to come to grips with the political realities of his period. The dominance of "decontrol" or "back to normalcy" forced him to abandon programs patterned in the New Deal's image.

Both Roosevelt's and Truman's Administrations attempted to use aid to veterans to promote broader welfare measures. Hence planners in 1942–1943 strove to bind their veterans' proposals tightly to more general needs, such as strengthening education and social security programs. This tendency shows up more clearly, of course, with Truman's efforts in respect to the Wagner-Ellender-Taft housing bill and the United States Employment Service—and with the national health program, not discussed in this study. This emphasis reflected both political expediency and the sincere conviction that separate treatment of nondisabled veterans was unwise. President Truman gave a good example of this orientation:

Adequate jobs for veterans is a major objective of this Administration. . . . We have proceeded on the basic thesis that jobs for veterans will be most plentiful if we direct our attention primarily to the expansion of the economy as a whole.[2]

Critics of this approach might observe that Roosevelt and Truman gambled, unrealistically, that the American people would continue to indorse New Deal objectives. Instead, perhaps, they should have undeviatingly and quickly applied their energies to meet specific veterans' needs—and then turned to broader objectives. Yet, this view would discount the validity of the contention that able-bodied veterans should not be singled out for special treatment. It also would suggest that only "back to normalcy" attitudes should have been heeded; that, in short, the President and Vice-President, who chose to interpret their 1944 victory as a mandate to continue the New Deal, should have repudiated their basic philosophy or styles. A more balanced view seems in order. At least two viewpoints clashed from 1943 to 1946: that of the natural desire to lift central governmental controls and "intervention"; and the concurrent belief that the New Deal's tasks needed to be completed. The first seemed to have triumphed; but that is not to say that the "losers" should have known this in 1943, hence, not even to have attempted to alter the outcome. To have done that would have been an abdication of Roosevelt's and Truman's claims to leadership.

How DID THE MULTITUDE of Executive agencies perform in the complex process of carving out a veterans' program? The Veterans Administration (VA) generally remained in the background in establishing policies. General Frank T. Hines and his advisers deliberately kept the VA out of the spotlight. They conceived of the VA as purely a service agency. It would draft legislation suggested by others—Congressmen or veterans' organization members—but not cast itself into an originating role. This attitude was comfortable; but in the long run it made the agency less influential in 1943 and 1944 than it might have been.

[2] Truman to Joseph M. Stack (Commander-in-chief, Veterans of Foreign Wars), July 16, 1946; Official File 190-J, White House papers of Harry S Truman, Harry S. Truman Library, Independence, Missouri.

Years of cautious management had not prepared the VA to perform the essential functions of planning for the needs of World War II veterans. The VA reflected Hines's conservatism; each benefit was viewed in light of the experiences of World War I doughboys. This was not an improper consideration; but the Depression and New Deal had changed concepts about the Federal Government's proper role. More was required of the central government; it now had to anticipate and stand ready to intervene in social and economic crises. Hines and the VA had been more modest, performing their tasks efficiently and with laudable economy. Neither Congress nor the White House objected to the VA's humility—until the rapid demobilization of veterans exposed the lack of the VA's preparation. Then the axe fell on the heretofore highly esteemed Hines.

Instead of adjusting its organization to meet the inevitable demands on it for service, the VA from 1941 to 1945 spent its energies defending its right to exclusive responsibility over veterans, as in the case of vocational rehabilitation and the GI Bill of Rights. Hines and some of his advisers responded to the new types of benefits with hostility or lack of enthusiasm. Their efforts to push adjusted compensation typified this attitude. Such a scheme would not only be most equitable for veterans, they thought; it would also make the VA's administrative burden easier to bear. No one can say whether the VA's preference for a bonus would have been a better solution—economically or psychologically—for nondisabled veterans. Yet, in the face of overwhelming Congressional and Executive sentiment to grant veterans a full range of educational and employment benefits, the VA's quiet crusade for a bonus was misdirected.

General Omar N. Bradley changed the supine attitude of the Veterans Administration. In a flurry of activity after September, 1945, Bradley asserted his agency's primacy in veterans' policymaking. He decentralized the VA's functions, so that an augmented regional branch system could process claims more rapidly. He brought in members of his European Army staff to reorganize the VA's mail room and medical corps. The result embroiled him in a spectacular controversy with the American Legion's national commander, John Stelle, concerning disabled veterans.[3] Most important of all, he had changed the VA's image in a fortnight from a conservative agency serving World War I veterans to a dynamic organization more in harmony with its times.

The planning functions that the VA might have assumed during the period from 1941 to 1945 fell to other agencies, particularly the National Resources Planning Board (NRPB). Up to its demise in the summer of 1943, the NRPB had begun to chart out a veterans' program. The planning vacuum caused by the ending of NRPB was not filled, as Bernard Baruch and John Hancock had hoped, by the Retraining and Reemployment Administration (RRA). That agency, due to lack of Presidential support and its own leadership, did not fulfill its projected task as planner and coordinator of veterans' affairs. Neither the Bureau of the Budget nor the Office of War Mobilization and Reconversion could make up for RRA's poor showing. The RRA remained little more than a paper organization under General Hines. The agency had been so discredited that General Graves B. Erskine had to spend valuable time in an effort to redeem it in the eyes of his fellow government officials.

The other federal agencies tended to play disruptive roles, creating barriers to smooth veterans' policymaking. The Departments of the Interior, Agriculture, and Labor, the Selective Service System, and the National Housing Agency especially fueled internecine administrative fires. Concerns about jurisdiction and about the agencies' future status helped make life for Frank T. Hines even more difficult. There seems to have been no way in which interagency bickering could have been avoided; indeed, much of the wrangling undoubtedly was desirable, for it brought disputes and legitimate concerns to the forefront. Yet, these quarrels helped sap the Executive Department's strength in achieving its goals.

Although the Washington bureaucracy did not always work in unison, it had nonetheless contributed to the series of piecemeal

[3] Jack A. Underhill, "The Veterans' Administration and The American Legion (1945–1947)," unpublished MA thesis, Columbia University, 1959, pp. 28–41.

measures that overall had coherence and relevance to the able-bodied veterans' needs. The process could have been quickened. Firmer guidance from the White House might have insured that the trio of necessities—planning for new benefits, administrative review of the VA's functions and readiness to execute policy, and measures to coordinate legislative-executive relations on veterans' affairs—would have been more successfully met. As it developed, only the first had been achieved.

CONGRESS, of course, did more than provide legal form to veterans' proposals conceived by the Executive Department and veterans' organizations. Individuals like John E. Rankin, Wright Patman, Andrew Jackson May, Elbert D. Thomas, Bennett Clark, Robert La Follette, and countless others mentioned in the preceding chapters helped shape the veterans' benefits. All collectively played an important role. To be sure, only a few benefits—the GI Bill and housing—were changed during Congressional debates. Yet, the work done in committees altered veterans' measures significantly. Representatives of the veterans' organizations, Administration spokesmen, and others gave valuable advice; the decisions to accept or reject that guidance, however, ultimately were made by Congressmen or Senators.

The traditional art of compromise marked the course of veterans' legislation. The superior committee structure for veterans in the House gave it a slight advantage. The lower chamber, through John E. Rankin's acquisition of jurisdiction over most World War II veterans' legislation, had organized itself to anticipate the flood of bills that inevitably flowed in for consideration. The Senate retained the Finance Committee's subcommittee system in handling veterans' legislation; this may have subordinated important bills to the parent committee's primary concerns. With the major exception of the GI Bill of Rights, the Finance subcommittee on World War Veterans' Legislation showed less energy than Rankin's committee in the House. Despite this organizational advantage, the House's contribution was matched by the Senate's in enacting the GI Bill of Rights and the Veterans' Emergency Housing Program. The Senate acted as a brake to the House's more generous cash benefits' policy in regard to mustering-out and terminal-leave pay. The Senate also seemed more willing to indorse the Administration's position—notably on the GI Bill, on mustering-out and terminal-leave pay, on the United States Employment Service's status, and on housing.

Both houses refrained from entering officially into either the demobilization or the seniority questions. They refused to do so partly because the Executive Department did not desire Congressional intervention. Equally as important, Congress undoubtedly did not relish the idea of handling those thorny matters. Demobilization, in addition to being controversial, remained securely within the purview of military policy—hearings could be held, notes of protests sounded in the chambers, and letters written to the President and to the War and Navy Departments; but that was about all. The seniority dispute had remained intramural within the Executive Department until it became a judicial question, obviating more direct participation by Congress.

Congress' desire to reassert its peacetime prerogatives was also important. Abolishing the National Resources Planning Board and defederalizing the United States Employment Service were but the most outstanding examples of legislative-executive relations affecting veterans. This Congressional mood helped frustrate Roosevelt's and Truman's efforts to achieve broader programs that would have involved veterans. Constantly sniping at the Administration, Congress materially affected Truman's veterans' housing and employment programs—aspects of which were stifled by hostility within the legislature.

An additional motive made Congress generally unresponsive to the broader integrative veterans' programs of the Executive. The Administration's attempts to violate the veterans' exclusiveness principle threatened to blur committee jurisdictional lines in Congress, as with the controversies affecting disabled veterans' vocational rehabilitation, and able-bodied educational and employment service. Since administrative agencies tend to mirror separations on the Hill, Congress naturally objected to combining civilian and veterans' functions.[4] To have permitted this combination, urged by experts in centralized management like Harold D. Smith, would have imperiled Congress's attempts to exert control over the administration of its legislative enactments. Thus, part of the fervor exhibited by John E. Rankin and Bennett Clark over veterans' exclusiveness reflected their intra-Congressional concerns. Rankin especially seemed more solicitous over his "Congressional" than over his "veterans'" interests.

In general, although Congress altered proposals for veterans prepared by the Executive and interest groups, the national legislature played a reactive rather than initiative role. To be sure, as late as 1942 Roosevelt had balked at his Budget Bureau's suggestion to present committee chairmen with a specific Administration bill for vocational rehabilitation. This delicacy, however, was but an aberration from the norm. By the next year, in the cases of mustering-out payments and the educational measure, the President had acceded to the presentation of officially indorsed substantive bills. Hence in veterans' affairs, as with other matters, the Executive followed a pattern that had been established during the early years of the New Deal. Big government had changed old relationships between the legislature and executive.

WHAT IMPACT did the various veterans' organizations have on the course of veterans' policymaking? There can be little doubt that they were influential. At most, the veterans' organizations actually participated in the legislative process. In addition to drafting the original GI Bill of Rights, these groups sat down with Congressmen and government officials to draw up both the vocational rehabilitation and civil service preference measures. At least, their reaction to proposals had to be anticipated and considered carefully. Hence in October, 1943, when Administration officials discussed veterans' affairs, no one seemed to have questioned the necessity of consulting

[4] See Richard E. Neustadt, "Politicians and Bureaucrats," in The American Assembly, Columbia University, *The Congress and America's Future,* edited by David B. Truman (Englewood Cliffs, N.J.: 1965), pp. 105–9. Cited hereafter as *Congress and America's Future.*

the veterans' organizations. In one instance—on the status of the United States Employment Service—plans to alter a program were not adopted because of the anticipated opposition of the American Legion, Veterans of Foreign Wars (VFW), and Disabled American Veterans (DAV). These organizations, with their effective legislative staffs, closely followed developments affecting veterans. Their mere existence, size, and past success as lobbyists could not be ignored by legislator or bureaucrat.

But it is easy to exaggerate these groups' influence. Although powerful, they were not omnipotent. In the past they had not been successful in punishing their opponents at the polls.[5] Instead, the extent of their power depended upon their own unanimity and the strength of their opposition. If other interest groups were weak or divided, the veterans' organizations usually had their own way—as in the case of vocational rehabilitation and civil service preference. But they were not always that fortunate. The GI Bill of Rights demonstrated the pitfalls of a divided veterans' lobby, with the VFW initially, and DAV consistently, opposing the Legion's efforts. When faced with a strong pressure group, like labor, the veterans' organizations either adroitly incorporated features to stave off dissent—as in the GI Bill of Rights' unemployment section—or discreetly refused to become directly engaged, as with the quarrel over the United States Employment Service.

Other circumstances curtailed their influence. The competition between the VFW and the Legion, particularly for a commanding position to attract new members from the ranks of World War II veterans, may have stimulated a rush to get legislative trophies; but it made unity and strength difficult to achieve. The general uncertainty, moreover, whether the World War II veterans would shun the older organizations and create their own may have made the older groups wary about alienating prospective members. The growing number of union-affiliated Legion posts might have dictated, for

---

[5] See V. O. Key, Jr., "Veterans and the House of Representatives: A Study of a Pressure Group and Electoral Mortality," *The Journal of Politics,* V (February, 1943), 27–40.

example, that organization's abstention from joining the United States Employment Service fight more significantly. Finally, the veterans' organizations too had learned from the bonus fight of the 'twenties and 'thirties. The hot plate, in short, made no distinction whose fingers it burned.

In summary, the veterans' organizations proved to be influential in the least controversial programs for able-bodied veterans, where they faced little or at most, divided opposition. Their force began to diminish as the benefits became more controversial or when they met more decided opposition from the Administration—as with the bonus, disguised in either the form of mustering-out or terminal-leave pay, the superseniority fight, the veterans' housing program, or the United States Employment Service battle. Their influence on the reconversion measures, information centers and surplus property, was mixed—unimportant with the former, and belatedly effective in the latter.

The veterans' organizations seemed to fade in significance after 1944. For one thing, they had achieved major legislative goals by June 1944 when the GI Bill of Rights had been enacted. For another, recruiting new members increasingly became a main focus of their activity. This involved, among other considerations, a reorientation of internal organization and attitudes. The Legion's leaders, for example, faced the task of impressing older legionnaires with the necessity of at least appearing to be willing to step aside so that the new recruits could assume roles in the expanded organization. Legionnaires also had to school themselves to refrain from the general hilarity that had characterized their national conventions; the new veteran, it was reasoned, was more serious, hence old attitudes needed to be modified. Thus, with legislative goals achieved and internal matters to occupy their time, the veterans' organizations receded from the glare of publicity during 1944 and 1945.

There is another reason for the diminution of veterans' interest groups' visible activity during the period after 1944. It has been maintained that during the twentieth century the Executive, in becoming more "representative," has been more responsive than Congress to the national interests that have emerged as a result of the so-called communications revolution.[6] As a result, nationally based interest groups have attempted to gain access to the government by way of the Administration rather than through Congress. During the period 1919 to 1944, for example, the veterans' groups, facing hostile Administrations, were forced to wage their battles for favorable policies in the legislature. The tactical situation required the Legion, VFW, and DAV to resort to major propaganda techniques to mobilize their members and public opinion for unified support. They had to sway, for instance, the House of Representatives, whose members represented diverse interests and were often insulated from mere appeals of the national veterans' headquarters. Hence, although these organizations influenced the day-to-day operations of the VA, they found it more difficult to affect policymaking, given the attitudes of Harding, Coolidge, Hoover, and Roosevelt. Thus, the veterans' organizations' activities captured headlines; with their successes in the bonus and Economy fights, they combined publicity and results, earning the adjectives "powerful" and "influential."

In 1944, however, the relationship between the veterans' interest groups and the Administration changed. Busy with war matters, President Roosevelt no longer adhered strictly to his earlier views. More important, the Legion patterned its GI Bill closely enough to the Administration's separate measures to avert a direct clash. The civil service preference legislation followed the omnibus measure by five days; it too demonstrated that a harmony of interest could be achieved on veterans' affairs. The veterans' organizations had gained access to policymaking by way of the Administration. To be sure, this relationship remained uneasy; the clash between the Legion's national commander John Stelle and the new VA chief Omar N. Bradley in 1946 had threatened to place the veterans' organizations and the Administration into hostile camps once again. But the unpopularity of Stelle's position among the Legion's rank-and-file closed off the dispute; the 1944 "rapprochement" proved to be durable.

[6] See Samuel P. Huntington, "Congressional Responses to the Twentieth Century," *Congress and America's Future*, pp. 16–17.

THE NATION had moved far since Calvin Coolidge in 1924 had averred: " 'We owe no bonus to able-bodied veterans of the World War.' " [7] Coolidge and many of his generation had viewed veterans with suspicion. At best, ex-servicemen were misguided when they clamored for a bonus; at worst, they were Treasury looters. No one disputed the legitimacy of disabled veterans' claims. But the healthy ex-serviceman needed no special assistance. The Republican Administrations of the 'twenties and 'thirties opposed such aid, since they believed that Americans would be helped best by creating a favorable climate in which business could flourish. Hence, Mellon's castigation of veterans' exclusiveness.

The New Deal ushered in a new era; its keynote would be advocacy of central governmental responsibility for the general welfare of its citizens. On the surface, this may have been seen as a good omen for the veterans who had been constantly rebuffed since 1920. Actually, the Roosevelt Administration agreed with its predecessors; veteran's exclusiveness was an anathema to Morgenthau as to Mellon. But the outward similarity of the New Era and New Deal on this matter obscured fundamental differences. The Roosevelt Administration, despite its Economy Act and its opposition to the early redemption of the bonus, listened to, and acted upon, the complaints of veterans. Jobless veterans worked on public construction projects and busied themselves, side by side with other unemployed Americans, at Civilian Conservation Corps camps. Help the able-bodied veteran, yes; but let that aid flow to him as it would to other citizens.

The New Deal's emphasis on national planning accustomed government officials during 1940 to 1946 to the responsibility of preparing for the new veterans. As a result, despite the urgency of purely wartime concerns, planners were permitted to lift their sights beyond the immediate horizon, and peer ahead into the postwar world. That it may seem today only natural that government officials in 1940 should have begun to plan for the readjustment of the Nation to peace even before hot war had erupted, testifies to the beneficial ef-

[7] Quoted by Gustavus A. Weber and Laurence F. Schmeckebier, *The Veterans' Administration; Its History, Activities and Organization* (Washington, D.C., 1934), p. 232.

fect of the New Deal. Yet, national planning had not meant dictatorship. The fact that Congress modified the GI Bill of Rights and other veterans' benefits, so that their resemblance to NRPB recommendations seems remote, showed how planning need not have had sinister connotations. At least Congressmen had something to alter.

The costs of the World War II veterans' program were high, but not unprecedented. Measured as a percentage of the total national budget, they did not reach the level of the 'twenties and 'thirties; the costs for the peak postwar year (1948) of veterans' expenditures amounted to 20.1 per cent of the total budget, compared with 29.1 per cent in 1931, the highest prewar year.[8] The former percentage does not include mustering-out and terminal-leave pay; nor should it be forgotten that the general rise of the total budget, due in large part to heavy national defense expenditures, masks somewhat the huge outlays for veterans. On the other hand, those payments include figures for veterans of all wars, disabled and able-bodied alike.

It is impossible to construct an accurate tally of all payments to nondisabled World War II veterans, but the total as of 1955 probably exceeded $20 billion, excluding insurance dividends, and intangibles such as civil service jobs, surplus war property, and guidance to employment by the United States Employment Service. The cost was indeed enormous; but as Governor Edward Martin (R-Pa.) had noted in 1944:

The men in the armed service will pay the largest amount of the bills which are now being contracted. They will not only do the fighting, but will also do much of the paying.[9]

In general, then, the cost can be considered as the Nation's investment in developing its own vital human resources.

By 1947 the Nation had extended a bountiful hand to its returning nondisabled heroes. Some veterans' benefits had limited appeal

---

[8] U.S., The President's Commission on Veterans' Pensions, *A Report on Veterans' Benefits in the United States: Staff Report No. II, Veterans' Benefits Administered by Departments and Agencies of the Federal Government, Digest of Laws and Basic Statistics* (Washington, D.C., 1946), Table 26, 190.

[9] Martin to Senator James J. Davis (R-Pa.), March 31, 1944; Container Number 26, Political Correspondence, Davis Papers, Library of Congress, Washington, D.C.

—guaranteed loans for businesses and farms, preference for surplus war property, and privileged access to homestead lands. But others have been more significant, such as the GI Bill's guaranteed home loans, readjustment and education benefits, and the mustering-out and terminal-leave pay measures. The scope of these benefits testifies to how generously an affluent society can repay its citizen-army for military sacrifices; to how well, amid confusions and distractions, a nation at war can fashion a comprehensive veterans' policy; and to how sensitive representative government can be to the needs of its citizens—a government responding, as it were, to the crosscurrents of its historical experiences with veterans of past wars, with depression, and with experiments in national planning.

The education benefits helped spur the development of America's schools and colleges; they also gave to the participating men and women opportunities that they might otherwise have missed; a generation of youth had reaped a rich harvest. The conclusions of The President's Commission on Veterans' Pensions summarizes the impact of the readjustment benefits: "By almost any test, the economic status of veterans compares favorably with that of nonveterans of similar age." [10] World War II veterans occupy, in greater proportion than nonveterans of comparable age, the highest paid professional, technical, managerial, and skilled positions. They also have, on the average, two more years of formal education; this explains in part their higher employment status. The median earned income of veterans exceeds that of nonveterans, and the gap promises to continue to widen. In addition, veterans own more homes proportionately than those who have not been in military service; as in the case of earned incomes, this proportion seems likely to grow greater. Finally, those veterans who had experienced the greatest break in their education, have utilized the readjustment benefits the most.

[10] U.S., The President's Commission on Veterans' Pensions, *A Report on Veterans' Benefits in the United States: Staff Report No. IX, Part A, Readjustment Benefits: General Survey and Appraisal* (Washington, D.C., 1956), 143. The remaining portion of this paragraph paraphrases The Commission's findings; *ibid.*, 143–44. It should be noted that veterans, by and large, probably represented the most able of American youth, due to the screening followed in the induction process. Thus, the differences reported by the Commission are only in part a result of beneficial governmental programs.

The benefits for the new veteran, to summarize, have acted as a flywheel, so to speak, to continue the impetus of the Federal Government's expanding promotion of the general welfare. Thus, when the steam appeared to have escaped from the engine of the New Deal by 1945, the World War II nondisabled veterans' benefits—by design and by chance—provided new sources of energy. Although specifically proposed to facilitate the veterans' return to civilian status, the bonanza has had an ever-widening influence on postwar America. New businesses have arisen, new occupations found, new land tilled, and new horizons seen. Each has required the Federal Government to maintain a watchful eye. They have, in short, expanded governmental services far beyond the immediate needs of 1945 and 1946. These services have an air of permanence. Later conflicts, like Korea and Vietnam, have spawned new generations of Ulysseses. The advances made in veterans' benefits during 1940 to 1946 have seemed so solid that they have been extended, with modifications, to these new warriors.

Policymaking for nondisabled World War II veterans thus is another chapter in the chronicle of the consequences of the Roosevelt revolution of 1933. The Nation has always been grateful to its returning heroes. Economic crises, or the threat of crises, have been present after each major war. Veterans have consistently organized themselves and made their demands on government. All three of these conditions in conjunction have constituted a repeating postwar pattern affecting veteran-government relations. The 1940–1946 period represents the crucial turning point. For the first time the government anticipated the needs of all its veterans. The notion that the disabled alone needed aid was discarded. The masquerades of the past were rendered obsolete. It was no longer necessary for the able-bodied veterans in need to sham "war" injuries to qualify for pensions, or to resort to undignified appeals to their government for charity. The New Deal's impact on veterans' affairs was indeed great.

The veterans' benefits, to conclude, have contributed to making the Ulysses of World War II more happy for having survived than bitter for having served. It is reasonable to suggest that these benefits have helped Americans avoid repetition of ugly veteran-civilian

clashes. The Federal Government, in giving aid liberally to nondisabled veterans in such an unprecedented fashion, had established an
important principle: Ulysses deserves a helping hand not only to get
him to Troy, but to ease him back into life in Ithaca.

WORKS CITED

MANUSCRIPT COLLECTIONS

I: ARCHIVES

The American Legion Archives, National Headquarters, Indianapolis, Indiana

The National Archives, Washington, D.C. Records of:
  Bureau of the Budget, Record Group 51
  Department of Agriculture, Record Group 16
  Department of Labor, Record Group 174
  Department of War, Record Group 319 (at World War II Records Branch, Alexandria, Virginia)
  House of Representatives' Committee on World War Veterans' Legislation, Record Group 233
  National Resources Planning Board, Record Group 187
  Office of the Housing Expediter, Record Group 252
  Office of War Mobilization and Reconversion, Record Group 250
  Retraining and Reemployment Administration, Record Group 244
  Selective Service System, Record Group 147
  War Manpower Commission, Record Group 211
  War Production Board, Record Group 179
  War Shipping Administration, Record Group 248

Veterans Administration, Legislative and Research Branch Files, Central Office, Washington, D.C.

II: LIBRARIES

Columbia University, New York, New York. Oral History Project, Reminiscences of:

Brophy, John
Keough, Eugene J.
Cornell University, Ithaca, New York, Papers of:
Cole, W. Sterling
Reed, Daniel A.
Taber, John
Duke University, Durham, North Carolina, Papers of:
Barden, Graham A.
Langston, John Dulles
Franklin D. Roosevelt Library, Hyde Park, New York, Papers of:
Kilgore, Harley M.
Roosevelt, Franklin D.
Rosenman, Samuel I.
Thomas, Elbert D.
Harry S. Truman Library, Independence, Missouri, Papers of:
Clifford, Clark (Files)
Truman, Harry S
Kansas State Historical Society, Topeka, Kansas, Papers of:
Capper, Arthur
Hope, Clifford R.
Library of Congress, Manuscript Division, Washington, D.C., Papers of:
Davis, James J.
Wadsworth, James W., Jr.
Memphis Public Library, Memphis, Tennessee, Papers of:
McKellar, Kenneth
Ohio State Historical Society, Columbus, Ohio, Papers of:
Vorys, John M.
Princeton University, Princeton, New Jersey, Papers of:
Baruch, Bernard M.
South Carolina State Archives Department, Columbia, South Carolina,
Papers of:
Maybank, Burnet
University of Florida, Gainesville, Florida, Papers of:
Green, Robert A.
University of Kentucky, Lexington, Ky., Papers of:
Spence, Brent
University of Missouri, Columbia, Missouri, Papers of:
Bennett, Marion T.
Cole, William C.
University of Nebraska, Lincoln, Nebraska, Papers of:
Wherry, Kenneth S.
University of North Carolina, Chapel Hill, North Carolina, Papers of:
Doughton, Robert L.

University of North Dakota, Grand Forks, North Dakota, Papers of:
Hancock, John M.
Lemke, William
University of Oklahoma, Norman, Oklahoma, Papers of:
Schwabe, George B.
Thomas, J. W. Elmer
University of Washington, Seattle, Washington, Papers of:
Mitchell, Hugh B.

PUBLIC DOCUMENTS

U.S. Bureau of the Census. *Historical Statistics of the United States, Colonial Times to 1957.* 1960.

U.S. *Congressional Record.* 76th through 80th Congresses.

U.S. Department of the Interior. *Government Aid to Land Acquisition by War Veterans, 1796–1944.* 1944.

U.S. *Federal Register.* Vol. IX, 1944.

U.S. House of Representatives, Committee on Appropriations, Subcommittee on Deficiency Appropriations. *Hearings on the Urgent Deficiency Appropriation Bill for 1946.* 79th Cong., 2d Sess., 1946.

U.S. House of Representatives, Committee on Appropriations, Subcommittee on Labor Department and Federal Security Appropriations. *Hearings on the Department of Labor-Federal Security Agency Appropriation Bill for 1946, Part 3: War Manpower Commission.* 79th Cong., 1st Sess., 1945.

U.S. House of Representatives, Committee on Banking and Currency *Hearings on H.R. 4420 . . . A Bill to Amend the Reconstruction Finance Corporation Act by Adding a New Title Thereto.* 78th Cong., 2d Sess., 1944.

———. *Hearings on H.R. 4761 . . . 1945 Housing Stabilization Act.* 79th Cong., 1st Sess., 1946.

U.S. House of Representatives, Committee on Education. *Hearings on H.R. 699 . . . Vocational Rehabilitation Education and Training.* 78th Cong., 1st Sess., 1943.

U.S. House of Representatives, Committee on Expenditures in the Executive Departments. *Hearings on H.R. 5125 . . . Surplus Property Act of 1944.* 78th Cong., 2d Sess., 1944.

U.S. House of Representatives, Committee on Labor. *Hearings on H.R. 2915, HR 4437, HR 5142 . . . United States Employment Service.* 79th Cong., 2d Sess., 1946.

U.S. House of Representatives, Committee on Military Affairs. *Hearings on H.R. 3742 and H.R. 3799 . . . Mustering-Out Pay to Members of the Armed Forces.* 78th Cong., 1st Sess., 1944.

———. *Hearings on Demobilization of Materiel and Personnel.* 79th Cong., 1st Sess., 1946.

———. *Hearing on the Operation of the Army Personnel Readjustment Plan.* 79th Cong., 1st Sess., 1945.

U.S. House of Representatives, Committee on Naval Affairs. *Hearings on . . . Sundry Legislation Affecting the Naval Establishment, 1946, Number 177.* 79th Cong., 2d Sess., 1946.

U.S. House of Representatives, Committee on World War Veterans' Legislation. *Hearing on H.R. 7661 and H.R. 7662 to Amend Certain Laws and Veterans' Regulations to Provide for Rehabilitation of Disabled Veterans.* 77th Cong., 2d Sess., 1942.

———. *Hearings on H.R. 3917 and S. 1767, to Provide Federal Government Aid for the Readjustment in Civilian Life of Returning World War II Veterans.* 78th Cong., 2d Sess., 1944.

———. *Hearings on Investigation of the Veterans' Administration with a Particular View to Determining the Efficiency of the Administration and Operation of Veterans' Administration Facilities.* 79th Cong., 1st Sess., 1945.

U.S. House of Representatives, Select Committee to Investigate Disposition of Surplus Property. *Hearings on H. Res. 385, A Resolution Relating to Disposition of Surplus Property,* Part I. 79th Cong., 2d Sess., 1946.

U.S. House of Representatives, Special Committee on Post-War Economic Policy and Planning. *Hearings . . . on Post-War Economic Policy and Planning,* Part III. 78th Cong., 2d Sess., 1944.

———. *Hearings on the Use of Wartime Controls During the Transitional Period.* 79th Cong., 1st and 2d Sess., 1946.

U.S. National Resources Planning Board. *After Defense—What?; Post-Defense Planning.* 1941.

U.S. Senate, Committee on Appropriations. *Hearings on H.R. 4407 . . . First Supplemental Surplus Appropriation Rescission Bill, 1946.* 79th Cong., 1st Sess., 1945.

U.S. Senate, Committee on Banking and Currency, Subcommittee on Housing. *Hearings on H.R. 4761 . . . Veterans' Emergency Housing Act of 1946.* 79th Cong., 2d Sess., 1946.

U.S. Senate, Committee on Civil Service. *Hearings on S. 1762 and H.R. 4115 . . . Preference in Employment of Honorably Discharged Veterans Where Federal Funds are Disbursed.* 78th Cong., 2d Sess., 1944.

U.S. Senate, Committee on Education and Labor. *Hearings on S. 2714 . . . Vocational Rehabilitation of War-Disabled Individuals.* 77th Cong., 2d Sess., 1942.

———. *Hearings on S. 1295 and S. 1509.* 78th Cong., 1st Sess., 1943.

U.S. Senate, Committee on Education and Labor, Subcommittee on S.

1456 and S. 1510. *Hearings on . . . United States Employment Service.* 79th Cong., 1st Sess., 1946.

U.S. Senate, Committee on Finance, Subcommittee on Veterans' Legislation. *Hearings on S. 2814 . . . and S. 2327 . . . on Veterans' Rehabilitation.* 77th Cong. 2d Sess., 1942.

————. *Hearings on Veterans Omnibus Bill.* 78th Cong., 2d Sess., 1944.

U.S. Senate, Committee on Military Affairs. *Hearings on Selective Service Extension.* 78th Cong., 2d Sess., 1945.

————. *Hearings on . . . Mobilization and Demobilization Problems,* Parts XV and XVI. 78th Cong., 1st Sess., 1944.

————. *Hearings on . . . Demobilization of the Armed Forces.* 79th Cong., 1st and 2d Sess, 1945–1946.

————. *Hearing on . . . Superseniority Rights of Veterans.* 79th Cong., 2d Sess., 1946.

U.S. Senate, Committee on Military Affairs, Subcommittee on Surplus Property. *Hearings on . . . Veterans' Priority for Surplus Property.* 79th Cong., 1st Sess., 1945.

U.S. Senate, Committee on Military Affairs, Subcommittee on War Contracts. *Hearings on . . . Mobilization and Demobilization Problems,* Parts XI to XIV. 78th Cong., 2d Sess., 1944.

U.S. Senate, Committee on Naval Affairs. *Hearings on . . . Demobilization and Transportation of Military Personnel.* 79th Cong., 1st Sess., 1945.

U.S. Senate, Special Committee Investigating the National Defense Program. *Hearings Pursuant to S. Res. 55,* Parts XXXI to XXXIII and XXXVI. 79th Cong., 1st and 2d Sess., 1945–1946.

————. *Hearings on Emergency Housing Program,* Part XXXIX. 79th Cong., 2d Sess., 1947.

U.S. Senate, Special Committee on Post-War Economic Policy and Planning. *Hearings, Part III, the Problem of Unemployment and Reemployment After the War.* 78th Cong., 2d Sess., 1944.

U.S. Senate, Special Committee to Study and Survey Problems of Small Business Enterprises, Subcommittee on Surplus War Property. *Hearings on . . . Problems of American Small Business,* Parts XCVI to XCVIII. 79th Cong., 2d Sess., 1946.

REPORTS

Disabled Veterans of America. *Twenty-Second National Report, Disabled American Veterans, 1942.* Printed as U.S. House of Representatives. *House Document No. 39.* 78th Cong., 1st Sess., 1943.

U.S. Department of Defense. *Annual Report of the Secretary of the Army, 1948.* 1949.

U.S. High Commissioner to Philippine Islands. *Final Report, September 14, 1945 to July 4, 1946.* Printed as U.S. House of Representatives. *House Document No. 389.* 80th Cong., 1st Sess., 1947.

U.S. National Resources Planning Board. *Demobilization and Readjustment; Report of the Conference on Postwar Readjustment of Civilian and Military Personnel.* 1943.

U.S. The President's Commission on Veterans' Pensions. *A Report on Veterans' Benefits in the United States, Staff Report No. I: The Historical Development of Veterans' Benefits in the United States.* Printed as U.S. House of Representatives. *House Committee Print No. 244.* 84th Cong., 2d Sess., 1956.

————. *A Report on Veterans' Benefits in the United States, Staff Report No. II: Veterans' Benefits Administered by Departments and Agencies of the Federal Government, Digest of Laws and Basic Statistics.* Printed as U.S. House of Representatives. *House Committee Print No. 262.* 84th Cong., 2d Sess., 1956.

————. *A Report on Veterans' Benefits in the United States, Staff Report No. IX, Part A: Readjustment Benefits, General Survey and Appraisal.* Printed as U.S. House of Representatives. *House Committee Print No. 289.* 84th Cong., 2d Sess., 1956.

————. *A Report on Veterans' Benefits in the United States, Staff Report No. IX, Part B: Readjustment Benefits, Education and Training, and Employment and Unemployment.* Printed as U.S. House of Representatives. *House Committee Print* No. 291. 84th Cong., 2d Sess., 1956.

————. *A Report on Veterans' Benefits in the United States, Staff Report No. IX, Part C: Veterans' Loan Guaranty and Direct Loan Benefits.* Printed as U.S. House of Representatives. *House Committee Print No. 270.* 84th Cong., 2d Sess., 1956.

Veterans of Foreign Wars. *Proceedings of the 42d National Encampment of the Veterans of Foreign Wars of the United States; Philadelphia, Pa., August 24 to 29, 1941.* Printed as U.S. House of Representatives. *House Document No. 537.* 77th Cong., 2d Sess., 1942.

PUBLISHED PAPERS, MEMOIRS, JOURNALS, AND DIARIES

Allen, George E. *Presidents Who Have Known Me.* New York: Simon and Schuster, 1950.

Baruch, Bernard M. *Baruch: The Public Years.* New York: Holt, Rinehart and Winston, 1960.

Byrnes, James F. *All in One Lifetime.* New York: Harper & Brothers, Publishers, 1958.

Drury, Allen. *A Senate Journal, 1943–1945*. New York, Toronto, and London: McGraw-Hill Book Company, 1963.

Farley, James A. *Jim Farley's Story: The Roosevelt Years*. New York and Toronto: Whittlesey House, McGraw-Hill Book Company, Inc., 1948.

Hoover, Herbert. *The Memoirs of Herbert Hoover*. 3 Vols., New York: The Macmillan Co., 1951–1952.

Ickes, Harold L. *The Secret Diary of Harold L. Ickes*. 3 Vols., New York: Simon and Schuster, 1953–1954.

Lerner, Max. *Public Journal: Marginal Notes on Wartime America*. New York: The Viking Press, 1945.

Millis, Walter, editor. *The Forrestal Diaries*. New York: The Viking Press, 1951.

Perkins, Frances. *The Roosevelt I Knew*. New York: The Viking Press, 1946.

Roosevelt, Elliott, editor. *F.D.R., His Personal Letters, 1928–1945*. 2 Vols., New York: Duell, Sloan, 1950.

Rosenman, Samuel I., Compiler. *The Public Papers and Addresses of Franklin D. Roosevelt*. 13 Vols., New York: Various publishers, 1938–1950.

Rosenman, Samuel I. *Working With Roosevelt*. New York: Harper & Brothers, Publishers, 1952.

Truman, Harry S. *Memoirs by Harry S. Truman*. 2 Vols., New York: Doubleday & Co., Inc., 1955.

Truman, Harry S. *Public Papers of the Presidents of the United States: Harry S. Truman, 1945–1947*. 3 Vols., Washington, D.C.: U.S. Government Printing Office, 1961–1963.

OTHER SOURCES

Interviews:

Guy H. Birdsall and Robinson E. Adkins, February 3, 1965, Washington, D.C.

Omar N. Bradley, May 6, 1965, New York City.

Leonard Outhwaite, March 30, 1965, New York City.

Samuel Lubell, January 20, 1967, New York City.

John W. Snyder, April 13, 1965, New York City.

Letters:

Scott W. Lucas to the author, February 1, 1965.

Wilson W. Wyatt to the author, February 20, 1965.

BOOKS

Abrams, Charles. *The Future of Housing*. New York and London: Harper & Brothers, 1946.

The American Legion. *Digest of Minutes, National Executive Committee Meeting, May 6 and 7, 1943*. Indianapolis, Indiana: National Headquarters, The American Legion, 1943.

The American Legion. *Digest of Minutes, National Executive Committee Meeting, April 30, 1944*. Indianapolis, Indiana: National Headquarters, The American Legion, 1944.

The American Legion. *Digest of Minutes, National Executive Committee Meeting, September 17, 1944*. Indianapolis, Indiana: National Headquarters, The American Legion, 1944.

Bailey, Stephen Kemp. *Congress Makes a Law: The Story Behind the Employment Act of 1946*. New York: Vintage Books, Random House, 1964.

Baruch, Bernard M., and John M. Hancock. *War and Postwar Adjustment Policies: Text of Official Report and Related Documents*. Washington, D.C.: American Council on Public Affairs, 1944.

Bernstein, Irving. *The Lean Years: A History of the American Worker, 1920–1933*. Baltimore, Md.: Penguin Books, 1966.

Blum, John Morton. *From the Morgenthau Diaries: Years of Crisis, 1928–1938*. Boston: Houghton Mifflin Company, 1959.

Bolles, Blair. *How to Get Rich in Washington: Rich Man's Division of the Welfare State*. New York: W. W. Norton & Company, Inc., 1952.

Buchanan, A. Russell. *The United States and World War II*. 2 Vols., New York, Evanston, and London: Harper & Row, Publishers, 1964.

Burlingame, Roger. *Peace Veterans: The Story of a Racket and a Plea for Economy*. New York: Minton, Balch & Co., 1932.

Bykofsky, Joseph, and Harold Larson. *The Technical Services; The Transportation Corps: Operations Overseas*, Vol IX of *History of United States Army in World War II*. Washington, D.C.: Office of the Chief of Military History, Department of the Army, 1957.

Coit, Margaret L. *Mr. Baruch*. Boston: Houghton Mifflin Company, 1957.

Davies, Richard O. *Housing Reform During the Truman Administration*. Columbia, Mo.: University of Missouri Press, 1966.

Dillingham, William Pyrle. *Federal Aid to Veterans, 1917–1941*. Gainesville, Florida: University of Florida Press, 1952.

Duffield, Marcus. *King Legion*. New York: Jonathan Cape & Harrison Smith, 1931.

Durham, Knowlton. *Billions for Veterans: An Analysis of Bonus Prob-*

lems—Yesterday, Today and Tomorrow. New York: Brewer, Warren & Putnam, 1932.

Fenno, Richard F., Jr. *The President's Cabinet: An Analysis in the Period from Wilson to Eisenhower.* Cambridge, Mass.: Harvard University Press, 1959.

Freidel, Frank. *Franklin D. Roosevelt: The Triumph.* Boston and Toronto: Little, Brown and Co., 1956.

Galbraith, John Kenneth. *American Capitalism: The Concept of Countervailing Power.* Cambridge, Mass.: The Riverside Press, Houghton Mifflin Company, Sentry Edition, 1952.

Gellermann, William. *The American Legion as Educator.* New York: Columbia University Press, 1938.

Goldman, Eric. *The Crucial Decade—And After.* New York: Vintage Books, 1960.

Greenfield, Kent Roberts, Robert R. Palmer, and Bell I. Wiley. *The Army Ground Forces: The Organization of Ground Combat Troops.* Vol. I of *United States Army in World War II.* Washington, D.C.: Office of the Chief of Military History, Department of the Army, 1947.

Gunther, John. *Inside U.S.A.* New York and London: Harper & Brothers, 1947.

Haber, William, and Daniel H. Kruger. *The Role of the United States Employment Service in a Changing Economy.* Kalamazoo, Mich.: Michigan State University Press, 1964.

Hobbs, Edward H. *Behind the President: A Study of Executive Office Agencies.* Washington, D.C.: The Public Affairs Press, 1954.

Howenstine, E. Jay, Jr. *The Economics of Demobilization.* Washington, D.C.: The Public Affairs Press, 1944.

Hurd, Charles. *The Veterans' Program: A Complete Guide to Its Benefits, Rights and Options.* New York and London: Whittlesey House, McGraw-Hill Book Co., 1946.

James Marquis. *A History of The American Legion.* New York: William Green, 1923.

Jones, Richard Seelye. *A History of The American Legion.* Indianapolis, Ind. and New York: The Bobbs-Merrill Co., 1946.

Key, V. O., Jr. *Politics, Parties, & Pressure Groups.* 5th ed., New York: Thomas Y. Crowell Co., 1964.

Leuchtenburg, William E. *Franklin D. Roosevelt and the New Deal.* New York: Harper Torchbooks, Harper & Row Publishers, 1963.

Love, Philip H. *Andrew W. Mellon: The Man and His Work.* Baltimore, Md.: F. Heath Coggins & Co., 1929.

Lubell, Samuel. *The Future of American Politics.* 2d ed., rev., New York: Anchor Books, 1956.

Lyons, Eugene. *Our Unknown Ex-President: A Portrait of Herbert Hoover.* Garden City, New York: Doubleday & Company, Inc., 1948.

MacDonald, Mary E. *Federal Grants for Vocational Rehabilitation.* Chicago, Ill.: The University of Chicago Press, 1944.

McKean, Dayton David. *Party and Pressure Politics.* Boston: Houghton Mifflin Co., 1949.

MacNeil, Neil. *Forge of Democracy: the House of Representatives.* New York: David McKay Co., Inc., 1963.

Metz, Harold W. *Labor Policy of the Federal Government.* Washington, D.C.: The Brookings Institute, 1945.

Minott, Rodney G. *Peerless Patriots: Organized Veterans and the Spirit of Americanism.* Washington, D.C.: The Public Affairs Press, 1962.

Moley, Raymond, Jr. *The American Legion Story.* New York: Duell, Sloan and Pearce, 1966.

Morison, Elting. *Turmoil and Tradition: A Study of the Life and Time of Henry L. Stimson.* Boston: Houghton Mifflin Company, 1960.

O'Connor, Harvey. *Mellon's Millions: The Biography of a Fortune.* New York: Blue Ribbon Books, Inc., 1933.

Powell, Talcott. *Tattered Banners.* New York: Harcourt, Brace and Company, 1933.

Rodwin, Lloyd. *Housing and Economic Progress: A Study of the Housing Experiences of Boston's Middle-Income Families.* Cambridge, Mass.: Harvard University Press & The Technology Press, 1961.

Rogow, Arnold A. *James Forrestal: A Study of Personality, Politics, and Policy.* New York: The Macmillan Company, 1963.

Rostow, W. W. *The United States in the World Arena: An Essay in Recent History.* New York: Harper & Brothers, publishers, 1960.

Schlesinger, Arthur M., Jr. *The Age of Roosevelt.* Vol. I: *The Crisis of the Old Order.* Cambridge, Mass.: The Riverside Press, Houghton Mifflin Company, 1957.

Seidman, Joel Isaac. *American Labor From Defense to Reconversion.* Chicago: The University of Chicago Press, 1953.

Sinclair, Andrew. *The Available Man: The Life Behind the Masks of Warren Gamaliel Harding.* New York: The Macmillan Co., 1965.

Somers, Herman Miles. *Presidential Agency, OWMR, The Office of War Mobilization and Reconversion.* Cambridge, Mass.: Harvard University Press, 1950.

Sparrow, John C. *History of Personnel Demobilization in the United States Army.* Washington, D.C.: Department of the Army, Pamphlet No. 20–210, July, 1952.

Steinberg, Alfred. *The Man From Missouri: The Life and Times of Harry S. Truman.* New York: G. P. Putnam's Sons, 1962.

Stouffer Samuel A., *et al. The American Soldier: Combat and Its Aftermath,* Vol. II of *Studies in Social Psychology in World War II.* Prepared under the auspices of the Social Science Research Council, 4 vols.; Princeton: Princeton University Press (1949–1950), 1949.

Truman, David B. *The Governmental Process: Political Interests and Public Opinion.* New York: Alfred A. Knopf, 1965.

Tugwell, Rexford Guy. *The Democratic Roosevelt: A Biography of Franklin D. Roosevelt.* Garden City, N.Y.: Doubleday & Co., 1957.

Waller, Willard. *The Veteran Comes Back.* New York: The Dryden Press, 1944.

Warren, Harris Gaylord. *Herbert Hoover and the Great Depression.* New York: Oxford University Press, 1959.

Weber, Gustavus A., and Laurence F. Schmeckebier, *The Veterans' Administration; Its History, Activities and Organization.* Washington, D.C.: The Brookings Institution, 1934. Institute for Government Research, *Service Monographs of the United States Government, No. 66.*

Wecter, Dixon. *When Johnny Comes Marching Home.* Cambridge, Mass.: The Riverside Press, Houghton Mifflin Company, 1944.

Wellman, Paul I. *Stuart Symington.* Garden City, N.Y.: Doubleday and Company, Inc., 1960.

Wheat, George Seay. *The Story of The American Legion.* New York and London: G. P. Putnam's Sons, 1919.

Williams, William Appleman. *The Tragedy of American Diplomacy.* Revised and enlarged edition. New York: Dell Publishing Co., 1962.

Young, Roland. *Congressional Politics in the Second World War.* New York: Columbia University Press, 1956.

PERIODICALS

Abrams, Charles. "Government and Housing," *The Nation,* CLIX (October 21, 1944), 498.

"Army Proposes, Fate Disposes and GI's Long for Boats to U.S.," *Newsweek,* XXVI (October 22, 1945), 56 ff.

"Baruch Plan," *New Republic,* CX (February 28–March 6, 1944), 263–64, 304.

"Behind Union-Veteran Deal: How Agreement Differs from the Law's Guarantee of Job Rights; Question Raised Over the Status of Ex-Servicemen Working in Closed Shops," *The United States News* (August 4, 1944), 38.

Bernstein, Barton J. "Reluctance and Resistance: Wilson Wyatt and Veterans' Housing in the Truman Administration," *The Register, Kentucky Historical Society,* LXV (January. 1967), 47–66.

————. "The Removal of War Production Board Controls on Business, 1944–1946." *Business History Review,* XXXIX (Summer, 1965), 243–60.

"Bluejacket Ranks Thin So Fast New Ships Couldn't Fight a War," *Newsweek,* XXVII (March 4, 1946), 30 ff.

"Bring Back Daddy," *Newsweek,* XXVII (February 4, 1946), 55–57.

"Broken Leathernecks," *Newsweek,* XXVII (March 4, 1946), 35.

Buehler, Alfred G. "Military Pensions," *The Annals of the American Academy of Political and Social Science,* CCXXVII (May, 1943), 128–35.

Camelon, David. "I Saw the GI Bill Written: Part One, The Fight for Mustering Out Pay," *The American Legion Magazine,* XLVII (September, 1949), 11–13, 46–50.

————. "I Saw the GI Bill Written: Part Two, A Surprise Attack." *The American Legion Magazine,* XLVII (October, 1949), 18–19, 51–57.

————. "I Saw the GI Bill Written: Part Three, The Wild Ride From Georgia." *The American Legion Magazine,* XLVII (November, 1949), 18–19, 51–57.

"Colossal Rail Snafu Holds Up GI's in Christmas Rush toward Home," *Newsweek,* XXVI (December 24, 1945), 27–28.

Couper, Walter J. "The Reemployment Rights of Veterans." *The Annals of the American Academy of Political and Social Science,* CCXXXVIII (March, 1945), 112–21.

Current History, n.s. V (September, 1943), 69–70.

Davenport, Walter. "Big Wind from the South." *Collier's,* CXVI (December 1, 1945), 66, 81–83.

Davidson, Bill. "Veterans' New Dealer," *Collier's,* CXVI (November 24, 1945), 24–25 ff.

Denlinger, Sutherland. "The Vets' Best Bet," *Collier's,* CXVII (April 27, 1946), 34 ff.

"Eligible or Not, GI's Whoop It Up Against Slowdown," *Newsweek,* XXVII (January 21, 1946), 59–60 ff.

"Erskine, Graves Blanchard," *Current Biography,* 1946, 182–84.

"The Fortune Survey (The Housing Shortage)," *Fortune,* XXXIII (April, 1946), 266ff.

"Fuller's House," *Fortune,* XXXIII (April, 1946), 167–179.

"Get Back in That Foxhole!," *Salute,* I (September, 1946), 14.

Gilpin, DeWitt, "Bread and Butter Front," *Salute,* I (April, 1946), 28–30 ff.

"The GI Revolt," *The Commonweal,* XLIII (January 25, 1946), 372.

"Guidebook to Surplus Disposal, Part One," *Business Week,* May 26, 1945, 43–75.

"Hancock, John M." *Current Biography, 1949,* 239–41.

"Hines, Frank T." *Current Biography* (April, 1944), 296–99.

"Human Demobilizer," *Newsweek,* XXIII (April 3, 1944), 70.

Kaplan, A. D. H. "Liquidating War Production," in *Economic Reconstruction,* edited by Seymour E. Harris. 1st ed.; New York and London: McGraw-Hill Book Company, Inc., 1945. 124–45.

Keating, Frank A. (Maj. Genl.) "Redeployment Jitters," *The Infantry Journal,* LIX (September, 1946), 38–40.

Key, V. O., Jr. "The Veterans and the House of Representatives: A Study of a Pressure Group and Electoral Mortality." *The Journal of Politics,* V (February, 1943), 27–40.

Kingsley, J. Donald. "Veterans, Unions and Jobs," *New Republic,* CXI (October 23, 1944 and November 13, 1944), 513–14; 621–23.

Kreager, H. D. "Community Action for Veterans' Housing," *Public Administration Review,* VIII (Winter, 1948), 29–33.

Lee, R. Alton. "The Army 'Mutiny' of 1946," *The Journal of American History,* LIII (December, 1966), 555–71.

"Legionnaires at Work," *Newsweek, XXIV* (October 2, 1944), 47.

Levenstein, Aaron. "Superseniority—Postwar Pitfall," *The Antioch Review,* IV (Winter, 1944–45), 531–43.

Lindley, Ernest K. "Bradley and the Veterans," *Newsweek,* XXV (June 18, 1945), 35.

Lippman, Leopold. "When The Veterans Come Home," *The New Republic,* CXI (September 4, 1944), 272–74.

Lisio, Donald J. "A Blunder Becomes Catastrophe: Hoover, the Legion, and the Bonus Army," *Wisconsin Magazine of History,* LI (Autumn, 1967), 37–50.

The Literary Digest, CXV (July 17, 1933), 3.

Luce, Clare Boothe. "Greater and Freer America; GI John's Future; Address to Republican National Convention, June 27, 1944." *Vital Speeches,* X (July 15, 1944), 586–88.

"Lying to Get Elected," *The New Republic,* CXI (October 16, 1944), 580.

"Mr. Roosevelt and the Future," *The New Republic,* CXI (November 20, 1944), 648.

"Mr. Wyatt's Shortage," *Fortune,* XXXIII (April, 1946), 105.

Neustadt, Richard E. "Congress and the Fair Deal: A Legislative Balance Sheet," in Carl Friedrich and John Galbraith, eds., *Public Policy,* V (Cambridge, Mass.: Harvard University Press, 1954).

The New York Journal American, 1942–1944.

The New York Times, 1941–1945.

Northrup, H. R. "Where's the Lumber?," *The American Magazine,* CXLII (December, 1946), 27 ff.

Novack, Max. "About That Bonus," *Salute,* I (April, 1946), 12–13.

"An Old Riddle Crops Up Again—," *Newsweek,* XXV (May 21, 1945), 76 ff.

"On Bringing 'Em Home Alive," *Newsweek,* XXVI (December 3, 1945), 56 ff.

Ordway, Samuel H., Jr. "The Veteran in the Civil Service," *The Annals of the American Academy of Political and Social Science,* CCXXXVIII (March, 1945), 133–39.

"People of the Week." *The United States News,* XVI (June 2, 1944), 62–64.

"People of the Week," *The United States News,* XIX (September 21, 1945), 78–80.

"People of the Week," *The United States News,* XIX (February 15, 1946), 72.

"Rankin, John E.," *Current Biography* (February, 1944), 555–58.

Redkey, Henry. "Rehabilitating the War Injured," *Survey Midmonthly* (May, 1943), LXXXIX, 131–33.

Reid, Bill G. "Proposals for Soldier Settlement During World War I," *Mid-America,* XLVI (July, 1964), 172–86.

Roher, Miriam. "Veterans and the Civil Service," *The American Mercury,* LXIII (December, 1946), 689–95

Roosevelt, F. D., Jr. "Sick and Tired of Doubling Up," *The New Republic,* CXV (December 23, 1946), 852–84.

Rosenman, Mrs. Samuel I. "The Racket in Veterans' Housing," *The American Magazine,* CXLII (September, 1946), 26–27 ff.

Schubart, Henry. "The Housing Crisis," *Political Affairs,* XXV (March, 1946), 240–53.

Schuyler, Jack. "Veterans and Union Rules," *The American Mercury,* LXI (December, 1945), 666–71.

Shishkin, Boris. "Organized Labor and the Veteran." *The Annals of the American Academy of Political and Social Science,* CCXXXVIII (March, 1945), 146–57.

"Smith, Harold D.," *Current Biography,* 1943, 710–12.

"A Stake in the Future," *The Christian Century,* LXI (May 10, 1944), 582–83.

The Stars and Stripes, London Edition, 1945.

——, Middle Pacific Edition, 1945.

——, Southern Germany Edition, 1945.

Stone, I. F. "Millionaires' Beveridge Plan," *The Nation,* CLVIII (March 25, 1944), 354–55.

" 'Superseniority' for Veterans: Far-Reaching Effects of Official Interpretation of Job-Preference Law," *The United States News* (September 1, 1944), 38 ff.

Time, XLVII (January 21, 1946), 21–22.

TRB. "Post-War Planning at Last," *New Republic,* CIX (October 25, 1943), 572.

————. "When Demobilization Comes," *The New Republic,* CIX (August 2, 1943), 139.

"Unrest of Veteran Troops: What Homesick Soldiers Say," *The United States News,* XX (January 25, 1946), 19–21.

"Unsuper Seniority," *Newsweek,* XXVII (June 3, 1946), 26.

"Veterans and Workers," *The Commonweal,* XLII (July 27, 1945), 349.

"Veterans Being Placed," *Business Week,* August 17, 1946, 83–85.

"Veterans Job Showdown Near," *Business Week,* May 19, 1945, 100–102.

"Veterans' Reemployment Litigation: Need For an Administrative Process," *Harvard Law Review,* LIX (April, 1946), 593–604.

"Veterans: Senior to Whom?" *Newsweek,* XXVII (April 15, 1946), 37.

"Veterans, Unions, Jobs," *American Federationist,* LI (August, 1944), 3.

Vivian, James F. and Jean H. "The Bonus March of 1932: The Role of General George Van Horn Moseley," *Wisconsin Magazine of History,* LI (Autumn, 1967), 26–36.

"Warning From the Ranks," *The Christian Century,* LXIII (January 23, 1946), 104–105.

The Washington Post, 1942–1945.

"Washington Whispers," *The United States News,* XVIII (March 23, 1945), 68.

"Washington Whispers," *The United States News,* XIX (August 17, 1945), 80.

"Washington Whispers," *The United States News,* XIX (August 24, 1943), 96.

"What Price Superseniority?" *Fortune,* XXXI (January, 1945), 111.

Whelan, Russell. "Rankin of Mississippi," *The American Mercury,* LIX (July, 1944), 31–37.

White, George A. "Cradle Days in the Legion," *The American Legion Weekly,* November 19 and 26, December 10 and 17, 1920.

"Why the GI's Demonstrate," *The New Republic,* CXIV (January 21, 1946), 72–73.

Woodbury, Coleman. "Objectives and Accomplishments of the Veterans' Emergency Housing Program," Supplement, *The American Economic Review,* XXXVIII (May, 1947), 518 ff.

"Work Choice of GIs," *The United States News,* XIX (February 15, 1946), 32 ff.

Yank: The Army Weekly, 1945.

OTHER SOURCES

Coldberg, Marshall R. "Federal Control of Construction Following World War II." Unpublished Ph.D. dissertation, U. of Mich., 1950.

Hennessy, Arthur. "Bonus March of 1932." Unpublished PhD. dissertation, Georgetown University, 1957.

Rogg, Nat. "A History of the Veterans Emergency Housing Program." Washington, D.C.: Office of the Housing Expediter, n.d., 488 pp. Mimeo.

Sneller, Maurice Paterson. "The Bonus March of 1932: A Study of Depression Leadership and Its Legacy." Unpublished Ph.D. dissertation, University of Virginia, 1960.

Underhill, Jack A. "The Veterans' Administration and The American Legion (1945–1947)." Unpublished MA Thesis, Columbia University Thesis, 1959.

INDEX

Adjusted Compensation, *see* Bonus, World War I
Agriculture, Department of, 119, 144–45, 197–200, 280
Allen, A. Leonard, 112–13, 116*n*, 117*n*
Allen, George E., 268–69, 273
American Association of Junior Colleges, 96
American Association of Teachers Colleges, 96
American Council on Education, 96
American Federation of Labor, 149
American Legion: origins of, 7–9; influence after World War I, 9–11; supports World War I bonus, 13–19; National Legislative Committee, 14; pushes World War I pension, 20–29; supports job retraining, 42–50; role in supporting Rankin in House jurisdictional battle, 74–78; role in mustering-out pay legislation, 78–82, 87–88; role in passing GI Bill of Rights, 98–107, 117, 120–24; and VA hospital investigation, 135, 137; and surplus war property, 212–13; and civil service preference for veterans, 194; influence on policymaking, 283–86
American Veterans Committee, 221, 270

American Veterans of World War II, 212–13, 247, 269–70
Armed Forces Committee on Post-War Educational Opportunities for Service Personnel, *see* Osborn Committee
Association of American Colleges, 96
Atherton, Warren G.: attempts to broaden Legion's wartime recruiting base, 77–78; launches campaign for mustering-out pay, 78–79; cooperates with Hearst press, 80; appoints committee to draft veterans' omnibus bill, 99; criticizes Rankin, 109; confers with FDR, 119
Auchincloss, James C., 176

Bailey, C. W., 134
Bailey, F. J., 198
Ball, Joseph, 221–22
Barden, Graham A., 42, 47–48, 112–15
Barkley, Alben, 83–84
Baruch, Bernard Mannes, 127–29, 131, 157, 158, 205*n*, 280
Bennett, Marion T., 210
Biddle, Francis, 153
Birdsall, Guy H., 120
Blandford, John Jr., 72–73, 244, 260*n*